D1746556

AUSTRALIA
-A GOURMET'S PARADISE-

Published by Focus Publishing Pty Ltd
ACN 003 600 360
PO Box 557, Double Bay NSW 2028
Telephone (02) 327 4777
Fax (02) 362 3753

Chairman: Steven Rich
Publisher: Jaqui Lane
Associate Publisher: Carolen Barripp
Managing Editor: Clare Wallis
Production Manager: Timothy Ho
Designer: Angela Brown

© Copyright 1995 Focus Publishing Pty Ltd

This book is copyright. Apart from any fair deaing for the purpose of private study, research, criticism or review as permitted under the Copyright Act, no part may be reproduced by any process without written permission.

ISBN 1 875359 21 4

Printed by Griffin Press
Film by Dot 'n Line (Aust) Pty Ltd
Picture research by Jacqui Mott

This page: A typical Barossa Valley Homestead enclosed by rows of vines
Previous page: Miniature vegetables nestle in Joe Chetcuti's hands

AUSTRALIA
-A GOURMET'S PARADISE-

Table of Contents

Advisory Committee
Page 6

Sponsors' Roll of Honour
Page 7

Foreword
Page 9

Introduction
Page 10

THE INFLUENCES
Tastes of Australia
Page 12

CHEFS & HEROES
Celebrating Rare Talent
Page 30

NORTHERN TERRITORY
An Ancient Land
Page 58

QUEENSLAND
Exotic by Nature
Page 68

NEW SOUTH WALES
Raw Energy
Page 86

TASMANIA
Treasure Island
Page 106

VICTORIA
Rich & Cosmopolitan
Page 132

SOUTH AUSTRALIA
Tradition with a Twist
Page 154

WESTERN AUSTRALIA
A Different Time and Space
Page 174

CELEBRATING
the Great Outdoors
Page 206

A WONDERFUL BOUQUET
Australia's Wine Heritage
Page 218

INTERNATIONAL PROFILE
Made in Australia
Page 238

Sponsors' Directory
Page 258

Photographic Credits
Page 286

Glossary
Page 287

Writers
Page 288

Advisory Committee

CHAIRMAN
John Gough AO OBE

COMMITTEE
Kelvin Aldred
Ken Allen
Bob Annells
Peter Bartels
Joan Campbell
Geoffrey Coles AM
Senator Peter Cook
Brian Croser
Jeffrey David
Catriona Fraser
Lee D. Gilham
Wolfgang Grimm
Sir James Hardy OBE
Dr Patricia Kailis OBE
Jim Kennedy CBE
Jaqui Lane
The Hon. Michael Lee
Rex Lipman AM
David McCulloch
Don McWilliam
Alberto Modolo
Dan O'Brien
Peter Rowland
Steven Rich
Leslie J. Schirato
John Schaap
Peter Shelley
Paul Simons AM
Rod Slater
Dr Bruce Standen
Lynden Wilkie
Bill Wright

Sponsors' Roll of Honour

LEAD SPONSOR

American Express International Inc.

MAJOR SPONSORS

Australian Meat & Live-Stock Corporation

Australian Tourist Commission

Cadbury Confectionery

Cantarella Brothers

Davids Limited

Pacific Brands Food Group

Qantas Airways Ltd

South Australian Tourism Commission

Spotless Catering

Western Australian Department of Commerce and Trade

Western Australian Tourism Commission

Woolworths - The Fresh Food People

GENERAL SPONSORS

Australian Dairy Corporation

BOC Gases Ltd

Bonlac Foods Limited

Camerons Oysters

Cascade Beverages

Cerebos (Aust) Pty Ltd

The Curtin Group

D'Orsogna Limited

R J Gilbertson Pty Ltd

Green's Foods Limited

Heinz & Co Pty Ltd

Hyatt Regency Perth

K G Palmer & Associates Pty Ltd

Lactos Master Cheesemaker

Margaret River Vineyards - Leeuwin Estate, Voyager Estate, Brookland Valley Vineyard

National Dairies Tasmania Ltd

Peters & Brownes Group

Rosemount Pty Ltd

Tabasco Pepper Sauce

Tasmania Department of Tourism, Sport and Recreation

Tasmania Development and Resources

Tassal Ltd

Tourism New South Wales

Tourism Victoria

Unifoods - A Division of Unilever Australia Ltd

The Western Australian Meat Marketing Corporation

Westinghouse Appliances

Winning Appliances Pty Ltd

Wise Winery

A sumptuous fig flan with Tarago River cheese

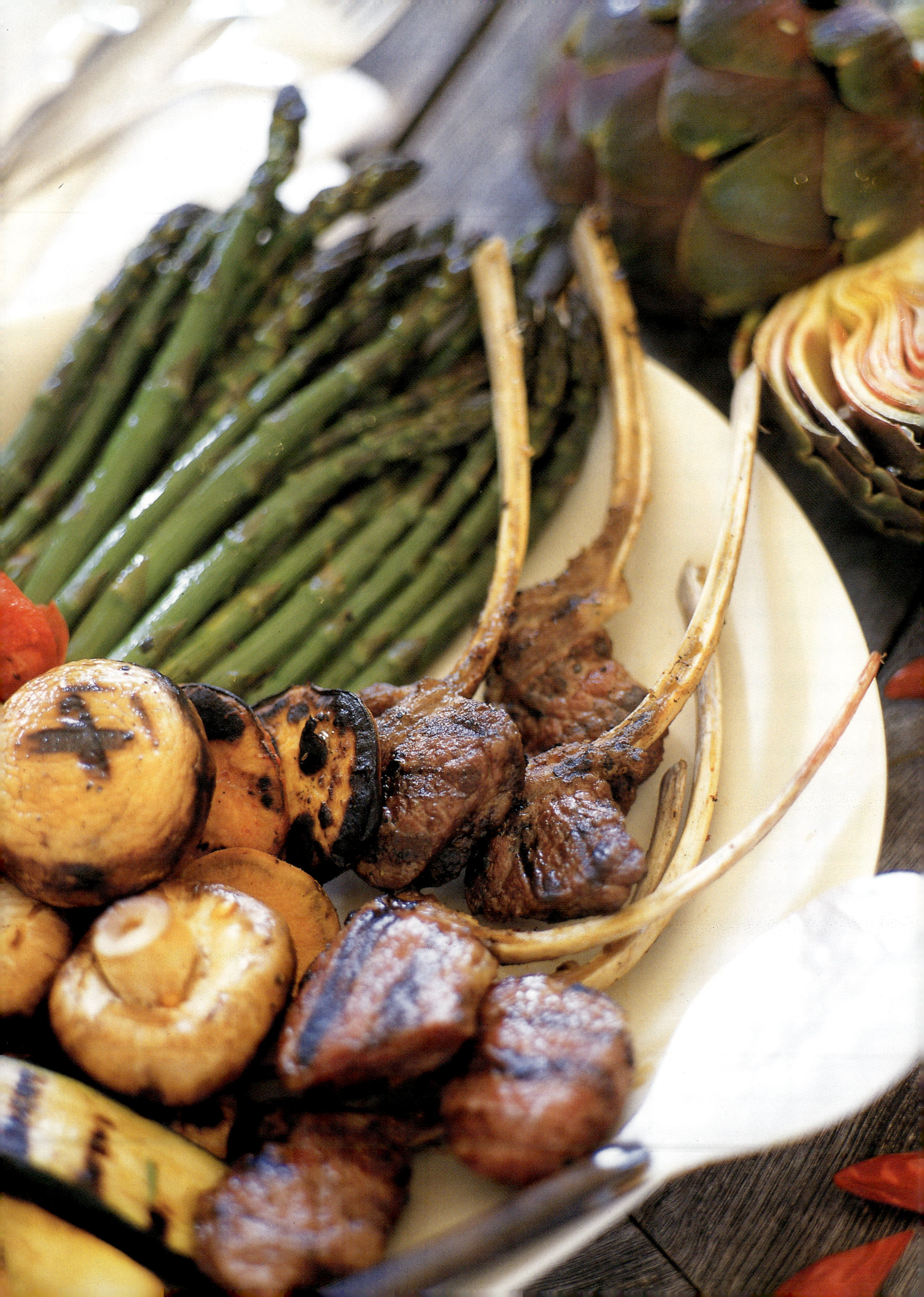

Foreword

HAIL TO THE CHEF!

Hail too, to the producers who are also heroes and without whom the chef would be able to accomplish little.

It's now pretty well universally acknowledged that Australian food is right up there with the world's best; that Australian chefs are unusually daring, imaginative and ever responsive to the brilliant produce that this country is delivering to market.

It has taken a little while for this truth to be widely admitted but gradually the doubters have come round—first the Americans, then the Brits, finally the French. Throughout the seventies and eighties, a slew of visiting chefs and food writers, sceptics all, arrived to check out this place they'd dimly heard of but knew little about. And what they knew least about was our food.

They came, they tasted and they were conquered. They learned that from the oceans around this mighty continent came wondrous seafood in unimaginable variety and from the north rare tropical fruits they had only seen and smelled in posh shops. In Europe such exotica cost a poultice. In Australia it was dirt cheap.

More recent visitors have remarked on the speed with which Australian producers have lifted their game, seeing the commercial advantage in producing foodstuffs other than rubber-skinned tomatoes and artificially coloured oranges.

They have remarked, too, on the way even suburban markets and stores have expanded the variety of produce they offer the adventurous consumer.

Change has been swift and comprehensive. Australia is now a food force to be reckoned with. And the first, most critical link in the chain is the supplier. May the chefs continue to be inspired, the producers continue to produce and the quality levels continue to rise. And rise.

LEO SCHOFIELD

Grilled gourmet fare

Introduction

I'M SITTING LOOKING AT AN OLD MENU from my catering days in the early seventies. It was for a party of 300 held at the Town Hall in Sydney. The menu was in French. We felt it was the right thing to do, even though the food wasn't French. We believed the French produced the world's greatest cuisine.

There was smoked salmon on the menu: 'Salade de lentilles aux poissons fumes'. I remember it well, it was the first of our Australian-farmed salmon trout to be smoked by Piers Ranicar of the Tasmanian Smokehouse.

We could actually buy fresh asparagus then, and there was a new variety of lettuce called 'cos'. But there were no vine-ripened tomatoes, no exotic shapes and colours, just plain tomatoes. There were three varieties of potato: pink, white and dirty. At the last count there were twenty-seven. Mangoes came once a year from Queensland, pineapples and pawpaws were plentiful but for a slice of papaya you had to visit Thailand.

There was only one thickness of cream, and cheese other than cheddar was only just taking off.

Meat was good but we were, of course, less demanding. There were no fancy cuts of anything. There were no game birds unless you went out and shot them yourself and we never talked, or even dreamt, about kangaroo as a table meat. As far as chooks were concerned, usually a man delivered them on Saturday for Sunday dinner. They were regarded as something special.

Seafood has always been plentiful but the Fish Market in Sydney only started as a retail outlet in 1970 and there was not a great variety of fish. There was no fresh salmon or salmon trout, no mussels, scallops or yabbies but plenty of prawns, some crabs and lobsters and, of course, oysters, but of little variety. If you drove up in the late afternoon outside certain pubs the fishermen would be standing ready with their catch of fish and prawns for sale.

But we did manage to cook good food in spite of the fact that we didn't have the enormous range of ingredients that we have today.

It was around this time that I first discovered the great worth of Leo Schofield! Leo headed up a series of trips overseas for dedicated cooks. On his return he would publish minute details of the food and the way it was presented, and I then tried to copy everything I could from his description of the dishes.

These exciting new dishes became more widely available later on in the seventies as a result of long-distance travel becoming faster and cheaper.

Australians travelling to Europe learnt to enjoy the cooking of France and Italy, especially Tuscany. From North Africa and all around the Mediterrean we discovered couscous, tagines, baba ghanoush and pickled lemons.

And there was Asia too. India, Thailand, Malaysia and Hong Kong were the favourite destinations, offering interesting new tastes and flavours, and newly arrived Asian immigrants also introduced Australians to their native dishes by opening some of the many take-aways and restaurants offering international cuisine. Our chefs are still travelling, returning to cook innovative new dishes from the lands they visit.

No-one could have foreseen that this country, with its conservative British taste buds, would so quickly respond to new and often strange flavours in the way that it has. And just as the growers of the many varieties of produce responded to the needs of the international chefs who came here in the late seventies, the younger generation of chefs has shown an energy and vitality that we are all proud of. They have developed their own style in preparing their dishes and have strong ideas about the way their restaurants are presented.

We are fortunate that our climate allows outdoor eating most of the year round. Our many street cafes celebrate this and create a lively city life that makes Australia a welcoming, hospitable place to visit.

I do think we have developed a distinctive Australian style, and the joy of it is that it is a mixture of influences from all over the world. I think that this book is an important document in tracking the development of the 'Great Australian Culinary Revolution' and it has been enormously interesting for me to witness such major changes in our way of eating over a relatively short period of time. It has been an enjoyable experience.

JOAN CAMPBELL

Above: Squid-ink paste surrounded by fresh scallops, oysters and crab from Il Centro Restaurant and Bar in Brisbane.

T H E   I N F

Right: Salmon gravlax on a crispy wonton with wasabi mayonnaise by Belinda Franks Below: (left to right) Neil Perry, Chris Manfield, Steve Manfredi, Helen Greenwood and Tony Bilson in Sydney; the elegant dining room at the Windsor Hotel, Melbourne

ENCES

Tastes of Australia

Contemporary Australia has reached a quite celebrated pitch of culinary quality and diversity. The enlightened hybrid that might be called Modern Australian Cuisine is a matter of influences—Asian, French, Mediterranean, Middle Eastern and North African, a little British—and of attitude, with the liveliest chefs working with an informed plurality and confidence. The *omnium gatherum* of produce, that now includes the indigenous meats and intense fruits of the desert culture too, makes it all a great adventure and a very accessible one in restaurants right across the country. It's happening in Perth, Adelaide, Brisbane and in Hobart of course, but most of all in greater Sydney and Melbourne, the major watering holes where the most intense culinary interaction occurs.

ORIGINAL INFLUENCES Tracking up and down the culinary heights in the history of these two cities points up the clichés, the well-worn truths, in their differences. Sydney is the lotus-eating capital, famed for its glamorous shallows, but not nearly as fickle as rumour has it. It has a vigour, and a growing Mediterranean sensibility in the business of eating out that Melbourne, traditionally the more interior place, the more serious about what it eats and drinks, does not. Melbourne's cool and lively cafe life has counterpointed an historic conservatism that is reflected in the formality of its fine-dining time warp. The perils of provincialism, in fact.

What were the original influences, who made it happen? Fifty-odd years ago Australia was a culinary desert, making it impossible to believe that fifty years before that there were first-growth clarets available on South Australian trains. After wars and depression, sophisticated eating and drinking was invisible, something the rich, travelled few enjoyed in private. In public, the Melbourne establishment, when not ensconced at the Melbourne Club, was dining at the

AUSTRALIA - A GOURMET'S PARADISE

Windsor Hotel, while the Sydney push dined and danced at the Hotel Australia and at two rather swish clubs, Prince's and Romano's. Romano aka Orlando Azzalin had been manager at the Ritz and Hyde Park hotels in London. At Prince's, the distinguished Tony Clerici, once maître d' at Claridges, cooked a celebrated steak diane. The other excitement of the day was chicken in a basket, but if these dishes were beautifully cooked and served, most menus were prosaic by today's standards, and there was little hope for diners until the next migrant wave of catalysts and connoisseurs came to the rescue.

Passionate modernist Georges Mora arrived from Paris, and in 1956 opened Café Balzac in East Melbourne. Considered Australia's first modern restaurateur, he made the Balzac a compelling mix of good food and wine, people and art. And he forbade garnish of any kind. In 1957 French chef Paul Harbulot came to run the kitchen of the new Johnnie Walker Bistro in Sydney. And in 1960 Hermann Schneider, a Swiss chef of meticulous French skills and sensibility, opened Two Faces in Melbourne's South Yarra. For twenty-seven years this was not only the restaurant where so many loved to eat but where so many chefs learnt their proper profession.

The 'spaghetti mafia' also rose through the fifties to become a powerful force in the cultural good life of the cities, but serious gourmet activity was concentrated in the wine and food societies, a freemasonry of the palate that flourished until sidelined in the sixties. Key figures were vigneron Maurice O'Shea, art dealer Rudi Komon, wine merchants such as Johnnie Walker, and the young Len Evans who was already masterminding legendary vintage dinners. If scornful young foodies were then heard dismissing 'the tinned salmon gourmets', it must be said that some of the finest aspects of French influence came through these societies, particularly the Society of Gourmets in Sydney. Two members, advertising men Deke Coleman and Ted Maloney, collaborated on a couple of witty and sophisticated cookery books. The first, and most influential, *Oh, for a French Wife*, was published in 1952, and by 1980 had been reprinted eighteen times in three editions.

CROSS POLLINATION The Toflerisation of the industry had started, and Australians travelled, broadening their minds and refining their palates in Europe and Asia, in Thailand and Bali in particular. Anyone with any feeling for the sensual pleasures of food and wine had oil-spotted copies of Elizabeth David, and books and magazines took off, greatly assisted by

Clockwise from top left: The ardent, sharp-witted Joan Campbell; tuna braised in olive oil served with slivers of fried eggplant and green garlic cloves, one of Gai Bilson's superb dishes; Melbourne chef Stephanie Alexander; Margaret Fulton, whose cookbooks grace most Australian homes

Influences · Tastes of Australia

local catalysts such as Margaret Fulton and later Joan Campbell. The ardent, sharp-witted Campbell, a cook whose proper knowledge may well be marinated in her bones, was most influential at *Vogue* magazine and the *Vogue Entertaining Guide* from the late seventies when she gave young chefs a platform beyond the kitchen. Restaurant critics sharpened their words. Leo Schofield was the most robust, and whether he mirrored the times or made them, as mentor or scourge, from the early seventies he certainly pushed them along. More and more, chefs assumed centre stage. Cooking schools opened, such as Diane Holuigue's French Kitchen in Melbourne in 1969. Young tyros went to Europe as apprentices (most often to the kitchens of the Roux brothers), on degustation tours, or if as usual broke, simply to sniff the markets. And star guest cheffery developed as an important factor in the international cross-pollination of ideas, the raising of standards. The idea of the chef as hero and superstar came out of France and struck Australia in the eighties, having most effect in Sydney. In Melbourne's considered view only ownership allowed celebrity.

From the mid-sixties passionate amateurs opened small unlicensed bistros known as BYOs (bring your own bottle) that tickled up the stuffier establishments. Like that of chef Stephanie Alexander's Jamaica House in Melbourne, most BYOs were earthed in French provincial cooking. There was also Yolande de Salis at La Causerie in Potts Point, Sydney, and from 1969 chef Patric Juillet, who started at Juillets in Potts Point with Chrissie Juillet, his significant nurturing front of house other, then went on to Juillet et Fils in Crown Street where he delivered pungent southern French cooking with detectable traces of Asia. After the important 1974 opening of Tony and Gai Bilson's Bon Gout, Juillet was the competition that spurred the Bilsons to greater heights.

Born in a scruffy corner of East Sydney, Bon Gout became a benchmark, a body and soul affair that with its freshly inventive soups and dishes such as saddle of hare, canard au cerises and ambrosial French pastries, developed along nouvelle lines. Bon Gout was seen to be parallel with, and then encouraged by, the lightening and liberating of food in France when rule-breaking was sanctioned. The Bilsons were the first Australian-born chefs to become

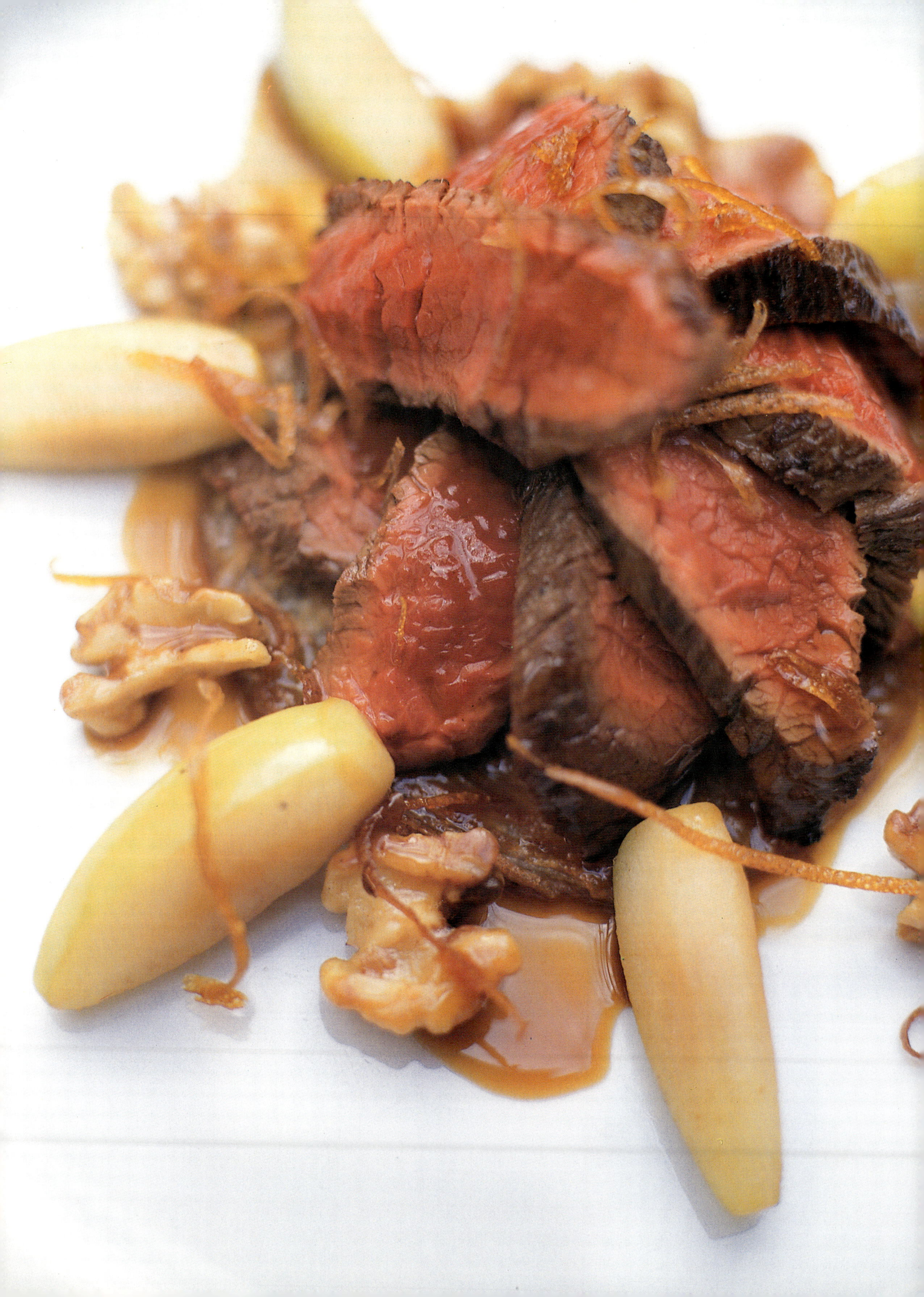

celebrities. They were influenced by the Japanese minimalist aesthetic and went on to open Berowra Waters Inn in 1977. A perfect dream site on a cliff at the northern reaches of Sydney, it was to become the iconic Australian restaurant, a culinary lighthouse. By 1980, the reconstruction by architect Glenn Murcutt complete, it possessed a breathtaking glamour and wonderfully exciting food: mushroom consommé, raw tuna wasabi, steamed brioches with toasted pinenuts, honey and lemon sauce. Both Bilsons were in the kitchen, Tony Bilson assisted by Leigh Stone Herbert, with Martin Teplitsky, Andrew Burley and Paul Merrony as apprentices. Anders Ousbäck and Michael McMahon were front of house. In local terms, this was the dream team.

This was roughly the moment that Sydney's culinary movers and shakers decided to appoint themselves the Gang of Twelve. A loose arrangement made up of chefs who liked to eat in each other's restaurants, it included both Bilsons and Leigh Stone Herbert (by now at Rostbif, his Cremorne milkbar conversion, merrily stuffing legs of lamb with asparagus). There was the cuisine minceur purist Jean-Luc Lundy at Bagatelle, Jenny Ferguson at You & Me in the city, Patric Juillet at Café Nouveau, and perfectionist Melburnian Damien Pignolet, who with his late wife, the fine chef Josephine Pignolet, had been working in Sydney with influential Danish chef Mogens Bay Esbensen at Pavilion on the Park. Later, in 1982, the Pignolets bought Claude's from maverick Frenchman Claude Corne. There was also the excellent Mark Armstrong at Yellow Book, later at Pegrum's, and the talented cheffing/surfing Northern beaches Doyle brothers, Greg Doyle at Puligny's and Peter Doyle working with Patric Juillet before opening his fine-dining Reflections at Palm Beach.

ASIAN INFLUENCES In the obsessive speculation about the provenance of cooking styles, the influence of Asia produces the most heated debate. At the heart of the matter, and absolutely not a new idea, Asian influences had filtered into Australian cooking and consciousness from the mid-nineteenth century arrival of the gold prospecting Chinese. Such influences now come from all directions, running through everything from Chinatown and all subsequent migrant cuisines of Thailand, India, Malaysia, Indonesia, Vietnam and Japan to the highly sophisticated Cantonese cuisine of Gilbert Lau at Flower Drum in Melbourne, the exquisite Japanese at the Unkai in Sydney's ANA hotel and the idiosyncratic brilliance of David Thompson at Darley Street Thai and Tetsuya Wakada at Tetsuya's in Rozelle.

But a few still think it's all down to Cheong Lieuw, the extraordinary Adelaide chef who through the eighties was zen master at Nediz Tu restaurant, teaching such stars as Tim Pak Poy. Adelaide's chef heroes must also include Le Tu Thai and Kate Sparrow (now partners in Nediz

Seared kangaroo fillet with glazed apple and walnuts, served with a lime and ginger sauce, by Kate Sparrow and Le Tu Thai

Tu), and Phillip Searle who while at Possum's enjoyed sparky culinary fencing with Cheong Lieuw before coming to Sydney to open Oasis Seros in 1987. Searle is the artist who taught himself the fine art of cooking, reaching an extraordinary pitch before returning to paint with a little consultant cheffing on the side. His star pupil Christine Manfield absorbed the consummate skills but has rather more consumer orientation. She actively encourages diners to eat in her Sydney restaurant Paramount.

If Asian and how East meets West is the great debate, and if Mediterranean is a given, for some years now, moving beyond the Italian influence to include the more aromatic reaches of the eastern Mediterranean, bush tucker, now elevated to Native Australian Cuisine, is a new dynamic. Taken up by innovative and market-aware chefs it is, despite the culturally blinkered, the latest and the last culinary frontier, defining a point where the intense, often bitter, flavours of a desert culture meet Western cuisine. For pioneer chef Jean-Paul Bruneteau it offers a whole new pantry of ingredients, and demand has created a wild food-farming and tribal-gathering infrastructure. With his partner Jennie Dowling he opened Rowntrees in 1983 and since 1992 has run the consistently fine and engaging Riberries 'Taste Australia' in Sydney's Surry Hills with young inner-city Koori apprentices.

A NEW DYNAMIC There are certainly different ways to go with these unfamilar flavours. The mildest is probably what happens in a sophisticated hotel dining-room, as with the last menus the late Juergen Zopf devised for Le Restaurant at the Regent Hotel of Melbourne, where he added lilli pilli sauce to the seared Queensland buffalo but abandoned the desert tomato as much too tricky. The wilder and more experimental is what Raymond Kersh is doing at Edna's Table in Sydney. The most Aboriginal is the Brambuk Koori Restaurant at Hall's Gap in Victoria where Sam Fairs is executive chef. The most cleverly tourist-market oriented is Andrew Fielke's Red Ochre Grill, a robust concept launched in Adelaide in 1992, now in Cairns and set to cross the country. Red Ochre declare they bring tropic and desert foods and traditional Aboriginal cooking methods to a modern kitchen and cuisine. Rodney Bodney, the Fielkes' Aboriginal pastry chef, did a much talked about yabbies in puff pastry when Red Ochre mounted an Native Australian Cuisine festival in New York.

Certain significant events marked the eighties and influence just how well we eat now and in what circumstances. Sydney journalist Cyril Pearl, who had written of the 1960s, 'wine was on their lips but beer was still in their bellies', could have carried on to say of the seventies, wine was on their lips and in their bellies, and of the eighties that food was on their lips while wine was in their bellies. Food was the buzz. Fine dining was whipped into even more of a

Left to bottom, top to bottom: Sydney's favourite brasserie, The Bayswater Brasserie, co-owned by Tony Papas; Anders Ousbäck when at the Wharf Restaurant, Sydney; fillet of kangaroo from the Red Ochre Grill; Hermann and Fay Schneider; David Thompson and Peter Bowyer from Darley Street Thai; Damien Pignolet, currently at Bistro Moncur; Andrew Blake's quail sausage roll; Serge Dansereau, executive chef, The Regent, Sydney; Gilbert Lau's renowned Flower Drum restaurant

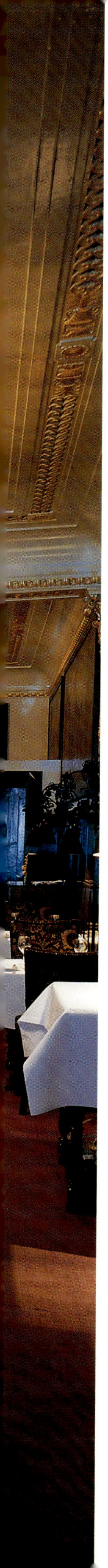
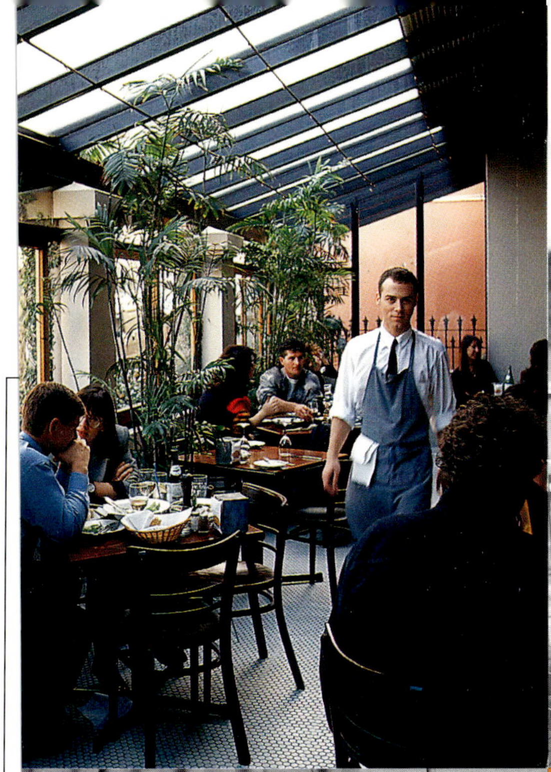
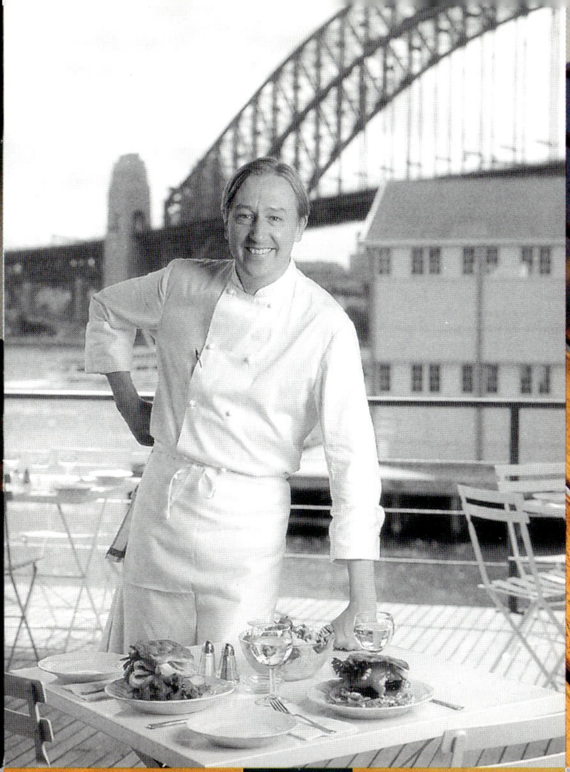
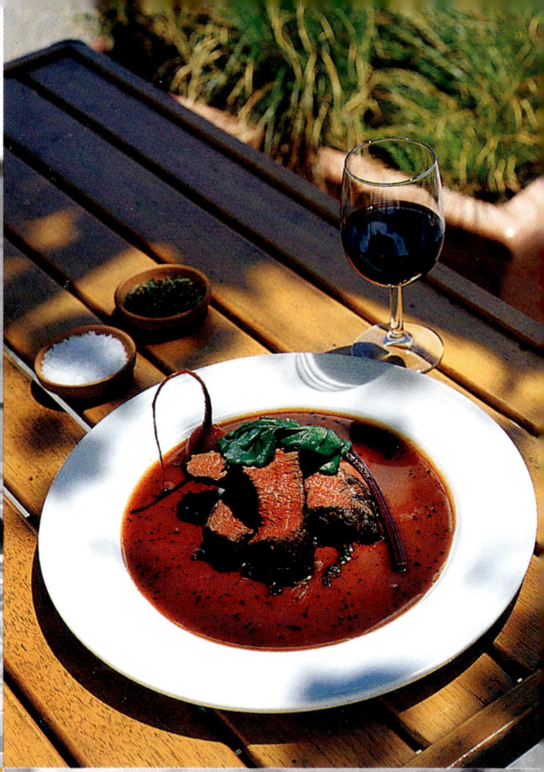
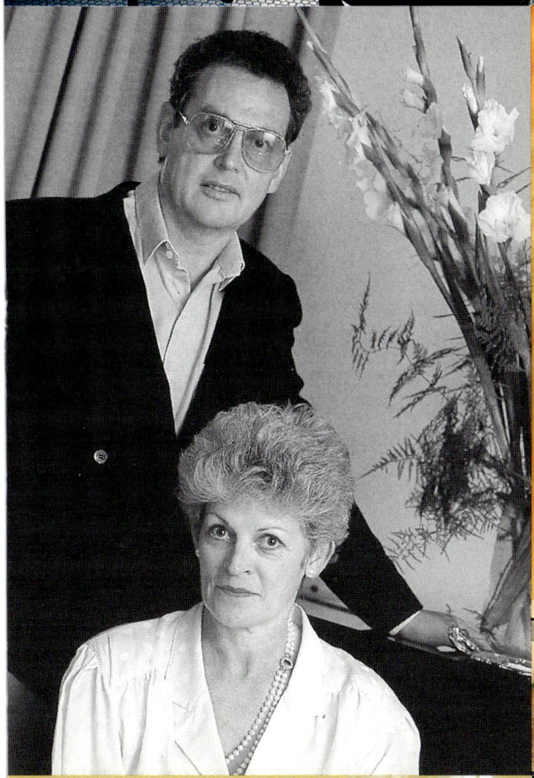
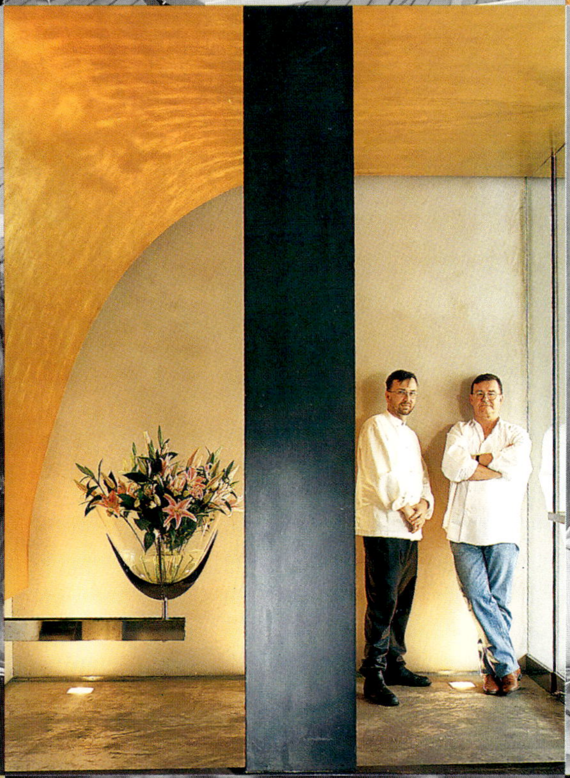
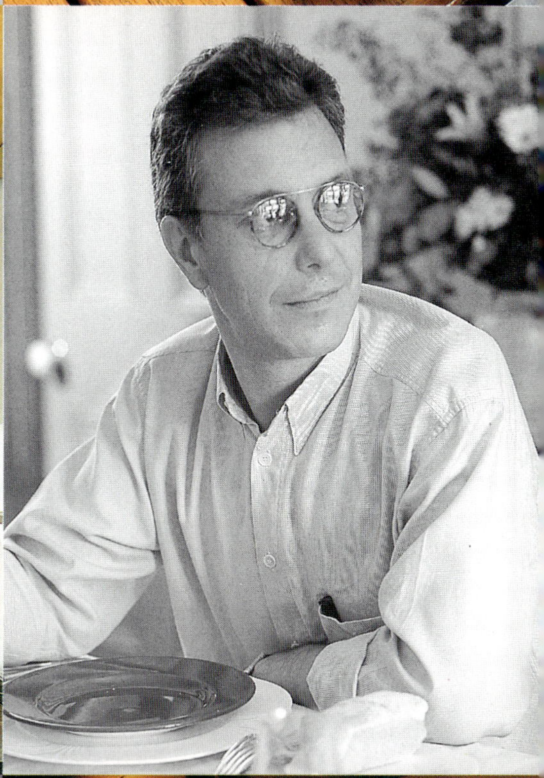
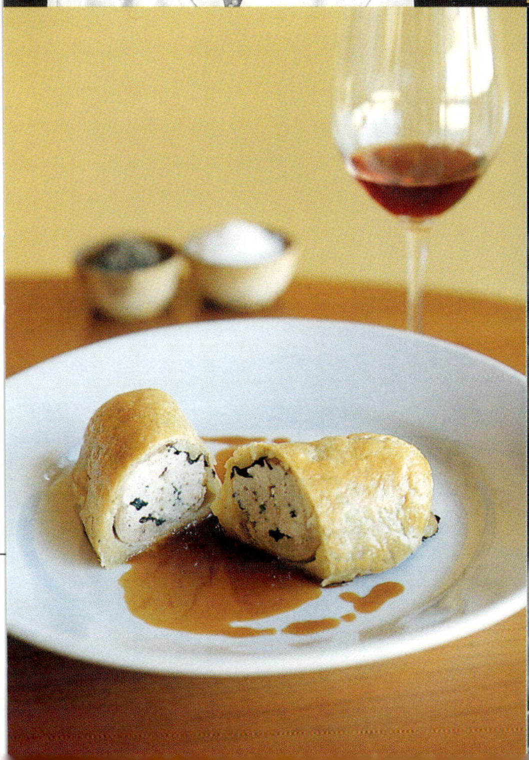
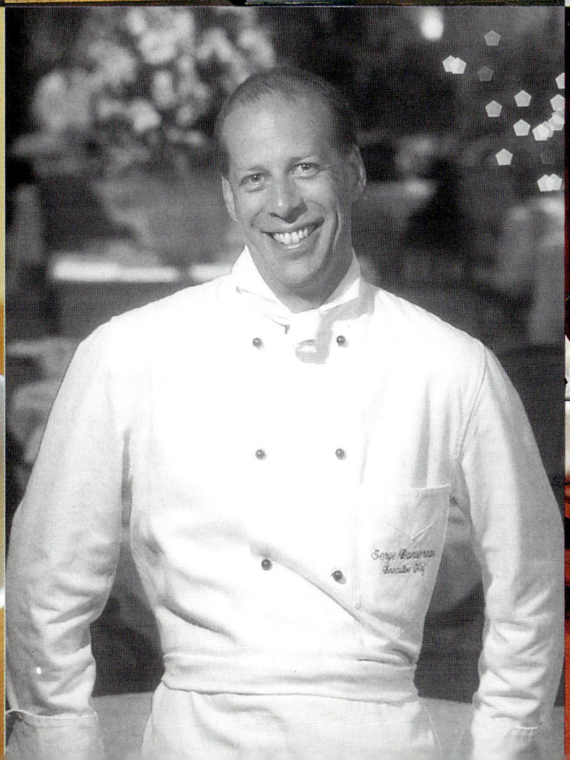
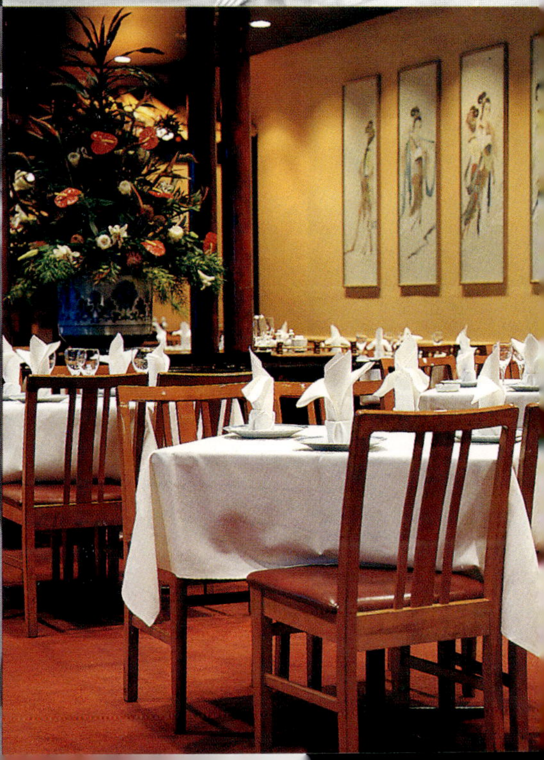

formal froth in Melbourne, with some excellent chefs opening serious restaurants: Stephanie Alexander moved Stephanie's Restaurant to an imposing Victorian villa in Hawthorn, Greg Brown was obsessively refining things French at Brown's in Armadale. And the clever Tansy Good was to open Tansy's Bistrot. It was the perfect moment for the Tsindos who did quite beautiful simple food in Bourke Street and for Bill Marchetti, vigorous chef owner of Marchetti's Latin and later Marchetti's Tuscan Grill. Restaurateur-cum-food stylist Gloria Staley was paying close attention to surfaces at the swish Fanny's and Glo Glo's before masterminding her Sydney challenge, the opening of Chez Oz in Kings Cross with her talented young chef Andrew Blake. And Ronnie di Stasio became partner in Rosati's, the implacably handsome Milanese-style brasserie that epitomised the histrionic moment.

In Sydney money and glamour pumped up the action with new recognition of the importance of position. Financier Leon Fink built Bilson's on Circular Quay as the star vehicle for Tony Bilson, Carol Jaggard and chef Neil Perry opened the Blue Water Grill (creating char-grill heaven on a Bondi headland), Victoria Alexander took over the Bather's Pavilion at Balmoral Beach and food and wine expert Anders Ousbäck was asked to run the Wharf restaurant at the Sydney Theatre Company's headquarters on Walsh Bay. He hesitated but after one look capitulated. Now Opera House catering consultant Ousbäck has a northern beaches background that is more Ibsen and Escoffier than surf and turf, and his impeccable provenance includes three years' apprenticeship with the great wine man Len Evans, three more in the kitchen and front of house at Two Faces with Hermann Schneider. Blissfully unconcerned about East meeting West, Ousbäck is 'of the school of poaching, frying, braising, proper stuff'. He did the Barracks Café, the Wharf, the restaurant at the Art Gallery of New South Wales, and Taylor Square and then Dov with Dov Sokoni. He could be held partly responsible for the fresh modern standards of absolute professionalism that we now enjoy. And if anyone wished to chart the rise and fall of trendy ingredients through the eighties all they need do is read the ten boxes of menus Ousbäck has deposited with the Mitchell Library in Sydney.

The clearest message of what was to come was the instantly successful 1982 opening of the Bayswater Brasserie when three clever Kiwis, Robert Smallbone, Dean Williams and chef Tony Papas, showed Sydney precisely what it needed: a sparky, highly professional non-stop restaurant suiting the ingrained laid-back local style.

5-STAR HOTELS Grand hotels were not all that grand until international changes in taste and demand upped the ante and in 1983 Melbourne and Sydney got their Regents. The opening of the Regent of Sydney launched the dynamic and fruitful partnership of general

Right: The opu...
Florentino—a Melbou...
Above: Rinaldi
from

Poached tomatoes with
Kervella goat ricotta from the
Bayswater Brasserie

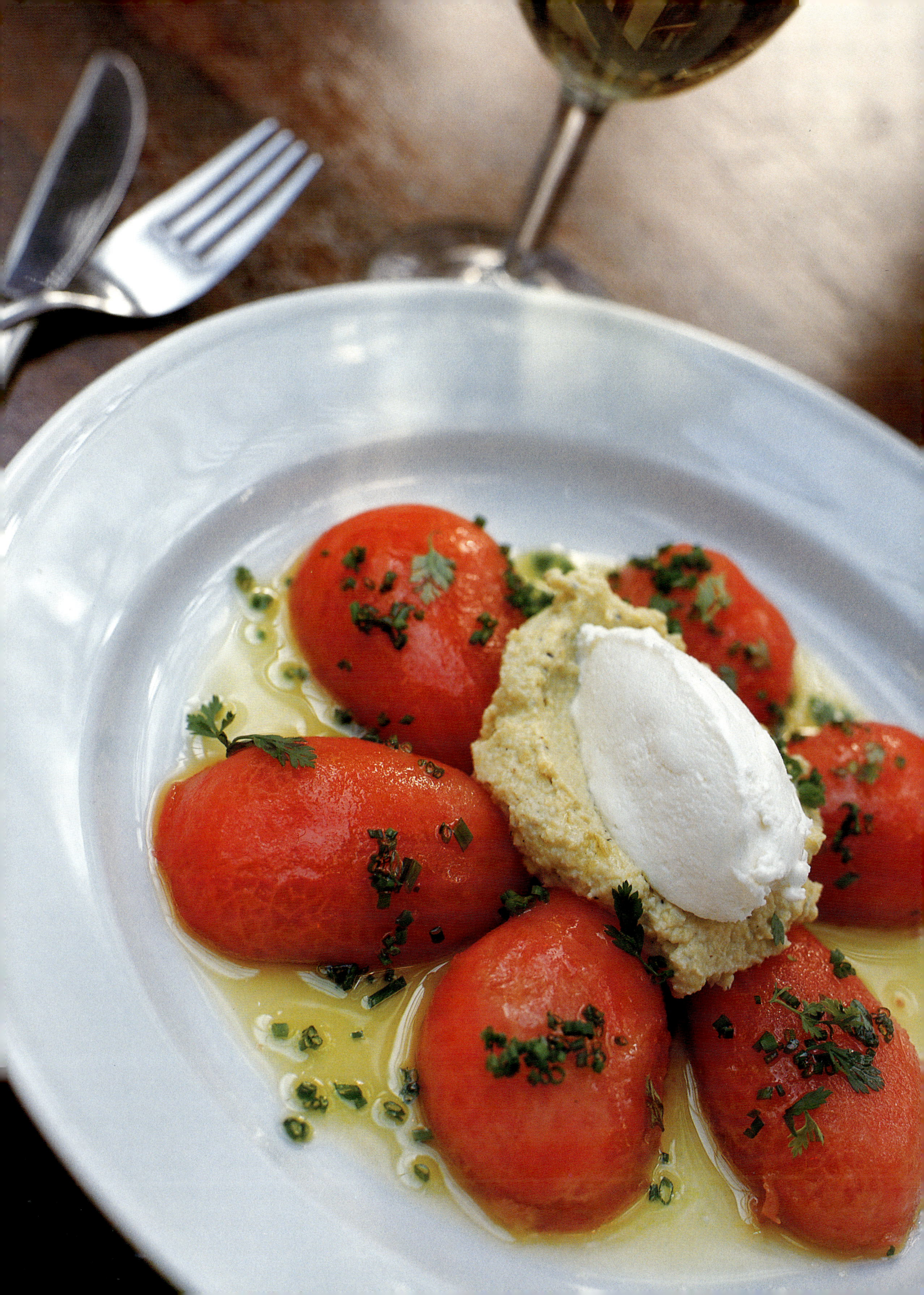

THE COFFEE EXPERTS

For nearly fifty years, the name Cantarella Brothers has been at the forefront of the Australian marketplace as a purveyor of impeccable quality gourmet products.

The Australian-owned company was founded by two brothers, Orazio and Carmelo Cantarella, in 1947. The brothers took the bold, entrepreneurial step in those post-war years—when Australia's migrant intake was burgeoning—by anticipating the demand among the new Australians for traditional flavours of 'home'. Chief among these was the demand for quality, freshly blended European-style coffee. And here, the Cantarella brothers excelled.

Many Australians still recall the pre-war years when the only coffee available was either ersatz or coffee derivative of questionable origin. Now, Australians have learnt the meaning of honest, robust coffee flavour, and the European coffee ritual has become an essential ingredient of Australian's everyday life. One has only to look at the boom in the cafe culture which flourishes not just in major metropolitan centres but provincial towns as well. Even more significantly, Australians with non-European backgrounds have fully embraced the habit of serving quality brewed or filtered coffee in their own homes.

To coffee connoisseurs in particular, the Cantarella Group's flagship brand, Vittoria Coffee, epitomises rich, full-flavoured coffee in the best European tradition. Coffee simply doesn't come any better.

The coffee is sourced from all over the world and is closely scrutinised by the group's own connoisseurs and master blenders to meet their exacting standards before it is distributed in the Australian marketplace.

Vittoria Coffee is roasted in Australia and contains only quality Arabica beans. While the primary and traditional source of the coffee beans used in the Cantarella Group's products is Brazil, there is also an Australian-grown component. Their Breakfast Blend actually uses Australian coffee grown high in the luxurious environment of far north Queensland's Atherton Tablelands.

The Cantarella Group are not only masters when it comes to roasting and

Right: Ripe Arabica coffee cherries from the Atherton Tablelands Far Right: A coffee plantation on the Atherton Tablelands

packaging. They also pioneered the vacuum pack—a 'brick hard' pack which seals in aroma and flavour, giving it lasting freshness. The group also distributes commercial equipment such as Espresso machines and bulk brewing equipment, as well as Espresso plungers and percolators for home use.

While Vittoria coffee is virtually a household name, several other products distributed by the group are also on the tip of the discerning consumer's tongue: the famous Norwegian cheese—Jarlsberg, Giralda olive oil, Barilla Pasta, and most recently King Oscar Sardines. This line-up alone almost makes a gourmet repast in itself!

The Cantarella Group—an established and highly-respected importer, manufacturer and wholesaler—is headquartered in Sydney, and through its six branches extensively services all states including country areas. Thanks to the group's highly advanced computerised distribution network and dedicated sales force—but above all—their commitment to quality, the group covers the nation. They also export to New Zealand and the South Pacific.

In short, the two founders, the brothers Cantarella, have more than met and matched the Australia/Pacific region's constantly evolving demand for 'good taste'.

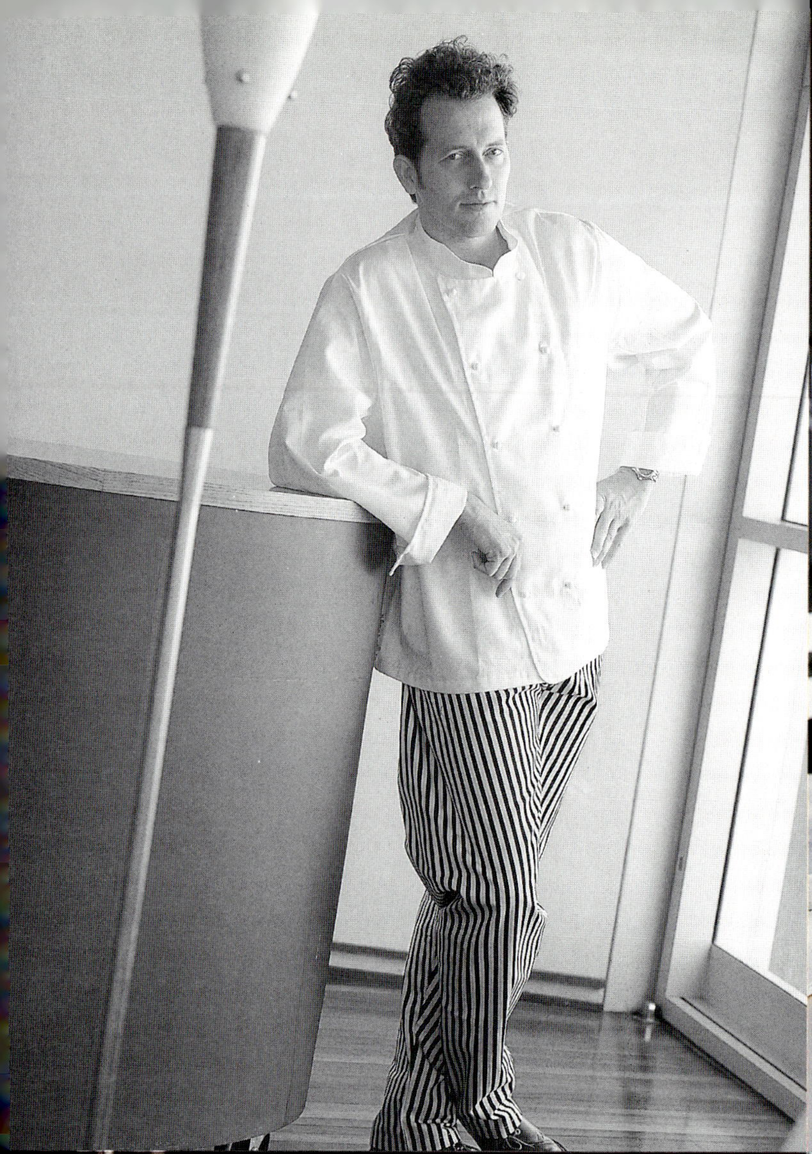
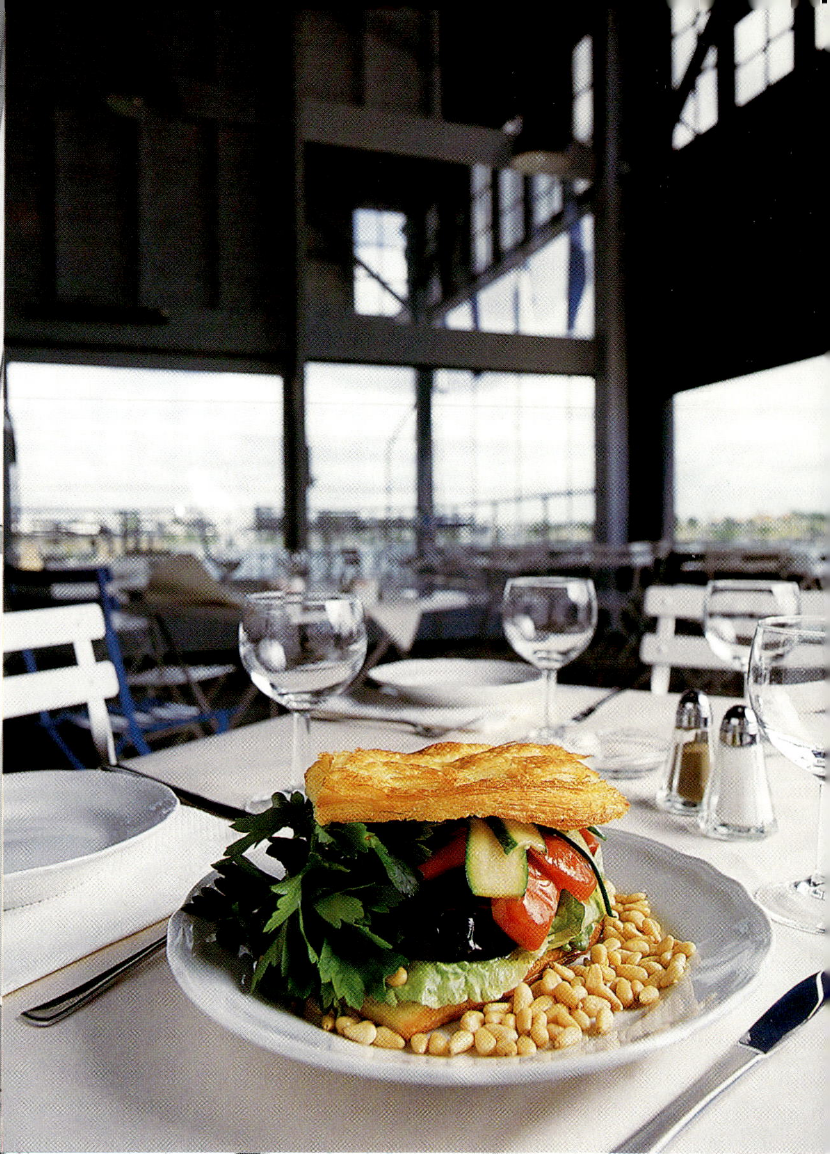
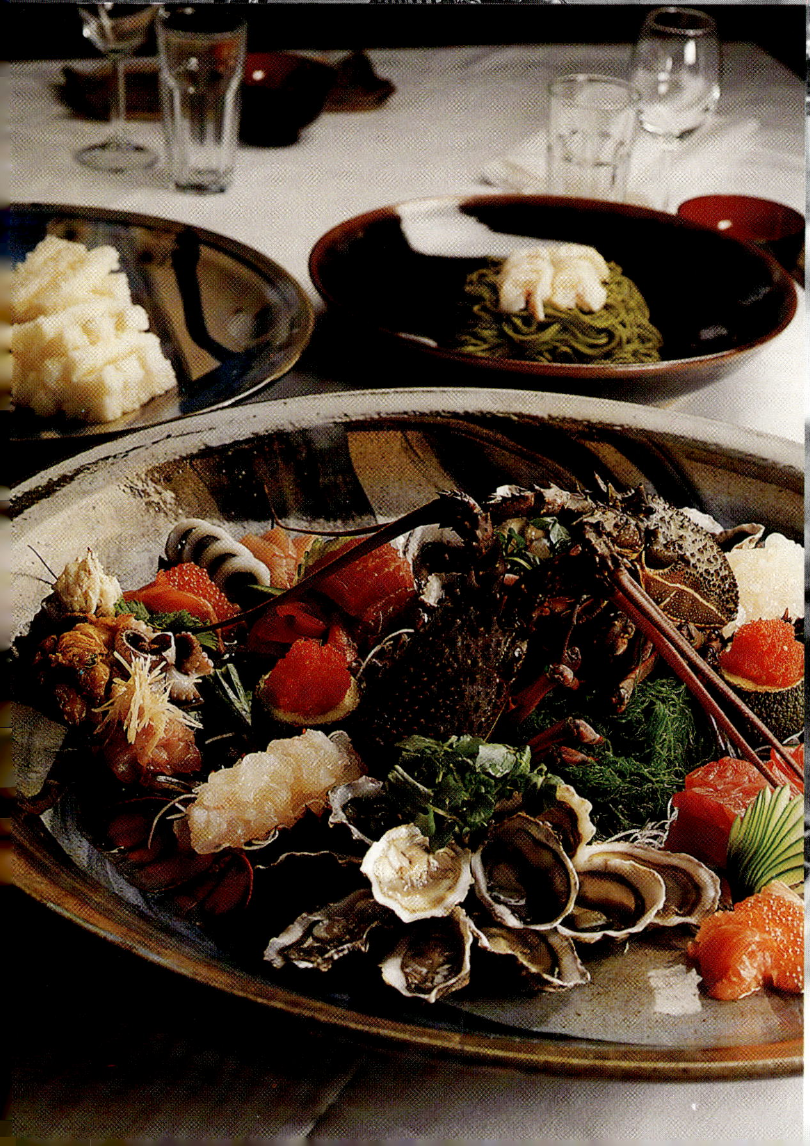
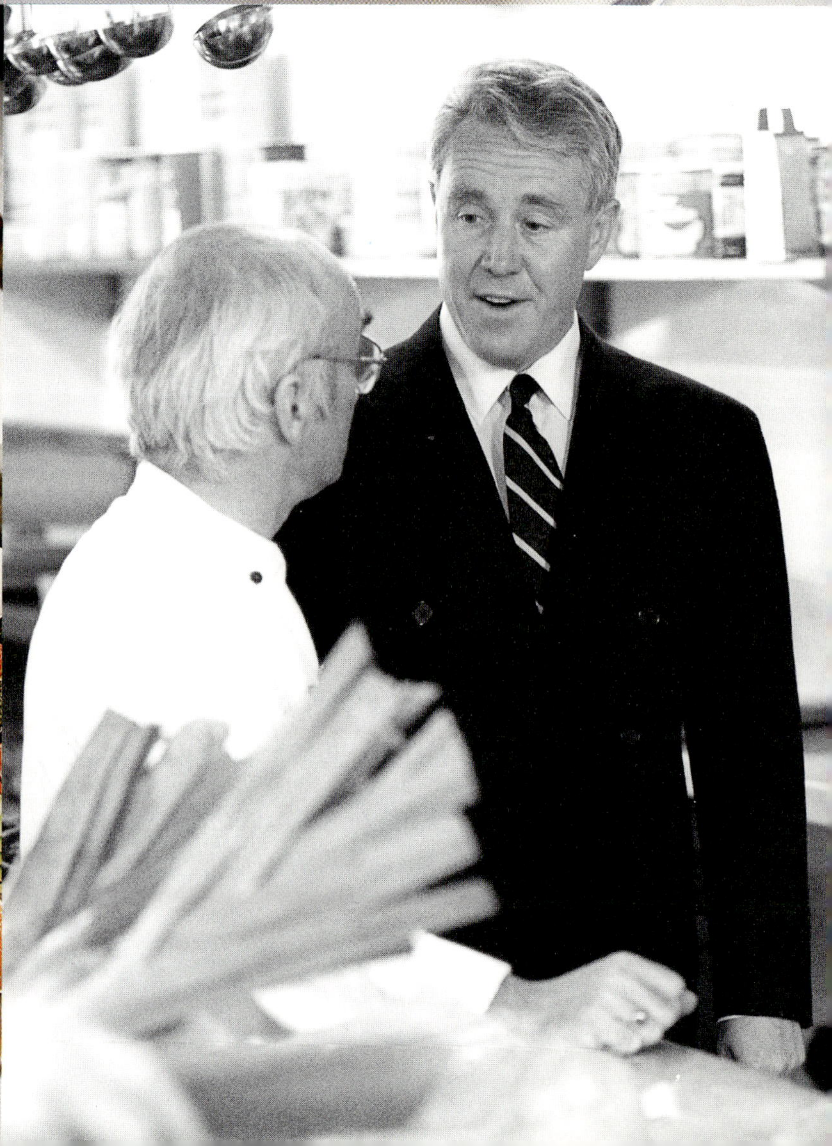

Influences · Tastes of Australia

manager Ted Wright and executive chef Serge Dansereau. To quote Anders Ousbäck: 'Never before had we seen such qualitative levels of hoteliering in this country. They opened with such sophistication and style and that filtered down. It set the standard, the precedent, made others come up to scratch. Its training programme started spitting people out back into the industry.'

Back home in Canada Dansereau had a useful history turning restaurants around by turning them into regional specialists. Backed by the healthy hotel budget this experience helped him become a prime mover in the development of the produce market, and not only to the benefit of the Regent's top restaurant Kables which is Dansereau's personal platform. Dansereau belongs to a Sydney chef/restaurateur network giving professional support with a generous camaraderie that would have been unthinkable in the more paranoid climate of Melbourne. Scenarios then included Dansereau discovering the first boxes of Florentine radicchio, ringing Anders Ousbäck and offering him a dozen boxes gratis. Scenarios now include Christine Manfield of Paramount borrowing betel leaves from David Thompson at Darley Street Thai and Armando Percuoco rushing truffled eggs from Buon Ricordo to his good friend Tetsuya Wakuda in Rozelle.

The brilliant maverick Lord McAlpine who was investing in his great love affair with Australia at the time became part-owner of Sydney's Inter-Continental Hotel, the nineteenth-century treasury building meshed with modern hotel that opened in 1988. McAlpine's involvement, combined with the powerful enthusiasm of general manager Wolfgang Grimm, probably ensured that from the heights of The Treasury Restaurant to the new wood-fired pizzas of it's Thirty Something brasserie this hotel operates at the highest levels.

Like the best hotels, catering has also changed out of all recognition. If in earlier times clever Sydney cooks such as Joan Campbell and then Anders Ousbäck set a certain standard, now catering is on a grand scale and no-one misses out. A level of cheffing and service operates all the way through from parliament to street, from the corporate military operations of caterers Spotless who fuel the governing stomach in Canberra and the Arts Centre in Melbourne, through Peter Rowland who in an historic thirty years of catering has done the tastiest and the classiest parties in Australia, to such modern, stylish and imaginative operators as Louise Lechte in Melbourne and Belinda Franks in Sydney.

As the taste of the town improves, the best of modern Australian cuisine filters through, and all life is catered for.

Antonia Williams

Clockwise from top left: Andrew Blake from Blakes; Fougaffe filled with eggplant, capsicum, tomatoes, zucchini and pine nuts from the Wharf; caterer Peter Rowland; a Tasmanian seafood platter Tetsuya Wakuda-style

THE WORLD'S FINEST

In an age where brand names come and go, 170 years of consumer loyalty to the Cadbury name is something in which to take pride. Cadbury confectionery has been available in Australia since the 1880s. In 1918 Cadbury merged with J S Fry (founded in 1728). In the 1920s they were joined in Australia by the firm of James Pascall Limited (started in 1866). The Australian company was then called Cadbury-Fry-Pascall, and it was this company which built the first Cadbury factory in Tasmania and began to produce Cadbury Dairy Milk™ Milk Chocolate, known for its famous 'glass and a half of full cream dairy milk'.

Since John Cadbury started his business in 1824 in Bournville, England, the name Cadbury has become synonymous with the world's finest eating and drinking chocolate. Because of their high quality and delicious taste, Cadbury products readily gained acceptance in Australia as the business went from strength to strength.

From these beginnings Cadbury has built a portfolio of leading brand names through a series of acquisitions, the creation of successful new products and through strategic moves into new confectionery markets in other countries.

In 1967 the Cadbury operation in Australia acquired MacRobertson Confectionery, a Victorian firm which began in the 1880s. Among its legacy of famous brand names are Old Gold Chocolate (1916), Cherry Ripe (1924) and Freddo, now Australia's most favoured children's confectionery product.

It was through MacRobertsons that Cadbury gained the factory at Ringwood which currently produces Cadbury's leading bar lines, children's lines, many of the Cadbury and Red Tulip Easter and Christmas lines and Cadbury cooking chocolates.

Red Tulip has manufactured traditional European-style fine milk chocolate and rich dark chocolate, specialty chocolates and seasonal gifts

Influences - Tastes of Australia

such as Easter Eggs in Australia since the 1940s, and became part of the Cadbury business in 1987.

In 1969 the Cadbury business merged with Schweppes—the famous soft drinks manufacturer. Ever since they have continually expanded in the consumer market place. Trade names such as Red Tulip confectionery, Europe health bars and Cottee's jams, cordials and desserts are now also part of the expanding Cadbury Schweppes business in Australia, New Zealand and Asia Pacific.

Cadbury also has a fast-growing food services business which supplies food professionals in the hospitality, restaurant, catering and industrial home food preparation industries.

A separate confectionery distribution business also services the needs of the confectionery retail market from warehouses and depots throughout Australia.

Today, Cadbury Australia employs people throughout Australia, New Zealand, Asia and the Pacific. With over $1 billion in annual retail sales, Cadbury Schweppes Australia is a major part of Cadbury Schweppes plc, the international parent company, which has its head office in London and manufactures in over twenty countries.

Left: The perfect couple—coffee and Cadbury's Cappuccino chocolates Above: Freddos on the production line

CHEFS &

Right: Reef fish with bok choy pancetta and garlic mayonnaise from Mesclun Below: Gai Bilson and Janni Kyritsis; Peter Doyle from Cicada, Sydney

HEROES

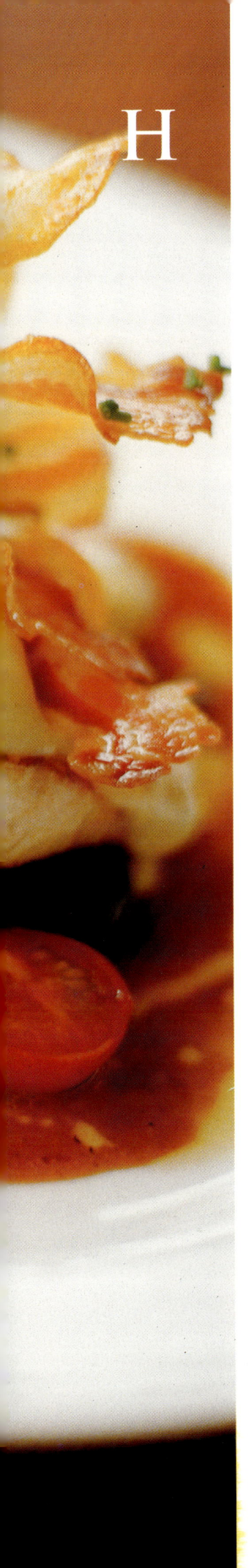

Celebrating Rare Talent

Who cuts the mustard now? As Melbourne and Sydney shrug off provincial attitudes and open up to their natural advantages with restaurants where the sharply designed quality of the fit-out is as much a given as the quality of the food, we celebrate the individual chef and the restaurant as hero. Despite herd instincts, there is a kaleidoscopic richness and character out there.

In Sydney, traditional territories get new injections of life. East Sydney, Darlinghurst and Kings Cross in particular pulsate with the openings of cafes, bistros, brasseries and restaurants. If the newest in Kings Cross are Rocket, Mesclun, Pond and Peter Doyle's wonderful revamped, relaxed, rechristened Cicada, the benchmark is the Bayswater Brasserie with chef Tony Papas still at the stove, doing such irresistible dishes as his Illabo lamb in a salt crust. A dozen years down the track and the Bayswater plays on with seductive, user-friendly consistency.

Sydney's new culinary geography embraces everything from far out west to key ozone positions on Bondi beach. At Ravesi's Hotel, the first floor brasserie offers idyllic blue views with fresh uncomplicated food, while at the Sportsbar Andrew Davies, who trained at the Blue Water Grill, Bayswater Brasserie and Streeton's, exemplifies the youthful surfing Sydney chef who sears and sizzles in full sight of the sea. His food: a whole roast snapper with fennel, sage and capers, perhaps, and a seriously good breakfast.

Old flavours include Italian and the traditions are strong. Beppi Polese is at Beppi's in East Sydney, founded in 1956. Norton Street, Leichhardt, is the flourishing heart of Italian Sydney. Chef restaurateur Armando Percuoco keeps the vigorous and proper traditions of Naples and Tuscany alive at Buon Ricordo where he currently cooks quite delicious food in tandem with Darren Taylor who is not revealing his decidedly French background. At Armando

Percuoco's second restaurant, Gastronomia Chianti in Surry Hills, the mood is more Milanese deli cafe. And Stefano Manfredi with the greater famiglia Manfredi produces a true strength of character and individuality in his cooking for the Restaurant Manfredi in Ultimo.

French still has its variegated and purist corners. An all-time favourite is the French Pacific Sydney flavour created by Chrissie Juillet and Jean Claude Wané at their tiny cafe Passion de Fruits relocated on a Surry Hills corner. At Cleopatra's in Blackheath in the panoramic bush of the Blue Mountains, Perigordienne Dany Chouet carries on cooking her classic cuisine grand-mère. With her partner Trish Mullene she has made this a perfect example of the nurturing boutique hotel not too far beyond the city where the indulgent diner can bed down for the night. (The best out-of-Melbourne example is chef Marieke Brugman and Sarah Stegley's Howqua Dale Gourmet Retreat.)

New flavours include the finer examples of Native Australian Cuisine with Jean-Paul Bruneteau and his Koori apprentices cooking at Riberries 'Taste Australia' in Surry Hills with a menu that may boast emu carpaccio, a bunya, myrtle and warrigal ravioli on a red centre of desert tomato and always the subtle signature rolled wattle seed pavlova. Raymond Kersh at Edna's Table in the city, initially influenced by Jean-Paul Bruneteau, has now set off on his own experimental course with native delicacies.

Grand hotels continue to make their mark. If the Nikko in Potts Point placed the best restaurant in the worst position, thereby enjoying only a fleeting star chef, the Observatory Hotel did nothing of the sort. They used guest cheffery to launch the Oriental Cafe with Anton Mossiman-trained Kit Chan flying in, cooking up a storm and flying out, leaving the stage to her number two, the Cipriani-trained Mark Clayton. A fine consistency describes Serge Dansereau, executive chef at the Regent of Sydney who applies as much thought to his delectable club sandwiches as he does with his chef's tables and menus for Kables restaurant, where a descriptive dish would of course be fish, the ravioli parcel of West Australian scampi with tomatoes various, otherwise the saddle of hare in a light pepper sauce. And, of course, there is the brilliant Tony Bilson, now chef and lord of The Treasury Restaurant at the Inter-Continental. As a schoolboy Bilson ran an account at the Balzac in Melbourne and on Georges Mora's recommendation became apprenticed to Paul Harbulot at Johnnie Walker's Bistro in Sydney. He believes that food in association with wine still commands the culinary heights, talks of 'playing a more interesting game with taste', of finessing technique and writing cookbooks. And the George Freedman crimson walls hung with big black and cobalt Michael Johnson paintings provide suitable background to his coddled salmon and veal flank pot au feu.

Italian style fave con pancetta (a traditional combination of beans and bacon) from Buon Ricordo

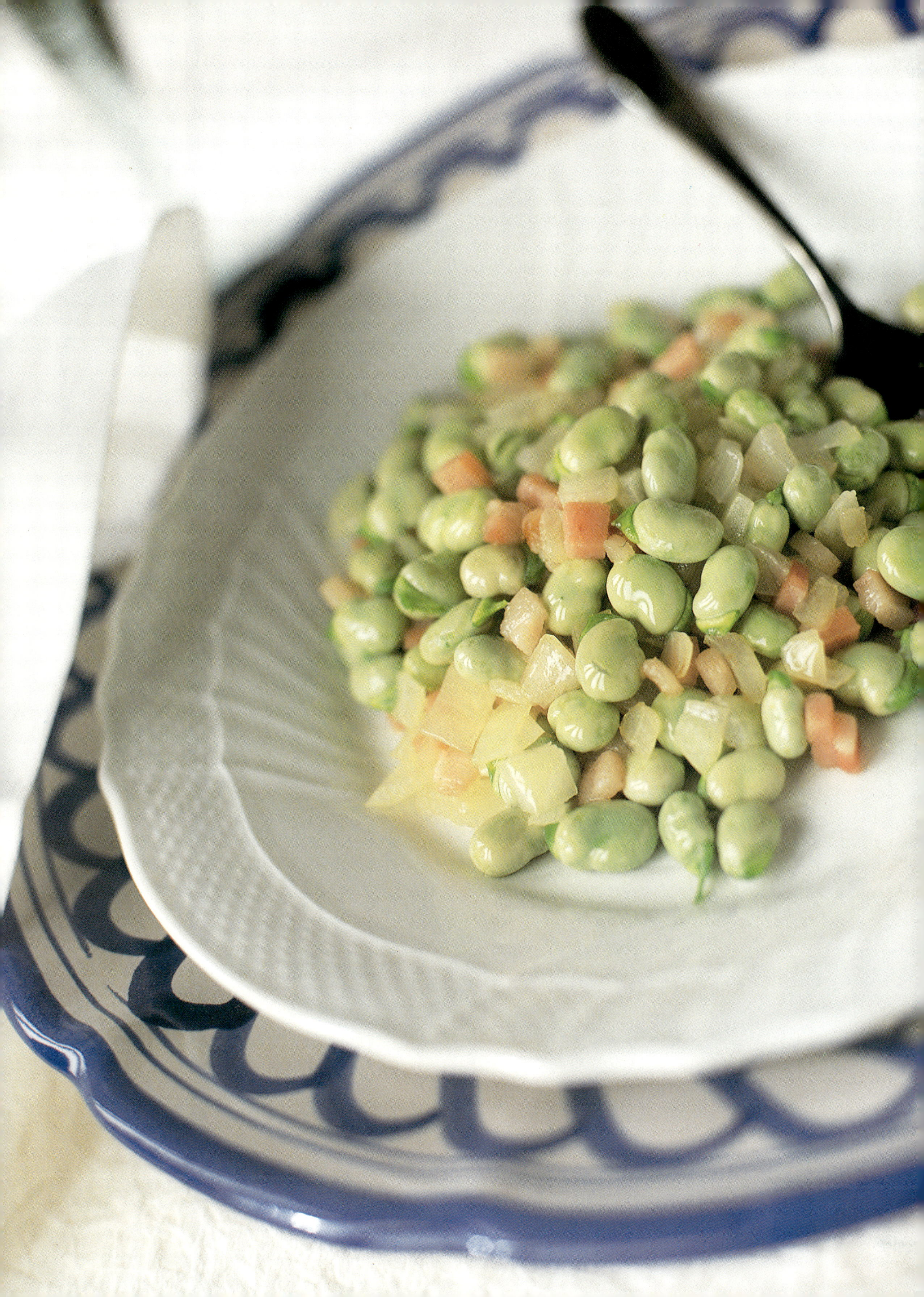

Right: Australian lamb cutlets seared to perfection on Gaggenau equipment Above: The ultimate luxury—cooking with Gaggenau

WINNING BY NATURE

From its beginnings in 1906, Winning Appliances has been a family business. It still is; in a showroom with the dimensions of an aircraft hangar, third-generation Winnings take you through the most comprehensive range of kitchen and laundry whitegoods on display in Australia.

It's always a pleasure to do business with Winnings. The family's knowledge of the industry is encyclopaedic, the staff has a thorough grounding, so everything you want to know about any model of any brand on the market is right there, saving you hours of searching. This is one-stop whitegoods shopping.

But the biggest factor in the Winnings formula is its after-sales service: thirty-five staff on the floor in three locations to give each customer full, personal attention, prices from any other store matched and, whether or not the product is in warranty, if there are any problems Winnings will try to fix them (staff keep details of all products, past and present). It's old-style service, where responsibility is taken.

In a cast of thousands, appliances are set out in semi-operational displays so that you can gauge on the spot what will and will not suit your needs. Half of total sales is made up of European brand names (Winnings was at least partly responsible for the growth in European appliances), but Australian products that do well are St George, Vulcan Chef, Westinghouse, Simpson and Kelvinator, and Fisher and Paykel from New Zealand. Winnings is franchised to sell everything.

Think about this: each day Winnings makes 100 deliveries, answers 1,300 telephone calls and turns over about $180,000 worth of stock. And this: business comes from word of mouth and from repeat customers (some fly in from Hobart, Melbourne, Hamilton Island, and some order from New York). It must be the personal touch.

It's Winning by name, winning by nature.

AUSTRALIA - A GOURMET'S PARADISE

Those in the know frequent the Oyster Bar at the Renaissance Hotel, the ANA's top floor Japanese restaurant Unkai and their Horizons Bar. If this delivers dazzling views from its thirty-sixth floor, the Park Hyatt's No 7 Restaurant on Sydney Cove—where chef Brett Patterson is cooking well—gives the full sea level harbour picture. The high octane positions are all filled these days with Sydney at last celebrating its unique physical gifts. It is amusing to recall that for much of this century the only way to enjoy water views as you ate was to go for the great fish experience at the Ozone, later Doyle's on Watson's Bay. You can now eat well, and sometimes brilliantly, at the vantage point of your choice. One time hotel chef Dietmar Sawyere directs hot corporate glamour spot 41 Restaurant and Bar on the forty-first floor of the Chifley Tower, and they have plans for a brasserie at a less dizzying level. Dov Sokoni runs the Wharf restaurant on Walsh Bay with a great user-friendly style which definitely includes the unfussy modern food. Michael McMahon's smart new Catalina, a ten am-to-midnight restaurant that eschews the word brasserie as too fancy, is buzzing on the old Caprice site at Rose Bay. The daytime view over sailboat-strewn waters may be dreamy but it's far too early to take a proper view of the food.

At the MCA (as in Museum of Contemporary Art) Café, a Neil Perry concession hard by his flagship restaurant Rockpool, there is the optimum terrace on which to eat something perfectly simple while gazing upon a pop opera postcard. And there is, of course, the icon on the cake, the Opera House itself, with a restaurant future that promises to be far more ambrosial than previous opera bouffe or buffet. As consultant to English caterers Gardner Merchant who have the $200-million twelve-year contract, Anders Ousbäck has summoned up Sydney's

Above: The Park Hyatt Hotel in the centre of Sydney harbour

*Above: Ravesi's, overlooking
Sydney's world-famous Bondi beach*

finest. Gai Bilson, exchanging one icon for another, will run the Bennelong, once architect Leigh Prentice has returned it to Jorn Utzon's original design intent, with supper club on the balcony. Bilson may be an impeccable pastry chef but her truest talent is in the synthesis of ideas that makes a good restaurant great. At Berowra Waters Inn she worked for a decade in symbiosis with the practical and gifted chef Janni Kyritsis and their professional partnership will continue at Bennelong where the thrust of the food is yet to be revealed but is certain to be both appropriate and, at times, gloriously theatrical. Bilson believes that cooking is an art to complement that of music and song.

VIRTUOSO CHEFS The innovative virtuoso chef is a rare beast. Sydney has several. There is no one the least like Tetsuya Wakuda who orchestrates an extraordinary taste game at Tetsuya's in Rozelle using European technique (learnt at cooking school in Tokyo) with a little injection of his native Japanese. He came here in 1987 and, a one man band, says 'If I'm not in the restaurant I don't open the restaurant'. There are Japanese ingredients (the wasabi mayonnaise), Chinese ingredients (the dried scallop soup) and to make the most of his love of variety in taste and texture, six courses for lunch and twelve for dinner. There is no menu and he may decide only minutes before opening how to treat the oysters. One dish might be the grain-fed beef fillet with a ragout of mushrooms and spinach, another the slow-cooked Atlantic salmon with braised red capsicums, leeks and konbu with parsley and caper oil. He has a licence but likes BYO as so many diners possess fine cellars. There are degustation nights and there is something wonderfully conspiratorial in the Tetsuya/customer relationship. Book early, then throw him a challenge at the last minute and see how he rises to the occasion.

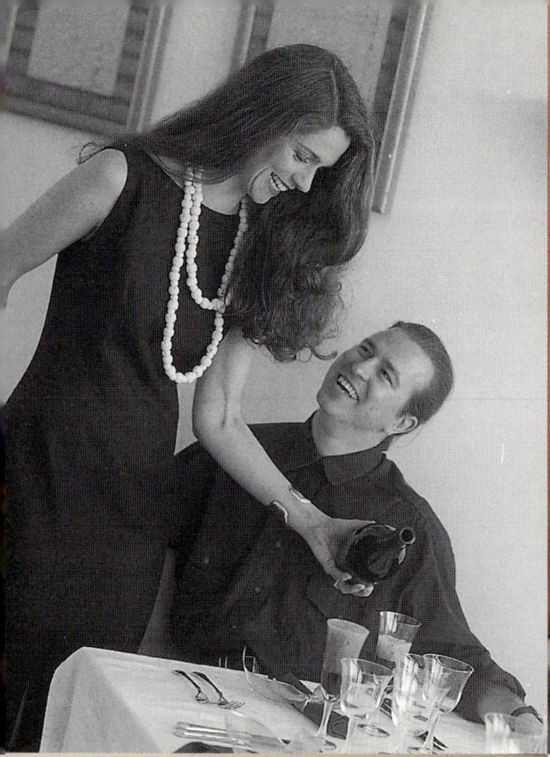
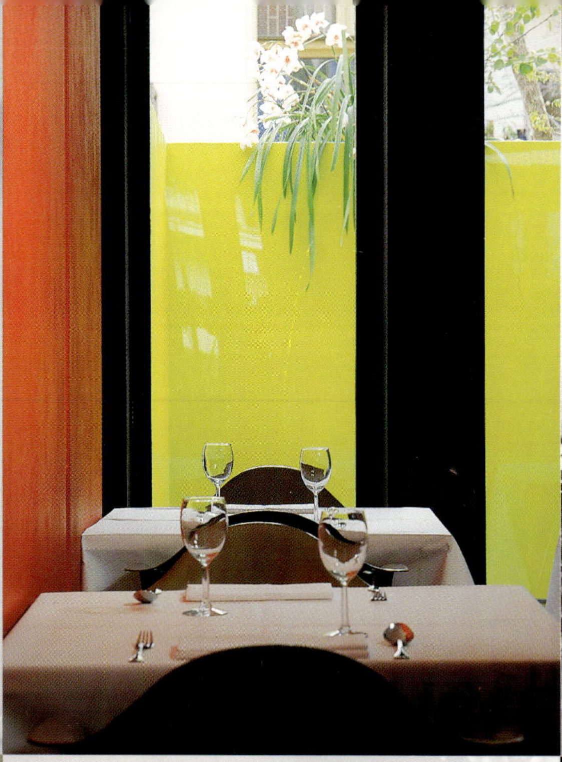
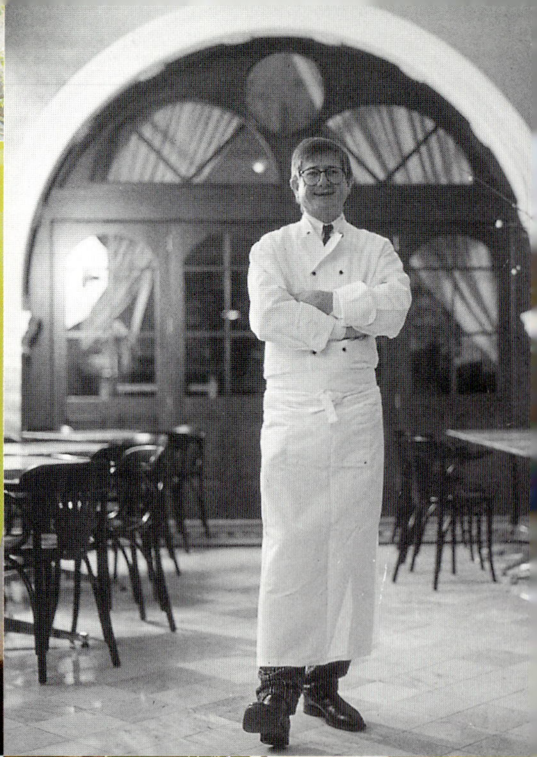
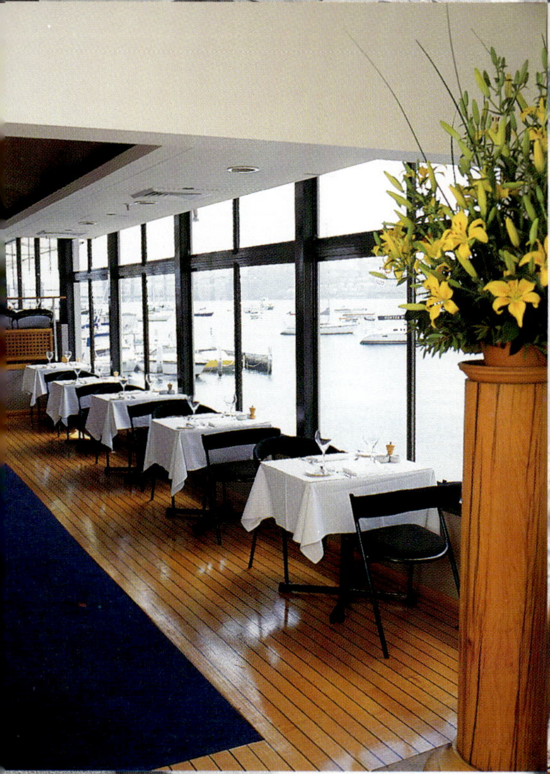
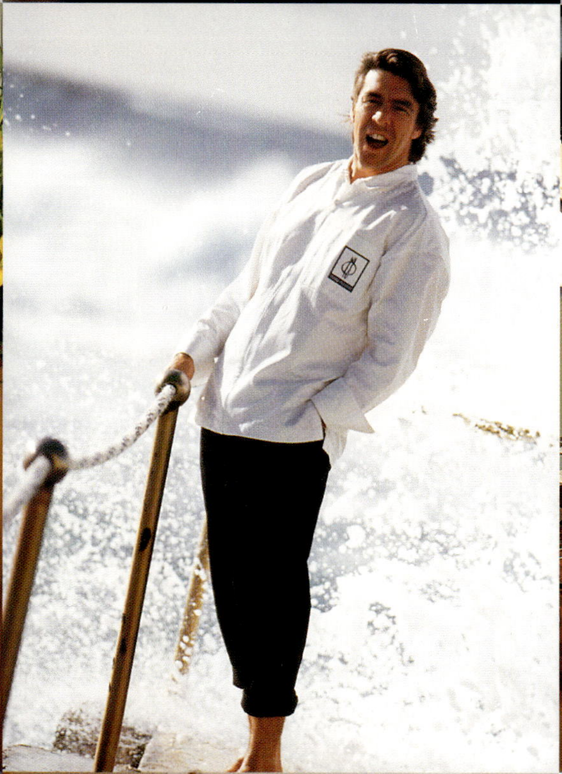
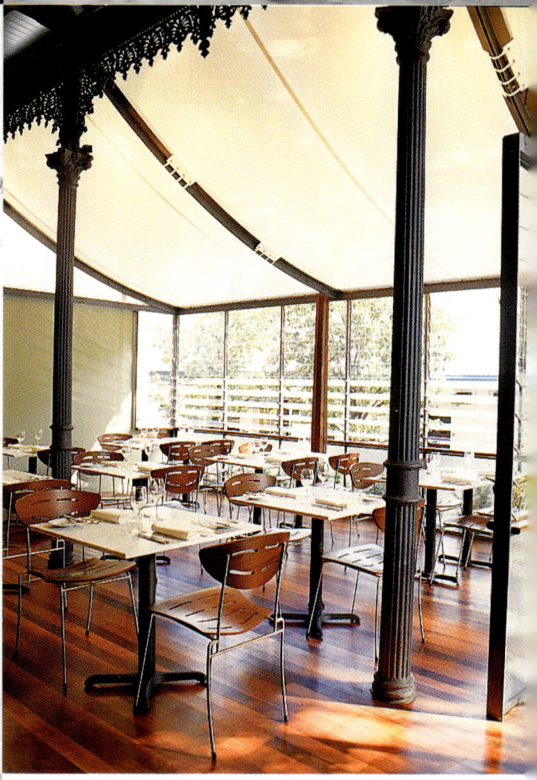
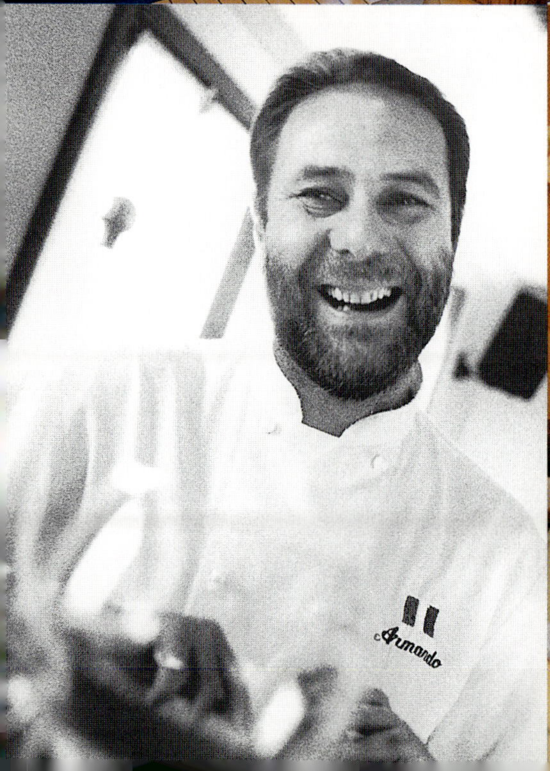
Armando
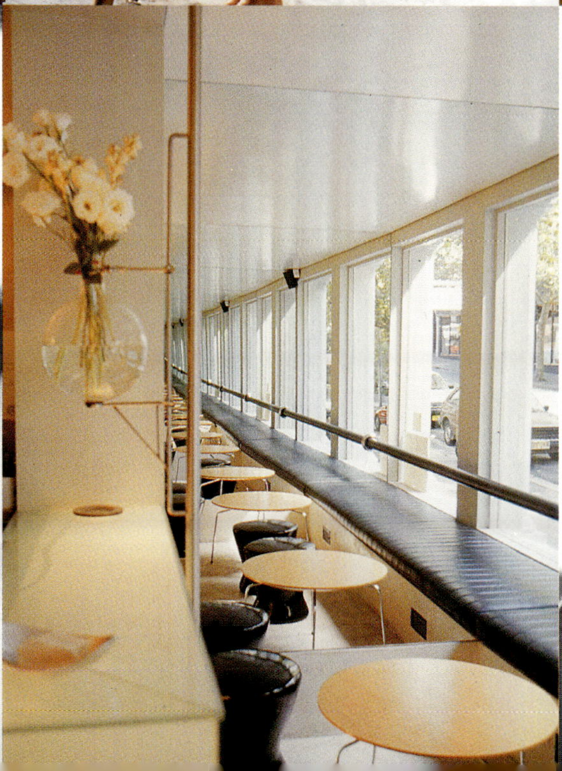
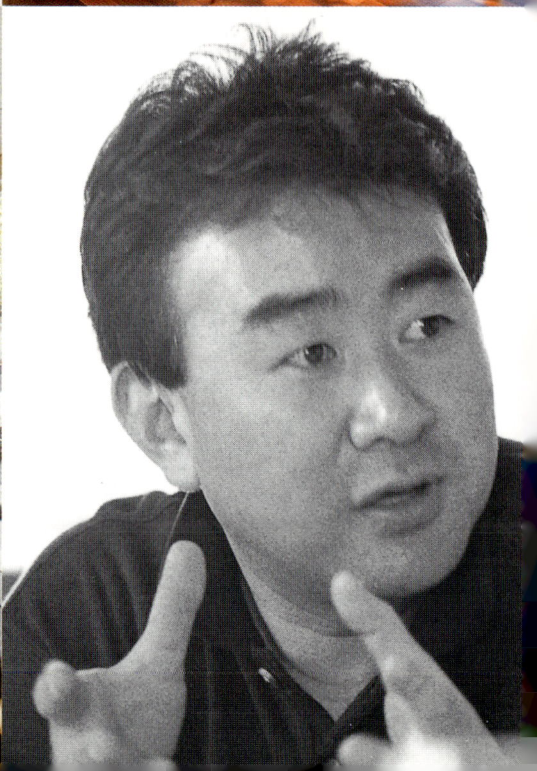

Twenty years ago David Thompson of Darley Street Thai was a chef at Rogue's who meant to go to Tahiti but ended up in Thailand. Now the Siamophile scholar chef, he finesses *rot chart*: 'the finely struck balance of extremes of flavour', which lies at the heart of Thai cooking. Where once he used fifteen ingredients in a curry paste he may now use twenty-two. The food is absolutely delicious and freshness being a Thai imperative the menu changes daily. How about the wine and spice relationship? Uncomfortable, at best de facto, says Thompson. Beer is less contentious. The Iain Halliday fit-out is brilliant and that's not only the Thai silk cushions. Front of house is run to a nicety by David Thompson's partner Peter Bowyer.

Tim Pak Poy is the consummate holistic chef and owner at Claude's, padding barefoot through the tiny greenish grey dining-room, hung with a collection of princely bird's-egg blue Limoges. His Cantonese/Scots background and a youth spent wandering in the orchards, ranges and salt marshes of South Australia have given him a strong sense of the vital connections. Of his apprenticeship with Cheong Lieuw he says, 'Cheong taught me how to eat. A fitness of taste.' He left East meets West a long time ago, and Adelaide at the right moment, coming to work with Damien Pignolet at Claude's in 1987. He likes the label New Australian Classicism, and speaks of love in the kitchen and of clearly defined focused flavour: 'Grilled salmon on beetroot with a glass of pinot noir. That can be the best.'

Of the influential chefs who saw themselves as the Gang of Twelve in the early eighties, a number are still providing the finest heady experiences in contemporary Sydney. Leigh Stone Herbert, after a stint at his family's renowned Gravetye Manor Hotel in England, is catering to the north shore. Gai Bilson is at the Opera House. Tony Bilson is at The Treasury at the Inter•Continental.

Then there are the original surfing chefs, brothers Peter and Greg Doyle. After seven years Peter Doyle has read the runes and with the aid of architect Luigi Rosselli transformed Le Trianon in Potts Point into the more laid-back but equally elegant Cicada. Front of house is run by Beverley Doyle, and it is all a perfectly balanced exercise. The most radical changes are to kitchen design, attitude and prices so it is amazingly good value, with the ravioli of prawns and escalivade terrine with tapenade and black olive bread dishes most expressive of Peter Doyle's style. Greg Doyle does something quite different at The Pier Restaurant in or rather on Rose Bay. His informative and proper kitchen training led to his opening Puligny's in the eighties, and he is the great fish man, an entrepreneurial consultant chef who manages The Pier with his partner chef Steve Hodges spending most time at the stove. A classically satisfying dish may be something as simple as the blue eye cod on mash followed by one of Doyle's

Left to right, top to bottom: Neil and Adele Perry of Rockpool and MCA Cafe; the distinctive design of Darley Street Thai; Tony Bilson at The Treasury, Hotel Inter•Continental; the epitome of dining on the Harbour, the Pier restaurant at Rose Bay; Greg Doyle; the latest addition to inner-city dining, Cicada restaurant at Potts Point; Armando Percuoco, Buon Ricordo and Gastronomia Chianti; the Paramount's mirrored bar; Tetsuya Wakuda.

AUSTRALIA - A GOURMET'S PARADISE

CATERERS FOR ALL

Spotless Catering Services is the major business of the Australian-owned public company Spotless Services Limited, providing catering and management services in over 700 locations in every Australian state and territory and New Zealand. The vastness and diversity of its catering operations firmly place it as the largest contracted services employer in the hospitality industry.

As a catering management company which provides services in host environments, it purposefully does not promote its own branded image. But its presence is very much apparent in the excellence of its product.

Spotless' expertise and streamlined operations mean that it can fully service a variety of locations, ranging from central activity districts to regional centres and remote mining sites.

With over thirty years' experience across a broad spectrum of the hospitality and tourism industry, Spotless is a proven provider of innovative and contemporary catering solutions for clients from the Prime Minister at Parliament House, Canberra, through to the public attending major sporting and cultural events. Spotless is retained by the leading organisations in Australia to cater for their complete hospitality requirements including Sydney International Airport, Taronga Zoo, Melbourne Cricket Ground, the BHP Company Ltd, Commonwealth Bank, Sydney Football Stadium, Victorian Arts Centre and the Australian Defence Force Academy.

Numbers are no object. Spotless can cater at individual locations from as few as fifteen people to as many as 100,000.

A core activity is its operation of catering facilities and hospitality services for companies operating in the corporate and manufacturing sectors. In addition, catering and hotel services are provided in residential locations ranging from university colleges, independent schools/training colleges through to nursing homes/hostels, including the provision of Meals on Wheels service.

Menus are developed on a site-by-site basis, tailored to the needs and conditions of climate, working environments and the requirements of the client.

Chefs & Heroes - Celebrating Rare Talent

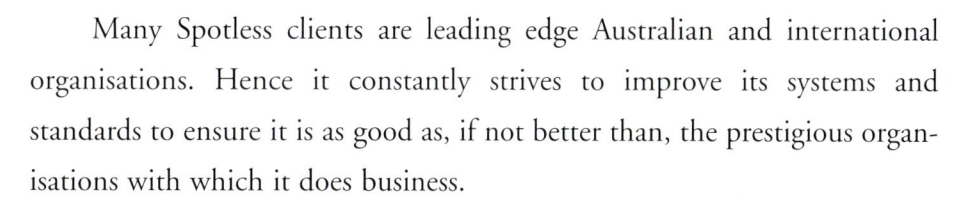

Many Spotless clients are leading edge Australian and international organisations. Hence it constantly strives to improve its systems and standards to ensure it is as good as, if not better than, the prestigious organisations with which it does business.

Spotless' services include complete financial and operational management combined with a significant purchasing network. The company has a national supply office which deals direct with growers and suppliers to procure product into the locations it services. The company policy is to use only leading brands, with preference always shown for Australian-grown and produced food items.

The enjoyment of food and the social activity of eating is a major focus with the emphasis on contemporary Australian cuisine. 'Fresh is best' is also a strong operational philosophy.

As one of the biggest employers in the industry, the company engages the skills of highly-trained executive chefs through to general staff. It also recruits and trains personnel and offers excellent career prospects for those keen for advancement. Spotless is the largest private employer of apprentice cooks in Australia, employing 140 Australia-wide. These apprentices are seen as being the skilled workers of the future.

Spotless is justly proud of its staff's achievements at the last Culinary Olympics held in Frankfurt. Its team captured an astonishing eighteen awards from eighteen entries—six gold, ten silver and two bronze medals. If proof were ever needed of the world class performance of Spotless, there couldn't be a better endorsement.

Prepared by Spotless: (left) The essential texture and colour of fresh vegetables; (above) delicious seafood and a wonderful view from Taronga Park Zoo, overlooking Sydney Harbour

delicate, dangerous prize-winning desserts. He always keeps an unadulterated crème brûlée on the menu.

Nicely rumbustious Kiwi Mark Armstrong was running Pegrum's before sensing a change in the air and opened the Macleay Street Bistro in 1986 with an easier 'T-shirt and jeans' menu. His eponymous north Sydney brasserie Armstrong's, one of the last expensive fit-outs of the eighties, survived and flourishes, feeding the needy northern CBD and those impelled to cross the bridge for his superb meat and game, cooked by Marcia Branson who has been with him since they opened. Now consultant chef to the Woollahra Hotel where he masterminds the popular Bistro Moncur, Damien Pignolet, another Gang of Twelve member, is the chef and fastidious technician who solves all Stephanie Alexander's knottiest problems. Pluses at Bistro Moncur: Colin Holt's excellent fresh French cooking and the sleek modern design by Alexander Tzannes.

A VISUAL FEAST In fact, with the fit-out adding so much to the charisma, designers may be heroes too. In Melbourne the modern visual feast is best expressed by Alan Powell's grasp of traditional Italian meeting contemporary art aesthetic for Café di Stasio, by Christopher Connell's clean and sophisticated cafe style at places such as Baretti and the edgy glamour of Denton Corker Marshall's heavenly bar and basement brasserie at the Adelphi Hotel.

Sydney's most dazzling marriages of food and design must include all Leigh Prentice's takes on monotone and minimal for Dov, for Ditto, and for the ritzy new Catalina on Rose Bay, Burley Katon Halliday's appropriate brilliance for Darley Street Thai and Paramount, and absolutely everything Bill McMahon has done for Neil Perry. McMahon art directs Neil Perry's dreams. And Perry of Rockpool, Rocket and the MCA Café is the quintessential and consummate Sydney chef who synthesises the excellence and fun that great Sydney style is all about. Clutching his bible *Great Chefs of France*, he polished his cooking skills with Stephanie Alexander and with Damien Pignolet at Claude's. He possesses 'a passion to do things properly, for having the best there is', which is reflected from the front of house-keeping to the stove at Rockpool in the Rocks, a series of sharply glamorous spaces, including the Oyster Bar, that reminds some of French Shanghai in the thirties. Here he perfects his tea-based cuisine with such dishes as the smoked trout with red braised shiitake mushrooms, such mushrooms being part of the Perry signature. His brilliant date tart is one more dish that sticks in the memory. Rocket, a non-stop brasserie, is another flavour entirely. The eastern Mediterranean comes through in such dishes as the tripe with chickpeas and the lamb ravioli with a garlic yoghurt

Clockwise from top left: The bar at Baretti; an attractive touch at Baretti's; rooftop bars at the Adelphi Hotel; The Adelphi restaurant

Payphone

BARETTI

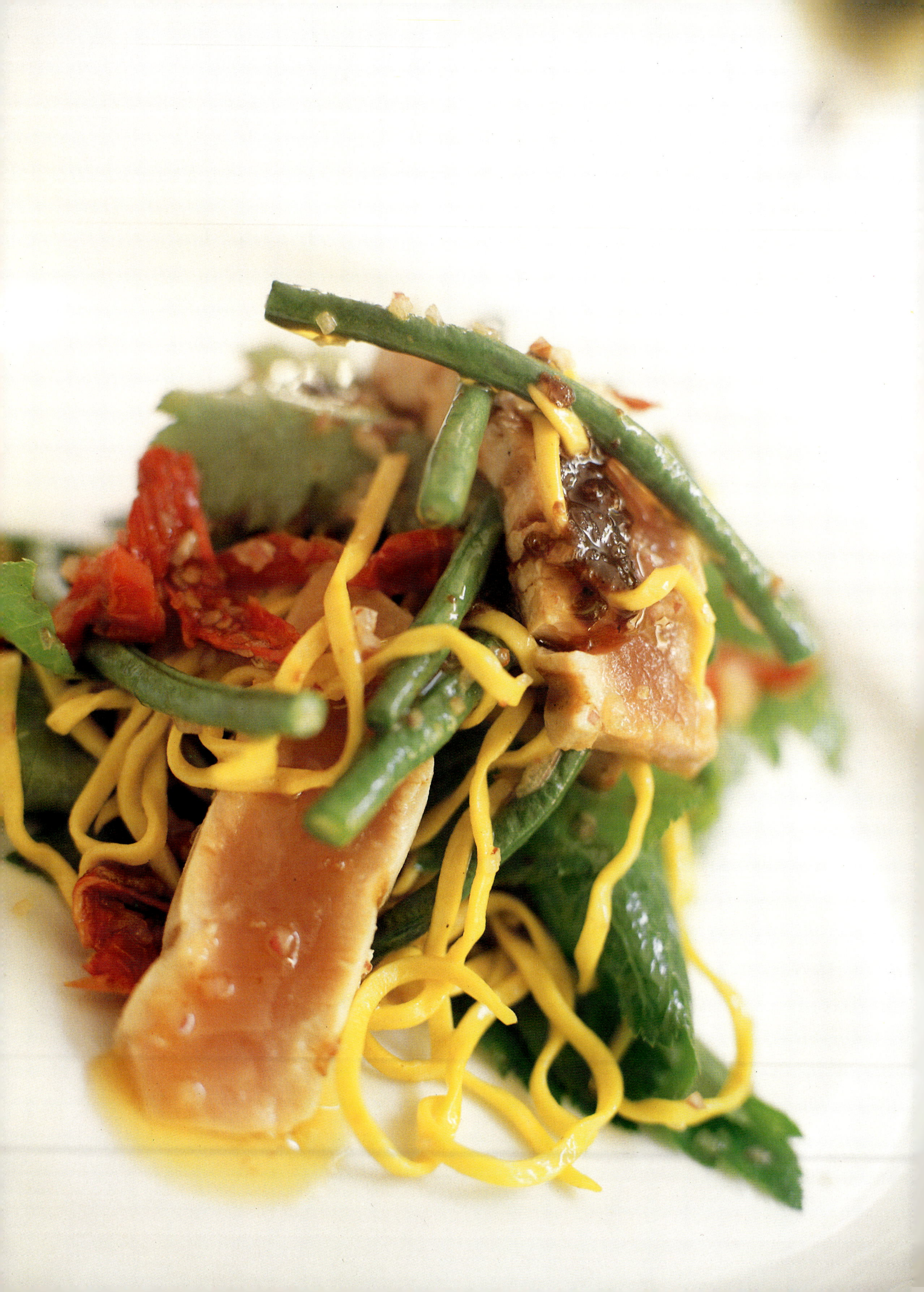

butter. It is always possible that any second now Neil Perry will have opened something else compellingly smart and edible.

Pure pigheadedness allied to natural gifts won Paul Merrony apprenticeships at, amongst others, the Berowra Waters Inn, the Gavroche in London shortly after it won its third star, and the Tour d'Argent in Paris. Now at Merrony's in the city, he does wonders with his refined rustic French food, with offal, game and beef as the pièces de resistance. A great Merrony dish is the braised beef cheek with brussel sprouts, parsnip and veal sweetbreads. Midway between the restaurant and home he has opened his own neighbourhood dining-room, cool cafe Ditto, where Jason Bird cooks up classic risottos and croque mesdames.

Christine Manfield ran away from Queensland at a tender age and, recognising a passion and ambition to become a chef, became apprenticed to Cath Kerry at the Bridgewater Mill Restaurant in the Petaluma winery in South Australia before arriving in Sydney in 1988 with the prime intent of learning from Phillip Searle at Oasis Seros. She did, then leased two pub dining rooms, built a reputation fast and in 1993 with partner Margie Harris opened Paramount in Potts Point with Iain Halliday doing the glistening lemon sorbet and steel fit-out. Manfield describes her food as labour intensive in the kitchen but easy on the plate and hates a feeble approach to flavour. Her five spice duck and shiitake mushroom pie with ginger glaze appears neatly European but contains a clearly oriental spectrum of flavours. Her kitchen supplies Paramount Stores, her mini Dean & Delucca next door.

Who will be the star chefs of Sydney 2000? Many of the above no doubt but interested diners should keep an eye on such new talent in the creation of fresh and simple modern Australian food as Matthew Moran at Paddington Inn Bistro, Mary Jane Hayward ex-Taylor Square at the Forecourt Café at the Opera House, Genevieve Harris at Bather's Pavilion, Gary Skelton operating with wood-fired enthusiasm and skills at The Edge, Anthony Massur, ex-Kit Chan's kitchen at the Observatory, and Stewart Kennedy who took a flying leap from Goodfellas in Newtown to Tribeca in Double Bay. And if one theory has it that chefs now quit their apprenticeships so fast there is no chance of their developing real knowledge or individual style, another theory firmly states that talent will always out. This is positively encouraged in the energetic democracy of Australian food.

If the chefs carry on as heroes, they may have to share some celebrity with designers and, given the increasing and extraordinary quality of the produce, quite a lot of celebrity with suppliers. There are not many daughters of Dansereau yet but there are several sons of Serge, such catalysts as Simon Johnson of providores McDonald & Johnson, Barry and Jamie

Grilled rare tuna with saffron noodles, snake beans and oven-dried tomatoes, a supreme experience from Margie Harris and Chris Manfield at Paramount, Potts Point

McDonald of B & J Lizard, suppliers of optimum fruit and vegetables, John and Don Wilson of Mohr Fish, Matt Brown of Greens and John Susman of the Flying Squid Brothers, suppliers of the best and freshest seafood and oysters.

MELBOURNE DELIGHTS Now that the great Melbourne restaurant thaw is underway there are restaurants for every mood and chefs for every taste. Hard times have made Melbourne diners more discerning across a far more interesting and relaxed spectrum but they have not entirely abandoned their love of formality and a handful of individual chefs and restaurateurs can still provide epicurean experiences in surroundings as swept up or as serious as the food. Philippe Mouchel carries the Bocuse torch for all of Australasia at the Paul Bocuse Restaurant high in the Melbourne Centre. The setting may be pure Magritte but there is nothing surreal about the food. It is fresh, light and fantastic. The brilliant Mouchel, originally from Normandy, has worked across the Bocuse empire, in France, Hong Kong, the United States and twice in Japan. He appears delighted with local levels of wine and food literacy and praises the quality and consistency of the produce which, often brought to his door by small producers, has improved by leaps and bounds since his 1991 arrival. Always on the menu is the signature truffle soup, the Tasmanian rib of beef and the Queensland barramundi in a puff pastry, Philippe Mouchel's variation on the Bocuse classic using seabass.

Gilbert Lau's Flower Drum Restaurant is an institution that has never failed in twenty years and the mandarin elegance of the dining-room is suitable foil to the exquisite food—haute cantonese if you like. The seafood is exceptional and it is this, too, that Lau believes gives a subtle, specifically Australian flavour and texture to the classic traditions. Lau also owns a small Flower Drum in the Casino and the wildly popular and more populist Purple Sands at Doncaster.

Stephanie Alexander's Stephanie's Restaurant is well-established in a large late Victorian villa in Hawthorn East. Here as owner chef, she and her partner Dur-é Dara create a richly varied dining experience in a series of comfortable rooms. Originally passionate about the country cooking of France, she has evolved over the years to somewhere more complex and individual. On her prix fixe spring menu for 1994, there is duck cassoulet or a black silky chicken with

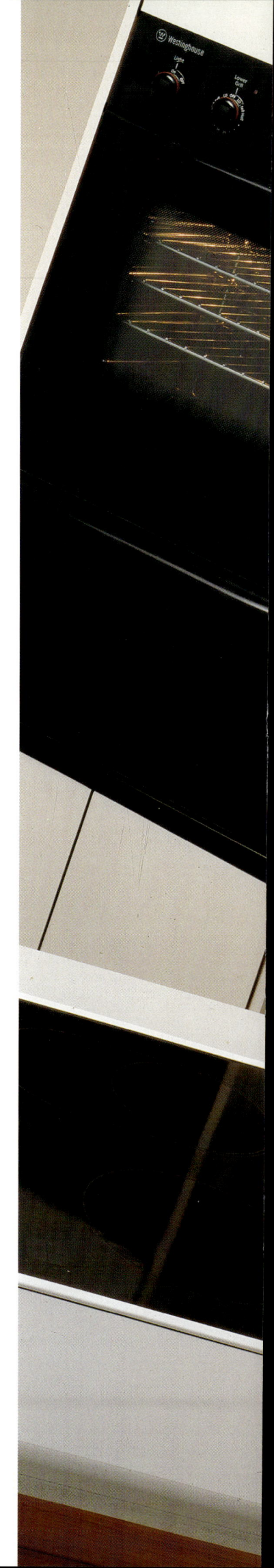

Sleek Westinghouse style and reliability

THE CHOICE OF GENERATIONS

The Westinghouse name is found on many different appliances in Australian homes. The range includes gas and electric cooking products, rangehoods, dishwashers, washing-machines, clothes-dryers, refrigerators, freezers and air-conditioners.

Generations of Australian families know and trust the Westinghouse name because they associate it with appliances which have made their lives more comfortable. Synonymous with superior performance, reliability and quality of workmanship, Westinghouse appliances are manufactured to exacting Australian and international standards. High-quality standards across the board mean that Westinghouse appliances are both technologically advanced and stylish, with an array of designs and features to suit a wide range of individual needs. As such, Westinghouse consumers can buy Australian-made Westinghouse appliances without compromise.

Technology has made an enormous difference to our lives, but has not always been friendly to the environment. Westinghouse appliances' leadership in dealing with environmental issues is manifest through the Aurora range of CFC-free and HCFC-free refrigerators and the energy efficiency and water-conserving qualities of other appliances in the range.

Westinghouse refrigerators have been produced locally since the 1940s and cooking appliances since the 1950s. The latest Westinghouse ovens and cooktops set new standards for Australian-made kitchen appliances. You would expect nothing less from the company with its name on the first Australian-made fan-forced cookers introduced in the 1970s. Australian-made Westinghouse appliances by Email Limited are also now being exported to an ever-increasing number of countries around the world.

Westinghouse appliances are sleek, flush-fitting and have smooth, continuous surfaces and, because everyone has different cooking needs, include a choice of multi-function ovens, large capacity double ovens, wall and under-bench ovens and a huge selection of cooktops including ceramic, square and rectangular models. The range also includes ovens with separate grill compartments—a feature for which Australians have shown a marked preference.

This is why Australian gourmets say, 'You can be sure if it's Westinghouse'.

ALLISON'S

purple congo mash, braised butter lettuce and a ragout of sweetbreads and morels. And those who want it plainest can always request Stephanie's Boiled Dinner. Alexander knows how to rise to an occasion. At one banquet celebrating the full gamut of Australian produce, it was her grevillea nectar ice-cream that lingered in professional memory. Her influence goes far beyond the restaurant, with her gifts as a writer in particular making her a seductive ambassador for the industry.

Mietta O'Donnell and Tony Knox continue to conduct the proper business of Mietta's with or without the accompaniment of music and song. Twenty years ago in North Fitzroy they opened a coffeehouse salon of Italian Asian flavour which paid homage to Mietta's heritage as granddaughter of the Vigano family of Mario's Restaurant. And then they fell for the wine culture and therefore French cuisine. Today their restaurant, in the hands of chef Adam Wood who trained with Anton Mossiman at the Dorchester, is more hybrid, seriously fine but not as specifically French as in the days of their French chefs Jacques Reymond and Roman Bapst. The salon may be the ideal place to drop into at 1 am for a glass of champagne and petits fours at the echoing end of a musical soirée. At such a moment it is possible to discover the proprietors, one volatile, one vigilant, in conversation with a quartet of musicians or an entire table of chefs.

Of all the older Italian restaurants Florentino, founded by the Massoni family in the twenties and now owned and run by Lorraine Podgornik with chef Mark Haynes at the stove, maintains a strong sense of traditional style and atmosphere from the bistro and ever-popular cellar bar to the panelled upper rooms enlivened by Napier Waller's art deco renaissance murals.

After twenty-seven years in Melbourne, then five running his revered Two Faces at Delgany House in Portsea where he and his wife Faye finally achieved the dream of Australia's first full Relais Chateau, doyen of owner/chefs Hermann Schneider is now enthroned at Arthur's Restaurant at Arthur's Seat on the Mornington Peninsula. With a restaurant, a bistro, a bar and vineyard and quite magnificent views across Port Philip Bay to distant city towers, he celebrates the local wine, the fish, vegetables, herbs and orchard fruits. Into his traditional but lightened French food he may now choose 'to intertwine Asian ingredients', and if a classic Schneider dish of the sixties was the rich creamy veal of Swiss Geschnetzeltes with roesti, at Arthur's the most characteristic would be the boned garfish with a sand crab farce fried in a crisp beer batter. Hermann Schneider is one of the very few who could and would actually fillet a garfish.

VARIETY IS THE ESSENCE Melbourne is very much a moveable feast. Traditionally

Jacques Reymond's paupiette of whiting

rich in cool cafe life, something to do with pervasive, stylish Italian influences, there is now a freewheeling confidence centred on the eating of great simple food in cafes, bistros and brasseries at whatever time and place you choose. In new culinary territory St Kilda you may pursue a great coffee with some style down Acland Street. But best of all you could settle into the George on Fitzroy Street, the food, wine and arts complex developer Donlevy Fitzpatrick is assembling bit by bit in a vast iced wedding cake of a Victorian pub. There is nothing quite like this in Sydney. In the bar, the most satisfactory experience might be oysters freshly opened on the shell at the end of an afternoon with the sun streaming in. The bread and pastries are by Melbourne's finest patissier Louis Vaussenat, and young English chef Jeremy Strode, trained at the Gavroche, the Waterside Inn and La Tante Claire in England and at Le Moulins de Mougins in France, cooks compellingly clear-flavoured French provincial dishes, including perfect rillettes, for the cafe. Donlevy Fitzpatrick has plans underway to open a vast restaurant and wine shop on the ground floor too; all senses should be on the alert.

There is great variety, and some great chefs. Asian Melbourne is as various as Akita or Suntory for immaculate Japanese; Flower Drum, Purple Sands, Chinois, and Mask of China for Chinese. At Chinois the pull is the great style and customer content as much as the East strikes West food of Allan Koh and Stanley Soares. At the Mask of China it is the imaginative refinement of Yeung Pui Ming's cooking with the clean modern design.

French Melbourne is not simply Philippe Mouchel in glory at Bocuse but oysters opened on the shell or a perfect steak, frites and salad prepared by Joachim Ignacio at Jean-Paul Prunetti's France-Soir. It's also the lightened haute cuisine of Burgundian chef Jacques Reymond at Jacques Reymond's Restaurant in Windsor where complex harmonies of flavour now include odd notes from the indigenous desert pantry.

You may consider the real Italians: fine traditionalists like Valerio Nucci, chef at the Café di Stasio in St Kilda, or Maurice Terzini, whose tiny trendy

Right: Abalone with preserved lemon salad and a fresh coriander sauce by Andrew Blake   Far Right: Cadbury's chocolate chef Aaron Marie shares his knowledge and pleasure of chocolate   Above: Jacques Reymond in the heart of the kitchen

CHOCOLATE ART

The use of chocolate in food preparation has come of age in the 1990s. And who better to demonstrate how to achieve first-class results with fabulous confections than Australia's best known pastry and chocolate chef?

At twenty-five, international patissier Aaron Marie is a member of the elite, invitation-only World Master Chef's Society.

Trained in Switzerland and the United Kingdom, Aaron Marie is a formidable talent and an expert at demonstrating the step-by-step process in preparing high-value, yet affordable confectionery and baking creations.

Since 1992, when he began his association with Cadbury Australia, Aaron has captivated chocolate lovers with his recipes and technical tips through Cadbury Cooking Demonstrations. From beginners to professional chefs Aaron shares his knowledge of how to expertly cook with chocolate and shows them how to make superb, imaginative creations using only quality ingredients and equipment found in every kitchen.

Author of three cookery books, Aaron Maree is a well-known newspaper columnist on pastry and baking, television personality and winner of prestigious awards nationally and internationally. In 1990 Aaron was voted Young Queenslander of the Year, an acknowledgement definitely well-deserved.

AUSTRALIA - A GOURMET'S PARADISE

chef at the Café di Stasio in St Kilda, or Maurice Terzini, whose tiny trendy Caffe e Cucina in South Yarra embodies rustic flavour and never fails with the coffee. If you do squeeze in upstairs you could feel close to the panfried fillets of John Dory even before they leave the stove. Tradition is intrinsic to even the most modern Italians. Rick Davis, a charming local Welsh Italian with a good cafe and deli history, owns the buzzily warm and stylish Arrigo Harry's Bar in the original Balzac premises in East Melbourne with partner and chef Joseph Cooper. It's a cafe-brasserie with Harry's Cellar Bar Express for speed snacking. And now they've opened Café Forza in Middle Park with chiaroscuro mood lighting, quattrocentoesque murals and a lively menu which may include a great artichoke omelette in a pastry parcel. Ted Manhal is cooking at the popular Ristorante Roberto's in the city. Roberto, alias Roberto Scheriani, out of the polished energetic school of di Stasio, keeps prices moderate and the food fresh and interesting, their pastas as good as their most distinctive dish, the spicy parmigiano gelato with bruschetta and greens.

You can enjoy the Middle East reinvented at O'Connell's pub restaurant by Lebanese Australian Greg Malouf who has worked in Europe and at Two Faces and Mietta's, and cooks in an imaginative, aromatic style, dishing up a saddle of young rabbit stuffed with spiced minced spinach, roasted with juniper berries and served with potatoes whipped with goat's cheese and such dishes as watercress tabouleh and Turkish coffee ice-cream that play with his childhood memories.

Melbourne has an extraordinary number of young English chefs and English-influenced chefs trained in some of Europe's toughest and most exciting kitchens. At Cambray's, Dean Cambray, most influenced by his apprenticeship with Jean Bardet in France and Bruno Loubet at London's Inn on the Park, serves roasted scallops on buckwheat polenta with braised endives sauced in a veal juice, braised pig's trotter filled with a pate of pork, and a gingerbread, cumquat and vanilla pudding with a sabayon of brown ale. Time should not be of the essence when dining here: perfectionist Cambray likes to mash his potatoes to order.

Right: Australian macadamia nuts bursting from their shells Above: Wine from Salisbury Estate, which uses BOC gases in its wine-making process.

TRAVELLING THE WORLD

Without the sophisticated gas technologies developed by BOC Gases Australia Limited (formerly CIG), Australia's gourmet produce might still be limited to regional and seasonal availability; instead, our epicurean wonders travel the world, transported and stored using BOC Gases' fast-chilling systems. So the same Port Phillip Bay scallops we savour in Sydney might find their way to Paris or Zurich.

BOC Gases is one of Australia's top 100 companies, and the Pacific region's leading manufacturer and marketer of gases and gas-related products. Employing around 2,000 people in Australia, its breadth of service to the Australian food industry is best illustrated with examples.

Australia grows the finest macadamia nuts in the world. For Macadamia Processing, Australia's largest producer (it exports 95 per cent of its crop), and Macadamia Plantations, BOC Gases devised a packaging system that ensures optimum freshness and longevity by reducing oxygen levels to 1.5 per cent or less.

Austrimi Seafoods produces Surimi, fresh Australian fish cooked to a 600-year-old Japanese recipe, for the export market. To maintain absolute freshness after production, the temperature of the fish is rapidly reduced with liquid nitrogen, using BOC Gases' cryogenic technology.

BOC Gases custom-designed the fast-freezing cryogenic system at Wollongong Fisheries: within hours of being taken from the sea, the day's catch is washed, trimmed, filleted, frozen and packaged.

In the journey from hatchery to rearing pen, SALTAS's Tasmanian salmon are transported in oxygen-enriched water tanks developed by BOC Gases.

Moorilla Estate Wines is a small winery with a concentration on high quality (its riesling has joined Qantas' First-Class wine list). At different points, BOC Gases-designed oxygen and nitrogen systems are employed in the process of winemaking, for the best results.

Each year, Bonlac, Australia's largest dairy plant, produces 300 million packs of Australian cheeses. A mixture of gases made by BOC Gases is used to modify the atmosphere in the packaging by flushing out harmful organisms, so extending the products' shelf life.

AUSTRALIA - A GOURMET'S PARADISE

At Carlton Place, Australians Brad and Gerardine French reveal their past, soaking up the disciplines and delivering fine cooking in the kitchens of Kensington Place and Launceston Place with such dishes as the petit salet of duck and the fillet of beef with bone marrow which Brad French does his way, split in two with whole roasted Yarra Valley shallots. At the fashionable Stokehouse restaurant, Londoner Michael Lambie, most recently engaged in the ego-fatigued kitchens of Marco Pierre White's Canteen, has composed a menu that is basically French but reveals a world of references: there is a fine escabeche—marinated red emperor with saffron and coriander. The first floor restaurant is very big with beautiful views over St Kilda beach; downstairs is a vast cafe, bar and terrace.

The new Southgate development on the Yarra provides great choice and opportunities for culinary treats with a river view, a first for Melbourne. It is wonderful on a summery night. On one first floor corner is the smooth Walter's Wine Bar, and on one ground corner the popular Blake's Café with terrace. Andrew Blake was the talented chef who in the mid-eighties spearheaded Gloria Staley's Melbourne offensive with Chez Oz, discovered that in Sydney chefs were hotter than their stoves and later imported the easy Sydney-style home. Blake's is significantly user-friendly and whether wood-fired or not the food has bite to it. Geoff Lindsay is the chef, there are American influences as well as Sydney ones, and praise for braised ham hocks, dessert pizzas and the smoked salmon with horseradish and game chips. There is a good wine list, intelligently matched to the food, and sparky, informed service. Like the George and Stokehouse, Blake's is one of the unaffected stars of Melbourne's new food culture.

Antonia Williams

Above: The Southgate development on the South Bank of the Yarra river has a multitude of restaurants, shops and promenades
Right: Andrew Blake's seared salt-cured salmon on a bed of mashed potato

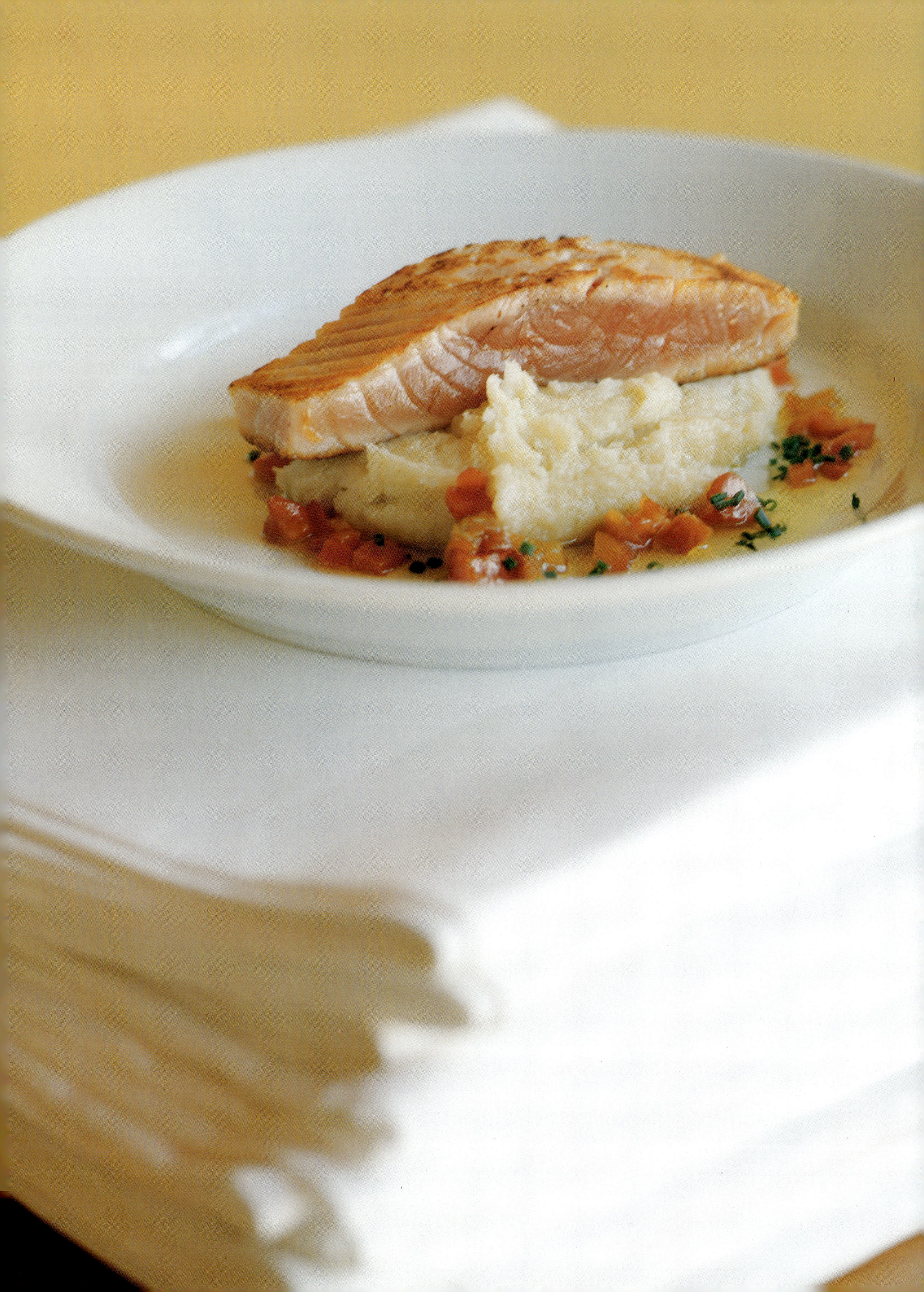

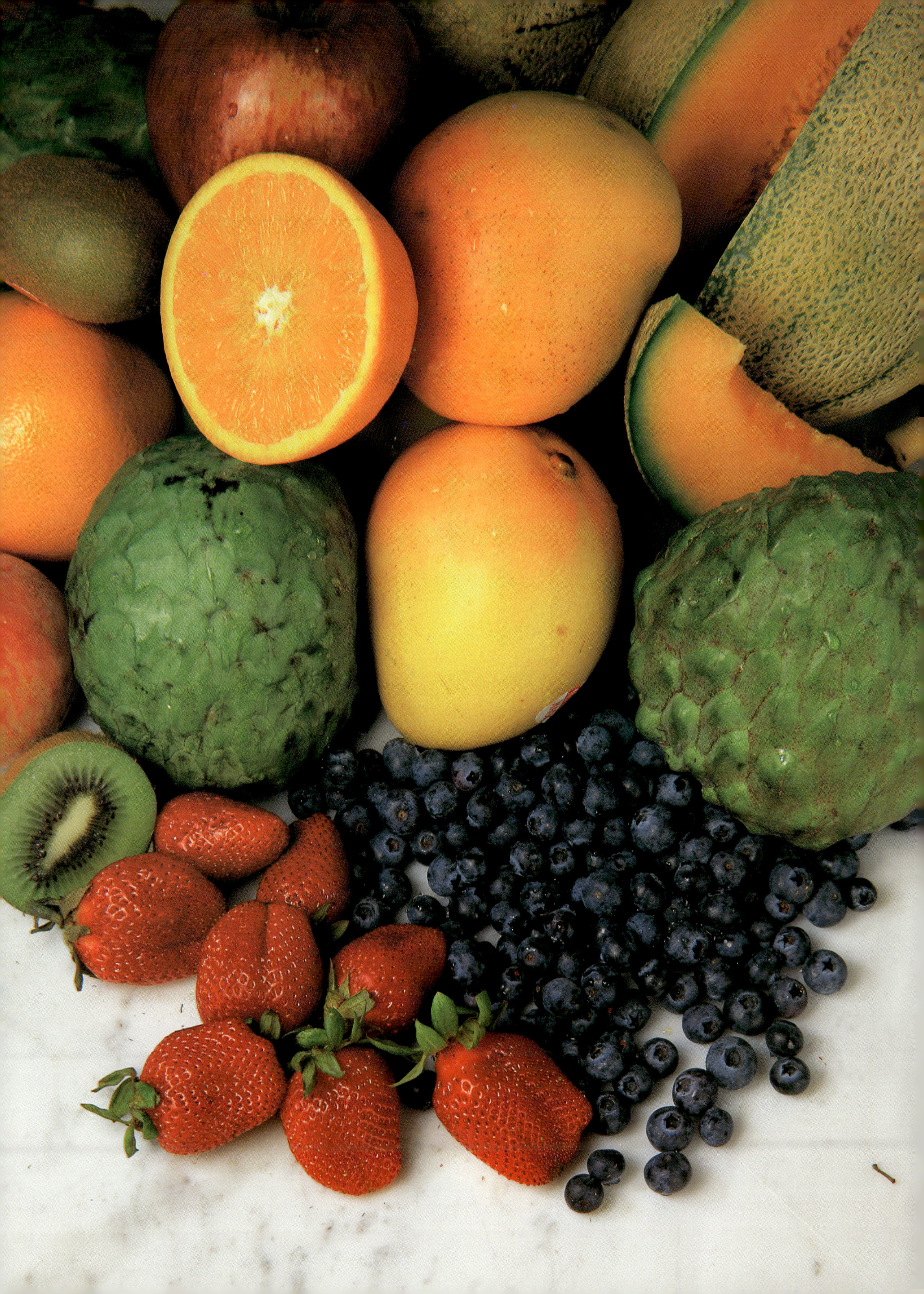

ADVISING THE EXPERTS

Suppliers of commercial cooking, refrigeration, dishwashing and ice-cream equipment to outlets big (the major fast-food chains around Australia) and small (the corner milkbar), the Curtin Group is a company that caters for caterers. What distinguishes Curtin Foodservice Equipment from others is the calibre of its clients—for example, Coles/Myer, Woolworths, Safeway, McDonald's, Ansett Australia, Qantas, KFC, Sizzler, Pizza Hut, Davids Limited, Southern Pacific Hotels and BHP ships all utilise Curtin equipment and Curtin's personalised systems. Clearly, with such big players on board, needs are met.

This is a full service of responsibility. Clients may have a new product idea, but won't know how best to cook it, for how many, how long, in what. The Curtin Group's team of experts undertakes a complete needs analysis of the proposed catering operation, the projected volumes, and the budgets and time restraints on the operators. Then the wheels are set in motion, with Curtin involved from the beginning to the end.

Australian-owned with 140 years in the industry, Curtin began as an iron-founder, making castings for trains and boats. Then came the evolution—importing overseas brands, beginning with the Zanussi range (still the flagship brand for the company)—until Curtin became the largest importer and manufacturer of food service equipment in Australia. This was achieved in stages, by building four divisions to cover every need: Curtin Queensland is responsible for the company's manufacturing; Curtin South Australia is a contracting arm; Curtin Butler provides quality tabletop ware and Curtin Foodservice Equipment is the imported cooking and refrigeration equipment division. Much of the company's continuous growth is due to its nationwide distributor network, with offices in Brisbane, Sydney, Melbourne, Adelaide and sole distributors in Tasmania and Western Australia.

Curtin's reputation has been built on the excellence of its performance, equipment, after-sales service and training. Curtin pioneered the concept of consultant chefs who train clients on-site. In aiming to look after the ultimate customer, the important people at the consumer end, and turning this into the company philosophy, Curtin has become an industry leader. And others follow.

Left: Curtin equipment keeps food fresher longer
Above: The art of fine cooking with Zanussi

NORTHERN

*Right: The Bush
Camp at Alice Springs
Above: Cashew nuts in their
natural state; Magpie geese in the
picturesque wetlands of Kakadu*

TERRITORY

An Ancient Land

Considered as one of the world's last frontiers, where the tyranny of distance has shaped its history, people and cuisine, the Northern Territory offers a romantic vision of Australia. Here you can find the 'True Blue' Aussie image of sundrenched stockmen and outback bushmen, a pioneer lifestyle mixed with the mysteries of an ancient culture, Arab desert dwellers, Asian traders and seafarers—amidst a land of contrasts.

A region of vast desert landscapes where food and water are scarce unless nurtured, it's where turquoise waters rim northern shores and lush exotic tropical foods abound. A harsh land, or a place to enjoy languid days on shuttered verandas, iced drink in hand, the soul enticed by vibrant sunsets and starry heavens before being enveloped in balmy nights.

Covering an immense area of central Australia, the Territory reaches from the harsh outback desert, north to the picturesque wetlands of Kakadu and Arnhem Land and is edged by the clear tropical waters of the Timor and Arafura Seas, which divide Australia from Indonesia. The region hosts the broadest melting pot of cultures within Australia and to many its appeal is hidden, but to those who come to understand this vast and often harsh wilderness, it can become a lifelong romance.

Many claim the Aboriginal people of the Territory's most northern tip at the Coburg Peninsula, some eleven degrees south of the equator, were the forerunners of today's multicultural Australian cuisine. Having roamed the ancient land for over 40,000 years, living off the land, hunting wallaby, magpie geese, turtle, snake, dugong and other bush foods, they understood how to survive in the 'Top End'. They welcomed their Macassan neighbours from the island of Sulawesi to the north, who until the early 1900s when immigration laws were introduced, annually voyaged south to the Coburg Peninsula to gather, cook and preserve trepang (sea cucumber). The Macassans brought with them Asian foods, herbs and spices, returning home after several months to trade their prized trepang cargo with China.

In 1838 the British, anxious to ensure their claim on this valuable Asian trade route prior to the Portuguese, French and Dutch explorers, established Victoria Settlement at Port Essington. They were the first to introduce a European lifestyle and cuisine to the Coburg region along with pigs, buffalo, Balinese banteng cattle and Timor ponies which can still be found amongst the crocodiles, dingoes, snakes, kangaroos, waterbirds and other native wilderness fauna. Unable to adapt to the isolation, harsh region and climatic demands of the seven local tropical seasons of the Aboriginal calendar—The Cloudless Blue, Lightning, Thundering, Rainmaking, The Greening, Wind Storming and Fire Raging, which have a strong influence on food supply, gathering and lifestyle—the settlement closed within a few years. The influence of the British, however, remains today as an integral ingredient within the mixing pot of Territory cuisine.

Japanese and Filipinos soon ventured to the northern coastline enticed by the lucrative pearling, fishing and prawning industries, bringing with them further flavours and tastes of the East. In 1838, Sir Charles Todd established Alice Springs. Cattlemen, gold prospectors and pioneer business men arrived, introducing a further understanding of desert produce and lifestyle. By 1869 Darwin, the Territory's capital city, was successfully established, attracting people from many cultures with a resilient nature and a pioneer spirit. By 1929, John Flynn brought the Flying Doctor Service to the outback providing much needed medical help and diminishing the tyranny of distance for many whilst enabling the establishment of long-term settlements and industries, the basis of today's successful desert economy.

LIVING IN HARMONY An understanding of how to live in harmony with the Territory began to grow, but even as late as the fifties, with the boom of uranium mining in Rum Jungle, many new residents—disappointed with the inability to grow cool-climate vegetables—anxiously awaited weekly planes from the south bearing cauliflowers, cabbages and other familiar treasures for their traditional Sunday roast, despite the sweltering heat. Others were already feasting on leafy Asian vegetables, fresh local seafood, tropical fruits and bush foods cooked in a variety of new styles gathered from other local inhabitants.

Nowadays, many outback houses continue to favour shady verandahs, while to the north some modern monsoon-proof houses retain their shuttered windows, but air-conditioning and fast, efficient refrigerated transport has resulted in a rapidly-expanding tropical produce trade, new opportunities and an easier lifestyle.

Capturing the spirit of the bush (left to right, top to bottom): Bush Broth from the Bush Restaurant, Alice Springs; edible flora; 'Spotted Dog'—damper with raisins; boiling tea bush-style, in a billy; a Northern Territory Aborigine; traditional Scotty's fare complete with a can of Territory Bitter; a Balinese banteng cow; a crocodile glides silently through the water; a typical barbeque, meat and potatoes

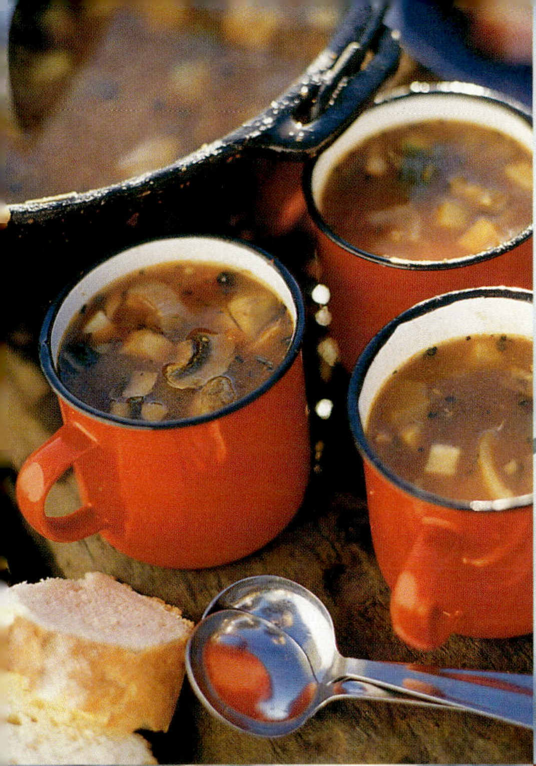
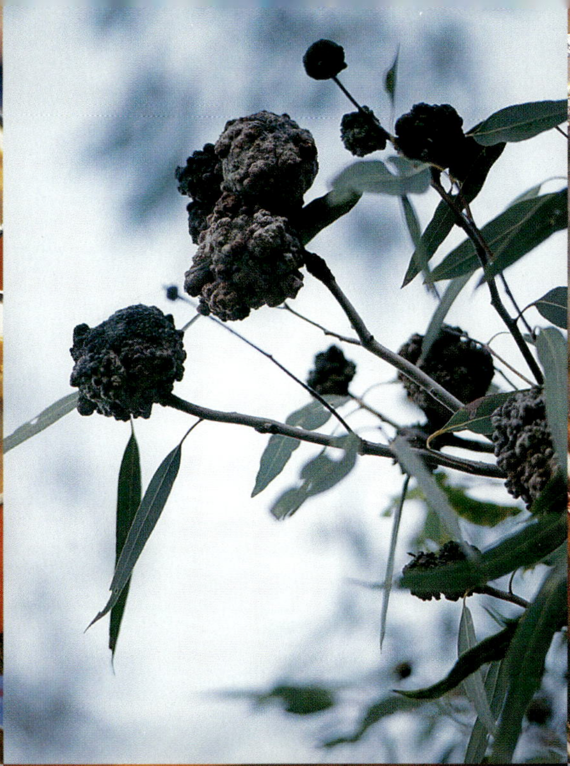
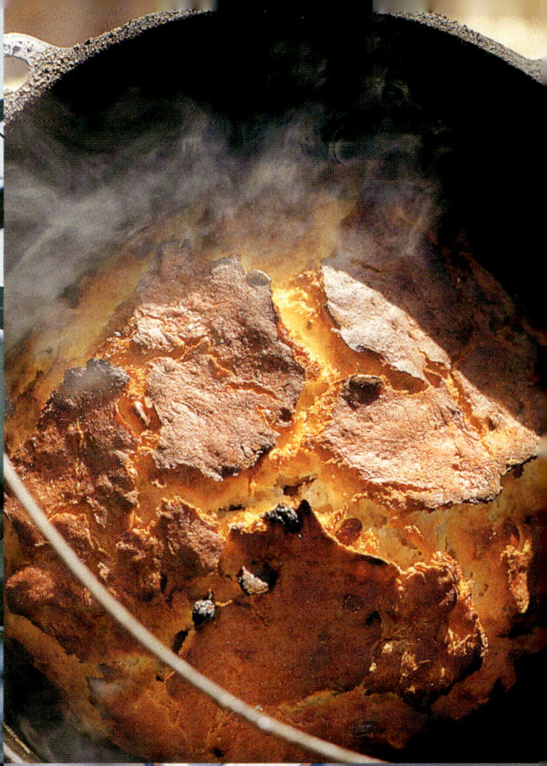
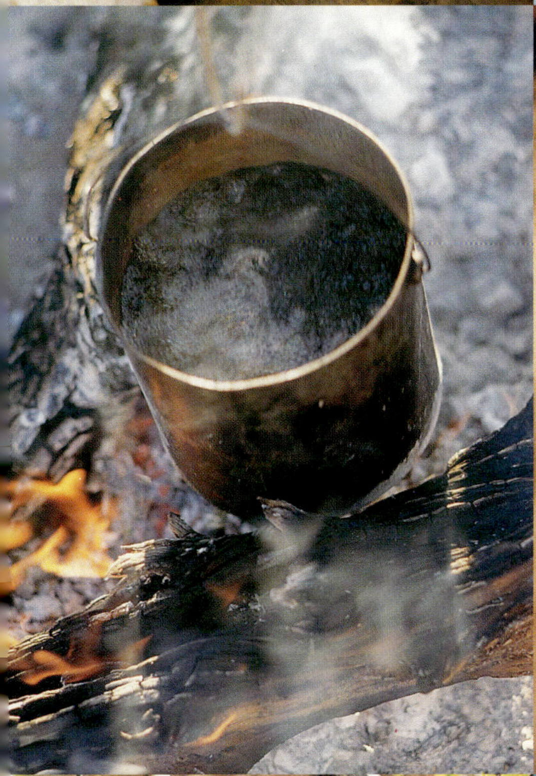
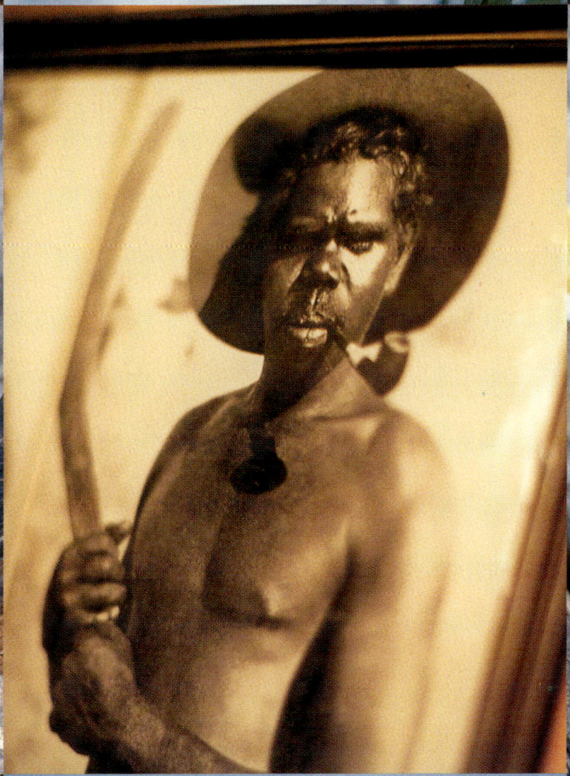
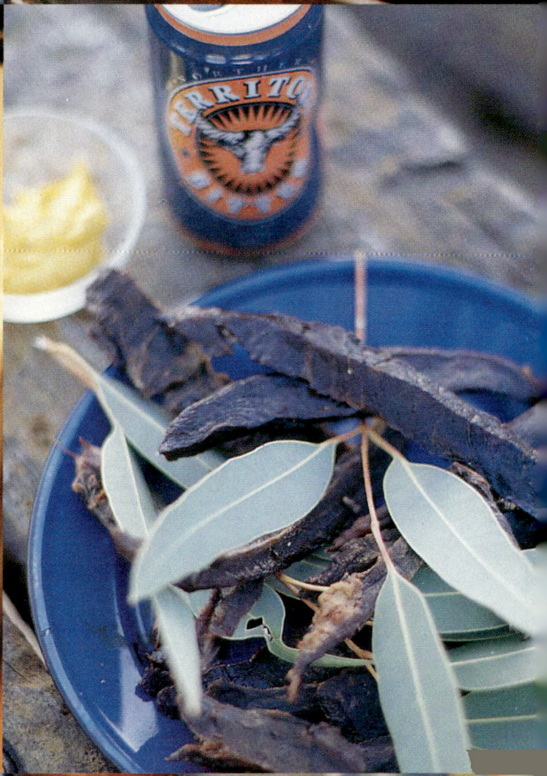
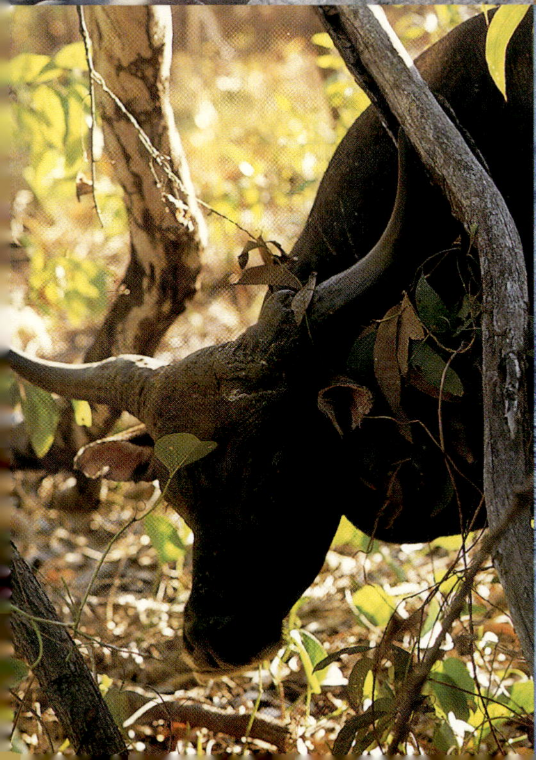
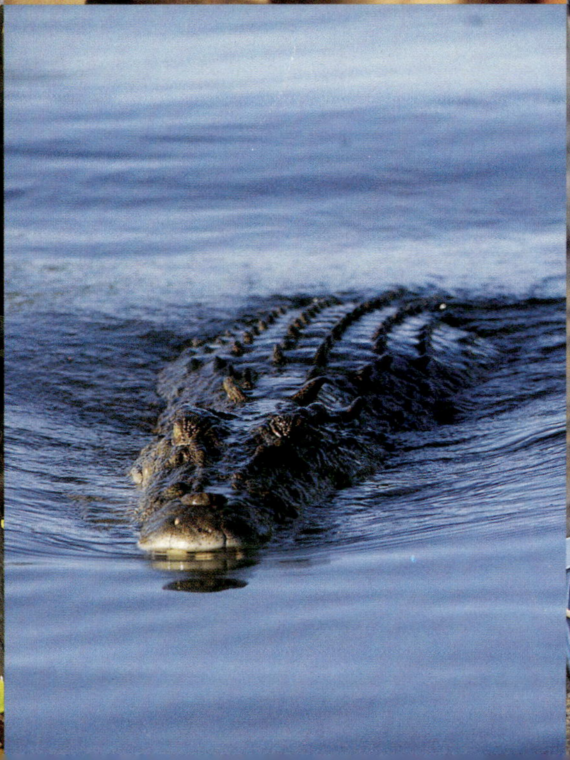
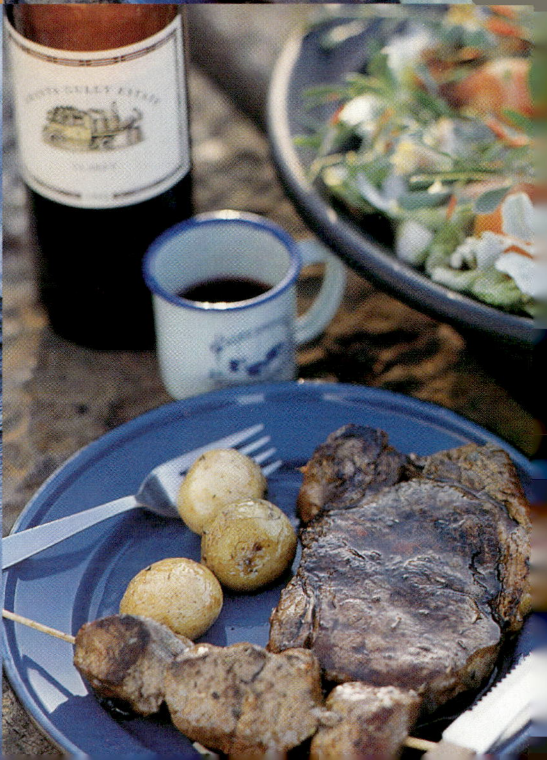

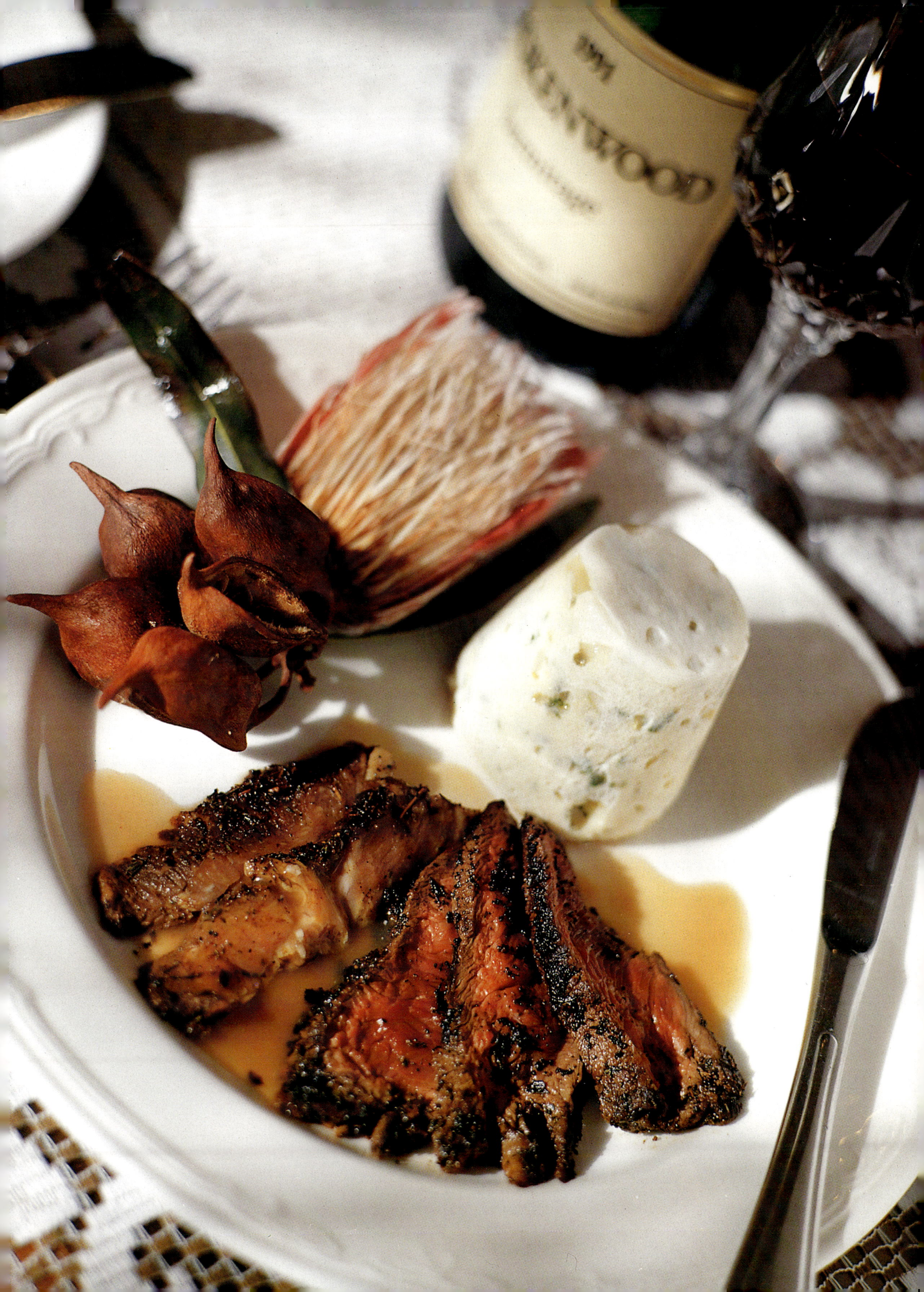
GOODWOOD

Visitors to Alice Springs today often choose the comfort and warm hospitality of the Diplomat Hotel and Miss Daisy's, where they can savour emu, kangaroo, buffalo, witchetty grub and other Territory favourites prepared with a French influence. They then venture outback to explore nearby 'Uluru'—Ayers Rock—before returning for a drink or two at Scotty's, a drovers' bar decked with memorabilia of prominent Aboriginals and early pioneers. Scotty's offers such Territory culinary delights as Flutter and Hop (emu and kangaroo), Wallow and Hump (buffalo and camel), Hop and Hump (kangaroo and camel), and Bait and Bite (barramundi and crocodile), all cooked outdoors on the barbecue as you sample a cold Territory beer and a yarn with the locals.

Nearby, Michelle and Nick Smail offer unique outback dining—'Take a Camel to Dinner'—where you can ride and dine Territory-style on local beef, wine, beer, table grapes, melon and other fruits. Along the way you can also visit the Mecca Date Farm, a thriving industry which supplies a range of fresh dates under the colourful 'Desert Fruit Company' label.

Historical dining at the Old Ghan Train is also available, while for those wishing to capture the authenticity of an outback stockman setting and campfire cooking, the Bush Restaurant on Undoolya Station offers a spectacular outback setting beneath the red orange escarpment of the MacDonnell Ranges. Here Ron Tremaine, Bob Barford and Ray Kelson provide billy tea, damper, a hearty bush broth of local vegetables, bush food salad (mix of old man salt bush, wild and local tomatoes and leafy greens) and beef, all prepared campside under the stars, with the strains of outback droving songs to mellow the heart and transport you into outback dreaming.

As you head north, overland through the dusty desert, you cross cattle and mining country where the erratic rainfall and vast distances give warning to check your water supply and advise authorities of your travel plans. The flavour and quality of Territory beef is well known, and simple cooking is regarded as the best here—meats barbecued campside, grilled, roasted or corned country style. The breeds Santa Gertrudis, Shorthorn and Brahman provide beef for both the Australian and the growing livestock export market to south-east Asian countries. Mining is the largest income earner for the Territory and it is closely followed by tourism, beef, pearling, fishing (including prawning) and tropical fruit farming.

NEW SENSATIONS At the 'Top End' Darwin offers a range of international hotels from the top echelon and glamour of the seaside Diamond Beach Casino to the mid-town Plaza Hotel, renowned for exotic tropical cocktails, or the modest backpacker accommodation.

Miss Daisy's duo of camel and kangaroo fillet seared in Cajun spices, served with witchetty grub soufflé, decorated with protea and gum nuts

AUSTRALIA - A GOURMET'S PARADISE

Dining in Darwin provides an amazing range of multicultural cuisine. The Diamond Beach Boardroom is regularly voted the top Territory restaurant and features a wide range of local produce and an Australian and imported wine list, all presented with international flair. The Hanaman Thai—winner of the best Asian restaurant of the 'Top End'—features Asian food and Nonya cooking (a blend of Chinese/Malay food traditionally prepared by women). Regular winner of the best BYO restaurant is Lindsay Street Cafe which offers innovative light Territory cuisine; here Jock Mitchell and Lesley Merrett present the latest blends of the best, including favourites such as Asian antipasto, golden snapper with lime leaf and coriander sauce, kangaroo fillet with ginger, onion jam and fresh basil and, as an epilogue, refreshing mango sorbet drizzled with golden pandan coconut cream.

Local markets such as Mindil Beach provide the widest food variety at bargain prices. Here you can stroll and dine beachside while enjoying the sunset as you savour new taste sensations from myriad food stalls. Tropical vegetables, herbs, spices, fruits, ices, steamed mud crab, Arafura prawns, grilled barramundi, crocodile, buffalo and green paw paw salad are on offer, as well as a variety of styles including Malay, Filipino, Chinese, Japanese, Portuguese, Indian, Lebanese, Creole, Greek, Spanish and Thai. You may be lucky to savour green paw paw salad or pearl meat simply pan-fried with lemon butter, a by-product of the South Sea pearl oyster farmed by the Paspaley family off Coburg and Broome. Its rarity makes it generally too expensive for the local market, but as a prized commodity for virility, high prices are gained from export to Asia.

Due to modern technology and netting to protect against birds, insects and flying fox, plus the availability to supply off-season to the southern states, the Territory's tropical fruit and vegetable market continues to expand. The world's largest cashew nut farm is now producing at Wildmans River, while Katherine, Fogg Dam and Howard Springs have plantations of banana, mango, paw paw, asparagus, eggplant, pumpkin, cucumber, melon, avocado and coconut.

Chris Nathaniel's rare tropical fruit farm at Bees Creek is producing the widest variety of tropical fruit from the Territory. Unable to meet present demand, he predicts the tropical fruit market, which sixteen years ago earned $800,000, will reach $30 million in the next few years. Rare commercial varieties already being grown include Glom Sali guava, Maltese St Johns figs, rambutan, sapodilla (a Kiwi-style fruit which yields 2,500 fruit per tree), carambolla or five corner fruit, abiu (a translucent caramel flavoured fruit), red and white pummelo (non-acidic forerunners to the grapefruit), Indian and Tahitian limes and Kaffir lime leaves, pittaya or

Mindil Beach Markets—a wide variety of produce and multicultural cuisine, a casual beach setting, sunset dining and a mixture of people from many backgrounds

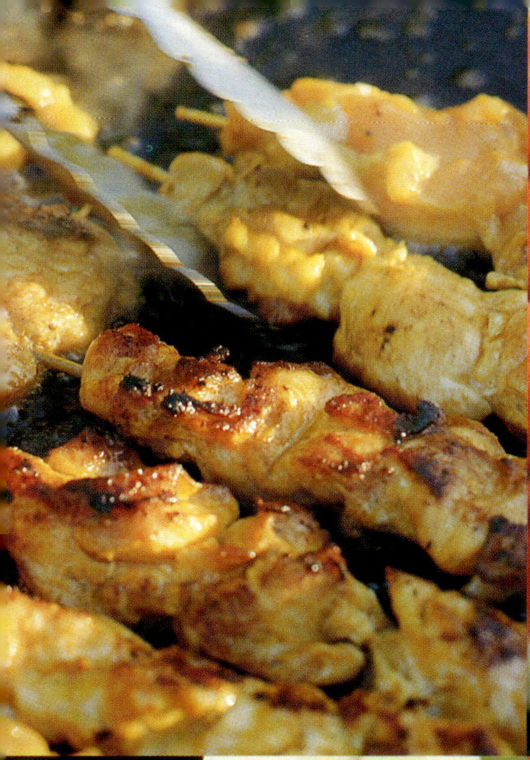
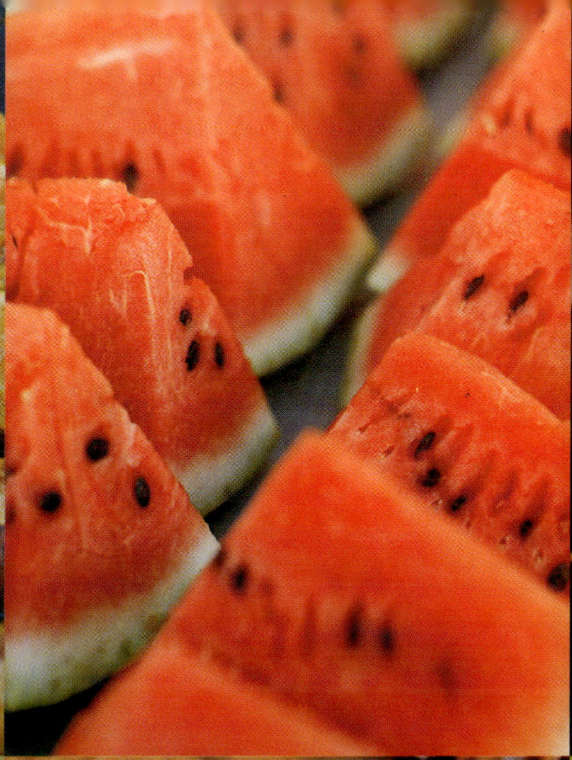
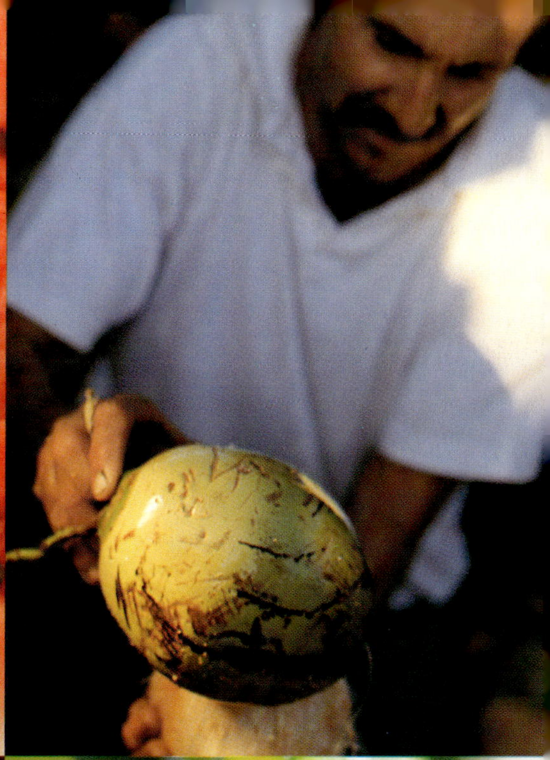
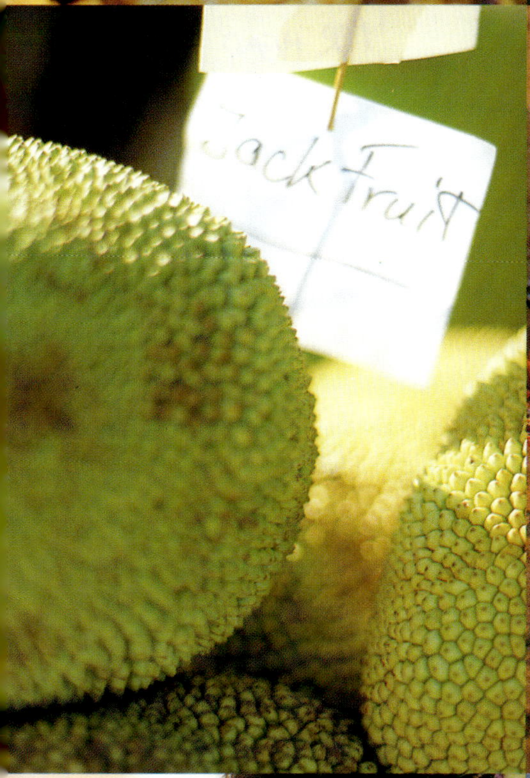
Jack Fruit
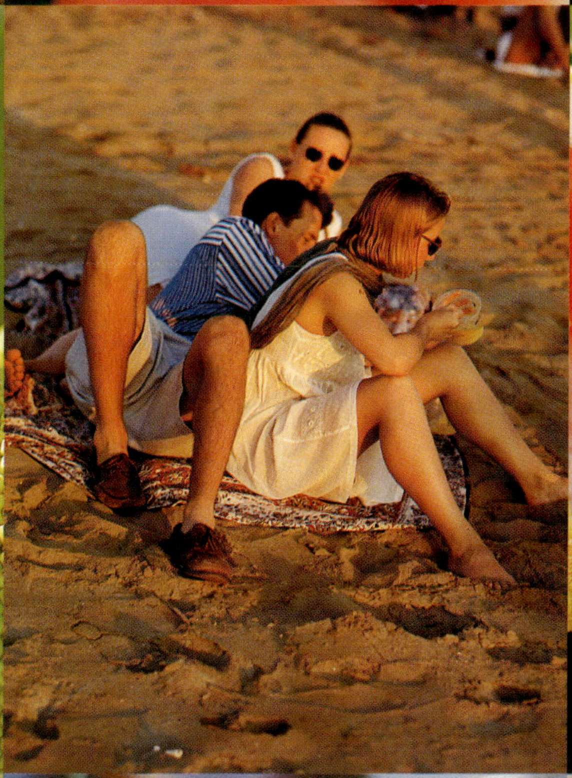
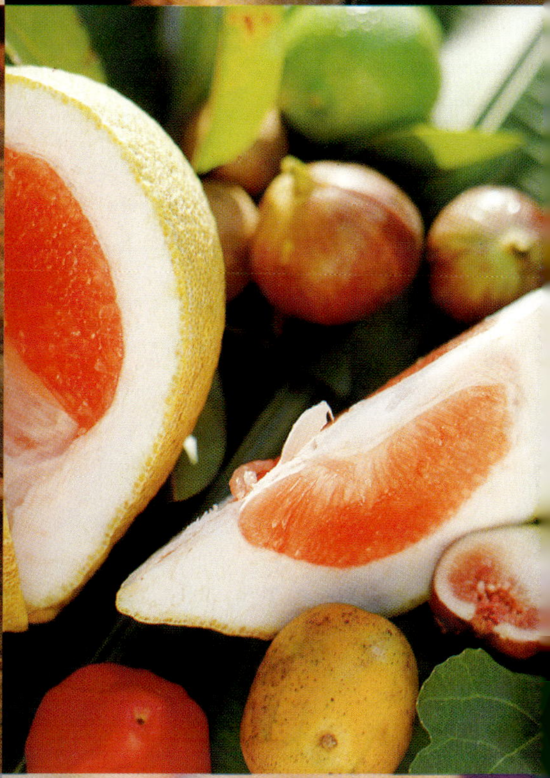
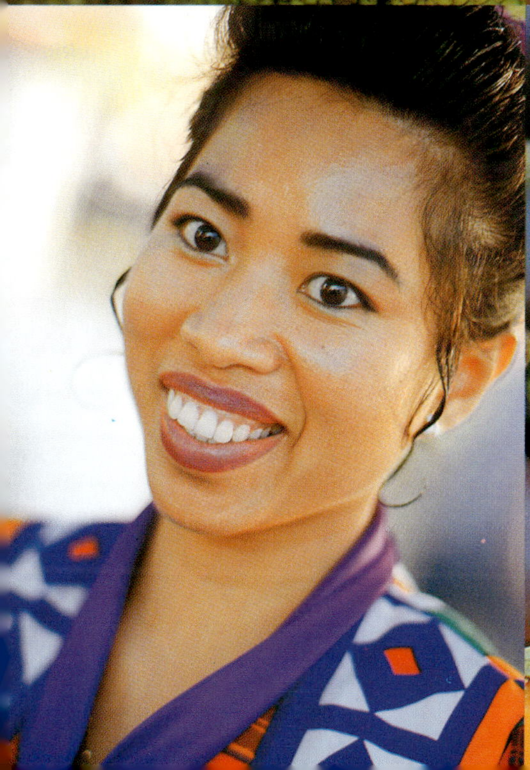
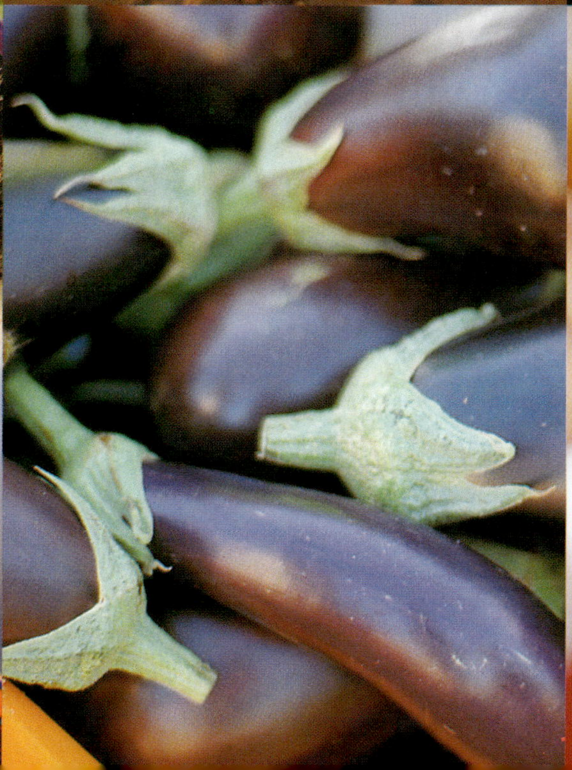
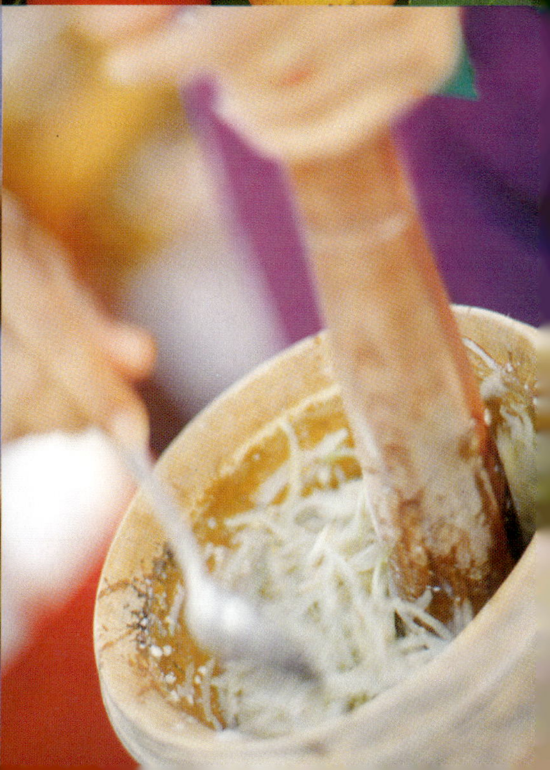

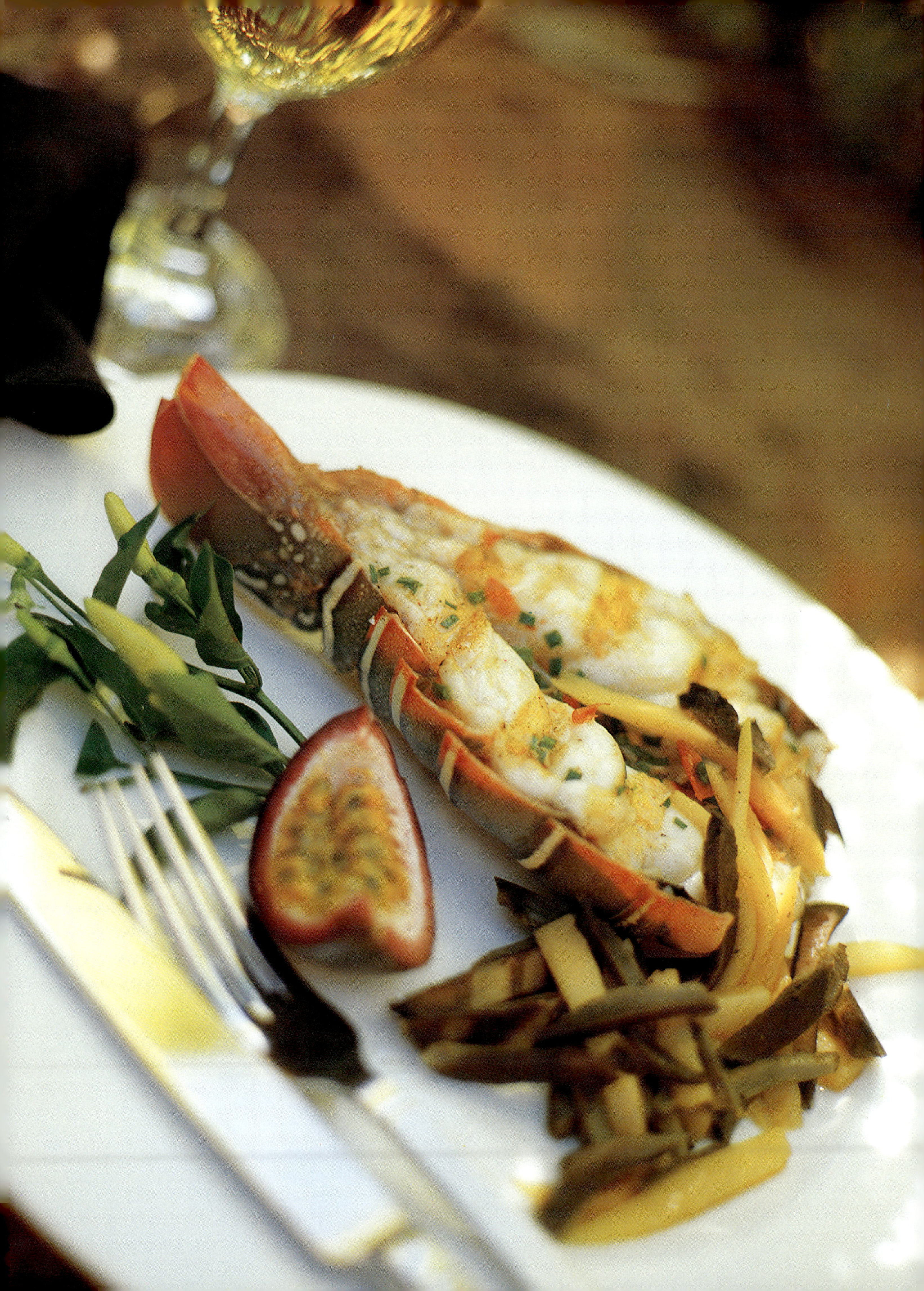

cactus fruit, black sapote or chocolate pudding fruit, lemons and mandarins. Growing fruit in the 'Top End' has the advantage of long periods of warmth and sunshine producing fruit of intense colour and flavour, low acidity and high sugar content which are desired by both the restaurant market and the home consumer.

At Palmeston, Geoff and Russell Read's Barramundi Farm, established in 1992, produces plate-size salt water barramundi. Russell runs regular taste tests to ensure flavour, consistent size and fine texture with fresh rather than frozen fish a speciality. By 1996 he plans to market 200 tonnes annually. Arafura Sea prawns, tropical painted crayfish, mangrove mud crabs and crocodile for both food and skins (often named handbag fish on more sensitive menus) are other northern seafoods treasured by both the local and international markets. Russell Read tells us Australians can also look forward to 'Barra Fish Tanks' in major Australian supermarkets, where consumers will be able to select live barramundi daily without the expense of a Territory fishing trip!

Coburg Peninsula now hosts Seven Spirit Bay, a five star eco-tourism resort near Port Essington and a regular winner of tourism awards. Perfectly in tune with the environment, it is a far cry from the early failure of the British to maintain Victoria Settlement in the same region. Today, the resort's chefs are conscious of the advantages of the region and use fresh local seasonal produce presented with stylish simplicity and an emphasis on harmony of flavour and contrasting textures, combining the best influences of Aboriginal, Asian and bush cooking, which results in flavoursome, innovative, multicultural Territory cuisine to delight the most discerning eye and palate.

Judith Hirst

Chargrilled painted tropical crayfish with chilli chive butter,
pandanus palm heart and fresh pawpaw, from Seven Spirit Bay, Coburg Peninsula

QUEEN

*Right: The glorious colours of
Australia's Great Barrier Reef
Above: Mud crab—a delicious
Australian seafood; a mango
orchard in Bowen*

SLAND

Exotic by Nature

The Queensland mud crab is a remarkable creature—a large and extraordinarily delicious crustacean, a prize of inestimable worth to serious food-lovers, but one which nature has equipped with a sturdy, almost impenetrable shell and a pair of claws powerful enough to remove a joint or two from a careless, investigative finger.

Such is life in the sun-drenched and ruggedly individualistic state of Queensland. The flavours that burst from much of the home-grown produce are heady and exotic, while some of the processes involved in harvesting and preparing that produce offer daily challenges well beyond those routinely encountered elsewhere in Australia.

For Queensland is the 'deep north' of the nation. Its tropical and sub-tropical latitudes spill across rich, well-watered, coastal strips—up and over modest mountain ranges to stretches of fertile, temperate tablelands with their grain crops, dairy herds and piggeries, and onwards through the grazing expanses of the state's near and far west which satisfy much of the nation's hunger for high-quality beef and lamb, ending in some of Australia's most unforgiving but endlessly fascinating outback regions.

The state forms the great north-eastern triangle of the Australian continent, and accounts for some 22.4 per cent of the area of the nation. Queensland settlement dates back to the establishment of the Moreton Bay Penal Settlement in 1824. That settlement later became Brisbane, the state capital, now Australia's third-largest city (after Sydney and Melbourne) and the nation's largest river port.

Queensland in the 1990s is a booming state and increasingly has an international profile as a unique tourist destination. With the extraordinary

AUSTRALIA - A GOURMET'S PARADISE

Great Barrier Reef guarding much of its eastern coastline and the incomparable surfing beaches of the Gold Coast and Sunshine Coast lying to the immediate south and north of Brisbane respectively, it is a tourist's paradise. Queensland exploded into life at the start of the 1980s, particularly by way of such events as the 1982 Commonwealth Games and the 1988 World Expo. And with its growing confidence have come many more changes to the fundamental nature of the state.

FRUIT FLAVOURS In the far, rain-forested north, for example, the lush stands of sugar cane that for so many years have lined the coastal strip to the exclusion of all other crops—source not only of sugars and syrups, but also of the fiery Queensland rums that power fashionable, fruity cocktails throughout the nation—are starting to give way to orchards of newer exotic fruits which find a ready market both in Australia and in the demanding Asian centres to the north. In addition to the magnificent, heavily fleshed and stringless 'Bowen' or Kensington Pride mangoes (perhaps the finest grown anywhere in the world), pungent durians (Asia's 'king of fruit') compete for orchard space with massive jack fruit and the indescribably delicious mangosteens, rambutans, lychees, rolinas, carimbolas and soursops, many of them brought to Australia in recent decades from Asia and South America.

In centres like Cairns and Port Douglas, jack fruit, mangosteen and soursop ice-creams can often be found on the menus of the more adventurous restaurants and are well worth experiencing, alongside the more familiar mango and fresh coconut ice-creams.

Australia's 'new food' revolution—largely driven from Sydney and Melbourne—is having its effect upon the output of Queensland's far north. The region's traditional yellow-fleshed 'northern papaws' are gradually making way for the more consistently delicious pink-fleshed papaya varieties introduced from Hawaii and the long, red-fleshed beauties from Thailand. The black sapote or chocolate pudding fruit, a relative of the persimmon, astounds all who taste its extraordinary flesh which, when allowed to overripen, can be mixed with a splash of fresh cream and a dash of Queensland's beloved Bundaberg Rum—easily the most memorable by-product of those sugar cane stands—and whipped into a very respectable chocolate mousse. There is also a white sapote which, treated like the black sapote, delivers an excellent white chocolate mousse—illustrating clearly that Mother Nature is nothing if not well attuned to prevailing food trends.

Most exotic of all is a curious piece of produce called simply 'miracle fruit'. The miracle it performs is to make anything eaten immediately after biting into its firm, pleasant flesh taste strangely sweet, so that the sharp segments of a fresh lemon or a bush lime, for example, would

Some of the Sunshine state's edible delights (left to right, top to bottom): Hydroponically grown strawberries; black sapote; harvesting mandarins; golden passionfruit; mixed tropical fruits; star apple; snow peas; spring onions; a pawpaw plantation in Innisfail

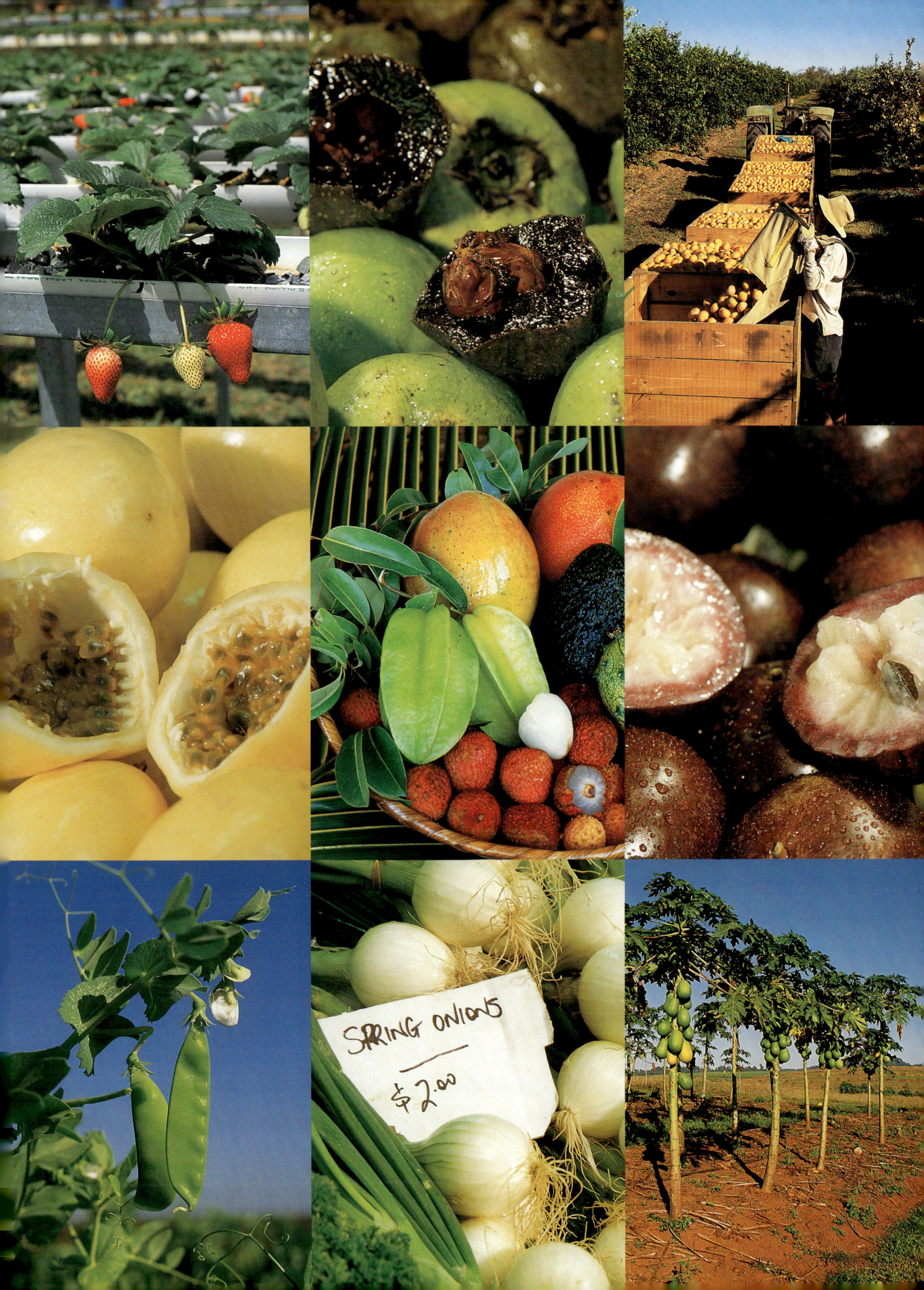
SPRING ONIONS
$2.00

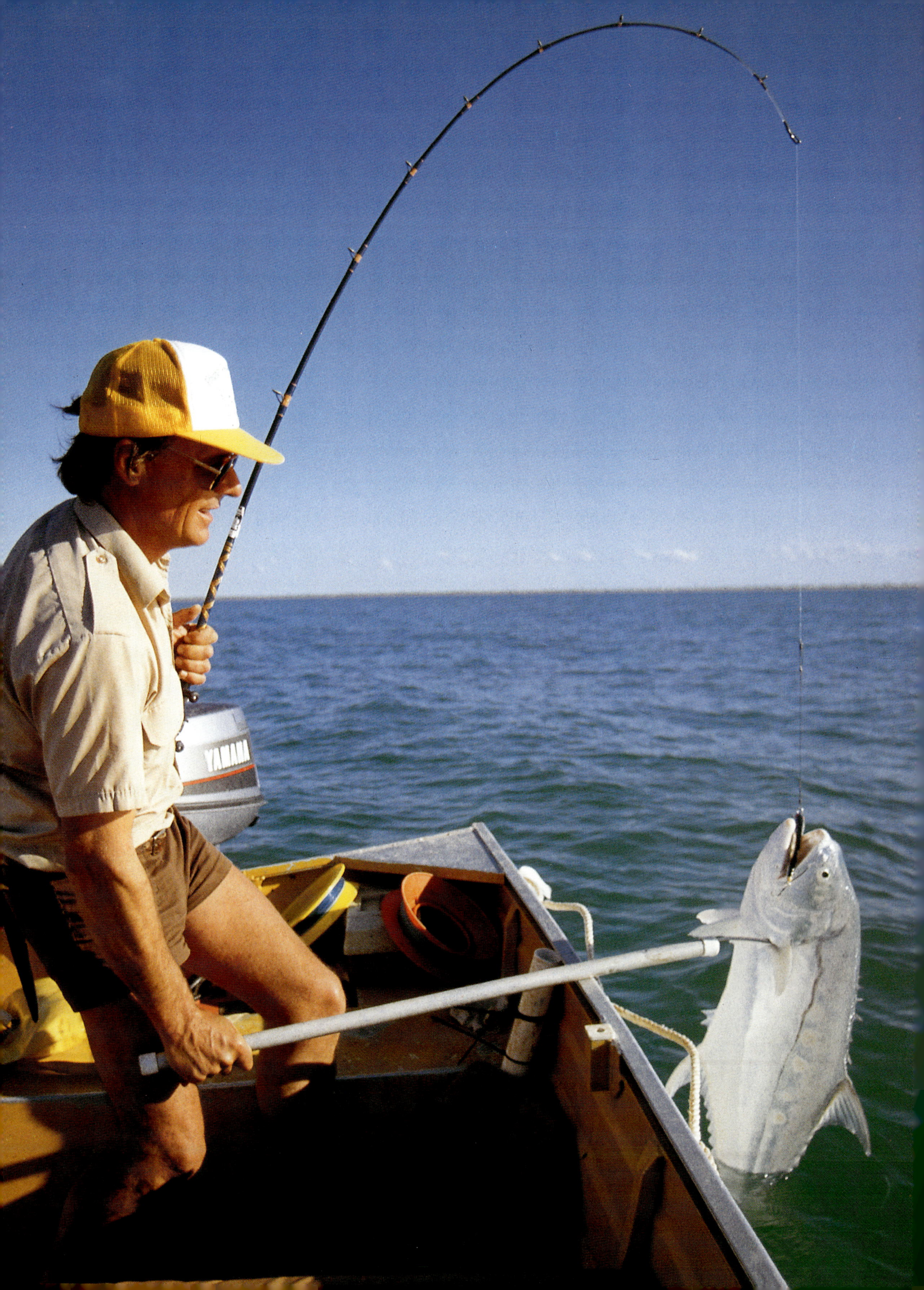
YAMAHA

become as delectable as the flesh of a navel orange. Miracle fruit can often be found in the far north Queensland markets such as the Mud Markets of Cairns or the morning markets of Kuranda, the charming little town at the other end of the scenic railway that snakes from the centre of Cairns, up the ridges of the foothills behind, to the edge of the tableland.

The north and far north coastal regions of the state also offer ideal farming and aquaculture conditions for the magnificent red-claw marrons—no, not chestnuts, but freshwater crayfish which are tender, delicately flavoured and, like so many products of this remarkable state, are significantly larger than life.

Inland, and by arrangement with property owners, licensed shooters 'harvest' kangaroos for their rich, wholesome and almost fat-free meat which is valued so highly by restaurant chefs, and wild pigs, mainly for export to European markets. Deer farms, producing the finest venison for home consumption—and collecting highly-prized deer by-products—are dotted throughout the coastal regions of the state, while just north of Brisbane, at Murgon, an Aboriginal co-operative runs an emu farm from which generous steaks and Flintstone-sized drumsticks from the affable birds are supplied to an enthusiastic restaurant market.

THE ENDLESS PACIFIC Many of Queensland's most exciting challenges and greatest gastronomic rewards, however, are more directly linked to the warm and highly productive expanse of the Pacific Ocean that laps at the state's seemingly endless stretch of eastern coastline and spills around Cape York into the Gulf of Carpentaria.

Determined game fishermen from around the world fly into resorts such as Lizard Island to charter game fishing boats and set off in pursuit of the mighty 'granders'—black marlin that weigh in excess of 450 kilograms and that will fight against capture for the best part of a day. Fit men have been known to die in the game-fishing chair to which they are strapped while fighting such fish. Less ambitious fishermen with smaller budgets and less stamina are content to tangle with fighting tuna, turrum and mackerel on light gear in waters regarded as perhaps the world's finest for game fishing. At certain times of the year, however, cyclones of astonishing intensity can lash Queensland's northern coasts and adjacent island resorts, reminding us once again of the conditions that nature has applied to the full enjoyment of Queensland's riches. Giant 'salties' or salt water crocodiles are a further reminder as they police the tropical streams from which dedicated and always alert fishermen pull the highly-prized barramundi, mangrove jack and king salmon for southern tables, while at sea, deadly box jellyfish and voracious sharks share the coral waters with spectacularly coloured and superbly flavoured reef fish such as snapper, coral trout, red emperor, pearl perch, parrot and wrasse.

Fishing the bountiful waters of Sweers Island Resort in the Gulf of Queensland

Not even catching the magnificent 'muddies'—which can be found all along the Queensland coast, but which are at their biggest, heaviest and most lethal in the tropical regions and in the Gulf of Carpentaria—is without risk or, at the very least, discomfort. The male crabs, often weighing two or more kilos, are generally to be found in murky, mosquito-infested and not particularly hospitable mangrove streams. Bagging them involves snatching them by hand from wire traps or 'pots' which are left overnight in the streams, and clamping their harmless back swimming legs with thumb and forefinger before a lightning snap of those mighty claws can fix on a finger. Veteran Queensland crabbers can seldom look forward to subsequent careers as concert pianists, and are inclined to be unreliable typists.

But as is so often the case in Queensland, the excellence of the produce more than compensates for the degree of difficulty involved in its capture and delivery. The Queensland mud crab is unquestionably one of the world's most delicious sea creatures. Its generous offerings of firm but delicate white flesh is equally impressive as the focus of a cold dish with a fine mayonnaise, as it is presented hot from the steamer—still in a shell which has been expertly and strategically cracked, and needing nothing more than a pot of sweet, melted butter, a pepper mill, and perhaps a crisp Queensland chardonnay or leafy sauvignon blanc to do it justice.

Smaller, thinner-shelled and rather less ferocious blue-swimmer or sand crabs are also caught in great numbers in Queensland waters. These are also delicious and generously fleshed at the peak of the season; they make a memorable bisque, but inevitably take second billing to the mighty muddies. More eye-catching are the alarmingly named Moreton Bay bugs, magnificent crustaceans comparable to the Mediterranean cigale. For decades, these prehistoric-looking creatures were casually tossed back into the sea by Queensland fishermen, or given to adventurous friends, until their true culinary and commercial value began to be understood in the sixties. Steamed bugs' tails are delicious cold, but the chunky tails are at their best quickly char-grilled, or wok-seared with Asian seasonings such as ginger or black beans.

And then there are Queensland prawns—ranging in size from the sweet, bite-sized school prawns from Brisbane's Moreton Bay, through king and tiger prawns, to the huge, crayfish-sized banana prawns of the deep water prawning grounds. Black tiger prawns are farmed at Cleveland, a Brisbane bayside suburb and, with the help of a unique chilling process which puts them into a state of suspended animation for around twenty-four hours, are sold live into Tokyo markets alongside the plentiful long tail tuna or even more delicious yellow fin tuna which are caught in Queensland's coastal waters. These fish are caught on lines, and treated

Pan-seared local seafood with a mixed grill of fennel, artichoke and asparagus with an anchovy and caper buerre blanc from Tables of Toowong

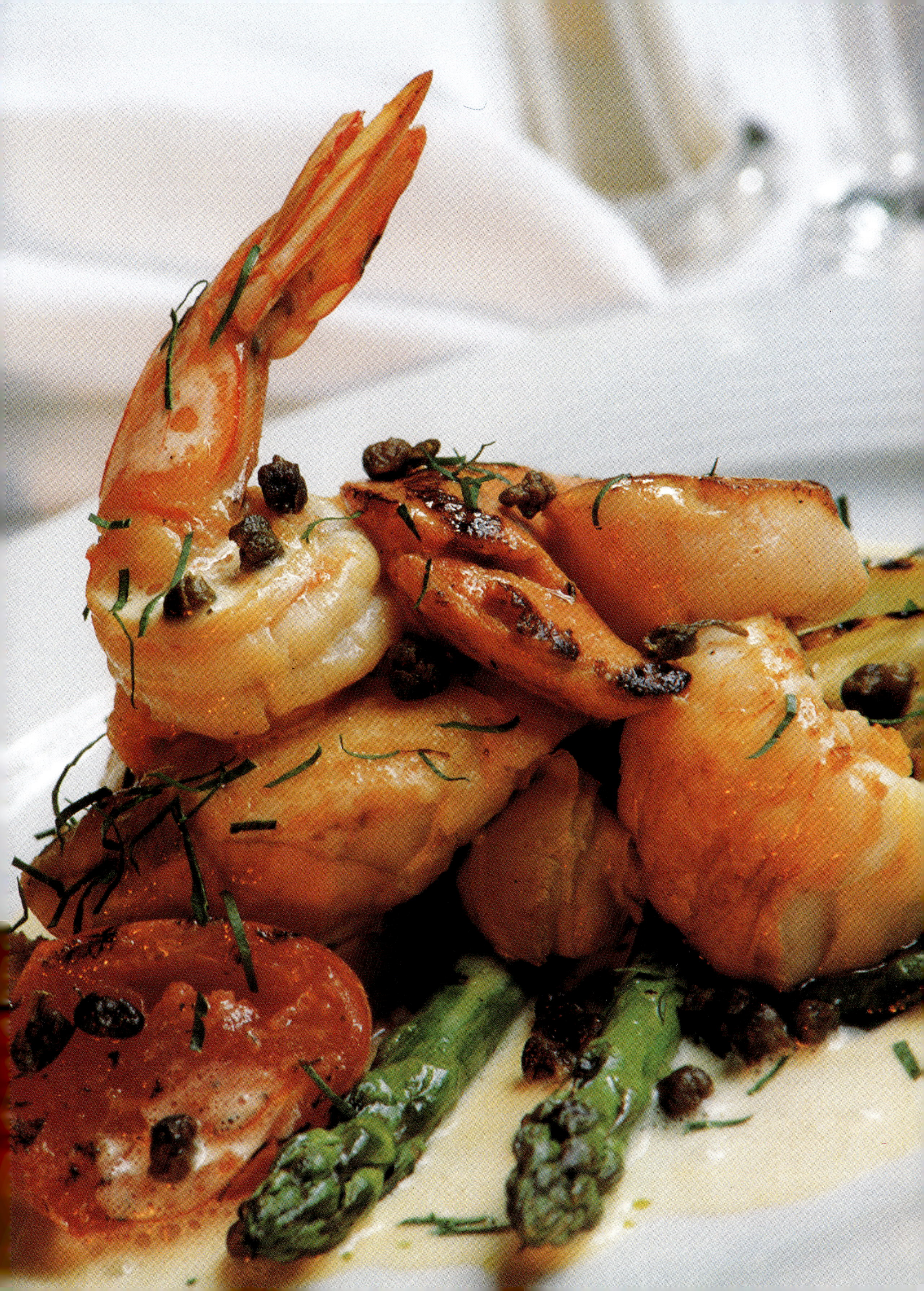

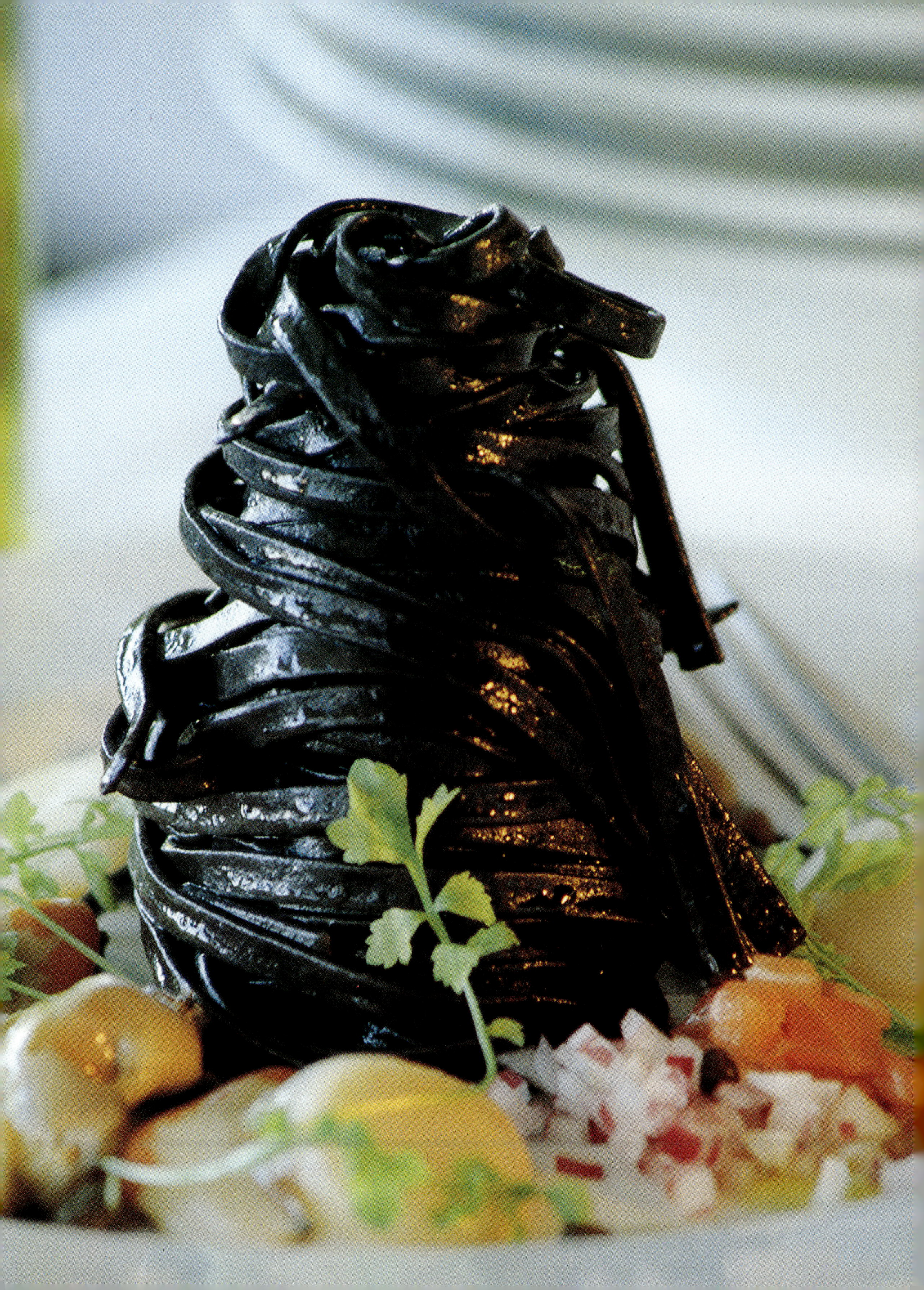

ikajimi style—the brain is quickly 'cored', a cable is fed down the spinal column to prevent shuddering, heart arteries are severed to bleed the fish which is carefully gutted through the gills and then it is chilled in an ice slurry, all to precise Japanese specifications.

INFLUENCES FROM JAPAN In particular, care is taken not to rupture intestinal tracts and thus reduce the quality of the highly-prized toro or belly flesh. The fish are not only exported to the hungry Japanese markets, but are served both as sashimi and as grilled tuna steaks throughout the state. The delicious, pale-fleshed knobby snapper pulled from Queensland's coastal reefs—not to be confused with the less impressive job fish or 'king snapper'—are treated just as respectfully as the tuna, also according to ikajimi dictates. The big, silver fish are spiked, but not bled, and are quickly chilled in an ice slurry and delivered—uncleaned, to maintain the integrity of the flavour—to markets throughout Australia and Japan. There is no doubt that in addition to lifting the market value of Queensland fish, the inspired Japanese teachings have also dramatically improved the quality of the product delivered to Queensland restaurants.

Nowhere in Australia is the Japanese gastronomic influence on our food felt as strongly as it is felt in Queensland. The restaurants that are to be found in Cairns, Townsville, at the Capricorn resort outside Rockhampton, in Brisbane and on the Gold Coast offer authentic Japanese food at prices far below those at which comparable food is offered in Japan. Sushi bar fare inevitably includes the exquisitely sweet whiting which teem around Queensland's coastal sandbanks, as well as the much admired snapper and red emperor flesh, and the live tiger prawns from Cleveland which are served as the traditional Japanese delicacy of 'sweet shrimp'—the quivering, translucent tail meat resting on a nugget of sushi rice, with the head and carapace removed but legs still attached, lightly battered and deep fried tempura style.

Seafood enthusiasts visiting Queensland have much to seek out and will seldom be disappointed. They should probably make it a habit to begin as many meals as possible with a platter of freshly-opened, live rock oysters—preferably from Brisbane's Moreton Bay. The curious geography of the bay, which is separated from the open sea by the long sand islands of Moreton and Stradbroke, means that with both incoming and outgoing tides, carefully positioned oyster leases are flushed through with fresh sea water rather than the outgoing river tides carrying silt and nutrients that wash through many of the leases in southern states. This gives the Moreton Bay oysters a bold, natural, salty tang which provides a perfect balance to the rich creaminess common to all Australian rock oysters. These oysters should be eaten with as few embellishments as possible—a grind of pepper, a squeeze of lemon (to which freshly opened oysters will respond by curling their lacy edges—a foolproof test of freshness), possibly

A spiral of squid ink pasta surrounded by seafood and fresh vegetables from Il Centro

a drop or two of good balsamic vinegar if you are following European traditions, or a splash of ponzu sauce if you are interested in joining the Japanese revolution in Queensland gastronomy. In all cases, the oysters should be served unrinsed, and should be eaten straight from the shell without benefit of oyster fork so that none of the precious juices are wasted.

Four establishments in particular have done much to consolidate the reputation of Queensland as the seafood state in recent years. They are Pier Nine and Gambaro in Brisbane, Saltwater in Noosa Heads, and Tawny's in Cairns. Each has its own, quite different approach to the business of presenting seafood, and each is quite outstanding.

In the heart of Brisbane's commercial district looking out over the busy waters of the Brisbane River, Pier Nine is the restaurant most likely to remain in the memory banks of visitors to Brisbane. A winner of the prestigious American Express award against all comers, the restaurant—operated by innovative young restaurateur Matthew Hill Smith—has set new standards for seafood service in the state. At any time, fresh oysters from as many as three different regions are on offer. They are opened to order and served unrinsed and attached unless requested otherwise. Mud crabs, steamed to absolute perfection, are served with drawn butter, Moreton Bay bugs are char-grilled, fresh tuna is quickly seared and served rare, and daily specials are built around only the finest of fresh fish available. Not surprisingly, Pier Nine is generally full and always alive.

Gambaro, a vast restaurant established in the 1950s by an Italian immigrant family and still owned and operated by that same family, is perched well above Brisbane's city centre in Caxton Street in the city's handsome, old Petrie Terrace district. It has long enjoyed legendary status among seafood enthusiasts in search of the creamiest oysters and the most perfectly prepared mud crabs. Gambaro plays an even more pivotal role in the Queensland seafood industry these days by being the state's largest wholesale supplier of oysters, mud crabs, and most fresh seafood.

Move north to Noosa Heads on the Sunshine Coast, and the township's buzzy boulevard, Hastings Street, these days seems to revolve around activities at a fashionable little seafood establishment called Saltwater. Operated by Steve and Lisa Cross, it functions as a fish-and-chippery and fresh fish retailer at street level, and a smart, state-of-the-art seafood restaurant on the level above. The menu is changed daily to align with market supplies, and most seafood is served unadorned but for the simplest of Asian or Mediterranean embellishments, and is simply but exquisitely cooked. The wine list is comprehensive and, coupled with the fine food and the view from the top, can leave diners feeling strangely at one with life and in love with Noosa.

Left to right, top to bottom: Michael Gambaro; Gambaro's prawns in a traditional Italian sauce with sun-dried tomatoes and basil; the magnificent cappuccino expresso machine in Gambaro's restaurant; Pier Nine's Storm Bay scallops grilled in an open shell with pesto linguine; Pier Nine's owner Matthew Hill Smith (left) and chef John Buchanan; oysters kaffir in sweet Thai lime vinaigrette, also from Pier Nine; About Face restaurant; pasture-fed eye fillet with asparagus, pickled walnuts and Australian wild mushrooms; Andrew Mirosch, chef and operator of About Face

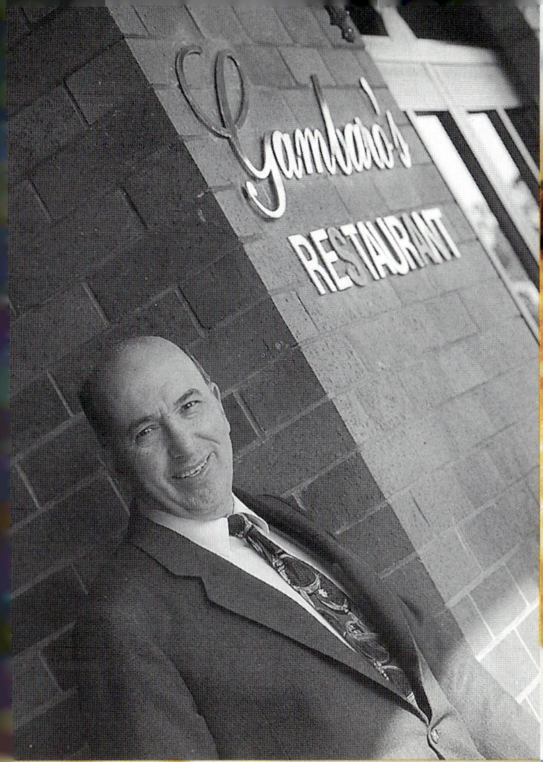
Gambaro's
RESTAURANT
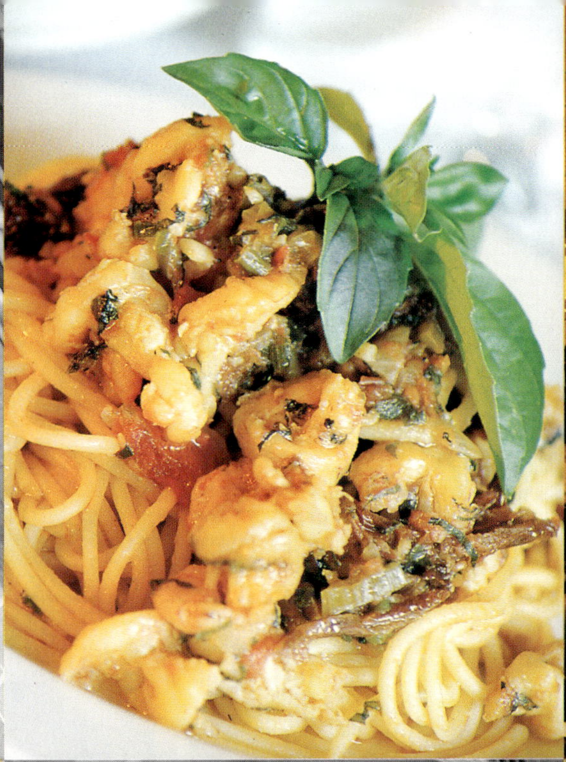
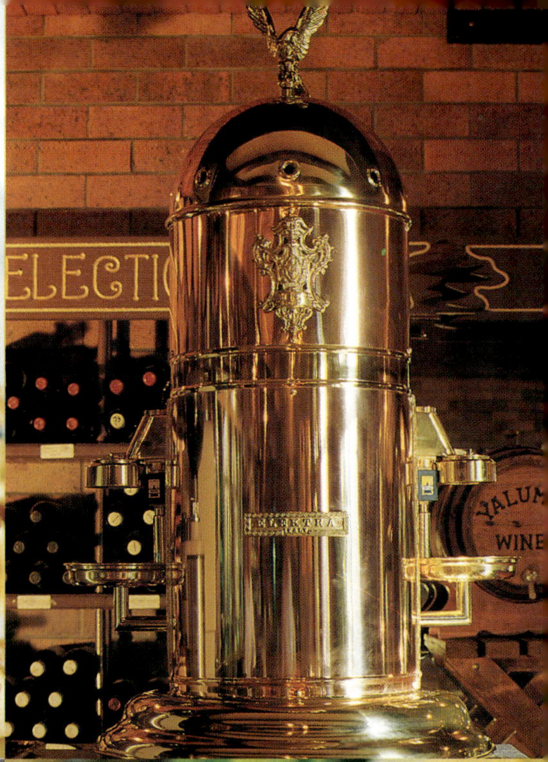
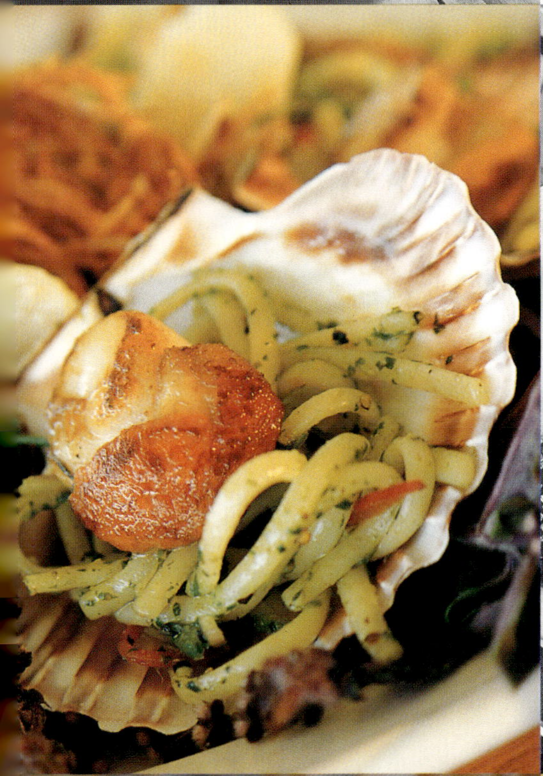
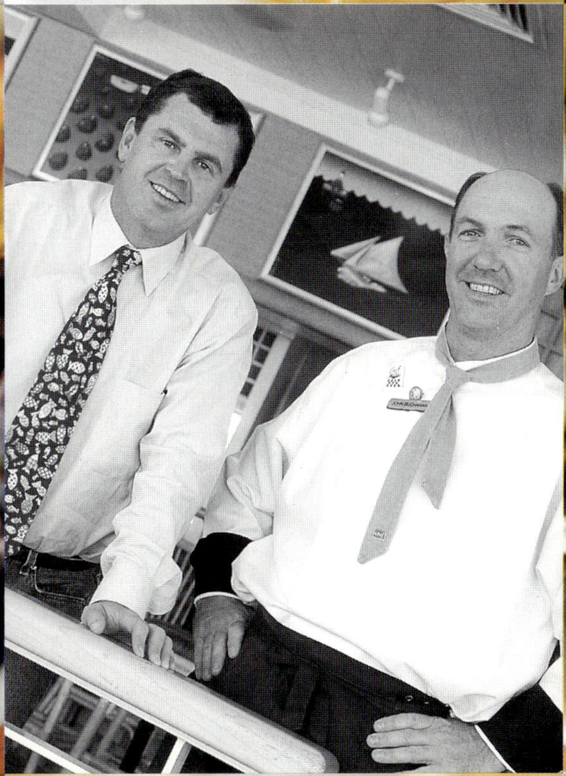
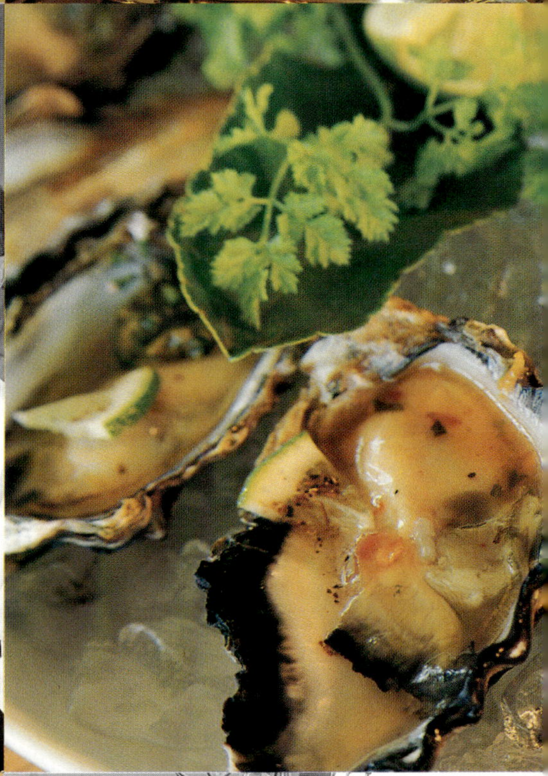
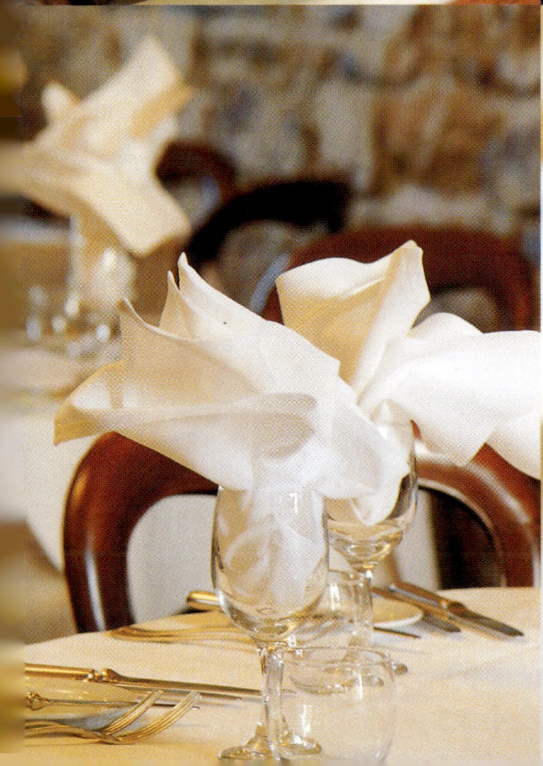
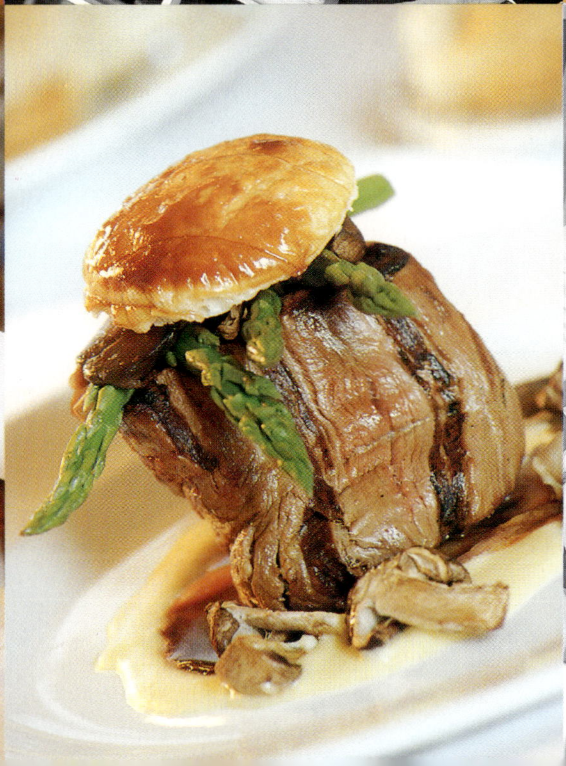
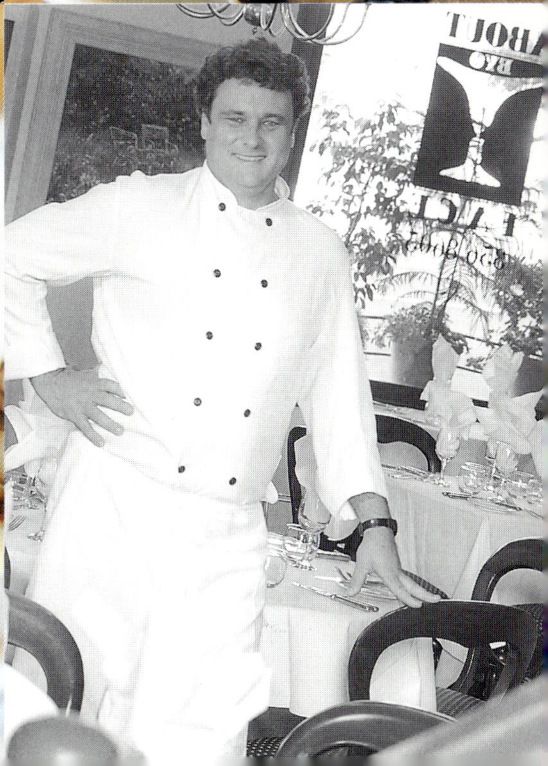

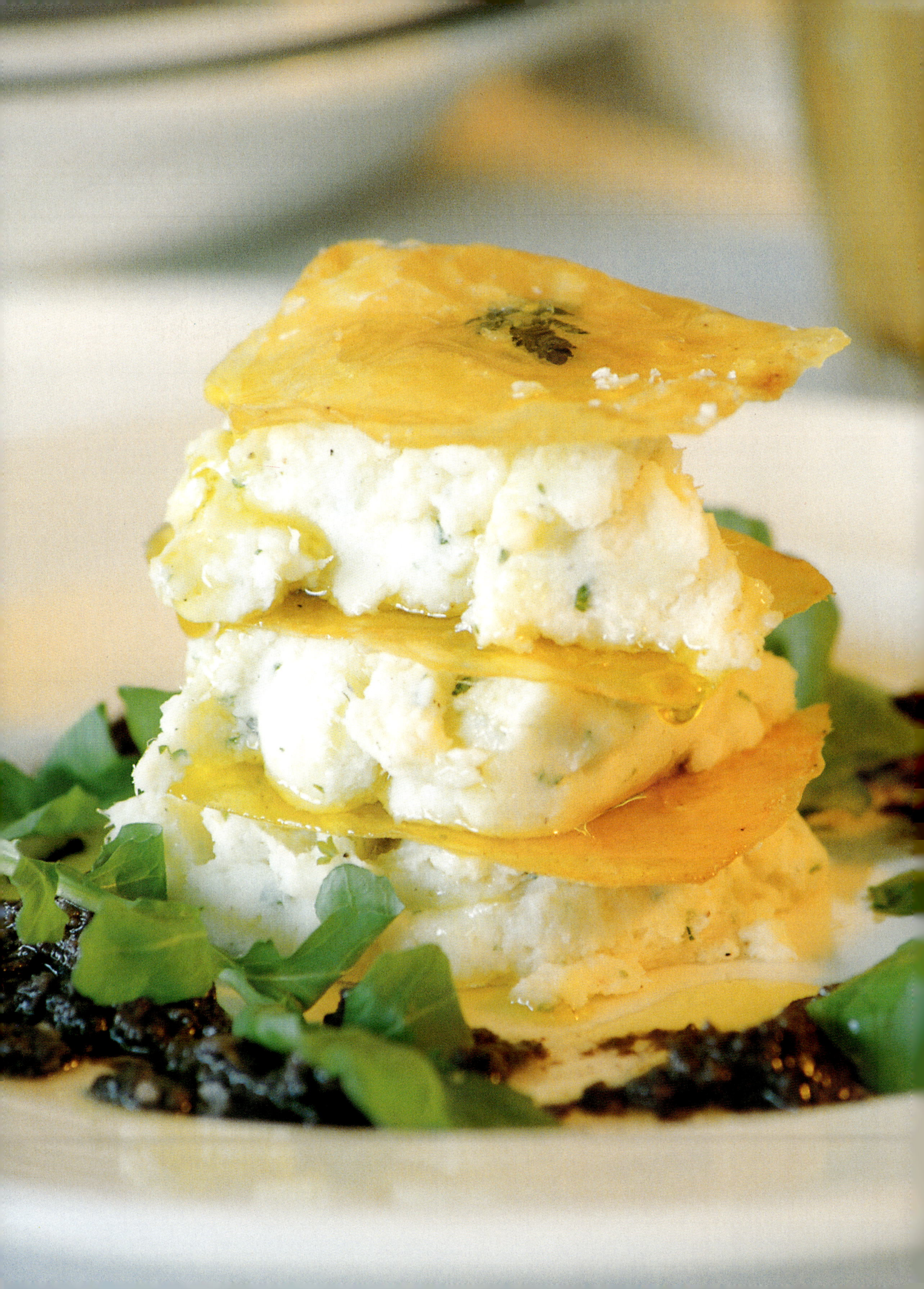

TROPICAL BRILLIANCE In all states of Australia, it is the most brilliant and innovative of the local chefs who set the gastronomic pace and keep the pressure on suppliers and growers to deliver nothing but the very best. And in Queensland, the chef who has set the pace is unquestionably Andrew Mirosch, now the owner and operator of the highly regarded About Face licensed restaurant in Brisbane's Kelvin Grove.

In 1992, Mirosch opened About Face as owner-chef, collecting all the awards and accolades on offer. His cooking—like Mirosch himself—is pure Queensland. It is robust and original, dependent on the finest fresh ingredients, and bursting with ideas he has woven around the unique and distinctive produce of the state, with just a hint of knowledge and exotica that has come from elsewhere in the world.

Widely respected as a master of game meats, his work with the racks of red deer venison and the magnificently flavoured, low-fat kangaroo cuts from Queensland's outback ranks with any in Australia.

Mirosch prepares the almost grainless kangaroo meat by searing whole sirloins on a charcoal grill, resting them, and serving them in fine, rare slices with braised Asian vegetables such as fresh baby corn cobs and bok choy, both widely grown in south-east Queensland. Other distinctive local produce to be found on a Mirosch menu will include corn-fed squab from Warwick on the Darling Downs, and the superb cuts of grain-fed beef—once again, tailored under Japanese instruction to the Tokyo markets—from Beef City feed lots outside Toowoomba. The fillets, cube rolls (also called rib fillets) and sirloins are from huge carcases which weigh in at between 300 and 400 kilograms. All of the meat is heavily marbled and meltingly tender.

And, as a complete contrast, Mirosch is an enthusiastic presenter of the small, sweet, farmed barramundi from the fish farms in Townsville and Cairns—ideally suited to being steamed whole, and presented with Asian vegetables and the range of locally produced fresh Asian herbs and spices, such as coriander leaves, lemon grass, fresh turmeric roots and premium ginger from the extensive ginger plantations at Yandina on the Sunshine Coast.

Mirosch is also totally dedicated to his home state. In return, the state has shared many of its secrets with him. He likes to catch his own fish—especially the richly flavoured fighting pelagics such as Spanish mackerel and black kingfish—in the waters of Moreton Bay on his free days, and often collects his own rare mushrooms during early walks around local golf courses. Southern chefs would be astonished by the morrells he collects from Milaney, a picturebook town in the hinterland of the Sunshine Coast, and the cepe-like slippery jacks he collects

Il Centro's salmon and potato stack, with green beans, shallot mayonnaise, boiled egg and olives

on Bribie Island, the resort and residential island colony between Brisbane and the Sunshine Coast. There can be no doubt that if Queensland has a taste of its own, then it is to be found, and will continue to develop, in the cooking of Andrew Mirosch.

At the Toowong establishment, Two Small Rooms, chef David Pugh is delivering food that is more delicate but no less inventive to a loyal and devoted clientele. Pugh has consolidated the reputation he developed as chef at the stylish Ascot eatery, Baguette. And no distance away another remarkable establishment—Tables of Toowong—continues to dazzle patrons just as thoroughly as About Face or Two Small Rooms through the wizardry of owner-chef Russell Amstrong. Eat in any one of these restaurants, order adventurously, focus on local specialties, and you will discover not only the highly distinctive tastes of Queensland, but food of a quality that will illustrate just why Australia is now regarded as one of the most complete food destinations in the world.

NEW VINTAGES With food, of course, goes wine. And while Queensland is far from being the most celebrated of Australian wine states, it nevertheless offers a range of distinctive wines of great quality and with clear, identifying characteristics. They are grown in Queensland's Granite Belt around the township of Stanthorpe—an area that attracted many of the early Italian migrants to Australia who chose to settle in the region and establish first the fruit-growing and later the wine-making industry, while a great number of their countrymen continued north to work in the sugar plantations and give many of the small coastal towns a strong Italian flavour.

There are now around a dozen good Stanthorpe wineries, several of them producing peppery shiraz, rich cabernet sauvignon, chardonnay, sauvignon blanc and buttery semillon wines that regularly either win or are in serious contention for medals at most Australian wine shows.

Above: The Brisbane skyline Right (clockwise from top left): Russell Armstrong and Charles Duffin (with cap) from Tables of Toowong; Tables' frozen parfait of Queensland ginger over a compote of summer berries and rolled 'cigarette' biscuit; David Pugh of Two Small Rooms restaurant and his roast cutlets with wood mushroom and black truffle risotto

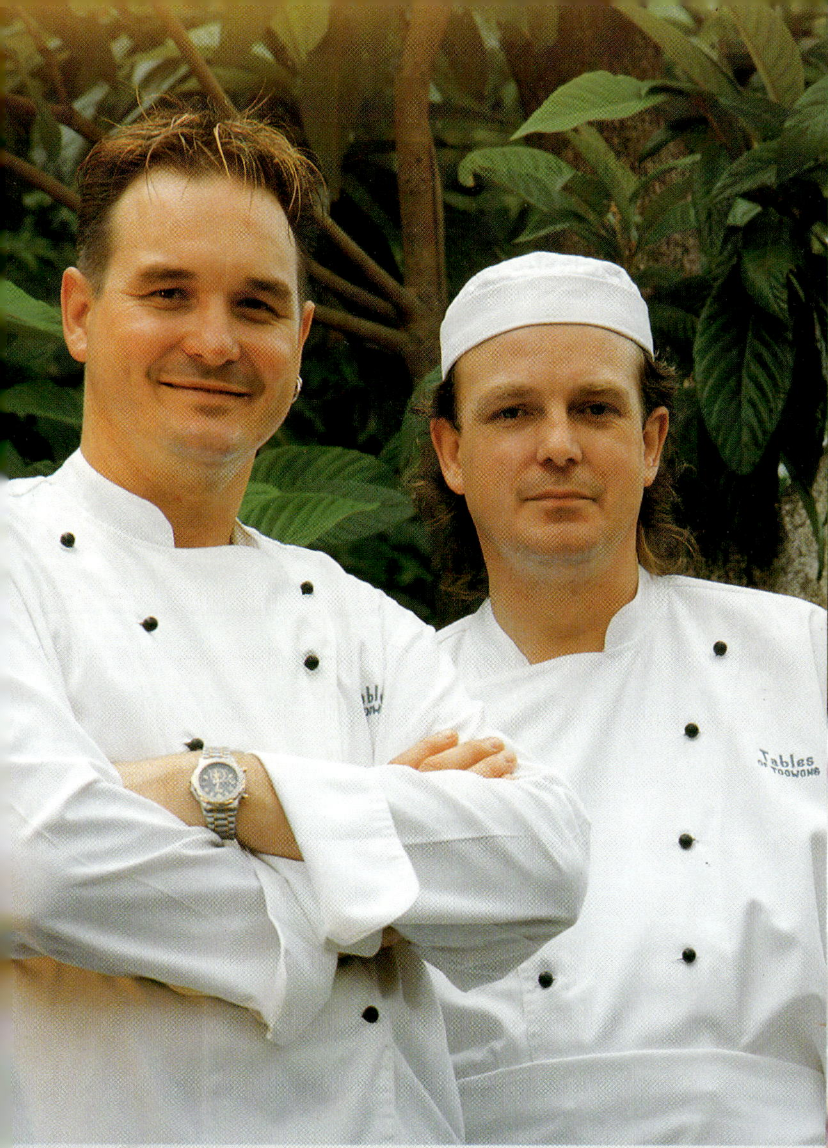
Tables

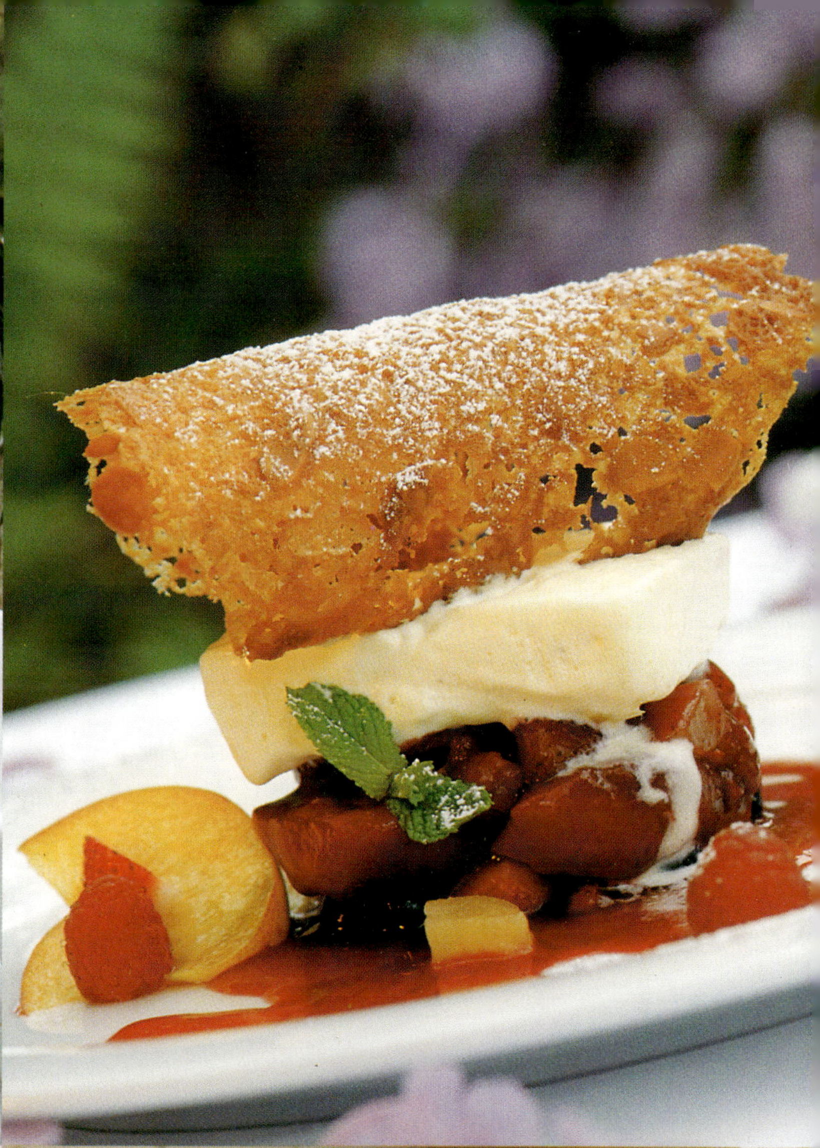

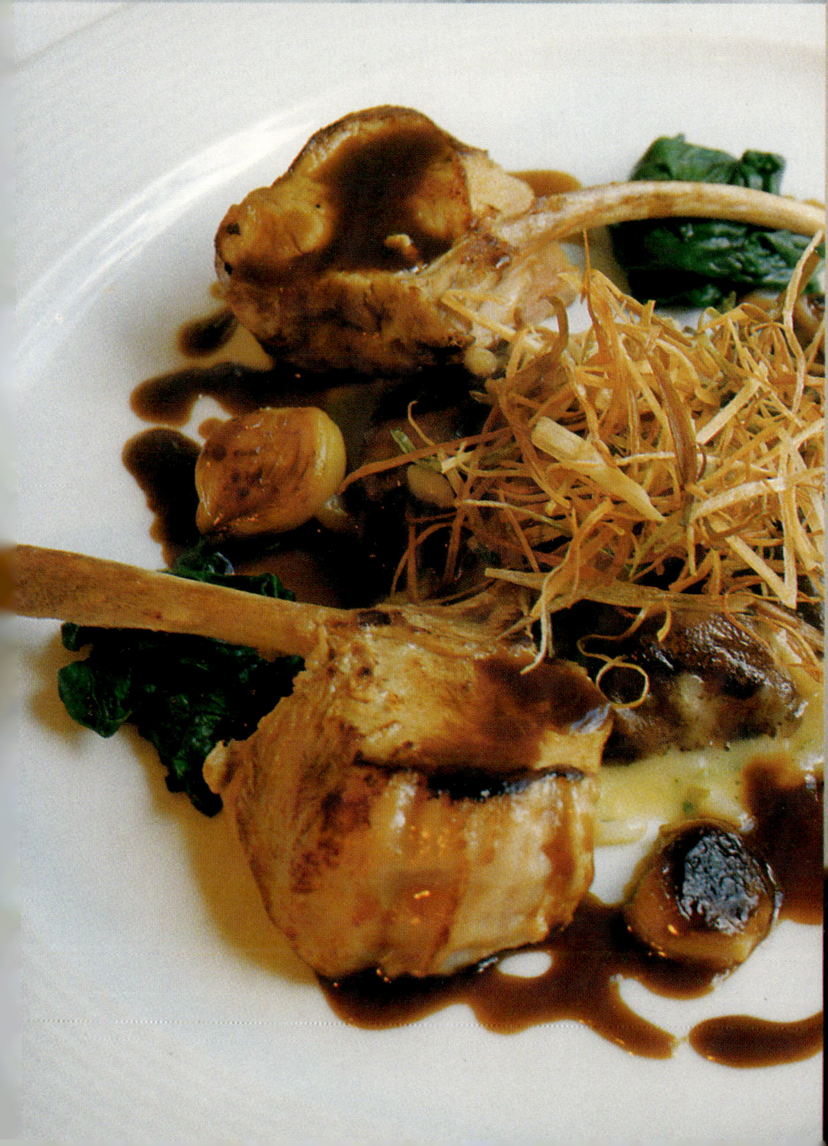

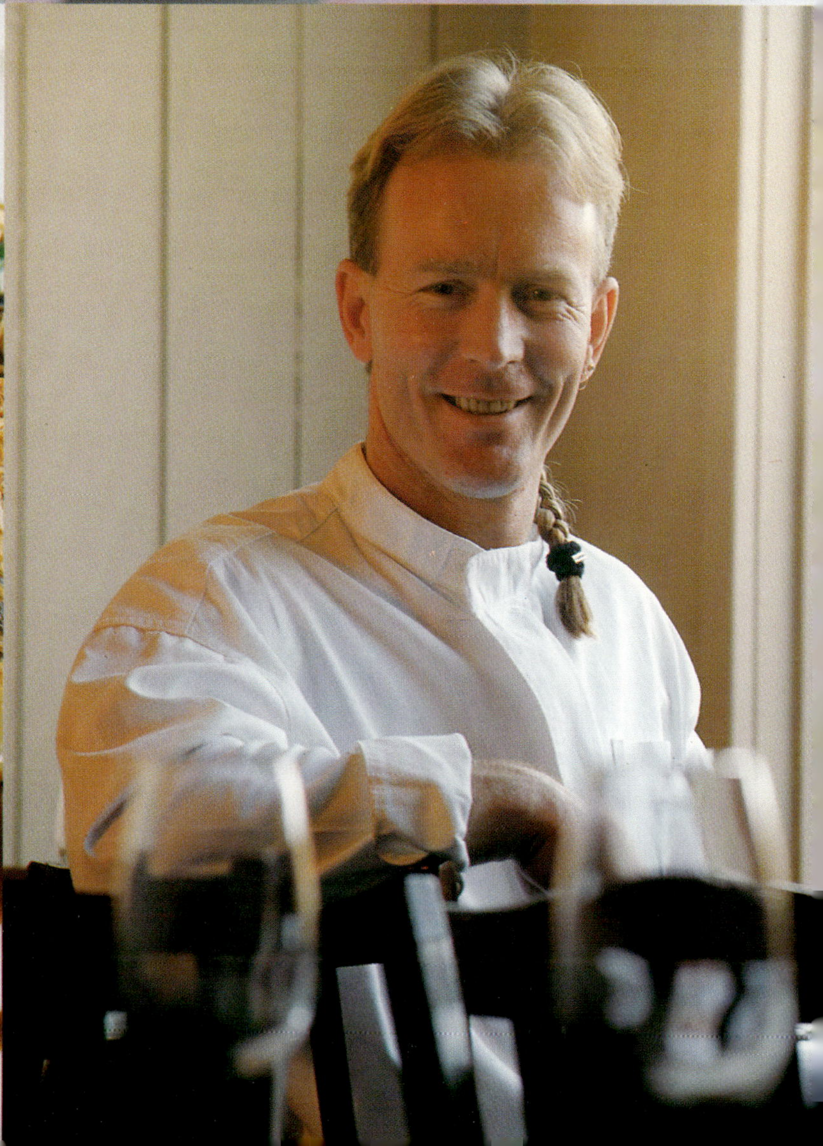

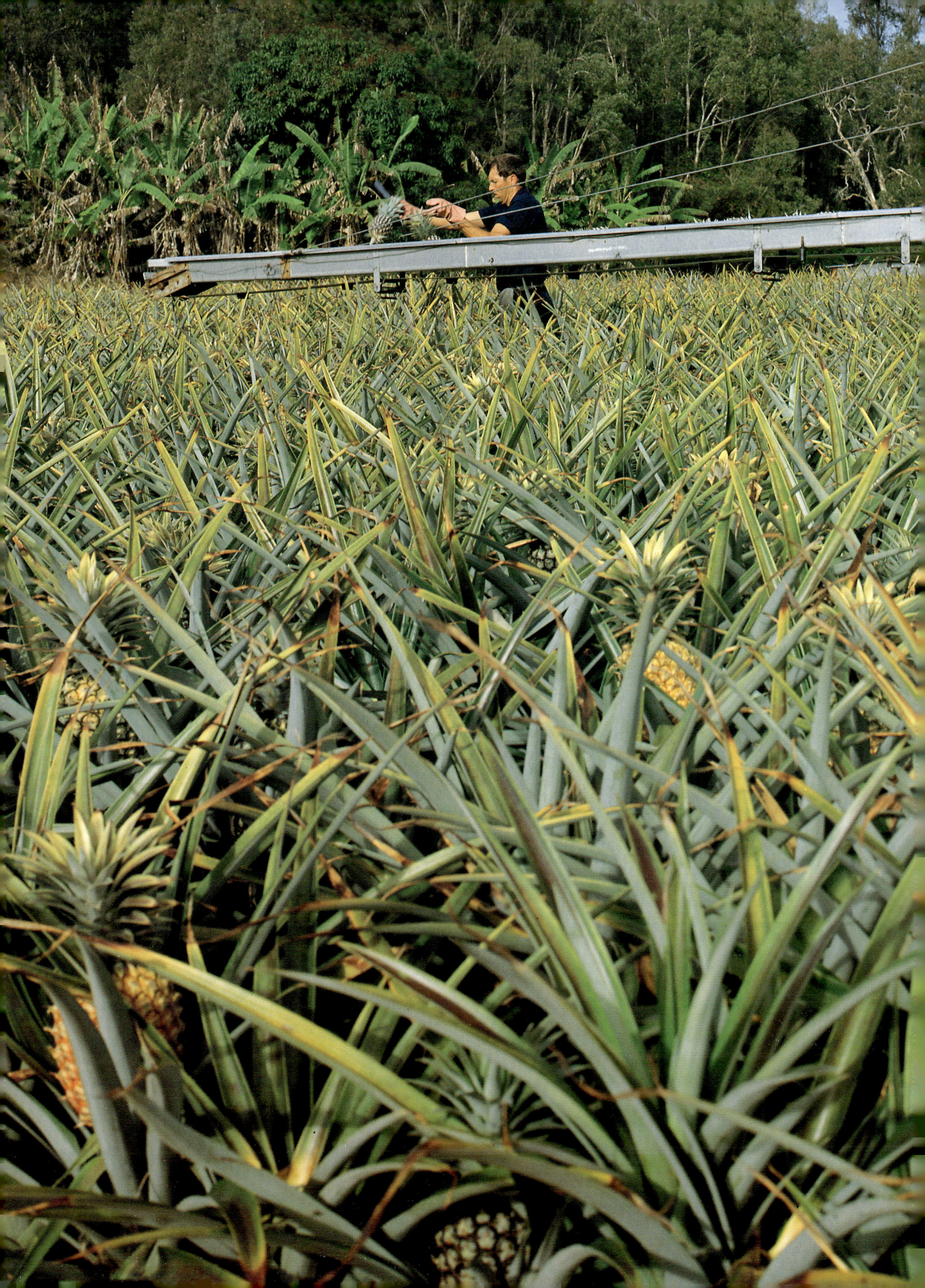

And as the name of the region suggests, the granite boulders that are an identifying feature of the landscape also contribute, through the decomposed granite in the topsoil, to the earthy and robust quality of many of the wines. Any bottle carrying a label from Ballandean Estate, Winewood, Bungawarra, Kominos, Stone Ridge, Mountview, Felsberg, Old Caves, Robinsons, Rumbalara and, especially, Bald Mountain, whose shiraz and chardonnays regularly astonish visiting wine enthusiasts with their brilliance, is worth trying. Wine lovers can visit the region—about a three-hour drive from Brisbane—and taste and buy at the cellar door. Visitors can stay overnight in any one of a number of establishments and enjoy superbly prepared local specialities at the award-winning Vineyard Café restaurant at Ballandean.

Lifting the awareness of Brisbane food enthusiasts is a role that has also been enthusiastically assumed by one of the local suppliers who caters to the demands of chefs. He is Peter Stergakis—a fruiterer who, like so many Australians of his calling, is of Greek extraction—whose Rock 'n' Roll Fruit Bowl is unlike any other establishment of its kind. Visiting food writers, chefs and foodies are inevitably directed to the huge barn of a place which occupies most of a block on Logan Road, a major thoroughfare through Brisbane's southern suburbs.

The principle is simple enough: if it grows in Queensland, is a fruit or vegetable, and it's good to eat, then you will find it at the Rock 'n' Roll. The calendar year begins with shelves bursting not simply with the usual array of Australian summer fruit available everywhere, but with tree-ripened peaches and nectarines whose perfume fills the place. While most fruit shops will offer the Kensington Pride mangoes during the glorious summer months, Stergakis will offer them in a range of sizes, and from a range of growers. And alongside them will be the R2E2 or 'bullock heart' mangoes snapped up from other remote corners of far north Queensland. And when the Stanthorpe farms deliver their berries—among them raspberries, loganberries, blackberries and young berries—you will find them first at Rock 'n' Roll, just as you will find the first of the fat blueberries and curiously delicious and versatile cape gooseberries from the rich Sunshine Coast hinterland.

'I love Queensland and I love the food that I can offer here. I love the look on people's faces when they taste something like a northern exotic fruit variety of some sort for the first time, and I push people into trying new, local produce rather than simply buying the same thing they have been buying for years,' says Stergakis.

'Most of all, though, I just try to remind people how lucky they are to live in Queensland. I am reminded of it myself every time I walk into my own shop and inhale.'

Bob Hart

Mechanical harvesting of pineapples near Buderim

NEW SOU

Right: Stunning Bar Beach near Newcastle, flanked by a cascading group of headlands Above: The distinctive red soil of Hunter Valley vineyards nurtures some of Australia's finest wines; Bilsons Restaurant overlooks the heart of Sydney Harbour, the Opera House and Circular Quay

WALES

Raw Energy

Socially, morally, intellectually, culturally, aesthetically and gastronomically, there is probably not a society on earth that has transformed itself so rigorously in the past two centuries as that of New South Wales.

Australian agriculture began in this state in 1788 when the eleven ships of the First Fleet dropped anchor in Port Jackson, but it was not a happy beginning. The first attempts to grow crops on the sandy soil at Farm Cove failed miserably, and for years the convict-settlers and their guards were close to starvation. It was only after three years, in 1791, that James Ruse, a farmer in his native Cornwall, was able to establish the first successful farm at Parramatta, showing the faintest hope that the infant colony might be able to feed itself.

What Sydney now eats is often described as fusion food—a collage of culinary influences which uses a splash of olive oil with one hand while tossing in chopped coriander and chilli with the other. The reason for this inspiring gastronomy is the ethnic bouillabaisse that is Sydney's population. Since 1945 the city's original Anglo-Irish population base has been enriched by successive waves of Italians, Greeks, Yugoslavs, Turks, Lebanese, Thais, Chinese, Malays, Indonesians, Vietnamese and Cambodians, each of whom have added their own cuisine to Sydney's diet.

In character, Sydney's restaurant dining tends to be more relaxed than that of Melbourne, but even so, the trend is away from the reverence that typified Sydney's fashionable restaurants of just a few years ago and in favour of a more relaxed and affordable style of dining. What has not been sacrificed is quality. Imagination, service, calibre of ingredients and attention to the essentials have, if anything, been refined as has the enthusiastic appreciation of an ever-increasing—and ever more well-educated—audience.

Indicative of the general raising of food consciousness, Sydney chefs have a higher profile than ever before, and the stars of the league such as Gai Bilson of Berowra Waters and advisor at the Opera House, Serge Dansereau of Kables in the Regent Hotel and Neil Perry of Rockpool, are familiar names on the Sydney scene.

A residual of this prominence has filtered down to suppliers such as the Flying Squid Brothers, Mohr Food and Enoteca Sileno, each of whom has played a pivotal role in inspiring these chefs with high quality and often esoteric ingredients. Even restaurant architects have been caught up in the fashionable whirl, and the partnership of Burley Katon Halliday, the names behind The Paramount and Darley Street Thai, are almost as well known as the restaurants they designed.

A RELAXED STYLE Food follows fashion, and having proven themselves on the catwalks, many of these star chefs are now opening second-label restaurants that offer stylish surroundings, quality ingredients, innovative cooking and cosmopolitan influences minus the trimmings and the expensive price tag—the culinary equivalent of prêt-a-porter. The result is Sydney's current fascination—the breezy, bring-your-own, open-early open-late cafe-bistro with prices and menus that come from the streets rather than the boulevards.

These cafe-bistros have transformed whole streets in East Sydney, The Rocks and the back streets of Kings Cross. Just off the southern side of William Street, the area between the city and Kings Cross has become Sydney's Gourmet Gulch, with Latin-inspired street cafes, gelateries and a sprinkling of well-proven restaurants favoured by Sydney's gastro know-alls.

One of the most interesting areas is Norton Street in inner-west Leichhardt, which has become Sydney's Italian eat street largely under the tutelage of the suburb's prominent Italian community. Comparisons with Melbourne's Lygon Street are inevitable, although Norton Street is higher on octane than ambience. Ever on the cusp of fashion, city-fringe Newtown shows promise with a choice of restaurants that grazes the culinary globe.

EXHILARATING VARIETY As a source of raw material, New South Wales is exhilarating. Given its size—which is just slightly bigger than France and the United Kingdom combined—it's not surprising that the state produces such an astonishing range of food, from apples to avocadoes, macadamia nuts, sugar cane, durum wheat, rice, wine grapes, pineapples, trout and tuna. As well as the large-scale, monoculture farming that is the bread and butter of New South Wales agriculture, many small-scale producers have responded to the increasingly sophisticated demands of the market by carving out a niche as suppliers of specialty foods.

Clockwise from top left: Coffee and dessert at Mesclun; Belinda Frank's chicken breast with herb pesto topping; a tempting treat—honey, chocolate and macadamia wafers from Mesclun; at the heart of the action—Kink Cafe, Oxford Street, Darlinghurst

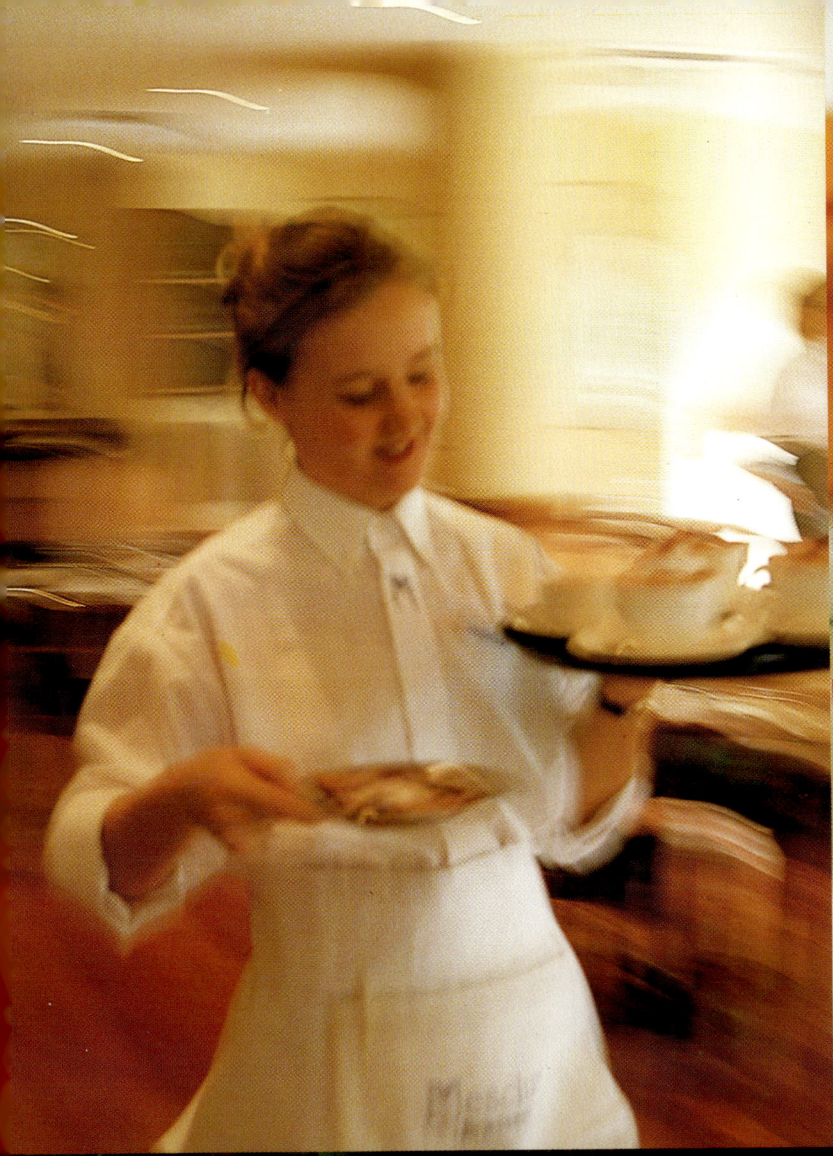
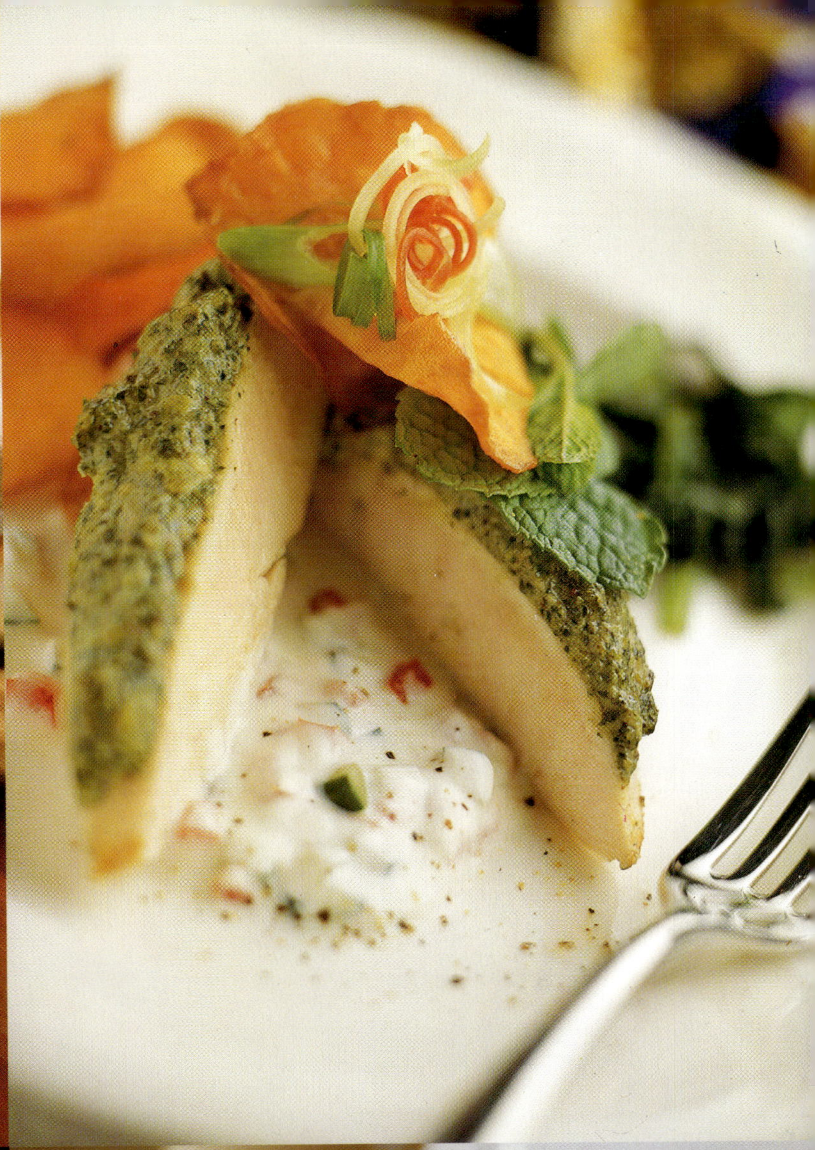
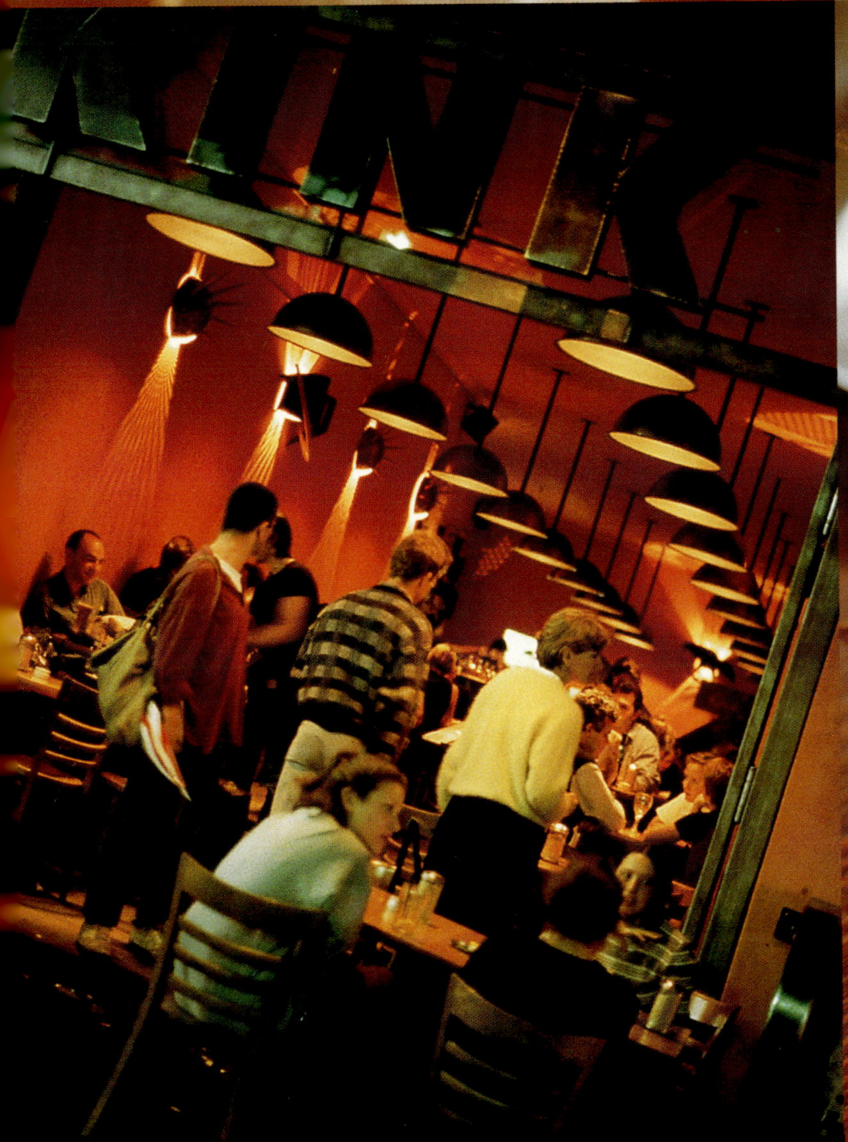
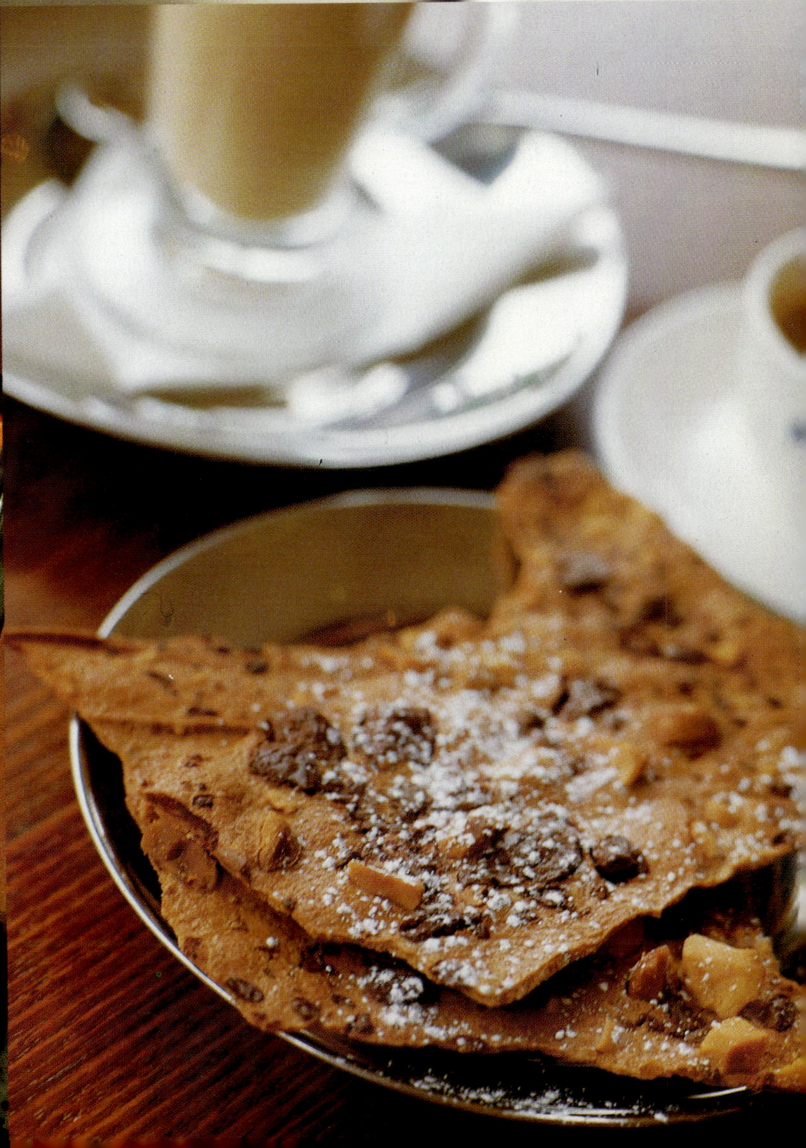

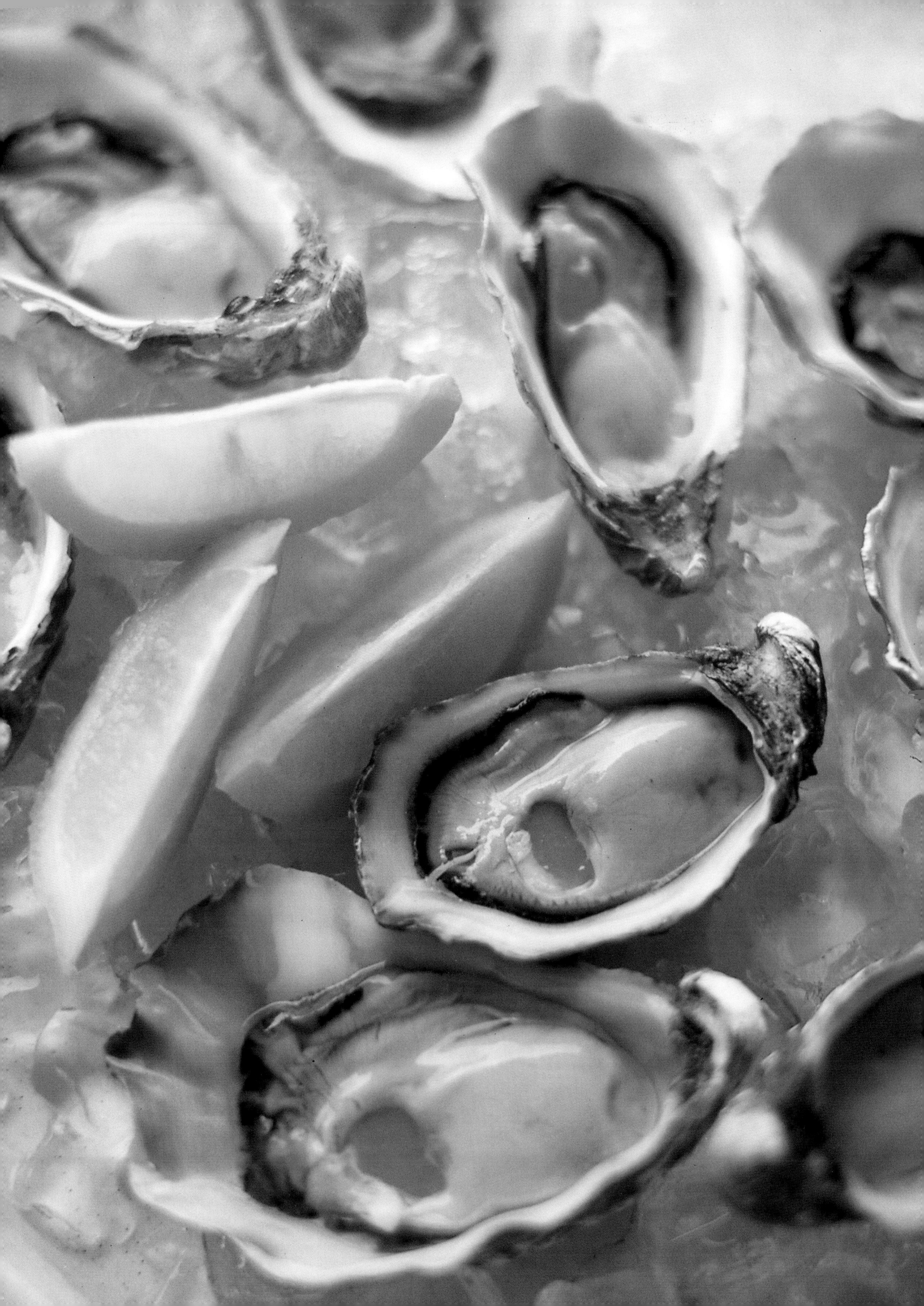

New South Wales - Raw Energy

Any gastronomic tour of New South Wales should begin at Sydney's Fish Markets. The market has anything up to 200 species on offer, making it second only to the giant Tsukiji market in Tokyo for sheer variety. 'The quality of our seafood is really sensational, and that's why species such as yellowfin tuna from the south coast of New South Wales find such a ready market in Japan,' says John Sussman of the Flying Squid Brothers, who together with partners Martin Groen and Geoff Warren, has been instrumental in bringing the finest from our seas to the Australian table.

Perhaps the single most representative New South Wales seafood is the oyster, which is grown commercially along almost the entire 1,900 kilometres of the state's coastline. Most common are the famous Sydney Rock oysters, the small, sweet crassostrea commercialis, which every New South Welshman believes to be the finest oyster in the world. At many places on the New South Wales coast, such as Jervis Bay, south of Sydney, these oysters are clotted on the rocks, and there for the taking. A great, flat sheet of blue water darkened by drifting clouds and ringed by forests and beaches, Jervis Bay is one of the reasons that Australia is still known as 'the lucky country'. Anywhere else on earth, the shores of the bay—only a two-and-a-half hour drive from Sydney—would be crowded with weekenders and marinas, yet apart from the summer holiday months the beaches are almost deserted and barely a sail crackles on the taut blue canvas of the sea.

From his base at Huskisson, at the back of the bay's throat, John Settree dredges for the Jervis Bay oyster, ostrea angasi, the big, plump oysters that lie on the bottom at a depth of about twenty metres. Jervis Bay oysters are frequently sold as Belon in Sydney restaurants. The famous French oyster is actually a different species, ostrea edulis, although there are similarities in this robust, luscious oyster with a taste that stays with you halfway back to Sydney.

'There's a Frenchman who comes down here and buys them from me and he's crazy about them. I sold him five dozen and I asked how much would these be worth in France and he said about $150. I sell them for six dollars a dozen. Nine dollars fifty in the markets.'

FROM EAST TO WEST The land mass of New South Wales can be divided into four distinct regions, from east to west. In the east is a coastal plain, which can be anything up to 100 kilometres wide. This plain is bordered by the Great Dividing Range, a chain of low mountains. On the western slopes of this range is a broad belt of fertile grazing country which gives way to the sheep pastures and wheat fields of the western plains, an arid, open, sparsely-populated region that occupies about two-thirds of the state.

Freshly opened rock oysters

AUSTRALIA - A GOURMET'S PARADISE

It is the rich, well-watered coastal plain that provides Sydney with much of its fruit, vegetables and dairy produce, but along with the cows, tomato fields and strawberry farms, there are several specialist producers of note. At Thirlmere, south of Sydney, John Meredith farms free-range, cross-breed ducks that he supplies undrawn to the restaurant trade. At Round Hill Farm in the Southern Highlands, Mark and Leigh Williamson grow herbs and vegetables of exceptional quality such as celeriac, kohl-rabi, leeks and carrots and at Mangrove Mountain, just north of Sydney, Phil and Jenny Smith are well known for their luscious, melt-in-your-mouth stone fruit such as peaches.

As well as skill, persistence and uncompromising dedication to quality, it also demands canny marketing abilities for such small, distinctive producers to survive. It also helps if you have a unique product and at Silverdale on the western outskirts of Sydney, surrounded by hobby farms and brick villas that hint at creeping suburbia, Joe Chetcuti hands me a box about the size of a brick. Inside are two red cabbages, a cauliflower, half a dozen lettuces, a head of broccoli, two pumpkins, two ears of corn, a turnip, a bunch of shallots and several carrots. They radiate colour and vigour, yet these bonsai gems are not baby vegetables but miniatures—fully grown, fully developed pygmies. The lettuces with leaves the size of a thumbnail are crisp and tasty. The Lilliputian carrots have been in the ground for six months, and a twelve-month-old red capsicum the size of a big marble spills out seeds when it's sliced.

Until 1989 Joe was a vegetable grower like any other, 'always trying to grow the large stuff, although I was always trying to grow it better than anyone else,' says Joe. Then a chance remark by a relation who worked as a purchasing officer at Sydney's Ramada Renaissance hotel planted the idea of growing miniature vegetables. 'I couldn't see the sense in it at first, but he said to me that growers have to be more creative and think up different products they could offer chefs.'

From his first success with a miniature cauliflower, Joe now produces about thirty vegetables, but while they might be tiny, the price is anything but. A single tiny carrot costs 50 cents—about the same as half a kilo of normal-size carrots. Non-root vegetables go for 75 cents each, but as Joe points out, each has been picked, washed, inspected and packed with a care that borders on reverence.

A feast for the eyes—grilled salmon with 'mini' vegetables served on Qantas First Class

New South Wales - Raw Energy

Chetcuti can't get them out of the ground quickly enough. His clients include several major Sydney hotels, as well as chefs in Hong Kong and Singapore. His produce has appeared on the plates of Queen Elizabeth II, George Bush and, sprinkled with gold dust, before the Sultan of Brunei. Qantas serves Chetcuti miniatures only to first-class passengers. 'I always thought their order would double, but they keep asking for more and more.'

THE FIRST VINES The history of viticulture in New South Wales began with the foundation of the colony itself. Vines from South Africa arrived with the First Fleet, and produced Australia's first wines which were judged to be 'tolerable'.

New South Wales was responsible for about forty per cent of Australia's wine-grape crush of around 720,000 tonnes for 1994, yet it consumes far more than it produces. The most productive wine-growing region is Griffith, in southern New South Wales, where the irrigated vineyards and hot, sunny climate yield the highest tonnage per hectare in the country, although with one or two notable exceptions the area is more remarkable for its quantity than its quality. Much of this wine is grown by the Italian families who settled in the area, and Griffith's Mediterranean accent can be plainly seen in the sidewalk cafes and the names on the business signs.

The most important wine-growing area in the state is the Hunter Valley, and in particular the forty wineries of the Lower Hunter, the low, rolling fields in the shadow of the Brokenback Range. Located 160 kilometres north of Sydney at the widest part of the coastal plain, these vineyards account for less than two per cent of Australia's wine output, yet in spite of a notoriously difficult climate, the Lower Hunter shows an almost inexplicable ability to produce soft, velvety, fragrant reds and voluptuous whites.

'It breaks most of the rules of a great wine-making area,' says Murray Tyrrell. 'It's much too hot, but we've got wonderful limestone soil and the Brokenback Range that surrounds us allows the breeze to come in the evening and cool the grapes down.

'When you've got a hot climate you get dehydration, which concentrates your fruit—the flavour—and you get better tannin and more sugar which gives you a sweetness up front in the palate that people love. The wines that we make are like Burgundy's—big, soft, full, easy drinking wines. We make the wines that people love to drink.'

Murray Tyrrell is the patriarch of one of Australia's great wine dynasties, unofficial ambassador for the Hunter and one of the most colourful personalities on the wine scene. It was Murray Tyrrell's great-uncle, Edward, who was one of the first to make wine in the area in the 1860s. Tyrrell's Long Flat Red—which Murray freely describes as his 'bread and butter' wine—is the second-biggest selling wine in Australia. Murray Tyrrell was the first to market chardonnay to Australian buyers and one of the first to grow pinot noir grapes.

The underlying strengths of the Lower Hunter are the wines made from semillon and shiraz grapes. 'These have been the great varieties,' says Tyrrell. 'They make the greatest wines in Australia. I don't think there's a better wine made anywhere in the world to go with fish than a Hunter semillon. The shiraz, given time, gives that lovely soft, full fruit of Burgundy. It's a wonderful wine with game; there isn't a better wine in Australia with quail or pheasant.'

Located 150 kilometres due west of the Hunter Valley on the inland slopes of the Great Dividing Range, the Mudgee vineyards are planted at an altitude of 500 to 800 metres, which means cooler nights, more sunshine and drier summers than the Hunter. While the Hunter makes the most of its well-deserved reputation for quality wines, the wines of the Mudgee region are consistently underrated. In part, this is due to the relatively small-scale wine-makers who are characteristic of the area—and whose promotional budgets are strictly limited. When you visit a Mudgee winery, there's a good chance that you might well purchase your bottle from the wine-maker who has tended the vines, picked the grapes, fretted over the fermentation and stuck on the labels.

Typical of these Mudgee wine-makers is Bob Roberts of Huntington Estate, who has made some of the district's finest red wines, and is as staunch a supporter for Mudgee as Murray Tyrrell is for the Hunter. Huntington Estate's crush is about 300 tonnes. Some of that is sold to the Hunter Valley wineries for blending, but about ninety-five per cent of the wine made under the Huntington label is sold at the cellar door. The same figure for Tyrrell's is less than one per cent, according to Murray Tyrrell.

Probably the most notable of Huntington's wines are the cabernet sauvignon and the cabernet merlot blend, both outstanding examples of Mudgee wines, although Roberts counters the popular perception that Mudgee is a reds-only area. 'Both Montrose and Craigmoor have won prestigious medals for their whites,' says Roberts. 'In just about any variety you could name, Mudgee wines have done very well at one time or another.'

New South Wales vineyards through the seasons

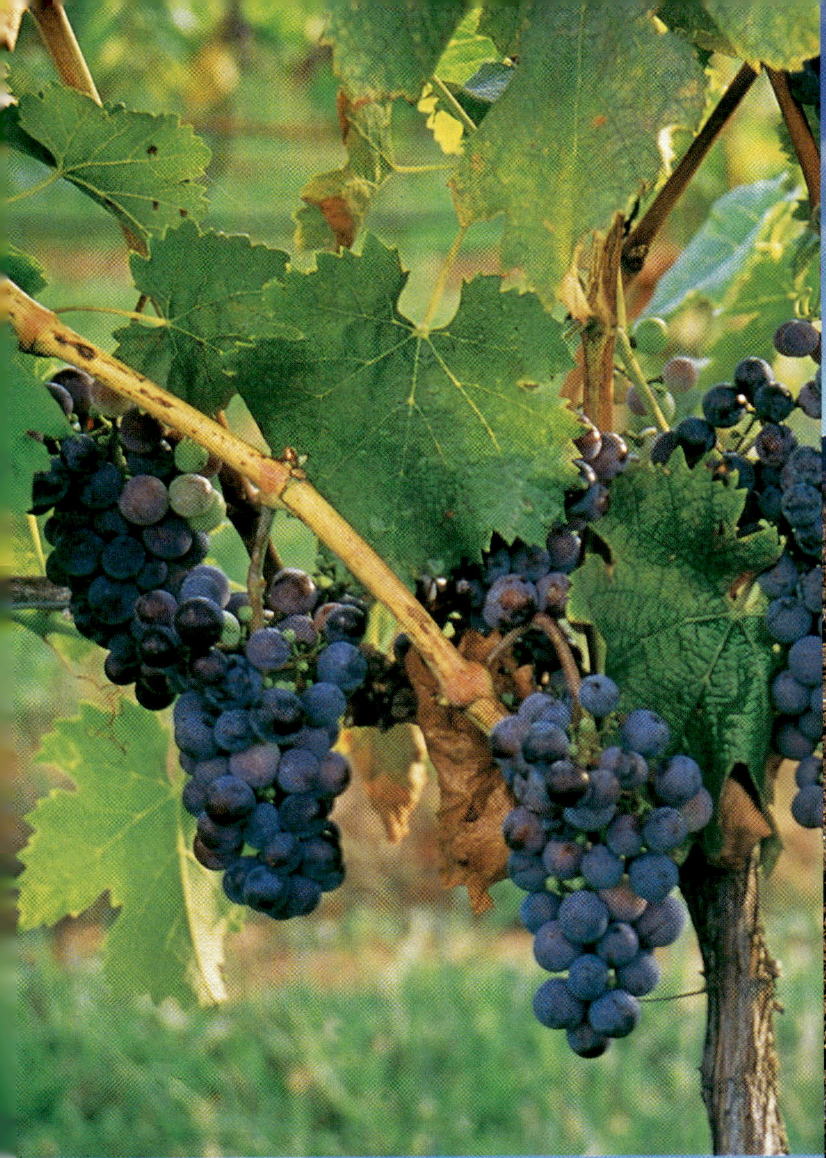
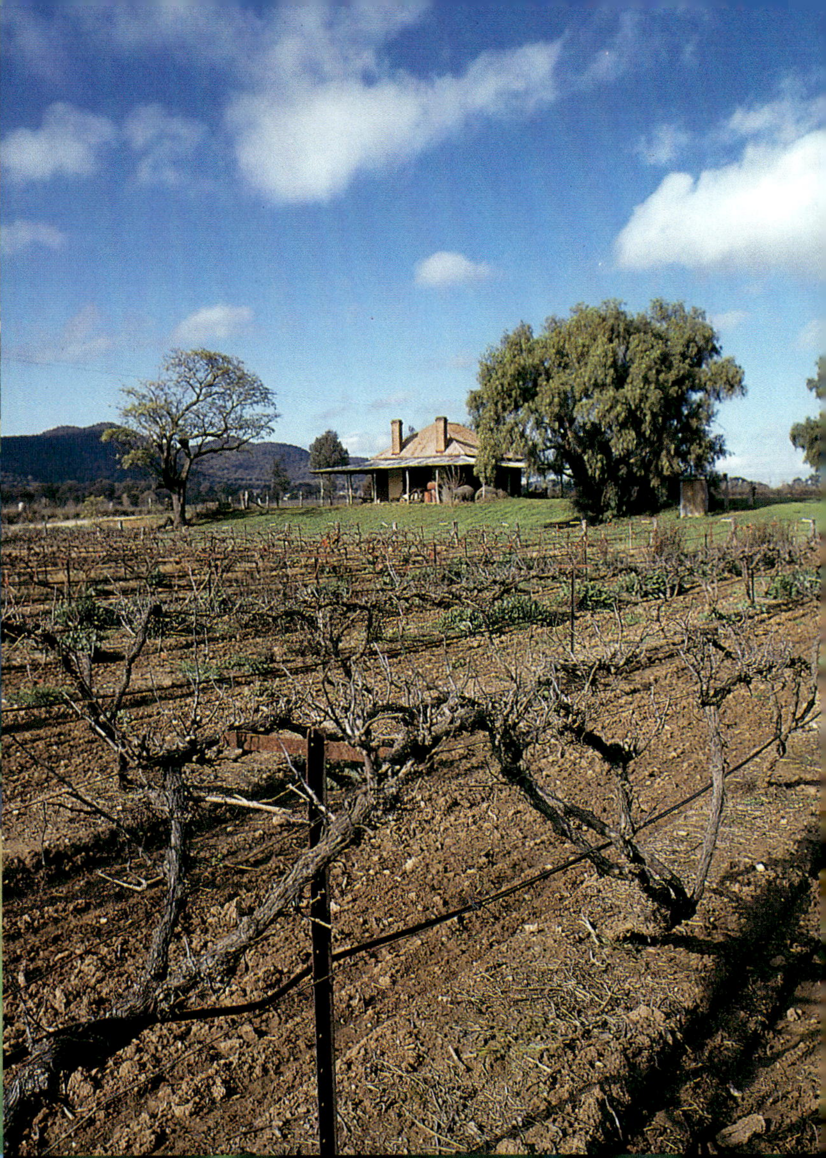
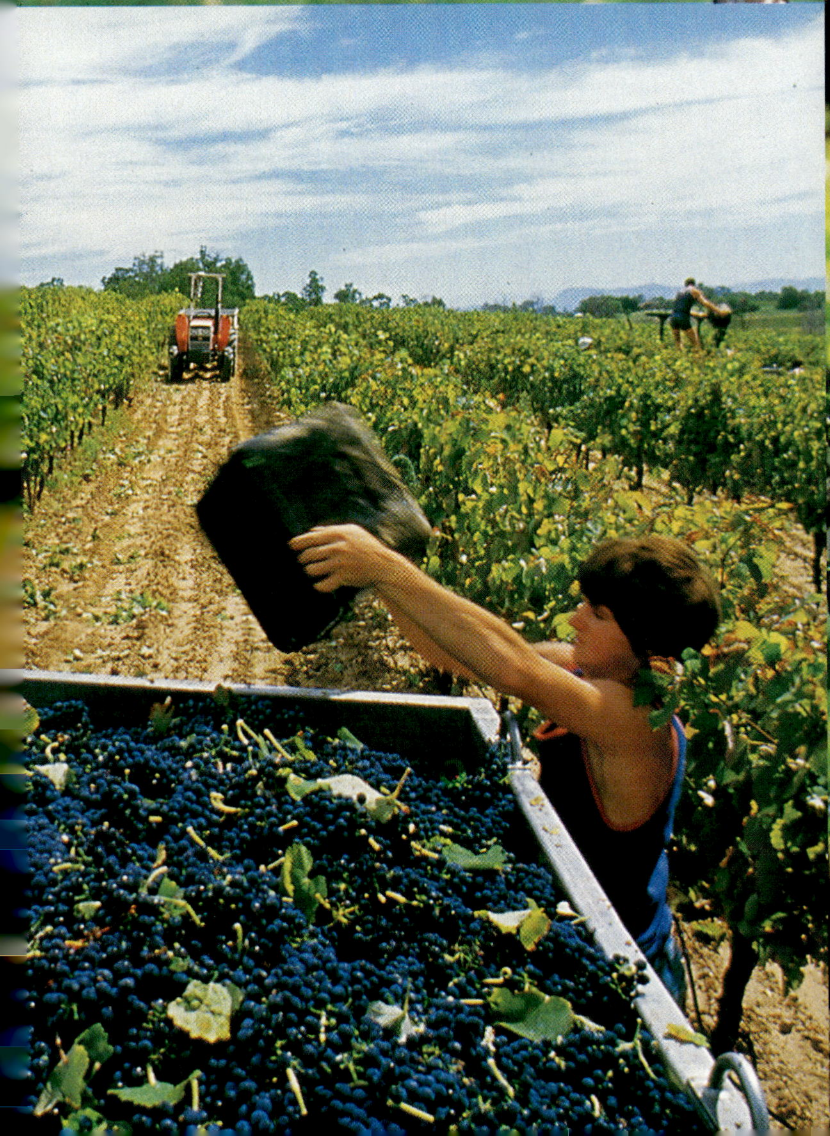
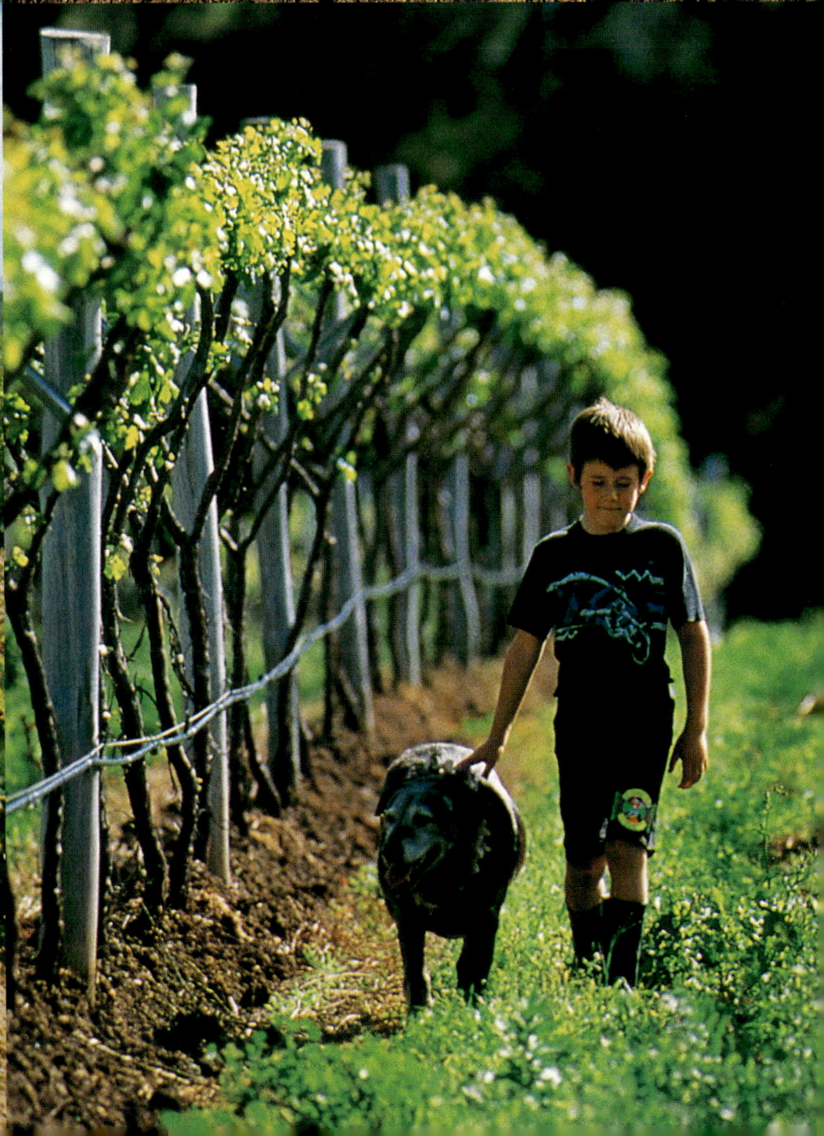

*Right: The tranquil waters of Jervis Bay, south of Sydney
Above: Hikers savour the stunning view over the Nande War Range from Mt Kaputar, near Narrabri; a burst of colour from a wattle tree in the Blue Mountains; enjoying the Sydney sunshine and character of Bondi beach*

DISCOVER THE WONDERS

When people travel, it's never just to see the tourist attractions. People want to experience another way of life, to feel how that is for themselves. So, even if they take photographs of the Sydney Opera House, their memories of it might include a performance they saw in the forecourt, or the colour of the sky and the water on that day. Memories are subjective, personal. On holiday, as in life, impressions are the sum of all the little things that happen.

And tourism is not just about leaving point A to get to point B. For Tourism New South Wales, a government organisation that markets holidays to New South Wales, tourism fosters social, cultural and financial benefits. It has five areas of activity: there's Marketing, Media and Public Affairs, Strategic Planning and Liaison, Sales and Information, and Corporate Services, and together they are working with the government and private sector to develop a Masterplan for the tourism industry to the year 2010 (beyond the Olympic Games).

One point of focus is bringing our rich cultural diversity into the mainstream of tourism. Australia is a country whose culture and cuisine is made up of many varieties, and whose national identity has evolved to include many elements that we have reinterpreted and made our own. But one major aspect of our culture that stands out as truly ours is our way of life, the Australian way of life.

And, according to the most successful advertising campaign Tourism New South Wales has ever launched, New South Wales is made up of Seven Wonders: mountains, beaches, the Outback, forests, rivers, country, Sydney. It's an overview of the state, a long vision, and it capitalises on New South Wales' diversity as its strength. In stretching from yellow sands over mountain ridges and forests to the red dust of the Bush and embracing everything between, Tourism New South Wales has created a single voice, strong and clear, with which all of New South Wales can speak.

Bob Roberts, who has been described as a renaissance man by wine authority James Halliday, epitomises the energetic craftsmen who are drawn to become small wine-makers. A lawyer as well as a self-taught wine-maker, musician and builder, Bob Roberts has most recently re-cast himself as an impresario. Over the past decade, Huntington has become famous for its annual winery concerts in early December, which feature the Australian Chamber Orchestra and attract an audience of several hundred for a series of concerts which span several days and which are broadcast by the ABC.

PAST THE GREAT DIVIDE Beyond the western slopes of the Great Divide, the landscape suddenly yawns and the tangled, olive-green chaos of the bush gives way to open sheep pastures and wheat fields. At the gateway to these plains, the city of Orange is the centre of the biggest apple and pear-growing area in the country, but increasingly, it is becoming known as a high quality source of rare and—in the Australian context—exotic produce.

'It's a special place because of the soil and climate,' according to Rob Robinson. 'It has four classic seasons, which means we get a large variety of crops here, and the main geographic feature of the area is Mount Canobolas, which has spewed rich volcanic soil over the area.'

Rob Robinson is a produce broker whose specialty is sourcing select foods of the Orange area for leading restaurants, wholesalers and hotels. 'Picking the eyes out of the local produce,' is how Rob describes it. A major line is the fungi that he collects from the wild, and which are highly prized by Sydney restaurateurs. 'We get saffron mill cap, boletus mushrooms, and also a winter mushroom, the lilac wood blewit which has a taste and perfume a little like new potatoes. There are also fairy ring mushrooms and the grey goose, which is another good variety of wild fungus. Plus of course traditional field mushrooms which also grow pretty well around here.'

'Some of our great assets are the soft berry fruits, which get a great depth of flavour here because of the chill factor,' says Robinson. 'We've sown fraise des bois, a wild strawberry that we got as seed from France, and that's had a very successful season.' Robinson also deals in chestnuts, figs, later ripening varieties of cherries which grow particularly well in the area, peaches, nectarines and plums. More recently, he has also been supplying Qantas with brook trout, a Canadian char that he farms along the Lachlan River.

Robinson is an outstanding example of the enlightened instincts that prevail among suppliers at the gourmet end of the food industry—an enthusiastic visionary, informed, lucid, in touch with restaurant trends and possessed of a keen eye for market possibilities. Most of all, he is a man of passion, and to hear him describing golden trout that he is currently experimenting with is enough to make your mouth water.

Expansive rice fields near Griffith, western New South Wales

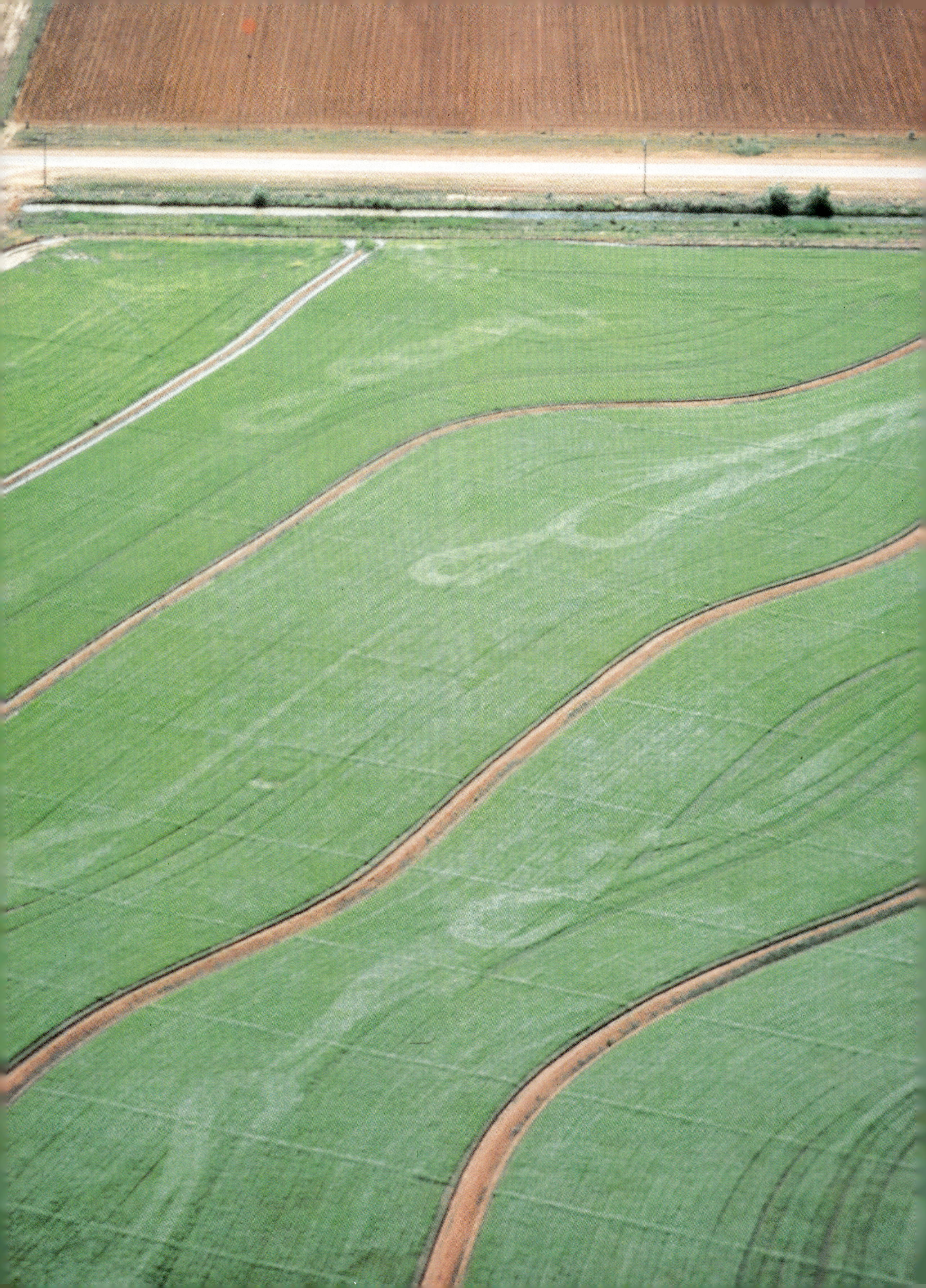

AUSTRALIA - A GOURMET'S PARADISE

A PROUD FAMILY TRADITION

In 1927, from humble premises at 91 Forbes Street in Sydney's Woolloomooloo, Joe David established a fledgling grocery business. Gifted with remarkable business acumen, he quickly expanded the business and by 1935 had seven stores—all managed by family members. It was the beginning of one of Australia's great success stories—the creation of the David family business. Today, the public-owned Davids Limited is widely acknowledged as Australia's leading independent grocery wholesaler.

Campbell's Cash & Carry, Australia's largest and most extensive cash and carry operator, is part of the Davids group and Davids has a fifty per cent holding in Australian Liquor Marketers, the country's leading independent wine and spirits wholesaler.

Davids supplies dry groceries, health and beauty care, perishables, general merchandise and liquor products to over 2,400 retail customers in all Australian states and territories. This includes servicing and supplying major banner groups such as Rainbow IGA, Festival IGA, Clancy's, Foodtown and Welcome Mart Supermarkets. In addition to supplying the Fleming family-owned supermarket chain, Jewel, Davids supplies the major convenience store chains.

Davids places considerable emphasis on retailer training and support services. They readily acknowledge their success is dependent on the success of their customers.

Their Retail Services division is dedicated to ensuring this success by guiding independent retailers toward achieving maximum long-term financial gain by helping retailers identify their particular markets and realise their potential.

Davids also offers up-to-date and efficient store-planning services and has pioneered a number of electronic systems in use today in the Australian grocery industry, including EFTPOS systems, cash registers, scanning, EDI and host support systems.

Another key factor in the Davids success story is their proven marketing and advertising expertise. Their Marketing Department closely liaises with manufacturers and suppliers to plan and organise promotions geared toward enhancing sales and profitability. At the same time, they closely monitor every industry trend and assist retailers in meeting the varying needs and preferences of their valued customers.

With their proud tradition firmly in place, the David family now sees the third generation of the family at the helm, and Joe David's philosophy—'if our retailers are successful then we will be successful'—remains as true today as when he first uttered the words.

Left and far left: A high standard of presentation is found in supermarkets supplied by Davids
Above: A Davids semi-trailer transporting another consignment of groceries

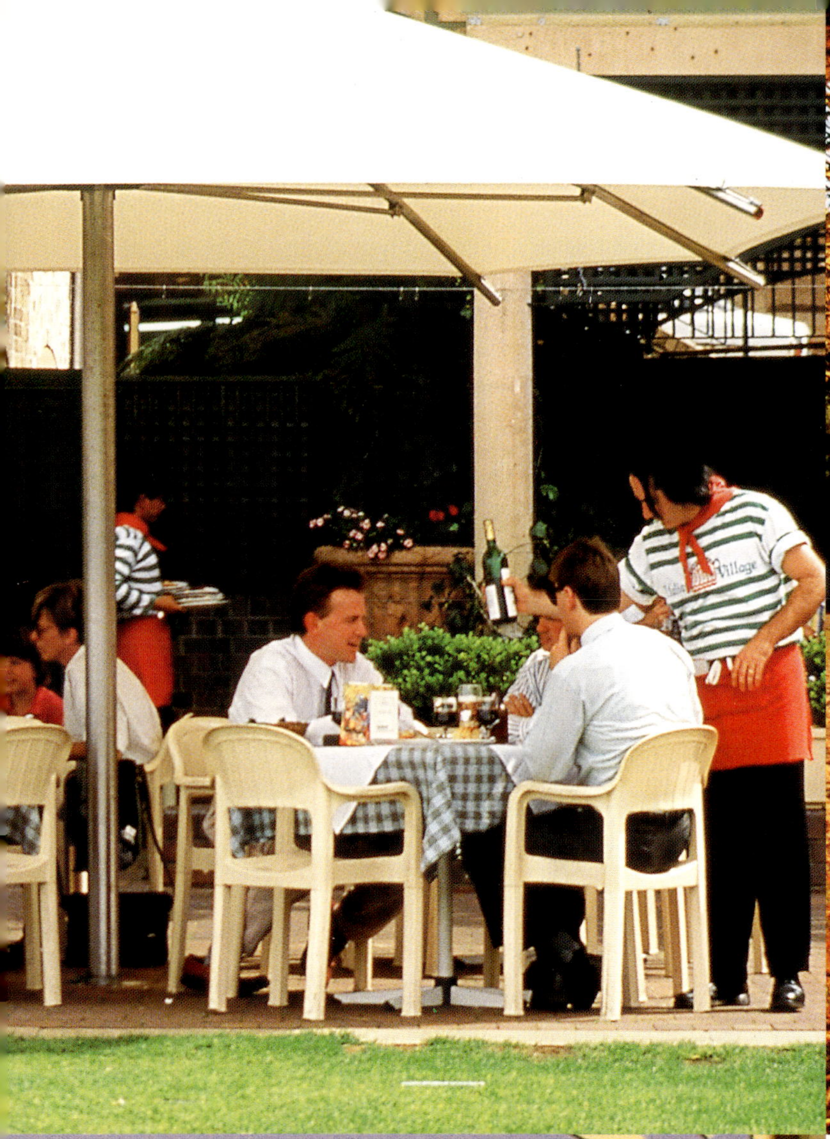

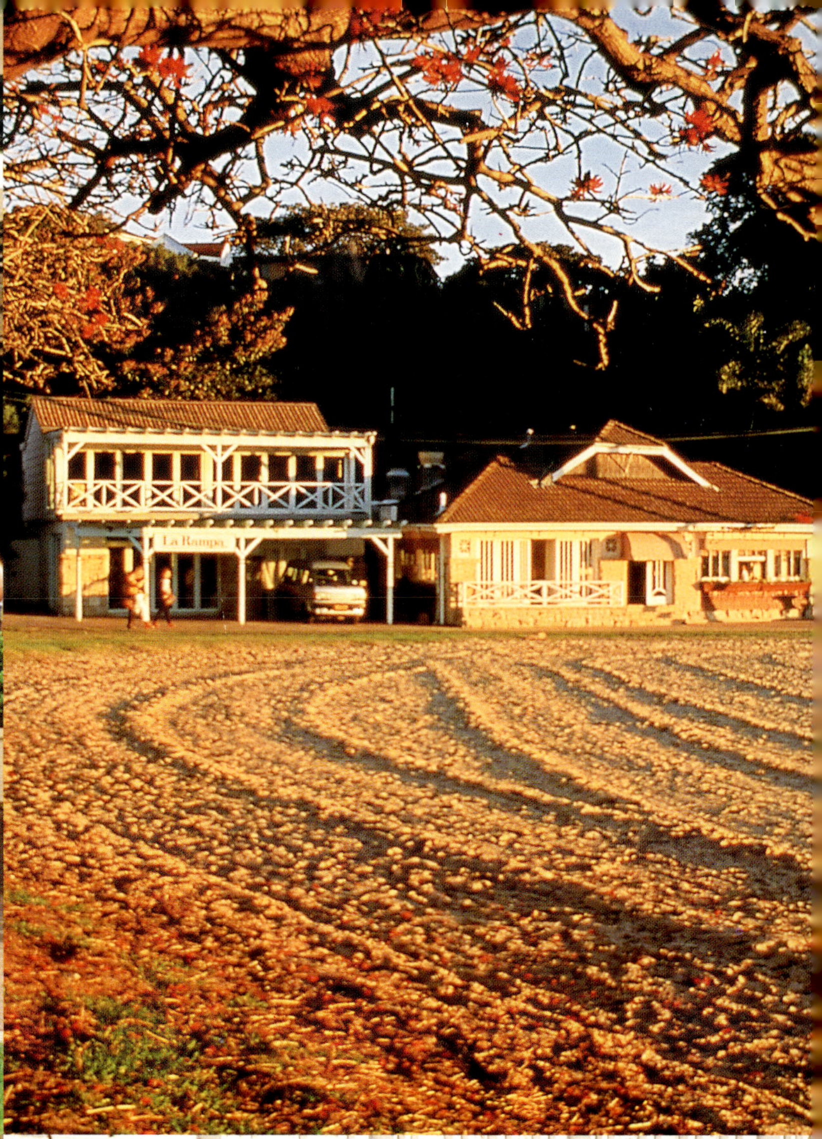
La Rampa

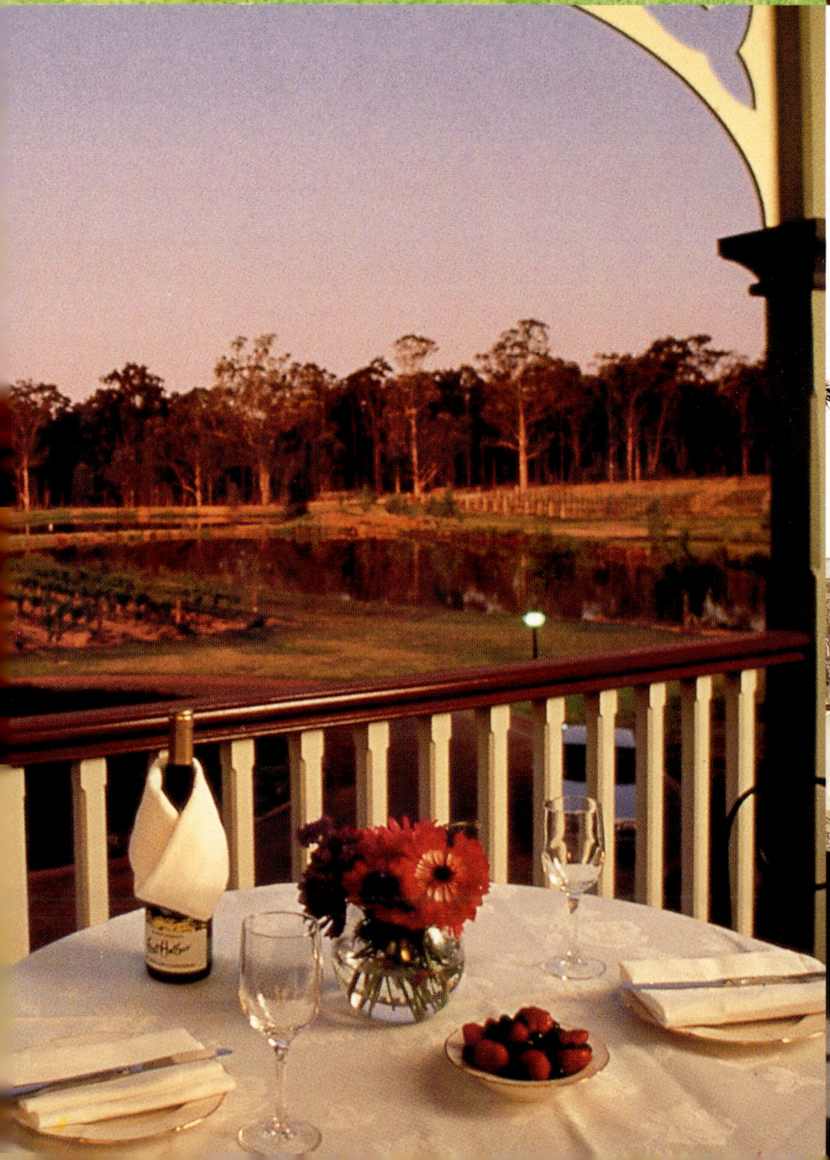

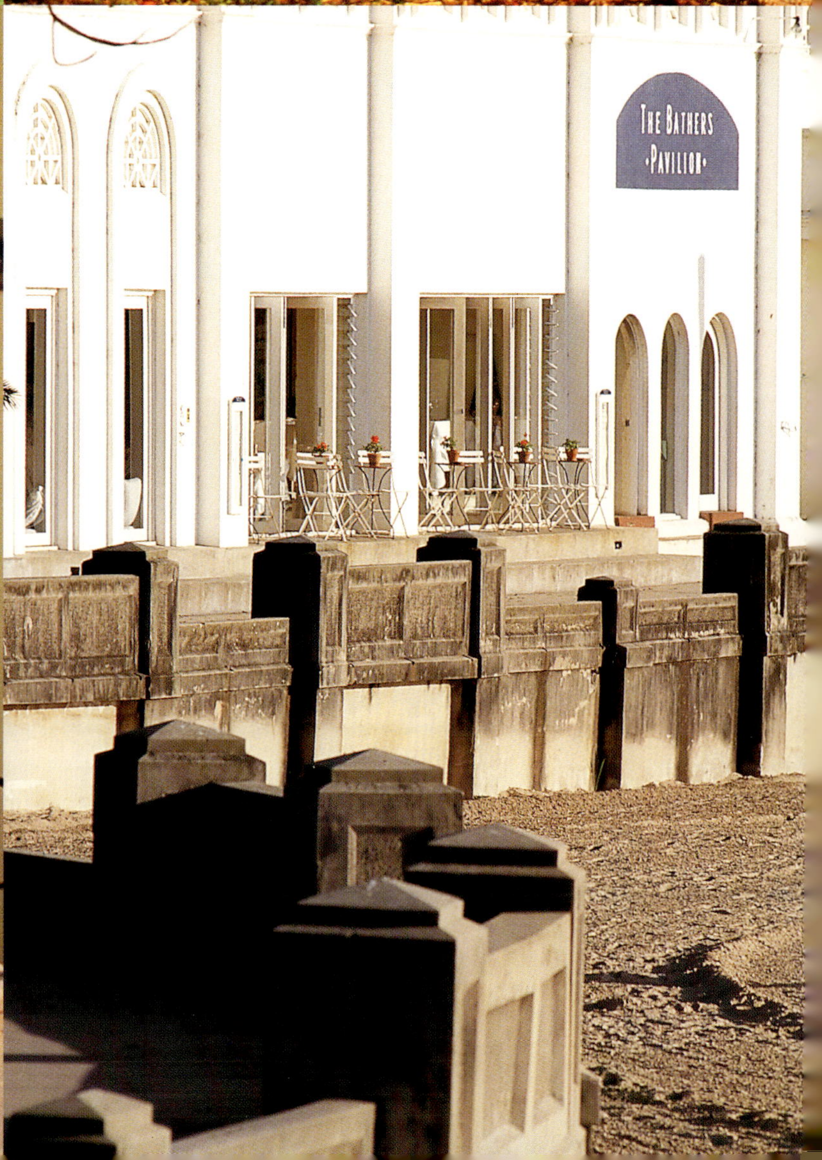
THE BATHERS
·PAVILION·

Rob Robinson recently set off for France to fertilise himself with some new ideas. 'Travel's always done that for me. You come back high, you come back motivated and put new energy into what you're doing.' More specifically, he was investigating truffles in the Perigord region. 'There aren't many places in Australia where you could even think about growing truffles, but Orange looks promising.' And as he says this, he bends over and picks up a handful of oak-leaf litter from beneath the trees and sniffs them lustily: a dream is materialising.

VAST LANDSCAPES Beyond Orange, the sheep pastures stretch interminably westwards. New South Wales is the dominant sheep state in Australia, with more than one-third the national total of about 180 million sheep. Most are Merinos, which are bred for wool rather than meat and which are especially well-suited to Australia's arid conditions.

Despite a premium product, domestic lamb consumption has declined and the Australian Meat and Livestock Corporation encourages farmers to grow lean lambs with less fat content. From his property Illabo, near Junee in southern New South Wales, Tony Lehmann is one grazier who has had considerable success in carving out a specialist market. Spurred by declining wool prices, Lehmann decided to market milk-fed lambs, and several premier Sydney restaurants now make a specialty of Lehmann's Illabo lamb. The lambs, a Border Leicester-Merino-Poll Dorset cross, are slaughtered at four to five weeks, when they yield a delicate, pale, buttery meat.

At this stage of the journey, something is happening to the scenery that can no longer be ignored. The elemental weirdness of the Australian landscape has become more shriekingly evident with every westward kilometre. The eucalypts along the roadside have drooping leaves that enable them to conserve water, and if you dig into the dry river beds, you find frogs that can await the coming of rains in a state of suspended animation for up to five years.

Against this backdrop of impoverished soils and unreliable rainfall that characterises much of the land mass of New South Wales, crops and agricultural techniques inherited from Europe have become sustainable only through massive irrigation projects. This is a weird continent, certainly, but productive—provided you know how to find and make use of its resources.

BUSH TUCKER There are powerful reasons why Australians should modify their diet in favour of native plants and animals, yet during 200 years of settlement, white Australians have merely flirted with the foods and flavours of wild Australia. Eucalyptus cigarettes, for example, were briefly popular a century ago, but recipes such as the bushman's for baked cockatoo (put a stone in the oven with the cockatoo; when the stone is tender, the

Clockwise from top left: Outdoor dining in the historic Rocks district of Sydney; Le Kiosk Restaurant, Shelly Beach, Manly; twilight at The Convent restaurant in the Hunter Valley; The Bathers Pavilion overlooking Barmoral Beach

cockatoo is done) show the gulf between European Australians and the food of their adopted land.

While the popular imagination still equates bush food with witchetty grubs and kangaroo tail soup, a quiet revolution has been going on in the kitchen. Yabbie tails with tomato and lemon myrtle jelly, yam gnocchi with sun-dried tomatoes, Warrigal olives and parmesan, pepperleaf blackened chicken breast served with a spiced honey dew melon salsa, wattle seed ice-cream—these days, there is scarcely a restaurant that subscribes to the fashionable 'modern Australian' label that does not have some bush food on its menu. The 'discovery' of native Australian produce is equivalent to a painter finding a whole new palette of colours. The bounty is astonishing, the flavours mobilise a new repertoire of taste sensations and chefs with skill and imagination now have a chance to stamp their mark by creating truly 'Australian' dishes.

At the forefront of the crusade to elevate bush food from the campfire to the starched white tablecloth is Vic Cherikoff, the owner of Bush Tucker Supply Australia, which acts as an interface between hunter-gatherers and the Australian stomach. Most of Bush Tucker Supply's range is sold as raw materials to the 400-plus restaurants that use bush foods. 'Chefs have been the most receptive, because they're always looking for a particular edge,' says Cherikoff. Bush Tucker Supply's catalogue lists forty-eight fruits, herbs, spices, seeds, nuts, meats, oils and preserves, but this is only a small part of the company's agenda.

Education has been critical to the wider acceptance of bush foods, and Vic Cherikoff runs courses and promotions and offers a fax-back 'bushing-up' service, which encourages chefs to add native ingredients to a traditional dish. 'For a dish of ocean perch in a lime butter sauce, we might suggest scrapping the lime and putting in a lemon aspen butter sauce—or maybe a shift to barramundi or even stingray.' One of Cherikoff's main tasks has been to address the misconception that bush foods are esoteric and require special cooking skills. 'It's just learning—how much to use, what goes with what, and what can negate the flavour of a bush food. Lemon aspen, for example, a rainforest fruit, has a complex citrus flavour that's interesting and exciting and one of its best applications is as a flavouring in sauces. Yet if you try and blend it with lemon juice, it kills the flavour.'

Having breached gourmet taste buds, native foods are now finding their way into processed foods, and although they are not yet common on supermarket shelves, bush foods are turning up in some surprising places. A range of pastas flavoured with native ingredients is proving popular and foods such as bush tomato chutney, wild rosella jam, lemon myrtle mayonnaise and wattleseed ice-cream are fairly easy to find.

Particularly for corporations searching for a distinctive 'Australian' feel to their cuisine, bush foods have been a startling success. 'We supplied Qantas with smoked emu for their business and first-class menus,' says Cherikoff. 'Initially they asked for three months' supply, but it was so popular they ended up buying it for about fifteen months.'

It's tempting to speculate what Australians might be eating today had they been more receptive to the idea of native foods from the very beginning. Remember those convicts who embarked from the ships of the First Fleet? While they starved, well-fed Aborigines looked on in amazement.

Michael Gebicki

Native Australian bush berries

T   A   S   M

*Right: Spiced oranges and summer pickles from Country Larder Preserves
Below: The unforgettable Cradle Mountain Range; freshly farmed salmon from Tassal*

106

A N I A

Treasure Islands

In George Mikes' 1968 book, *Boomerang—Australia Rediscovered,* the British/Hungarian humourist pointed out the obvious in a refreshingly sly way. 'Tasmania, of course, gave up any idea of seceding from Australia; perhaps because it has, in fact, seceded. It did not secede politically . . .Tasmania seceded first of all geologically.' Twenty-odd years later, Tasmania has again made a bold breakaway move, this time surging forward to become a major player on the Australian food scene way out of proportion to its physical size. It seems more than poetic justice that much of the credit goes to the Apple Isle's original assertion of independence: geology and position.

Nature has played clear favourites with Tasmania. Its tight grip on the title of gourmet state rests on such impossible-to-duplicate advantages: air so clean it feels freshly scrubbed, cool waters largely free of pollution, the richest soils, consistent rainfall and the absence of threatening animal and plant diseases such as the Mediterranean fruit fly which is endemic to the rest of Australia. Couple this headstart with the fact that dedicated locals (and others lured to the state by its beguiling beauty and opportunities) are almost messianic in their mission to produce only the finest quality foodstuffs—from raw ingredients to wonderful shops presenting finished products to restaurants serving the hippest of modern Australian cuisine. This goal is made more easy to achieve by the firm commitment and backing of the government via Tasmania Development and Resources, and the dedicated marketing of food products as Tasmanian rather than generically Australian.

Tasmania has been responsible for two of the most important landmark products in recent Australian culinary history—farmed salmon and sea-run trout. The state's smoked salmon, adhering to the traditional Scottish method, now outshines the original. King Island and other Tasmanian cheeses, especially from such leading companies as Lactos, have made it unthinkable for Australians to 'make do' with imported cheeses. Tasmania's apples, berries and pears have enjoyed world renown from the early days of European settlement and are now making a new impact throughout the world, especially in Asia. In a country where the transportation values of fresh produce frequently outweigh the taste factor, Tasmania is bringing back varieties of potato such as the now-chic Bintjes and Bismarcks that are packed with that solid, true potato flavour and mouth-feel.

To most Australians Tasmania still conjures up mental images of stacked-up apples, and although the state no longer rests entirely on these legendary laurels, the state's industry is still responsible for eighty per cent of Australia's export apples. Generations of families, many still prominent in the business, have contributed to the resurgent strength of Tasmania's apple industry, bounding back from a period of stagnation and diversifying strongly into apple products such as the purest of juices used by leading companies like Cascade Beverages.

The most popular apple varieties (Red and Golden Delicious, Croftons, Democrats) have now been joined by new varieties, including Mutsu, Fuji and Pink Lady, which are in high demand in Japan. While the idyllic Huon Valley remains Tasmania's most important growing region, the Tamar and Spreyton regions in northern Tasmania are also important apple-growing districts. Organic growers can also be found throughout the state's open-air produce markets—a popular variety being heavily juicy Sturmers. For those who want to delve deeper into the history of Tasmania's traditional agricultural money-earner, the Huon Valley Apple Industry Museum at Huonville presents an overview of the life of Tasmania's apple growers—now and then—and a complete rundown of the state's continuing pursuit of excellence as an apple producer of world standing.

Tasmanian pears are just as deserving of high recognition. For unabashed luxury you can't beat Doyenne du Comice pears eaten by hand—the gourmet pear of Australia. Other pear stalwarts include Packham, Josephine, Winter Cole and Beurre Bosc varieties. Heavily laden orchards notwithstanding, the Huon Valley grows the first and last raspberries and cherries in the world (depending on which hemisphere you calculate your seasons from). Other Tasmanian fruit crops to ask for in quality shops are apricots, nectarines, blueberries, strawberries and blackcurrants. Further exciting developments in the Huon Valley centre on mushroom growers working with the University of Tasmania to produce premium grade shiitake mushrooms for the Asian market, and almost meaty brown mushrooms with a far 'wilder' taste than standard-issue button mushrooms.

Left to right, top to bottom: Red Delicious apples; King Island delicacies; jug of whole milk; raspberry kirsch, jam with sour-reduced cream; Cascade Brewery; espaliered Golden Delicious apple blossoms; blackcurrants; Democrat apples; Packham pears

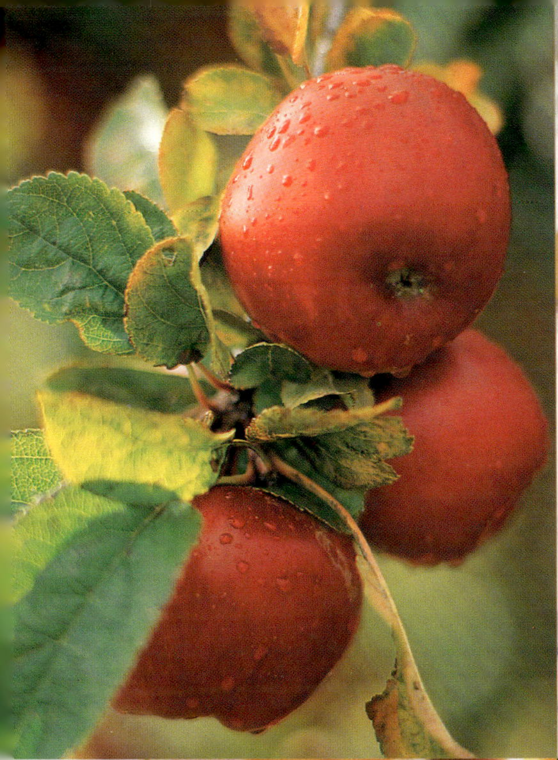
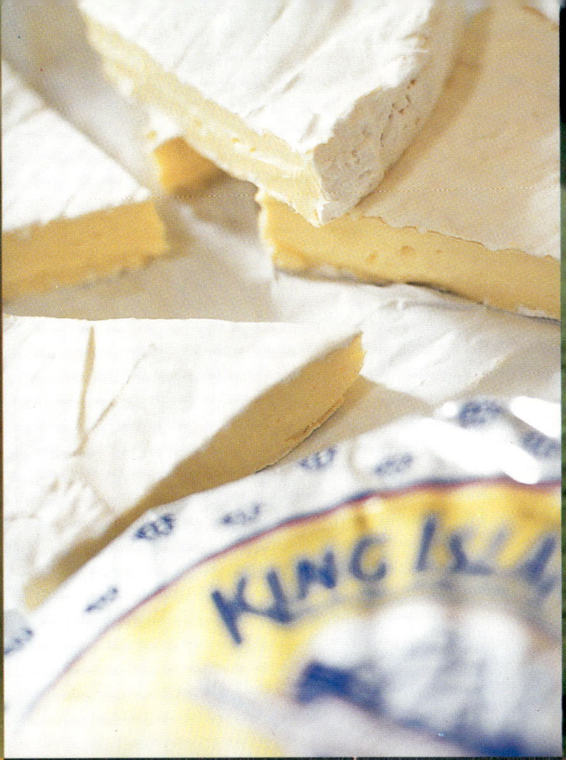
KING IS
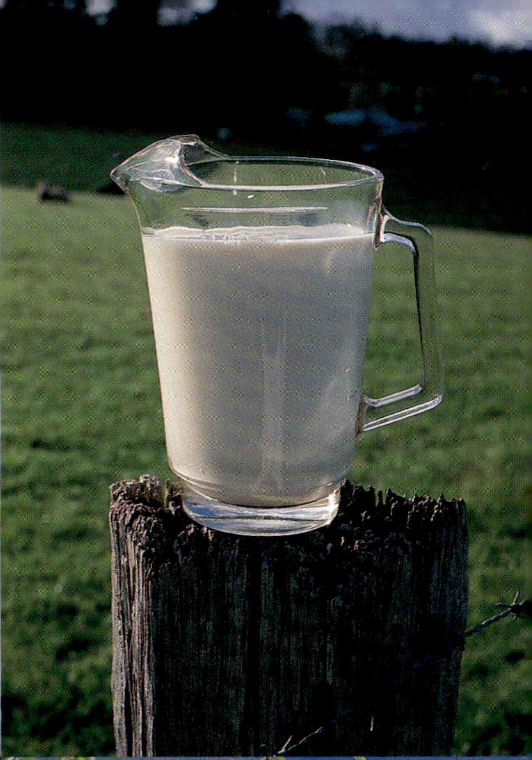
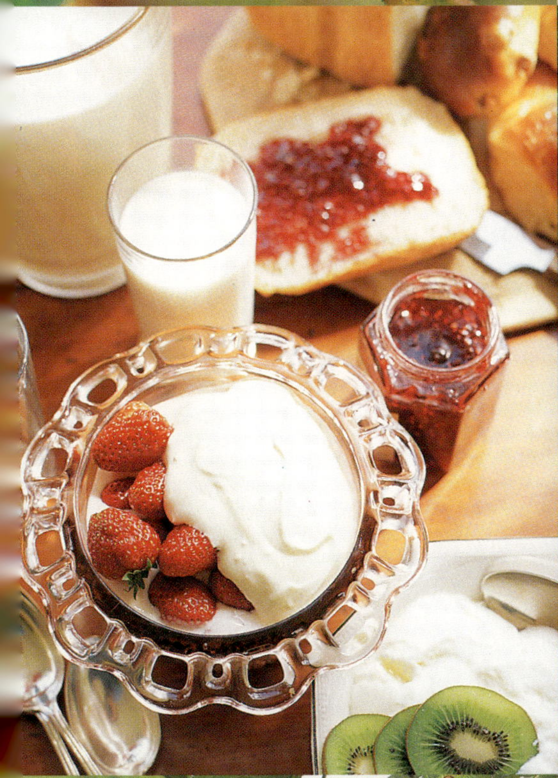
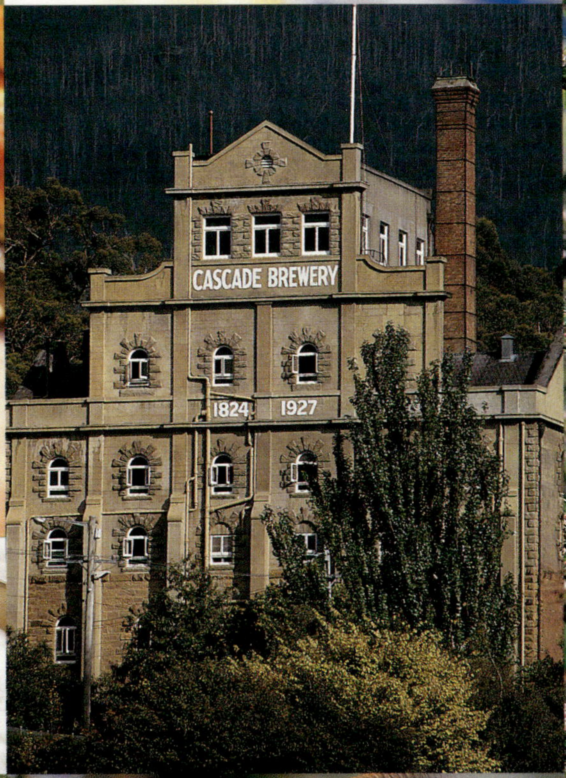
CASCADE BREWERY
1824 1927
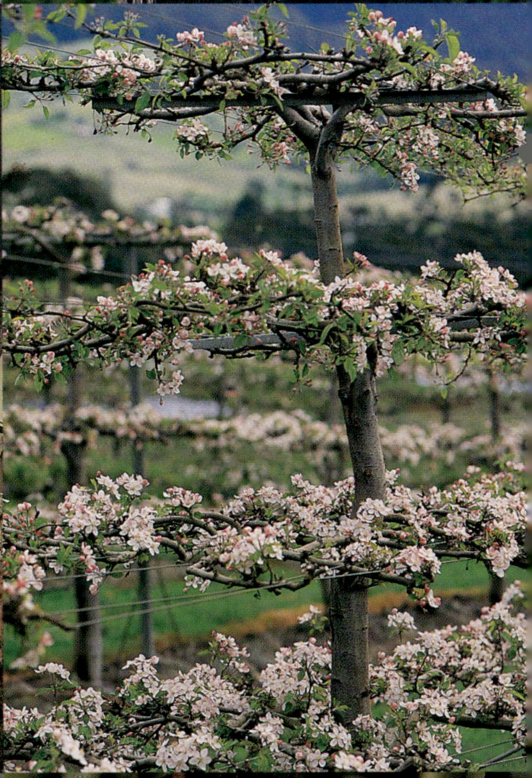
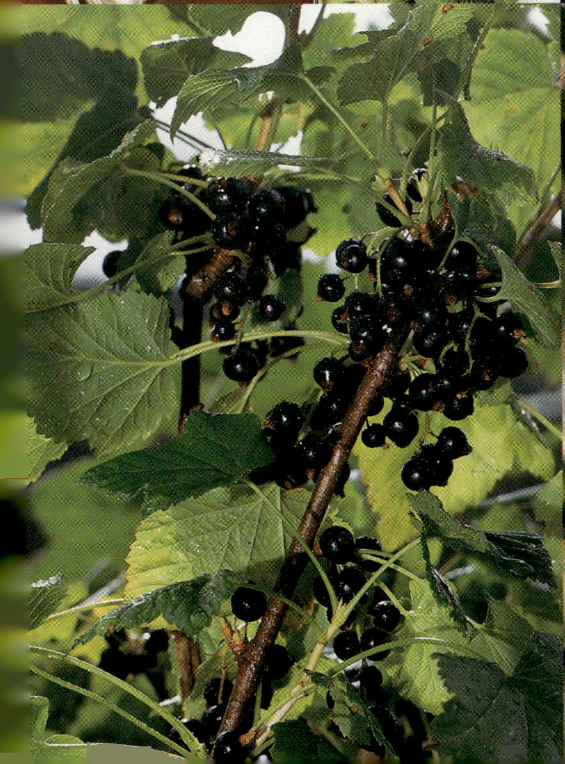
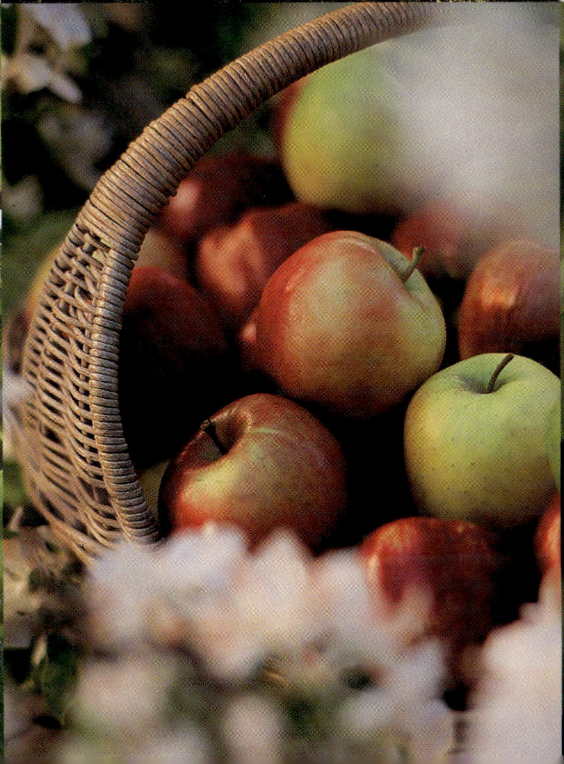
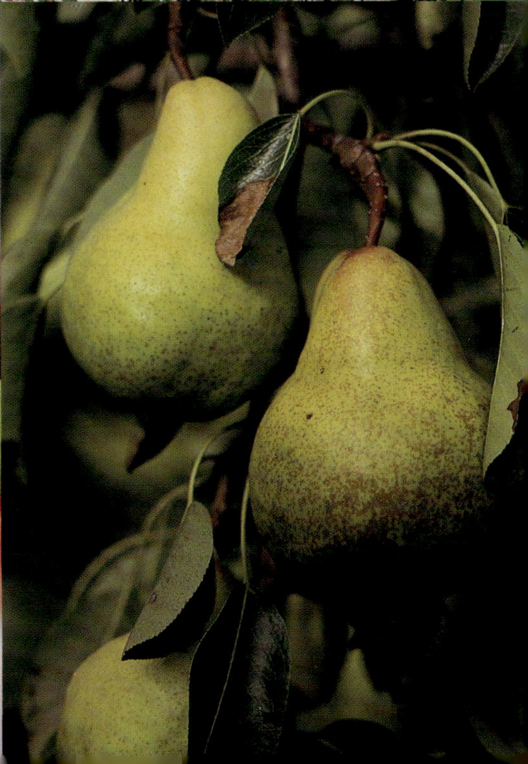

*Right: A selection of Lactos'
DOMAINE cheeses
(from left to right) DEEP BLUE,
RED SQUARE (also above) and
SUNRISE CAMEMBERT*

CHEESE MASTERS

Lactos Pty Ltd is Australia's leading specialty cheesemaker, the Australian company that has exchanged cheese technology with France. Sixty-five million litres of milk per year go into the making of a distinctive array of cheese—hand-made brie, camembert, True Blue, Double Cream, Cannonball, Fol Epi, St Claire Swiss, Mersey Valley Vintage Club, Edam, Gouda and DOMAINE soft–ripened cheese. Over thirty per cent of Lactos' annual production is exported, mainly to Japan, south-east Asia, the South Pacific, New Zealand and the United States—an annual export turnover of $15 million.

Lactos is based in Burnie, on Tasmania's North-West coast. Its most recent range of cheese, the HERITAGE brand, reinforces the Tasmanian origin of Lactos' cheese—a line-up that includes Camembert, Camembert with Peppercorns, Brie and True Blue. Introduced by Lactos in 1990, True Blue—a soft-ripened brie-style with a white mould coating—has grabbed the lion's share of the Australian blue cheese market. Little wonder it is one of only five cheeses selected for the Australian Cheese Platter served at all official Australian state dinners.

Founded in 1955, this multi-award winning cheese company uses only the purest quality milk from 145 hand-picked Tasmanian farms. Lactos was acquired by leading French cheesemakers Bongrain in 1981 but that's as far as foreign influence goes. Managing Director, Russell Paterson, stresses that Lactos remains a completely autonomous Australian company—better still, a Tasmanian one.

Lactos won the major award in the 1993 Tasmanian Export Awards for consistent international growth over the past five years. Says Russell Paterson: 'Over the past few years our 244 employees—through our Lactos 2000 Quality Programme—now believe in themselves and believe we produce the best cheese in the world. This attitude has strengthened our commitment to do better, and has shown in our success in the Asian market. Our assertive marketing and product development philosophy is reaping rewards, enabling us to continue to grow and strengthen our position as Australia's leading specialty cheesemaker'.

SPECTACULAR SUCCESS Few Australians can now possibly be ignorant of the deep-rose coloured flesh of Tasmanian salmon—large steaks of this unctuous, intensely flavoured fish are found in suburban fish shops throughout the country and on the plates of Australia's finest restaurants. For an industry that only started up in 1984, a fitting description for its success and high impact on local and overseas markets is spectacular. In 1990 Tassal Ltd, even then the industry's major producer of Atlantic salmon, merged with the second-largest producer Tasmania Atlantic Salmon Ltd to dominate salmon production. Other leading players are Aquatas and Nortas Aquaculture.

The harvest weight of Tasmanian salmon is around 3.5 kilograms—a target reached much faster than anywhere else in the world due to Tasmanian growing conditions. During the fresh salmon season—from September to March—fully grown fish are processed at the rate of twenty-four tonnes a day at the big plants. Enthusiastic markets for Tasmanian salmon are well-established in Japan, Singapore and Hong Kong. Over a million 70 gram smolt (eighteen month-old salmon) enter the sea-run farms of southern Tasmania each year from the hatchery. Tasmania's annual salmon harvest is now in excess of 3,000 tonnes and is expected to reach 8,000 tonnes by the end of the decade.

Tasmanian salmon is prepared for catering and retail sale only metres from the cages in which they were raised—largely as cutlets, boneless fillets or whole fish. Cold-smoked Tasmanian salmon, pin-boned and premium-packaged, has also carved out a highly-esteemed reputation at a whip-crack pace. Tasmanian salmon roe ranks as the delicacy of delicacies and other salmon products that warrant a trip to Tasmania are Mure's Boronia-cured salmon, Tasmanian Traditional Seafoods' whisky-cured smoked salmon and Tassal's Swedish-cured gravlax.

Cold water fish tastes best and that's a fact nobody will deny after a visit to Tasmania. Tasmanians revere their fleshy, striped trumpeter fish, but the state's stellar rock lobster, mussels, blue grenadier, albacore, bluefin and yellowfin tuna, orange roughy and trevalla could never be considered as second-best. Tasmania's Pacific oysters are the only Australian oysters permitted by United States authorities to be imported in an unprocessed form. Tasmanian freshwater trout and eels, both fresh and smoked, are also excellent quality.

King Island crabs and Tasmanian scallops are victims of their own popularity and are getting as rare in the shops as they are expensive, due to overwhelming demand in Asia, the United States and mainland Australia. Depleted scallop beds have been re-seeded in recent years using Japanese technology and the Japanese are also playing a pioneering role in the harvest and export of sea urchin roe. Several ventures are now underway to farm abalone on

Tasmanian smoked salmon served with creme fraiche and baby capers from Dear Friends

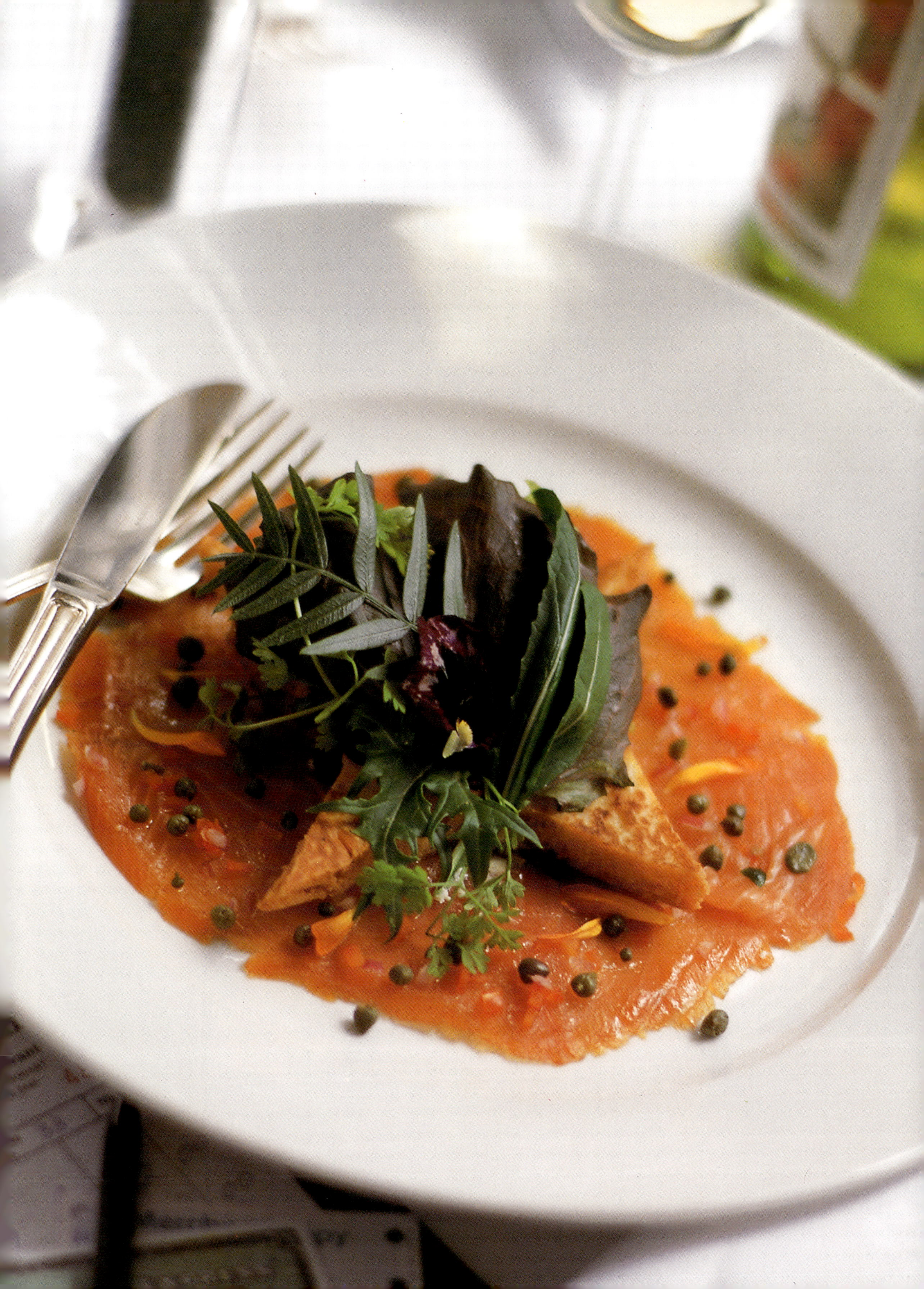

AUSTRALIA - A GOURMET'S PARADISE

the state's east coast and Bass Strait islands, heartening news for gourmets worldwide as Tasmania's 'wild' harvest is much sought after.

The restaurant and shop meccas for any fish-lover visiting Tasmania are Stingray in North Hobart, a retailer who will provide you with the makings of a seafood alfresco lunch straight out of a lavish movie set, and Mure's Fish Centre, a polished timber architectural triumph of a restaurant on Hobart's Victoria Dock. For twenty years it has anchored the city's seafood restaurant scene and rightly so. Choose from Mure's fine dining restaurant, or The Lower Deck which dishes up fish and chips that belong on a Wedgwood plate, not yesterday's newspaper.

LUSH PASTURES Tasmania's lush pastures are the 'secret' behind the outstanding quality of its beef and lamb—hailed by many to be the finest flavoured meat in Australia. In the north west of the state, in particular, the soil is so fertile there is year-round grass growth on which steers constantly graze, guaranteeing a level of tenderness usually the preserve of lot-fed cattle. Japanese importers are seeking to double their purchases of pasture-fed Tasmanian beef. Gilbertsons, Tasmania's biggest producer, has got the process of meeting the market down to such a fine art at its Longford and King Island properties in Tasmania that it measures the amount of marbling in a steak down to exact requirements. The state's significant lamb production reaches its apex with lean, 'elite' stall-fed lamb currently being snapped up by Asian markets and Australia's leading chefs. An exciting new gourmet direction in the prime meat area is capretto—milk-fed kid.

Deer were introduced to Tasmania in the early 1900s and today Tasmanian-farmed venison is the only disease and parasite-free deer meat in the world—grain-fed to retain a gamey flavour along with a light, lean texture. Fallow Venison Traders of Tasmania and many other Tasmanian deer farmers are now producing tender, juicy venison as fresh meat, smoked meat and sausages for both local and overseas markets.

Right: Catch of the day—fresh Tassal salmon Above: The distinctive colour of Tasmanian smoked salmon

DELIGHTS FROM THE SEA

Tasmanian salmon has exploded onto the global food scene with the impact of a comet. In the space of ten years, Tassal Ltd has become one of the largest fully integrated salmon producers in the world and the dominant figure of the Tasmanian salmon industry. A leader in scientific research, modern production techniques, sales and marketing innovation, Tassal has secured over seventeen major business awards for excellence, including the prestigious Commodities and Primary Products Export Award in the 1993 Australian Export Awards.

Exports account for just over half of Tassal's annual harvest which produces $21 million in export sales, making Tassal the largest salmon producer in the southern hemisphere. Tassal operates nine sea farms with the main site located in Port Esperance near Dover. During the cooler months Tassal's intake of almost one million 12-month old salmon is transferred from state-of-the-art Wayatinah Hatchery to the Tassal nursery sites before entering their 100 per cent seawater sites.

Expansion remains a cornerstone of Tassal's future. In 1993 Tassal bought the Tasmanian businesses of Safcol and Tasmanian Smokehouse Pty Ltd, paving the way for further diversification into processed lobster and abalone, mainly for the export market. The company has also been granted an experimental lease site at Great Taylors Bay near Bruny Island in southern Tasmania to allow further fine-tuning of its technology and research programme. Tassal's salmon-processing facility at Dover was the first fish processing plant in Australia to attain the world-recognised AQIS certification.

In addition to its Royal Tasmanian Salmon product range, Tassal is also one of the world's largest suppliers of abalone. The company's Royal Tasmanian lobster—with its firm white flesh and delicate sweet flavour—is in aggressive demand throughout the Pacific Rim. On the home front, New South Wales consumes fifty per cent of domestic salmon and lobster, but Queensland is opening up as a new marketing area for Tassal, particularly in the far north. These results are evidence of Tassal's continuing success.

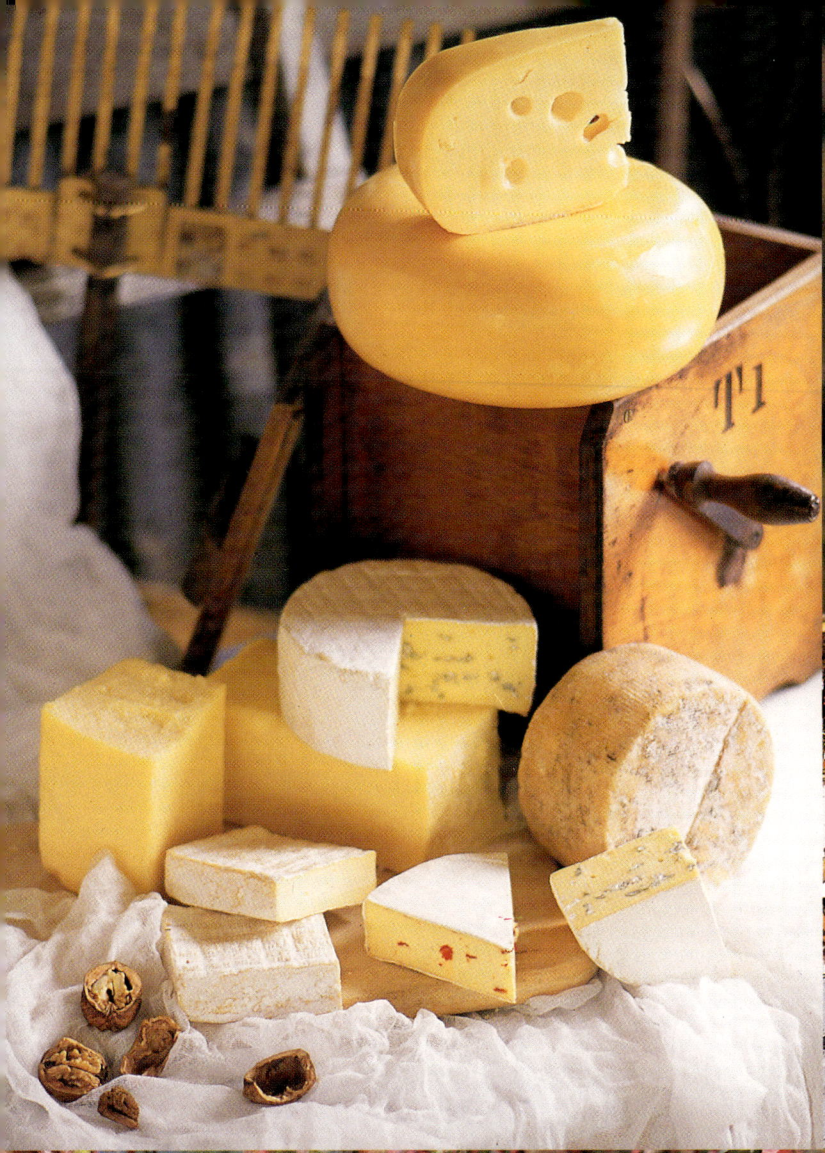

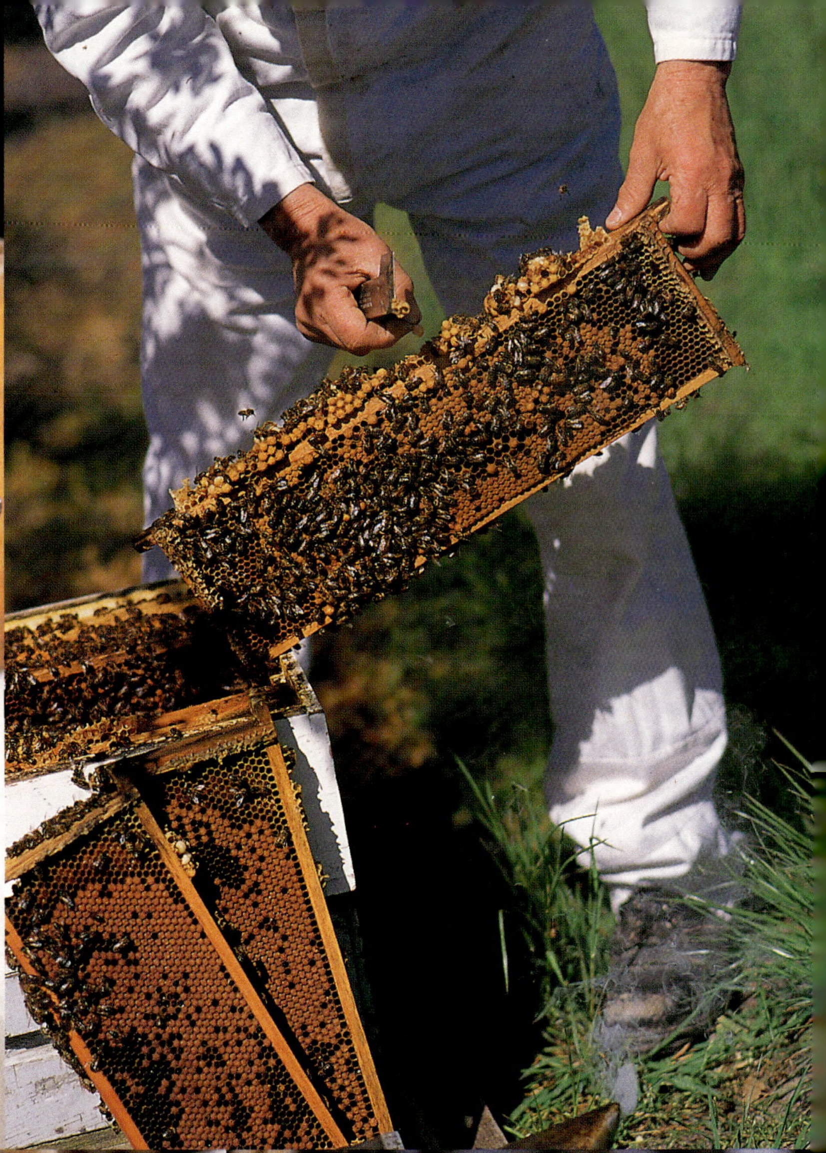

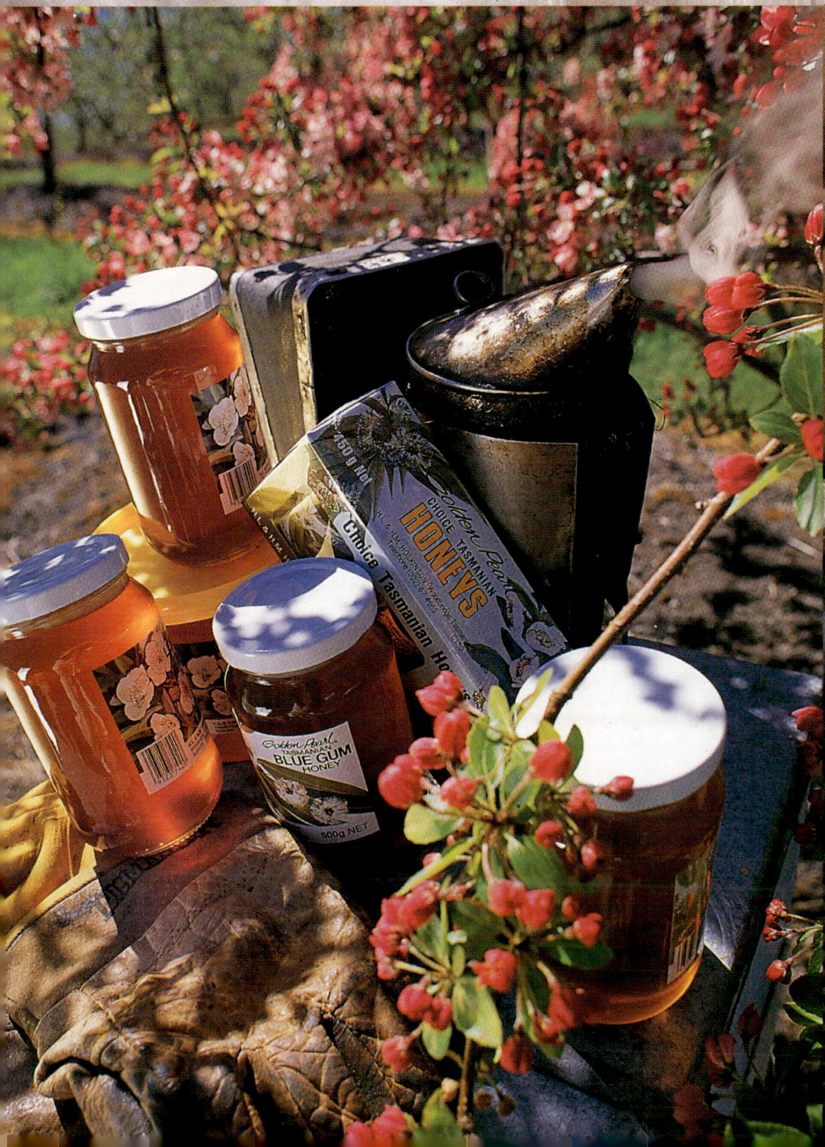
HONEYS
BLUE GUM
HONEY

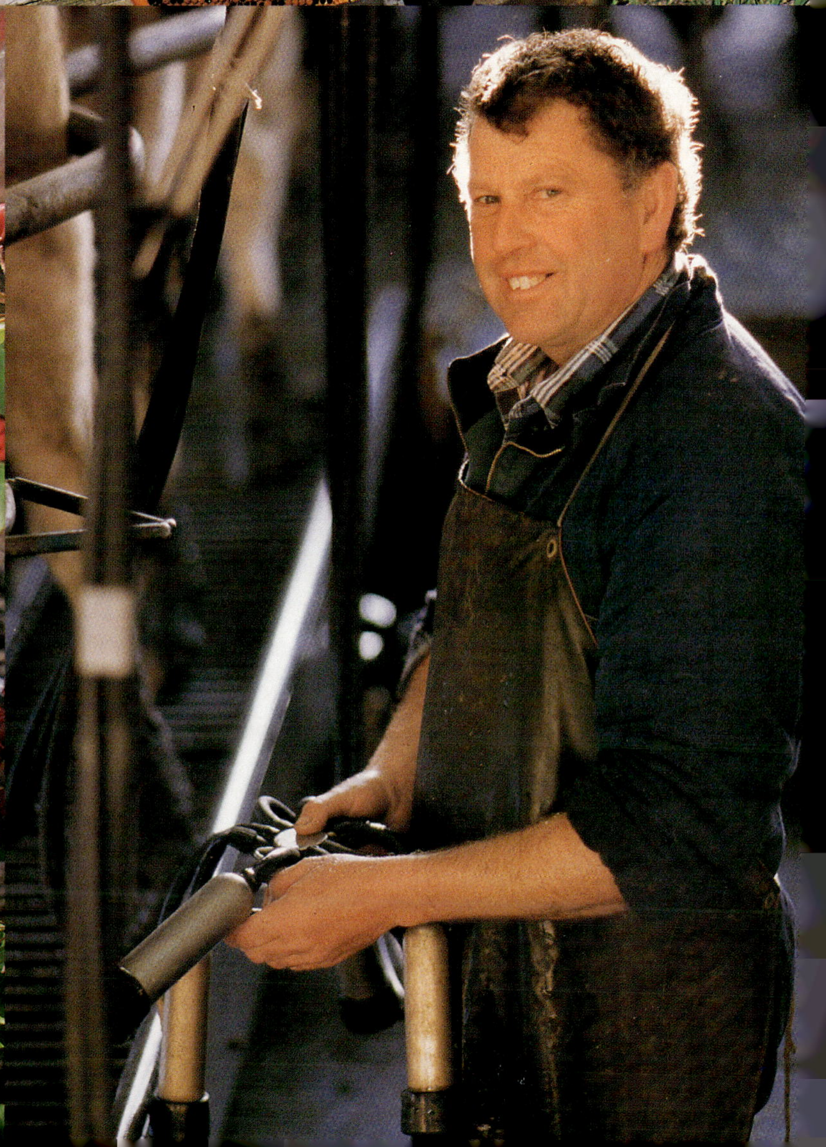

Leatherwood honey, hailing from the great temperate rainforests of the state's West Coast—a pristine wilderness that promotes a strong, exotic flavour—is unique to Tasmania. But although leatherwood deserves its far-flung fame, there are other, less full-bodied Tasmanian honey names that are worthy of wider circulation. Plain bush honey for a start, followed by river red and blue gum, white box and prickly bush. Honey stalls do a rapid business at Hobart's Salamanca Market but if you want to go straight to the top of the tree head for R. Stephens of Mole Creek, near Launceston, the company whose honeys are stocked by Macy's in New York. The factory is open for inspection during normal working hours for tasting and buying, just the spot to sample the famous 'golden bee' honey, redolent of clover and blackberry leaves.

As well as spearheading the return of potatoes with real taste, Tasmania is a leading supplier of onions, peas (sixty per cent of Australia's total crop), runner beans and 'boutique' gourmet crops like green kabichi squash, musk melons and salad cress. Large onion producers like Vecon are carving out significant market shares in Asia, Japan and Europe by providing fresh, crisp onions at a time when their northern hemisphere counterparts are suffering from the effects of extended storage. At Vecon, onions kept in the vast four-storey storage 'bins' receive twenty-five complete changes of air an hour to keep them in fresh condition. High-quality buckwheat destined to metamorphose into soba noodles in Japan, and walnuts that truly emulate the much sought-after French varieties, are other Tasmanian fine food products tailor-made for a golden future.

DELECTABLE CHEESES Time was, most Australians shunned home-produced cheeses out of inverted snobbery but these days views have taken a 360-degree turn. Only the woefully insecure would consider serving up a platter of imported cheeses buoyed up by a single Australian entrant. King Island cheddars, brie and camembert from the renowned gourmet island in the Bass Strait started Tasmanian cheese's run for glory, and the ball has been taken up vigorously by leading companies such as Lactos, where the highly-motivated research team has 'sculpted' cheeses to suit the highly discerning Australian cheese market. True Blue is a particular success, a cheese with a creamy camembert body shot through with Roquefort blue veins. Even the traditional camembert cheese boxes once imported from France are now made in Tasmania.

Swiss cheesemaker Frank Marchand came to Australia to work for Lactos but after ten years with the company decided to branch out on his own. The result is the highly acclaimed Heidi Farm Cheese company, producing cheddar, ricotta, cottage cheeses and cooked cheeses

Clockwise from top left: Cheeses for the discerning palate; a beekeeper works on a hive at Cygnet; milking time at Cygnet; Golden Pearl honey

such as gruyere, Heidi Barrel and raclette made from the milk of Marchand's seventy-five hand-selected Friesians. In Tasmania you can enjoy Heidi Farm cheeses made from unpasteurised milk, but on the mainland government rules require that cheese be made from pasteurised milk. A pity for Australians in other states as the unpasteurised versions have fuller flavours and creamier textures. Other Tasmanian cheese treasures are montasio, now back in production after a manufacturing break, and Taralen goat's milk ricotta—soft, tart and creamy.

Premium Lager from the Cascade Brewery, Australia's oldest brewery, was singled out as one of the four best beers in the world after its international launch. Premium sports the Tasmanian tiger on its label but don't begin and end your exploration of Tasmanian beer there. Cascade's Pale Ale, Boag's Export Lager and Tasmanian Breweries Classic Bitter are the leading trio of other top-shelf attention grabbers. Tasmanian Breweries and the Cascade Brewery run informative and enjoyable day-tours of their beautiful premises. Still on the alcoholic beverage trail, there are several mead (the original honey-flavoured ale of northern Europe) producers in Tasmania. Try Taverner's Good Ale Mead and Horehound Mead—strong and well-chilled.

After the tidal wave popularity of mineral waters around the world in the 1970s and 80s, questions started to be asked about the purity of some brands. Tasmania sits easy on that score with some of the world's purest natural mineral waters sourced in the island state. Subtly-flavoured Hartz mineral waters, available plain or in wildberry, peach and lemon/lime flavours, are rightly enjoying great success in Australia and overseas. The rainwater that teems down on Tasmania's west coast is amongst the purest in the world and was shipped in large quantities to Australian athletes at the Olympic Games in Barcelona.

GOURMET DELIGHTS A true gourmet culture, however, doesn't rest solely on producing the finest raw ingredients; it encompasses a rounded world view of shops, manufacturers and restaurants showcasing sophisticated end-products. Tasmania follows through in this respect with a food scene rivalling any to be found in Europe or the United States. Even in the small northern town of Devonport, you will find culinary lodes like Klaas's

FROM THE APPLE ISLE

The Cascade Brewery holds pride of place in the Australian drinkers' lexicon as Australia's oldest brewery, tracing its origins to 1824. But Cascade Beverages also has a pedigree that stretches back over 100 years—1883 to be exact. Older eyes still grow misty at names like Dandelion Ale, Sassafras Lager Ale, Kola Champagne and Orana. A far cry from the company's dynamic, revamped soft drinks spearheading new export markets in Asia in the 1990s.

Cascade's cordial and cider operations were moved to their present site in the foothills of Mount Wellington in Hobart in 1923. By 1956 their cordial and cider factories were so successful, the importance of Cascade's soft drink 'operation' forced a company re-structuring and the division's birth as a separate entity. In 1971 the division acquired the Port Huon Fruitgrower's Cooperative Association, also bringing Mercury Cider, considered one of Australia's finest cider producers, into the Cascade fold.

Tasmania's nickname of 'Apple Isle' isn't just a travel brochure cliché; at Cascade Beverages it's a title that still has highly profitable currency. The company purchases around 5,000 tonnes of Tasmanian juice apples per year, the majority destined for Cascade Apple Isle Sparkling Apple Juice. Cascade Apple Isle—no colours, flavours, sugars or preservatives—is now being aggressively marketed as a refreshing alternative to alcoholic drinks in many of Australia's leading restaurants. It is being shipped to Sri Lanka and New Zealand and Cascade now sells large quantities of Golden Delicious apple juice concentrate to Japan.

Export is again the path forward for Cascade's Ultra-C Blackcurrant Fruit Juice Syrup—this time to Singapore and Malaysia. This healthy, delicately flavoured drink has also increased its profile on the mainland eastern seaboard states.

The early 90s have seen an exciting leap for Cascade Beverages in terms of new equipment, new product lines and new export potential, not only for the revamped products but also for such high volume favourites as Real Apple 100% Crushed Apple Juice, Cascade Fruit Cordial and Mercury Cider Vinegar. With this track record, Cascade is in a strong position to pursue greater success in the future.

Luscious blackcurrants waiting to be picked

AUSTRALIA - A GOURMET'S PARADISE

Bakehouse where you can feast on Belgian, Dutch and Australian pastries heavy only with butter, and Beautiful Baskets, where you can buy picnic hampers packed with smoked salmon, chicken, cheeses and fruit tarts to fortify your wanderings along the wild north coast.

Honey pilgrimages aren't the only reason to centre a trip to Launceston; the region is a metaphorical lode of fine-eating experiences. In Deloraine you can eye-ball the Tasmanian hardwoods used for such delicacies as smoked salmon, trout and eel and choose on-the-spot purchases such as smoked seafood pates, salmon roe caviar and gravlax. Or direct your appetite to Hunters Larder, who specialise in local game—squab, guinea fowl, pheasant, venison, kangaroo and possum meat. The best restaurant in Launceston is Fee and Me—the 1993 Tasmanian entrant for the prestigious Gourmet Traveller magazine Best Restaurant of the Year Award.

Hobart, smack on the Derwent River and wedged in the foothills of Mount Wellington, is Australia's second oldest city—only sixteen years younger than Sydney. Salamanca Place, a restored sweep of mid-nineteenth century warehouses, is the backdrop to the renowned Salamanca Markets, held every Saturday, which serve as a continuous advertisement for Tasmania's seemingly endless fruit and vegetable bounty—pinkeye potatoes mixing it with mangoes, limes, the creamy cauliflowers from Forth Farm Produce, Asian vegetables like bok choy, and organic raspberries and strawberries. Tucked in between are stalls laden with huge focaccia sandwiches, bulging pies and crisp baguettes.

Hobart's fine-dining scene reflects Tasmania's gourmet thrust forward. Trendy new cafes such as Cafe Who, Atlas, The Cove Food Fair and Retro Cafe flesh out a scene crowned by Dear Friends, a restaurant long granted reverential status throughout Australia for a menu insouciantly and elegantly serving up dishes like rare-roasted fillet of hare with potato puree and a rich game sauce.

Floating punts on Constitution Dock offer Tasmania's finest fish and chips and Ali Akbar is frequently fingered as the best Lebanese restaurant in Australia. If you're a take-away fanatic at the highest level, the Caesar's restaurant occupies icon status—oh, you can pick up Malaysian curries, Amaretto-flavoured bread and butter puddings, homemade charcuterie and the finest German sausages. The Moorilla Wine Centre at Berriedale offers the best one-stop look-see of the Tasmanian eating scene—enjoy a sweep of Tasmania's finest wines with marinated trevalla,

Right: A prickly treat—sea urchin from the Atlas restaurant in Hobart
Above: Tranquil Hobart nestled behind Constitution Dock

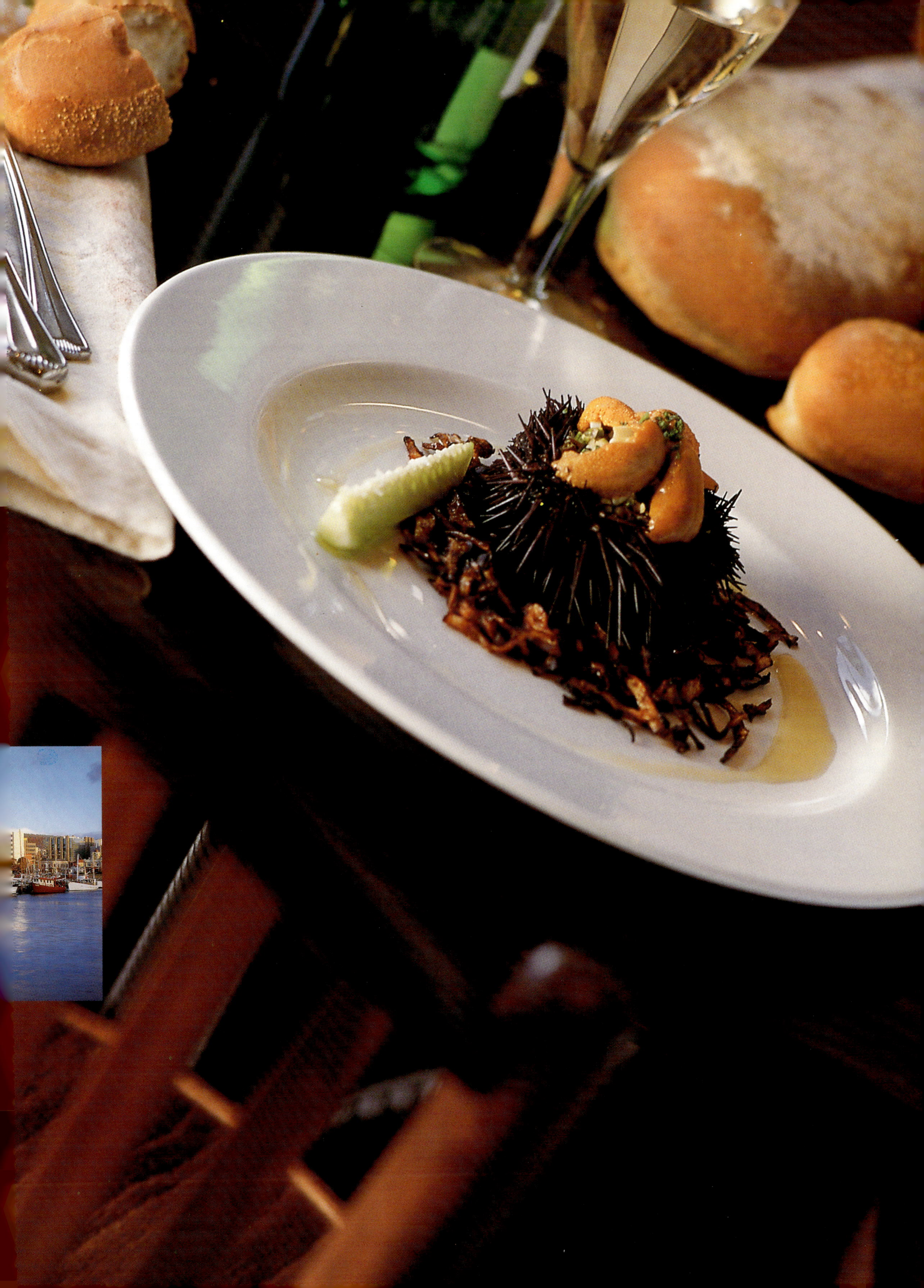

A HEALTHY STATE

Tasmanians down two million litres of their own rich cream each year, the lion's share of which comes from National Dairies Tasmania (NDT). NDT, which traces its origins back nearly seventy years, is the number one dairy product supplier in Tasmania, producing seventy-eight per cent of the state's milk, eighty-nine per cent of its flavoured milks and eighty-seven per cent of its cream. In keeping with its own healthy products, NDT sponsors many of Tasmania's athletic and sports clubs.

NDT began as a family milk delivery business in the 1930s. Every decade since then has seen expansive growth, particularly in the 1980s with the introduction of an extensive range of Tasmanian-made dairy products. Three sites in Hobart, Devonport and Launceston process 42 million litres of milk each year from seventy-three top quality Tasmanian farmers. NDT's biggest marketing success in recent years has been the two-litre plastic milk bottle introduced in 1992, which now represents forty-two per cent of the company's total sales.

Low-fat milk sales in Tasmania have surged since the late 1980s—at 185,000 litres a week, they now account for twenty-five per cent of NDT's total milk sales.

NDT's flavoured milks—such as Killer Shake and Milo—are firm favourites with Tasmanian families. And their new dessert products under the National Soft Dairy banner—which include Fruche and Peters Farm Yoghurts—have enticed a new generation into enjoying dairy products by NDT's innovative marketing and quality production.

NDT's success also rides on the fact that the Tasmanian dairy industry is at the most advanced stage of deregulation of any state in Australia. Tasmania's quality milk producers are permitted to sell statewide and the price of milk products is set by market demand. The Tasmanian Dairy Industry Authority still controls the price processors must pay for milk, but beyond the farm gate the consumer is the winner.

Dairy cows make their way to the milking shed

THE WELL-TRAVELLED ROAD

The most well-travelled road in Tasmania must be 'Cadbury Road'.

If you love chocolate, then take a trip down this road. There you'll find Australia's best-loved and most famous chocolate factory.

Cadbury is the market leader in all segments of the Australian chocolate market and holds a strong position in the sugar confectionery market with its Pascall brand. Cadbury products are just as likely to be served at the finest restaurants and hotels or enjoyed in everyone's homes.

Every year tens of thousands of overseas and local visitors tour the Cadbury Claremont Confectionery Factory nestled at the end of Cadbury Road. Located near Hobart on the estuary of the Derwent River, the Claremont plant has been producing top-quality Cadbury products since 1922.

Claremont was selected as the site of Cadbury's first Australian factory because it offered the right ingredients for success: an excellent supply of top-quality fresh milk from dairy farms throughout north-western Tasmania; clean air and moderate temperatures; plenty of hydro-electricity; good shipping facilities and, of course, access to Australian sugar, fruit, nuts and flavourings from the mainland.

Today visitors to the plant can witness the progress that has been made over the decades. They will find a state-of-the-art confectionery plant-manufacturing products such as Cadbury Dairy Milk™ Milk Chocolate—the company's flagship product—as well as Cadbury and Red Tulip boxed assortments and Cadbury Cocoa, first made at Claremont. A similar manufacturing upgrade has taken place at Claremont's sister factory at Ringwood in Victoria.

GRAIN
OATMEAL
OLIVE & SUNDRIED TOMATO
ROSEMARY & PECAN
50% WHOLEMEAL
BAGUETTE

VEAL NOISETTE
VEAL CHOPS
LAMB NOISETTE
WITH AN APRICOT AND ALMOND FILLING

venison terrine or Claudio's salad of fresh greens combined with goats cheese, cherry tomatoes and croutons.

Situated in the Lenah Valley, The Wursthaus features routinely in any article covering Tasmania's edible treats. Over twenty fabulous sausages from German bratwurst to Indonesian lamb satay are on sale each day. A smoker par excellence, The Wursthaus also specialises in smoked chicken, venison, river and sea-run trout. And for the keen but sometimes lazy cook, the shop's marinades are better than homemade.

Tasmania's Cadbury chocolate factory is a pilgrimage for families on holiday to Tasmania but if you want something to grace the dinner table, Anvers chocolate truffles made from the finest Callebaut chocolate are now a dinner party expectation in Tasmania.

Like any region with more than thirty per cent of its land mass set aside for agriculture, Tasmania's produce ranges of jams, jellies, pickles and chutneys are as spectacular as its World Heritage scenery. Doran's Fine Foods heads a growing list of companies selling the fruitiest redcurrant, raspberry and spiced apple butter preserves. Old-fashioned quince and medlar jellies are the trademarks of Ingleside at Evandale. Mustard and herb addicts should track down the seeded, smooth and flavoured mustards of Hillfarm Herbs.

But perhaps the ultimate all-Tasmanian push comes from Launceston's Pepper Berry cafe which specialises in products using the wild foods of Tasmania. In 1993, after creating restaurant dishes like warrigal greens and wild limes with Tasmanian salmon, the cafe released a small range of conserves and cheeses with a 100 per cent Tasmanian flavour. Think of wild rosella jam and chutney, pepper berry sauce and soft cheese fragrant with pepper berry leaves.

BRILLIANT WINES Tasmania is the only Australian state with a government-controlled appellation system that guarantees that only 100 per cent Tasmanian grapes are used in the production of the wine. A fitting development when you consider that the first Tasmanian vineyard was planted in 1823, in spite of much of the modern hype that suggests that Tasmanian wine is a 'new idea'. After this early start, however, it is true to say that the situation languished until 1956, when French engineer Jean Miguet planted a hectare of vines at La Provence, twenty kilometres north of Launceston, a development consolidated two years later by the founding of Moorilla Estate, north of Hobart, by local textile manufacturer, Claudio Alcorso. Today, with just over forty wineries dotted around the state, the late 1950s is now looked upon as the great renaissance of Tasmanian wine.

Piper's Brook vineyard is the 'big' name Tasmanian winery, with four vineyards in the north of the state and an impressive export record, particularly to Britain. Heemskerk, the

Left to right, top to bottom: A selection of locally produced wines from Wursthaus Kitchen; rainbow trout on smoking rack; freshly baked bread; harvesting Pinot Noir grapes, Elsewhere vineyard, Glaziers Bay; gourmet meat; a copse of oil and vinegar; chargrilled tuna from Mures in Hobart; bunches of Pinot Noir grapes, Elsewhere vineyard; Wursthaus smallgoods manufacturer Ray Coates

NURTURING GOURMET QUALITY

Whenever the subject of Tasmania's overwhelming success in promoting itself is broached, talk always hinges on the role of Tasmania—Development and Resources (TDR). This progressive state government organisation's prime mission is to formulate, promote and deliver industry support services to nurture the development of Tasmania's key resource and industry sectors. The state's gourmet push is considered to be so important that TDR has two key departments specific to the Tasmanian food and beverage industry—the Development Division and the Marketing and Export Division.

TDR's Development Division offers advisory and support services which help Tasmanian food and beverage companies to become more competitive within Australia and overseas. The Marketing and Export Division focuses on market expansion and investment promotion, honing Tasmania's market reputation as a recognised source of premium quality food and beverages through intensive marketing campaigns. It also conducts further marketing and promotional projects that assist the Tasmanian food and beverage industry in securing new market opportunities and sustainable market growth.

The results of this synergy have produced export successes that are now the envy of other states. Over two-thirds of Tasmania's total exports now go to Asia, the giant among customers being Japan. On the food side, the Japanese alone spend almost $70 million per year on Tasmanian foods, from Atlantic salmon to skim milk powder for baby formulas.

The United States too has turned its tastebuds to Tasmania—buying up an annual shopping list of $35 million worth of Tasmanian fish, $23 million of meat and $6 million of dairy products. In Europe, Germany is Tasmania's best customer, spending $13 million a year on fruit and vegetables. Tasmanian abalone is exported to Taiwan and Singaporeans have a decided taste for Tasmanian confectionery.

In its own words, TDR encourages a quality food culture throughout the community committed to the concept of Tasmania as a source of excellence. The results prove that the statement is no mere platitude.

OYSTER OBSESSION

Founded in 1970, Cameron of Tasmania is the largest oyster producer in Tasmania, specialising in prime Pacific oysters including the newly developed 'golden oyster'.

The company's hatchery and nursery on the Denison Canal at Dunalley can produce over 60 million oyster spat each year for its own use and sale to other leading Tasmanian and South Australian oyster farmers.

Cameron of Tasmania is an innovative company, and as a leader of the industry, is responsible for many new and exciting technological advances. One such innovation is the 'Flupsy' or floating upweller system. These are aluminium punts with twenty bays, capable of holding 500,000 oyster seeds per bay. They were developed because existing systems were incapable of holding the volume of oyster seed Camerons' produces.

It takes between eighteen months and two years to grow an oyster to a marketable size. Once the oysters leave the Flupsy system they are taken to the inter-tidal lease at Boomer Bay. They remain there until they reach 40-45 millimetres in length. At this stage the oysters are transferred to the deep-water depot at Eaglehawk Neck, a facility capable of handling 250,000 oysters a day. Grading is done by machine before the oysters are placed into specialised modules. The modules are then taken by barge and attached to longlines on one of the company's two deep-water leases for further growth and final conditioning.

Cameron's mature oysters currently fill two market niches—whole live and frozen half-shell. The market for live oysters is the most competitive. The company markets large quantities of premium oysters both live and frozen across Australia. Frozen oysters provide access to markets that cannot be serviced by fresh product, for example, the outback.

Cameron of Tasmania is a dynamic company which is continually expanding and developing within new and exciting areas of the aquaculture industry. Its objective is to lead Australia in the technological development and economic production of premium quality oysters.

Cameron's newly developed Golden Pacific oysters

state's biggest producer, is the other name that immediately springs to the lips of anyone discussing Tasmanian wine, a label responsible for talked-about chardonnays, pinot noirs and Tasmania's finest sparkling wine to date, Jansz. Moorilla Estate, befitting its pioneer status, crafts some of Tasmania's leading pinot noirs and chardonnays. In March 1993, Moorilla Estate secured Tasmania's largest-ever wine export order of 10,000 bottles to Japan.

Louis Roederer, the famous French champagne company, is in partnership with Heemskerk to produce a benchmark sparkling wine. In the meantime, Clover Hill, a vineyard under the direction of Victoria's Taltarni Wines, has produced an exemplary sparkling wine which has attracted excited reviews. Other up-and-coming names with further developments to watch are Tolpuddle, Rochecombe, Holm Oak and Freycinet vineyards. Right now, Tasmania's varietal strengths across the board are rieslings, chardonnays, pinot noirs, gewurztraminers and semillon. The future is guaranteed to see the scarcity factor that has frustrated lovers of Tasmanian wines consigned to yesterday's news.

The last words on Tasmania's deep commitment to its quality food and wine future belong to Greg Dodds, Austrade's senior representative in Japan and Korea. 'In 1990-91 Tasmania's main export to Japan was minerals—ore and concentrates to the value of $130 million. In 1991-92 falling prices and mine closures reduced that figure by twenty per cent to $97.4 million. What could have been a disaster for Tasmania was avoided by a lift in food exports over the year by seventy-two per cent from $67.5 million to $116.3 million. Tasmania's best selling point is that it is environmentally pristine. In Japan this counts for a great deal. As it does and will continue to do so in Australia and the rest of the world.'

Elisabeth King

Right: Pol Hereford cow and calf at the Tasmania show
Above: Lush vibrant pastures at Deloraine

PREMIUM BEEF

The Altona plant of Gilbertsons in Victoria stands unchallenged as Australia's most efficient meatworks. This fact ranks as 'normal' when you consider the full profile of a company that has played a leading role in the national economy as one of Australia's leading beef producers—a tradition begun in 1928. With an annual turnover in excess of $300 million, Gilbertsons is synonymous with supreme professionalism in all aspects of the meat processing industry from breeding to delivery, whether the final destination is in Australia, North America, Asia or Europe.

Gilbertsons easily captures the title of Tasmania's leading meat exporter, outdistancing their nearest competitor by over two to one. The company's Longford plant in north Tasmania and another on King Island are situated in two of Australia's leading beef-fattening and agricultural regions. The reasons are nothing more devious than Tasmania's clean, natural environment, a cool, moderate climate and consistent rainfall combining to ensure a year-round pasture dense with nutrition and protein.

With such an armful of natural advantages, it is hardly surprising that the cattle from these two prestige Gilbertsons properties produce beef of only the highest quality. Even the least culinary-minded can attest to the above-average tenderness, texture, taste and controlled meat colour of this premium Tasmanian beef that has acquired status symbol throughout the world.

Like all of Gilbertsons' production staff, the Tasmanian personnel are acknowledged experts in their field, stringently enforcing specification standards, hygiene, cleanliness and AusMeat guidelines. All cattle on the Tasmanian properties are hand-picked to meet Gilbertsons' strict breed, age, weight, meat colour and fat-marbling guidelines. Not content with meeting only current standards of excellence, Gilbertsons also adheres to a strategy of continuous review of improved processing techniques and the changing demands of respective markets.

Right: The inspiring Cradle Mountain range
Above: Trout fishing in Brumby's Creek, Norfolk Plains District

SPIRIT OF ADVENTURE

More than 450,000 tourists visit Tasmania each year and much of the credit is due to the forceful efforts of Tasmania's Department of Tourism, Sport and Recreation. When Tasmania mounted a virtual saturation billboard campaign in Melbourne in 1990, Melbournians signed up for a mini-migration. This is hardly surprising when you consider that one-third of the island state is preserved for all time in reserves, National Parks and World Heritage areas.

Tasmania's vast waterways, mountains, highland lakes and clean air represent significant drawcards for most mainland and international visitors. The state has forcefully introduced other lures into the 'holidaying in Tasmania' equation—gourmet produce in shops, restaurants, hotels and guesthouses, remnants of a British colonial history and the pleasures of four distinct seasons, just to name a few. The spirit of adventure is also encouraged in Tasmania—with some of Australia's best bushwalking trails, whitewater rafting, climbing, trout fishing and sailing.

Special events are assuming even greater importance in the island's promotions. The finish of one of the world's great bluewater classics, the Sydney-to-Hobart yacht race, continues to draw visitors from all over the world. Tasmania also hosts the five-day around-island touring rally—Targa Tasmania—with a multi-million dollar line-up of classic cars, the Reno-style air pylon racing of SkyRace Tasmania, world-class floral festivals and the annual Irish Festival at Port Arthur.

Tasmania capitalises on the fact that the state is comparatively small in comparison with other Australian states. Its compactness makes car touring a joy and visitors are still guaranteed great natural contrasts and diverse activities. Promotional campaigns may change for the Department of Tourism, Sport and Recreation, but its success rests on the state remaining virtually the same—a grand destination for those on nature's discovery trail.

V I C T

Right: A breathtaking view of the Twelve Apostles from the Great Ocean Road
Below: The unique entrance to Queen Victoria Market in Melbourne; geometric patterns of the Nursery Market Garden, Werribee

O R I A

Rich & Cosmopolitan

The year is 1889. The scene is Melbourne's bustling Queen Victoria Market at 6 am on a crisp autumn day. Although the sun has barely risen, Elizabeth Street is a blur of activity. The unmade road has been churned into quicksand by the shuffling hooves of the carthorses, who lumber forward under their heavy burdens, their breaths hanging in the chilly air.

Chinese market gardeners pushing handcarts expertly dodge and weave as they thread their way through the clamouring crowds of bargain hunters. Most of them have been walking since just after midnight from their market gardens located around the fringe of the fledgling city. The market is full to bursting point as red-faced stall holders spruik at the top of their voices, loudly promising to fulfil dreams and fill stomachs. The market grows by the minute as temporary stalls are set up in the streets and a sea of bodies promptly engulfs each new stall. Probing hands furtively grasp at full plump cauliflowers, and testing fingers tap against taut firm cabbages as if they were kettle drums.

For two bob, you can buy a whole side of mutton. If you're flush, and you can stretch to three and six pence, you can make it a side of lamb.

Aisle after aisle beckons, with their tempting vistas of neat yellow blocks of freshly churned butter laid out on crisp cheesecloth, counters piled high with hands of pickled pork, tubs of shiny apples, and newly laid eggs packed like precious jewels in fresh chaff.

There is nothing particularly new about Victoria's unashamed obsession with food. At the turn of the century, Melbourne had no less than eight produce markets with three of them located smack in the city centre. The driving force behind the markets was the Chinese, who had flocked to the gold-fields in the 1850s. Natural and gifted gardeners, they soon found that they had an affinity with the weird and wonderful vegetables that the predominantly English and Irish population could not live without. They grew carrots, spinach, peas and cabbages that were bigger, brighter and tasted better than anyone else's.

By 1924 it was reckoned that sixty-five per cent of the stallholders at the Queen Victoria Market alone were Chinese. 'Chinatown' in Little Bourke Street was first established as a staging post for the Chinese, many from the See Yap (Four Districts) of Guangdong Province who passed through Melbourne on the way to the gold fields.

In 1854 there were 2,341 Chinese in Victoria. By 1861 there were nearly 25,000 and Melbourne's Chinatown quickly developed into an exotic, bustling, dynamic centre that remained pretty much unchanged until the 1950s.

In the fifties, the air was thick with chatter and the constant clacking of mah jong pieces, and the scent of fresh roast suckling pig was as clear and as sweet as spring's first blossoms. 'The best roast pork was from the Fun Kee. It was exquisite,' says Elizabeth Chong, cookery teacher and food writer. 'You could see the blood from the slaughtered pigs running down the streets like little red rivers'.

By the turn of the century, other ethnic groups were rapidly making their presence felt, particularly the Jewish communities of Eastern Europe and, of course, the Italians. The two groups established popular eating houses with names like Cafe Tel Aviv, Cohen's Kosher Cafe and Fasoli's, a famous bohemian hang-out where one could discuss the ills of the world while enjoying a glass of good red, a dish of home-made pasta and a life-enhancing osso bucco. Italian soon became the flavour of the month, and has been ever since.

The power behind the popularity of Italian eating lay firmly in the hands of the so-called 'spaghetti mafia'. Tony Virgona opened a wine cellar in Brunswick Street which became the Casa Virgona, Rinaldo Massoni founded the venerable Florentino restaurant in the city, Camillo Triaca established the Latin in Exhibition Street, Rino Codognotto began The Society in Bourke Street, and Joe Molina put his family name to Molina's in Lonsdale Street.

TALENTED CHEFS Then, in 1954, a young and enterprising Italian called Gino Di Santo imported Melbourne's very first Cimbali single piston espresso machine, which was quickly installed at the then Lexington Cafe. Overnight, Melbourne's famous cafe life was born. In the fifties, it flourished on the outskirts of the city in Carlton, which soon turned into one giant social club for the local Italian community. When Nando Donnini and his brother-in-law Gianni Milani opened the University Cafe in Lygon Street in 1954 as a 'real Italian eating house', you could buy a plate of spaghetti bolognese or a thick veal cutlet for just

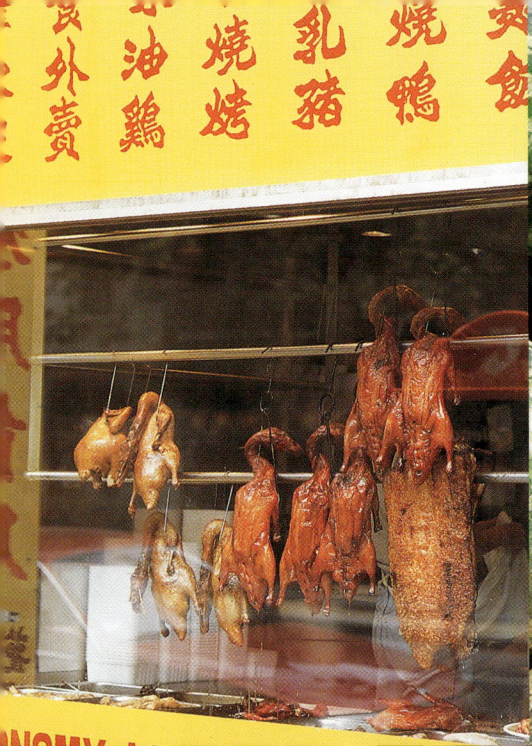

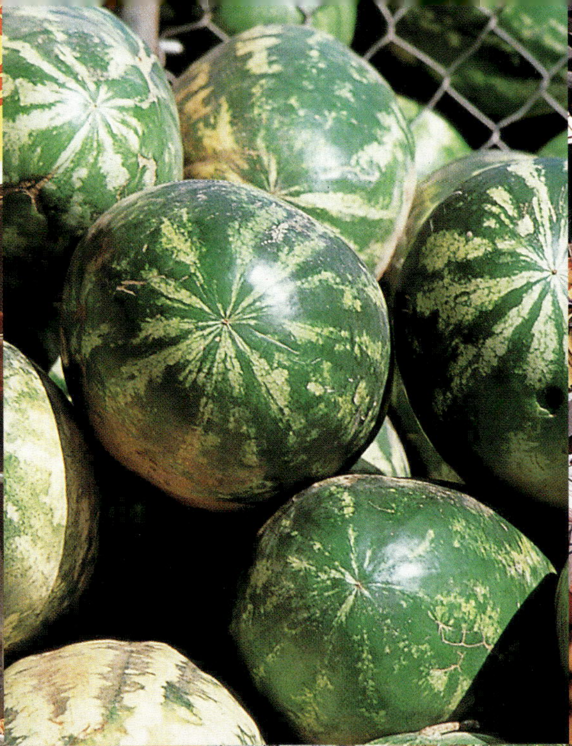

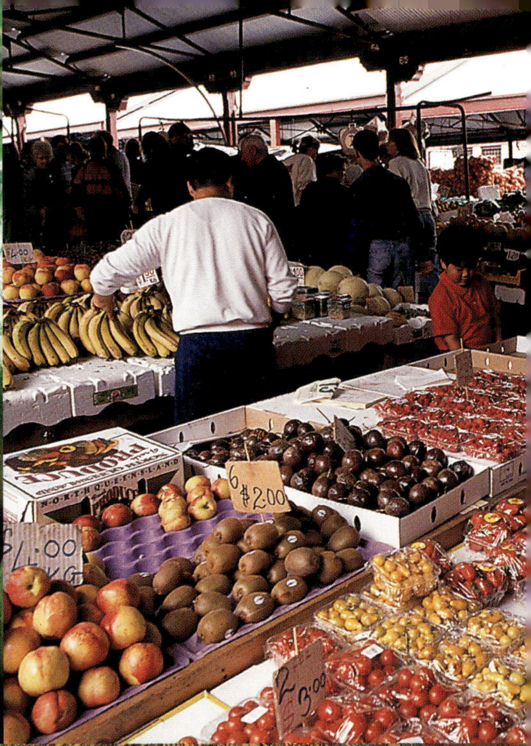

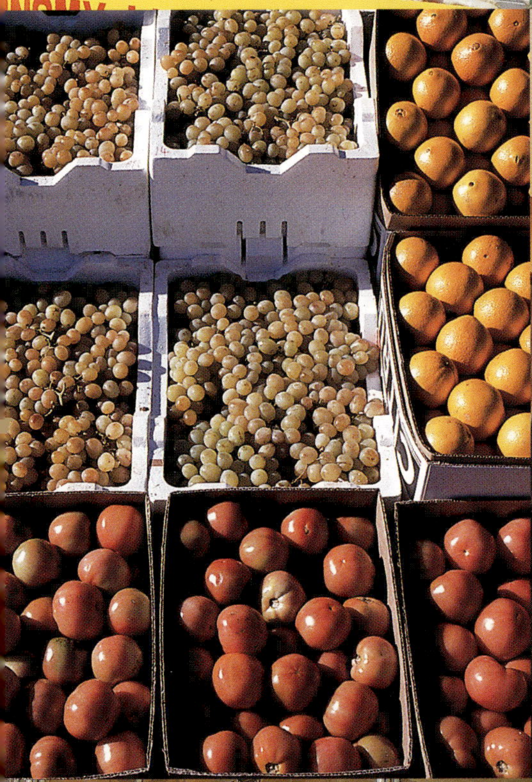

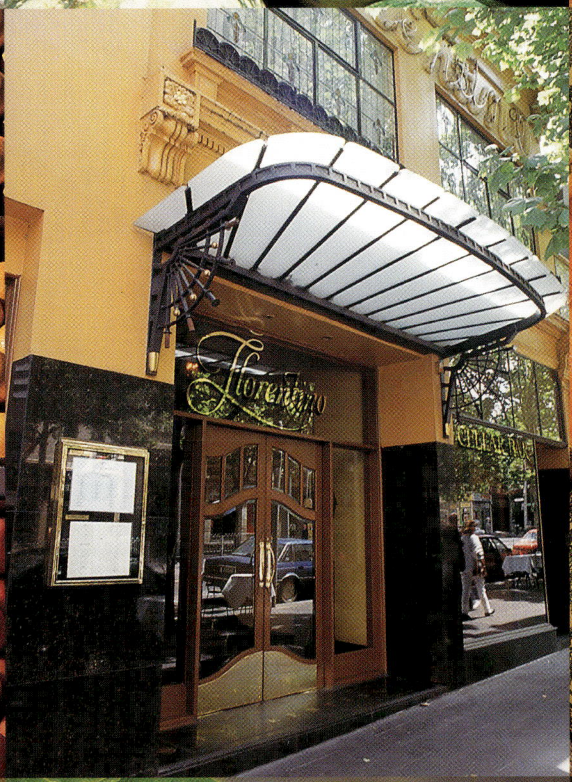
Florentino

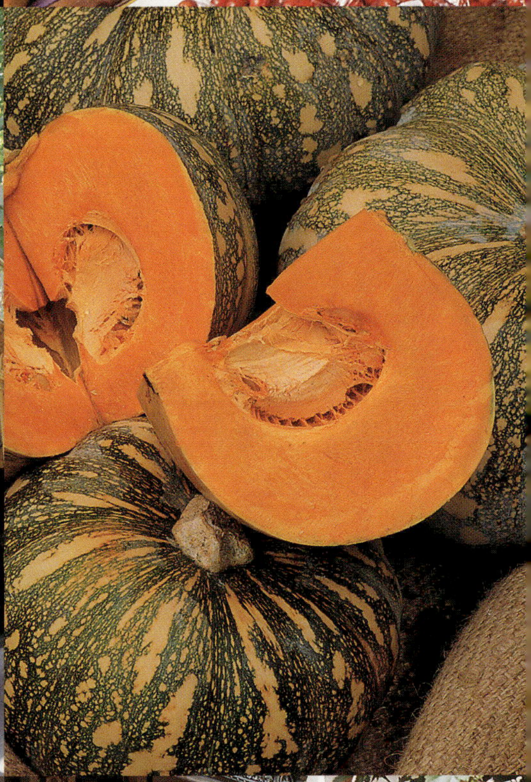

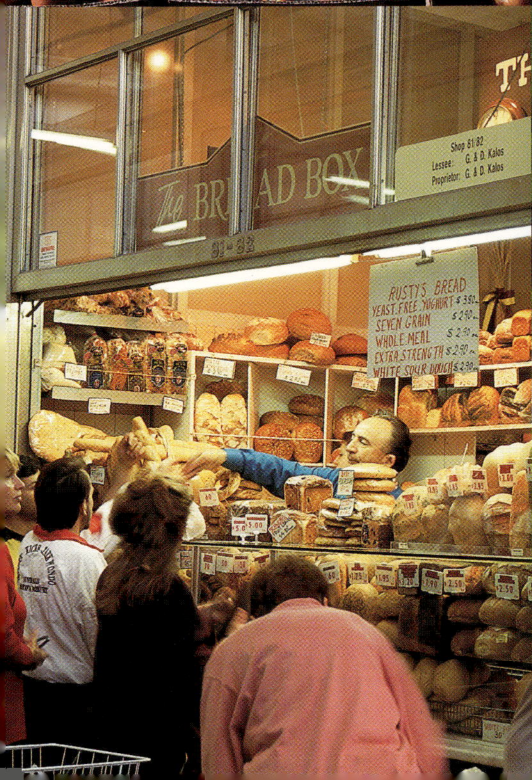
The BREAD BOX

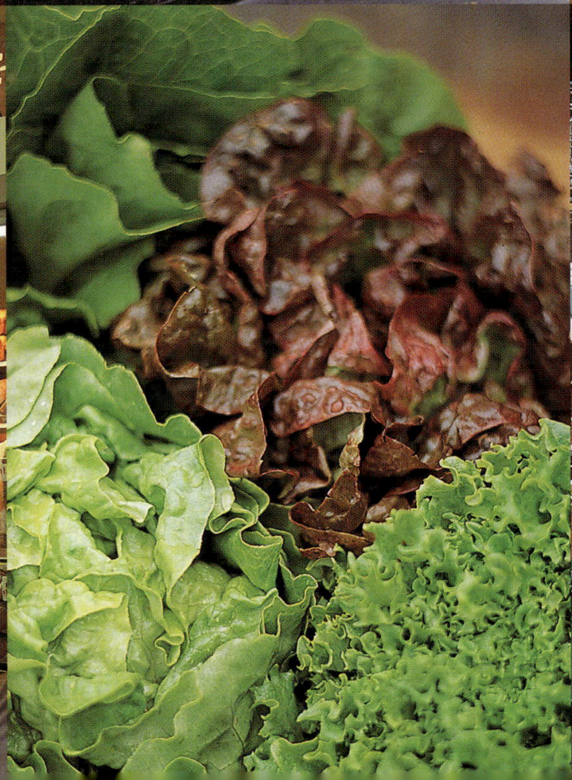

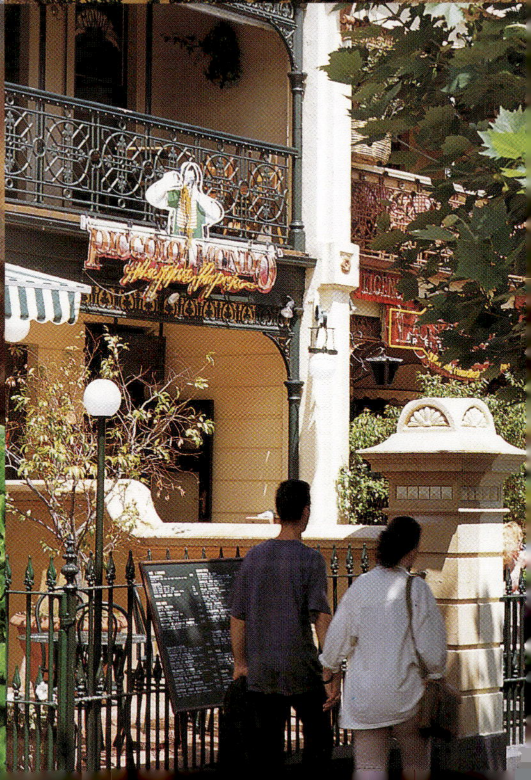

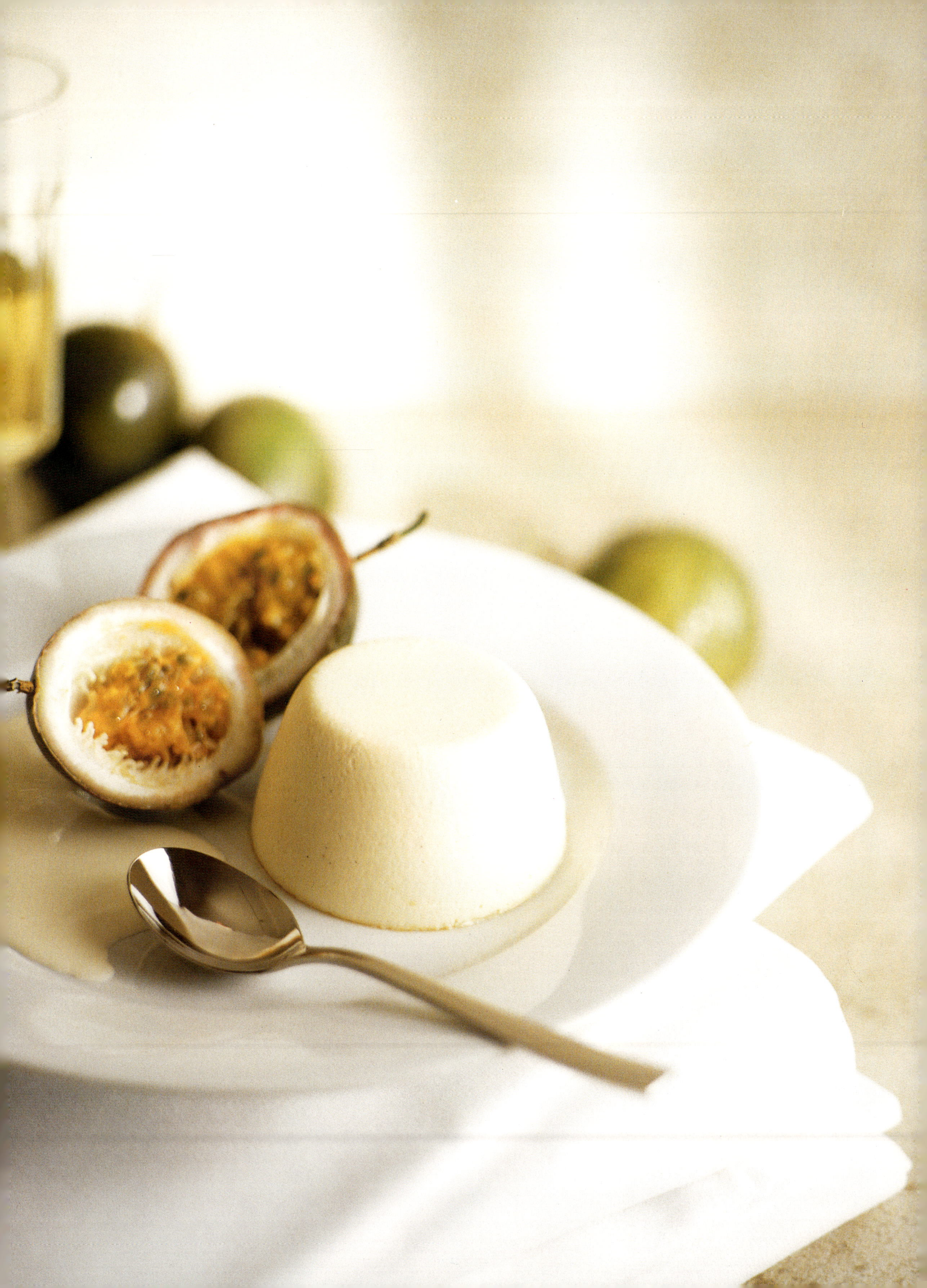

four shillings. The place soon became so popular that the queues reached down to the Grattan Street corner, and other eating houses began popping up in the area like porcini mushrooms.

It was in the fifties, too, that a certain sophistication invaded Melbourne's eating habits. We began calling the top section of Collins Street the 'Paris end' and we fell in love with all things French. We went to the French Exhibition at the Exhibition buildings and ate snails, and sampled the refined cuisine of visiting three-star French master Raymond Oliver of the renowned Parisian three-star restaurant, Le Grand Vefour.

Then, in 1956, Melbourne was plunged into the very middle of rampant multiculturalism with the staging of the Olympic Games. Not only did countries from all over the globe send some very talented athletes, they also sent some very talented chefs. One of them was Swiss-born Hermann Schneider, who stayed on after his team returned home, and became the founding father of modern cuisine in Melbourne.

Schneider's Two Faces restaurant in Toorak Road was soon the unofficial gastronomic headquarters for local food lovers who would speak breathlessly of his sweetbreads with morels, his salmi of pot roasted wild duck, and his fillets of wild rabbit with forest mushrooms.

In 1980, Peter Joyce, president of the Wine and Food Society of Australia, called Two Faces 'undoubtedly the finest restaurant in Australia'.

Melbourne was unanimously hailed as Australia's eating capital, a fact reinforced by the emergence of an exciting, adventurous, new breed of chef and restaurateur, including the likes of Stephanie Alexander, Mietta O'Donnell, John Smith, Iain Hewitson, and later Jacques Reymond, Marc Bouten, Tansy Good and Greg Brown. These were people who weren't afraid to take chances, and who knew that the quality of dining related directly to the quality of the produce that was available to them.

FLAIR FOR 'NEW FOODS' They encouraged growers to experiment, to pick their vegetables younger, to try out new varieties. Cheesemakers were given a chance to shoot for the stars, and agriculture suddenly turned into the new glamour industry. The chefs found wild mushrooms growing in our forests and provided a market for the fresh-picked baskets of dusky brown beauties. They persuaded people to age goat's cheese, to clot cream, to smoke eels, to produce oil from locally-grown olives and to sun-dry tomatoes. As the quality of dining improved, so did the quality of the produce in our shops. Suddenly, eating in became just as exciting as eating out. Victoria's reputation for its produce grew to a point where even Sydney chefs were showcasing Gippsland beef, Wimmera quail and squab, and herbs and young salad greens from the Mornington Peninsula.

Iain Hewitson's goats milk baravois with passionfruit

AUSTRALIA - A GOURMET'S PARADISE

Here were the first signs of the growth of distinct regional differences in food that older cultures like France and Italy took for granted.

Serge Dansereau, chef of Kables restaurant at Sydney's Regent Hotel, went so far as to stage a north-east Victorian dinner in 1992 featuring cheeses, lamb, hare, smoked products and nuts and vegetables from the area, accompanied by a selection of wines from the Milawa region, including Brown Brothers. Even the mustard and honey was locally sourced.

But perhaps the real success story of the past ten years has been the rise of Victoria's specialist farmhouse cheese industry. This is hardly surprising when you realise that the state produces nearly seventy per cent of the country's milk.

By definition, farmhouse cheeses are made on the farm using only the farm's own milk. Naturally, they depend heavily on local influences such as the climate, the quality of the feed—and therefore the milk—and the ability of the cheesemaker to adapt to his conditions. The cheeses therefore take on distinctive regional characteristics that make them unique in every way.

Bill Studd, Australia's most respected cheese consultant and our first member of the Guilde de Fromagers, was quick to see Victoria's great potential as a cheese producer. 'In 1980, there were no local farmhouse cheeses at all,' he says. 'People wanted air-freighted cheeses, because we had nothing to equal them.'

According to Studd, the first real breakthrough took place in an unprepossessing domestic garage on a Gippsland dairy farm in 1982. When local cheesemaker Richard Thomas, who had been working in Italy with one of the great gorgonzola producers, teamed up with fellow cheesemaker Laurie Jensen and dairy farmer Robert Johnson, something magical happened. It was called Gippsland Blue, a creamy, rich, thoroughly European-style cheese that set local foodies on their ears. When the three men took Gippsland Blue to Bill Studd, he was quick to include it in his range at a comparable price to the much-lauded imported cheeses he was handling. From there, the cheese industry matured at a rapid rate.

Right: Luscious tomatoes, a valuable ingredient in many Heinz's soups Above: Farfalle with creamy seafood sauce

QUALITY ASSURED

Heinz products have a selling history in Australia dating back to the nineteenth century. In 1935 however, H J Heinz Australia was established, becoming the fourth oldest affiliate of the corporation after the United States of America, the United Kingdom and Canada.

Today, H J Heinz Australia is an established market leader within its areas. Core products are soups, baked beans and spaghetti, tuna and tomato-based products. Globally, the corporation is one of the largest producers of baby foods.

The corporation adopts a Total Quality Management (TQM) approach to all aspects of its internal and external operations. In Australia, Heinz has its own Quality Assurance department which continually checks the quality of ingredients and looks into innovative packaging. For example, Heinz was the first company in Australia to change from a soldered side-seam can to a welded one and was the first organisation to introduce the ring-pull can end for food products.

No artificial colourings, flavourings or preservatives are present in any Heinz brand products and all raw ingredients are Australian-grown.

As tomato paste is an integral component of many Heinz products, the company meets regularly with tomato growers globally to keep abreast of new species. The same is true of other ingredients.

The company's Greenseas tuna brand also has a strict, dolphin-safe policy sourcing product from suppliers who use only traditional harvesting methods and fish in areas where there is no incidence of dolphin schooling with tuna.

All of Heinz baby foods are pesticide-free, clean, green and constantly tested and monitored to ensure exacting standards. Heinz has its own Baby Foods Advisory Service, consisting of a team of professional nutritionists who regularly liaise with health authorities, mothers groups and infant well-being organisations.

H J Heinz Australia acknowledges that its future lies in developing export markets while maintaining leadership in the domestic market. Heinz is committed to maintaining its presence as a major supplier of quality recipe products to the Australian domestic market and utilising its expertise to increase its presence as an international supplier to the Asian market.

Humble beginnings also begat some fine cheeses over on the other side of the state at a place called Timboon in the Western District, when bio-dynamic dairy farmer Herman Schultz invited German cheesemaster Hans Siegfried to Australia to teach his family cheese-making skills. The lessons were conducted on the verandah of the farmhouse and, within five years, Timboon was producing around 100 tonnes of cheese a year, including the Schultz's popular camembert, a brie, quark and gourmet feta.

In 1988 Haberfields of Albury combined with a Swiss-based consortium to produce a range of washed rind, surface-smeared cheeses under the Swissfield label at Wodonga. Production was supervised by Swiss cheesemaster Andy Eberle, whose prodigious output included a nutty, full-flavoured raclette, a good, smooth-textured tilsit and the amazing Mungabareena, a soft-washed rind-style flavoured with gum leaves.

Laurie Jensen popped up again 'next door' to Gippsland Blue when he set up another farmhouse cheese operation at Jindivick and produced a wonderfully creamy brie and Jindi supreme, a mould-ripened cheese made with Jersey cow's milk enriched with extra cream.

Jensen's former colleague, Richard Thomas, also made a return performance after a spell at King Island, by setting up a cheese factory at Milawa in the north-east with partner David Brown. They were soon turning out a veritable rainbow of cheeses including Milawa Blue, Milawa Gold and Milawa White, a tradition that David Brown continues today.

Thomas went on to help develop Fitzroy Conservatory clotted cream, before moving to Meredith near Geelong to produce a range of sheep's milk cheeses including Meredith white cheese, Meredith sheep's washed rind, and Meredith Blue, the closest Australia has come to the mighty roquefort of France.

Today, the cheeses keep coming thick and fast, particularly in Gippsland, where Fred Leppin, a one-time German architect, is producing a mind-boggling array of cheeses under the Top Paddock brand, including a wine-washed rind, a soft, full cream curd cheese called Whitelaw (the darling of Sydney's wood-fired pizza oven set), a striking orange yellow soft cheese coated in white mould called Cromwell, and a stunning new gruyère style.

Leppin started making cheese just a few years ago, for the simple reason that he liked eating it. With encouragement from Bill Studd, he began by specialising in English style cheeses, including the very distinctive Bass River Red, based on the classic Red Leicester. He has never looked back.

The nearby Faudel family, although relative newcomers to the business, are already making a range of goat's cheeses that are every bit as distinctive as the Anglo Nubian goats they

Choose your favourite from this variety of cheeses by Richard Thomas

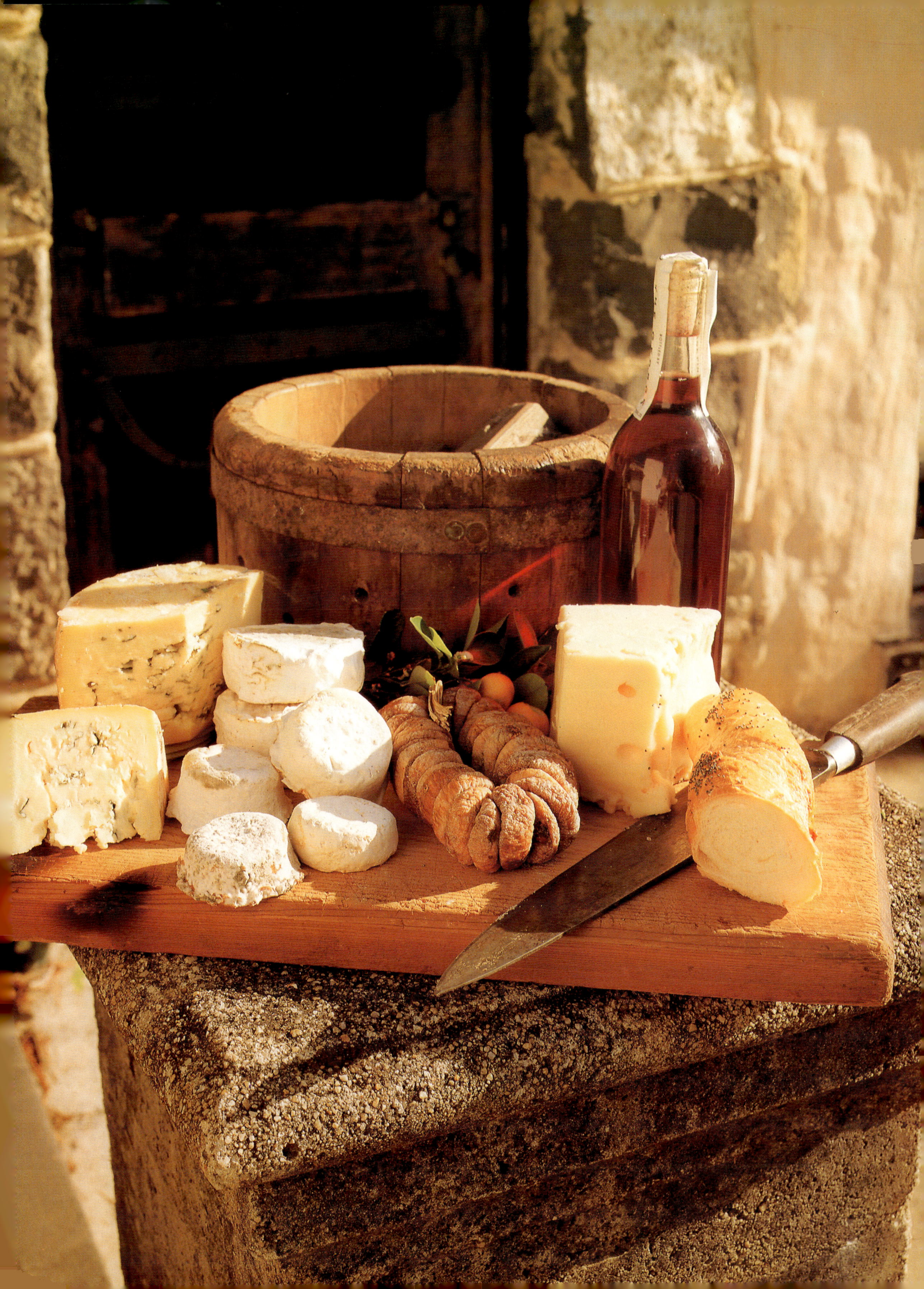

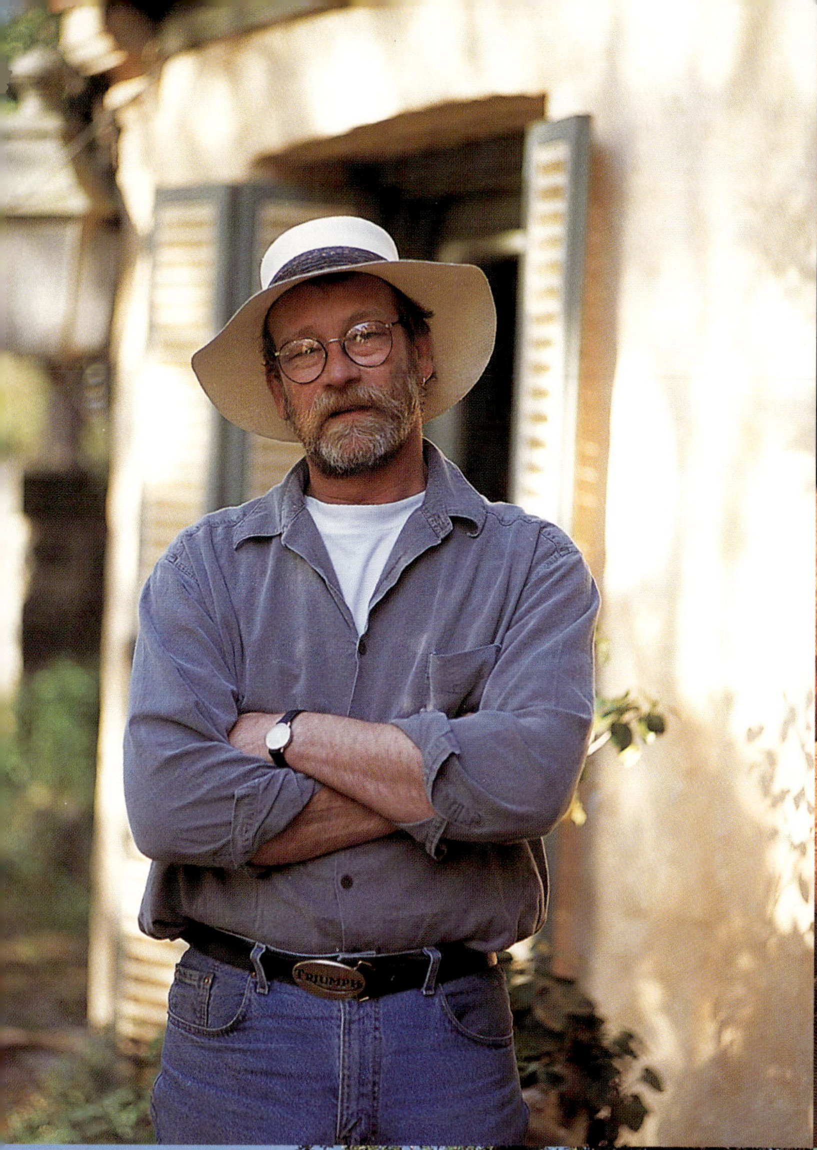

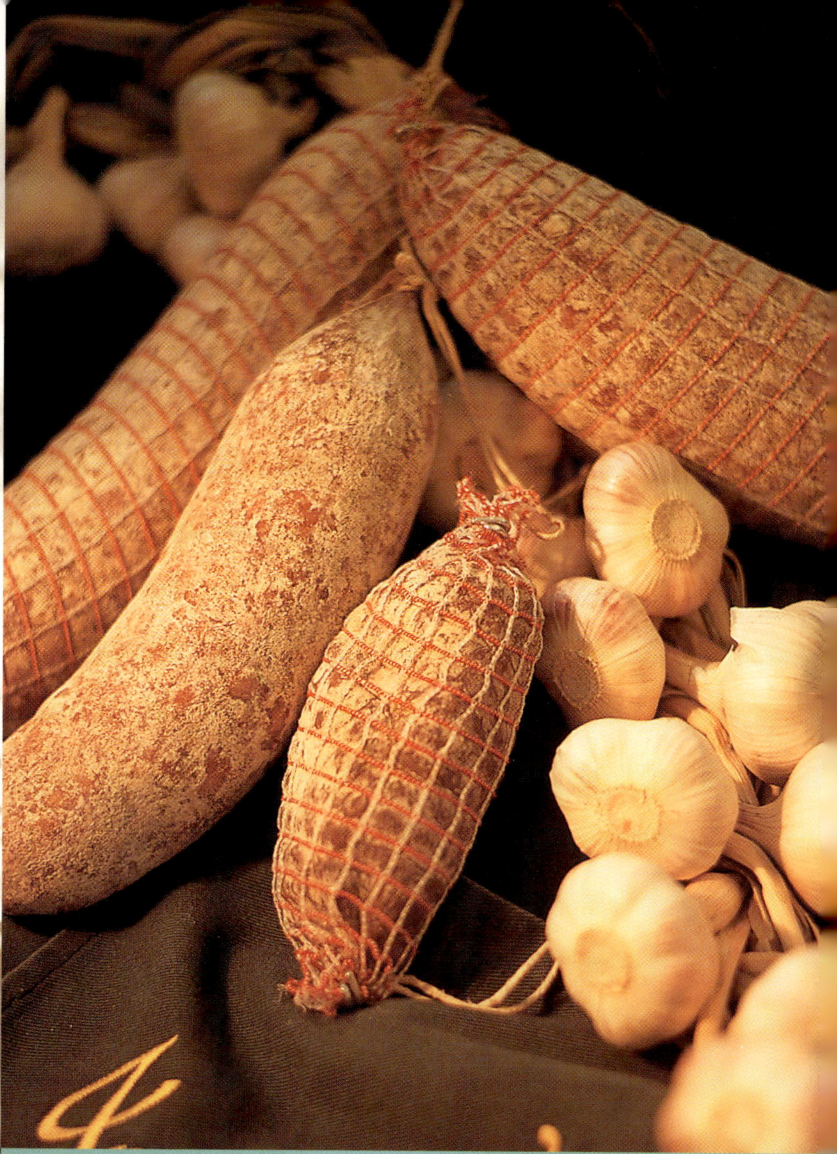

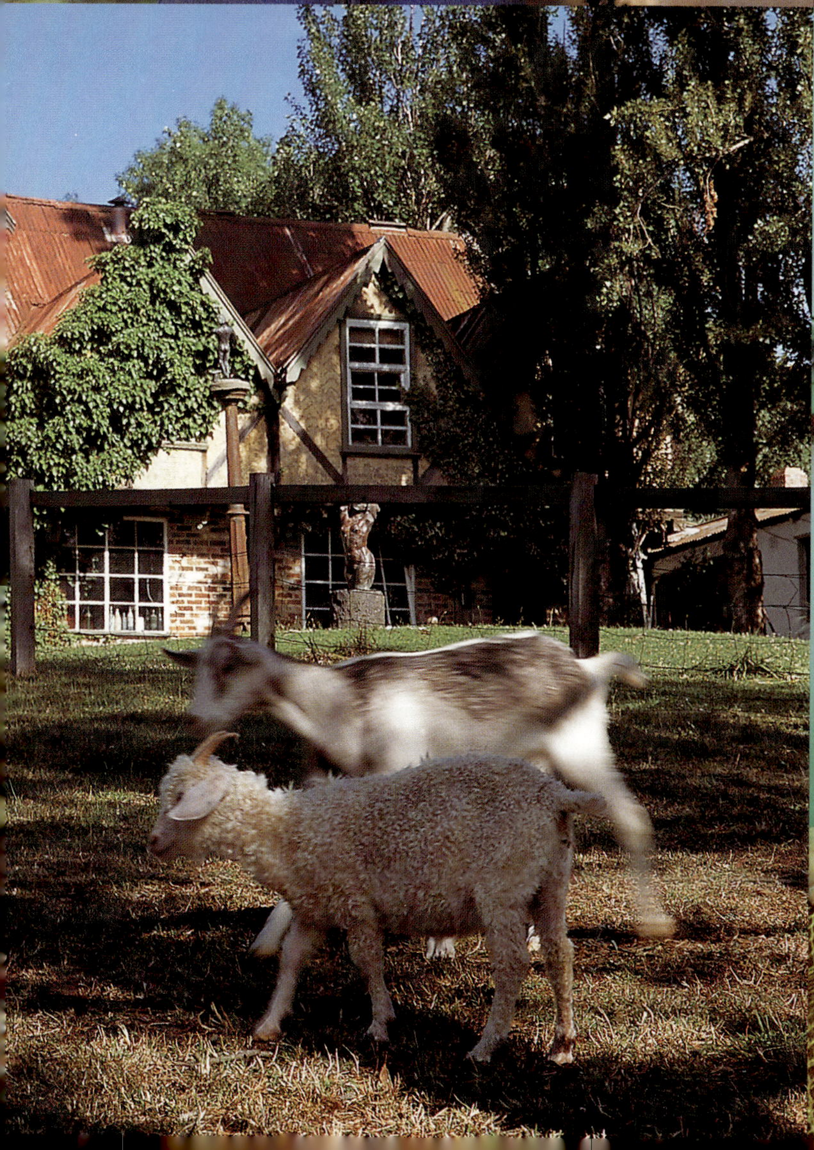

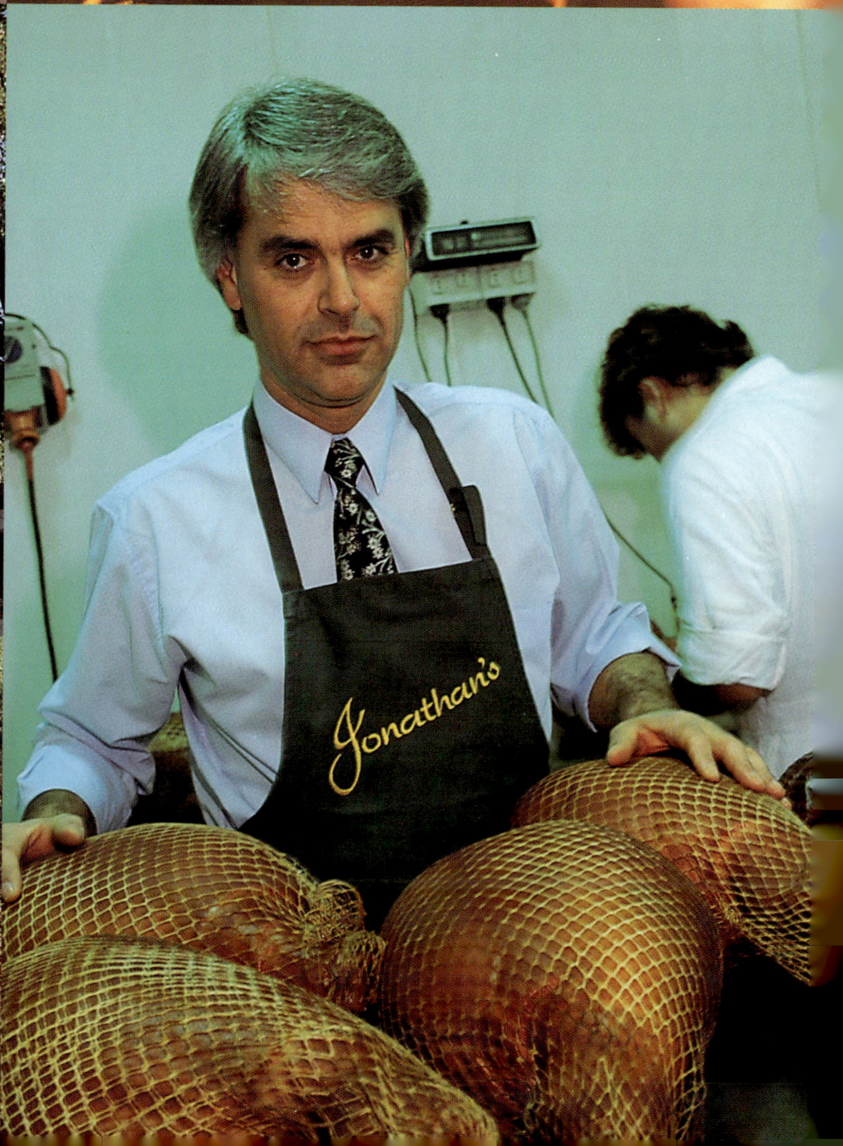
Jonathan's

breed on their Whitelaw property near Korumburra. Their fresh, handmade fromage de chevre is a sheer delight with its chalky, milky texture and clear, citrus-fresh flavours. Also impressive are their crottin and South Gippsland Chevrotin.

As for the future, keep your eye on Richard Thomas, who is quick to play down his role in the development of the Victorian cheese industry. 'My original sin was my greed for Italian gorgonzola,' he says. 'Then people said Victoria could never produce a good blue cheese, and that set me off.'

After a stint producing fresh herbed fromage blanc, Thomas is currently working hard 'in a benevolent laboratory' building a case for traditional (that is, using unpasteurised milk) cheeses. 'I'm looking at the interference of technology, of refrigeration, of pasteurisation,' he explains, 'while working with cheeses in a very traditional manner.'

PASSIONATE PRODUCERS Thomas is typical of that very special breed of Victorian—the passionate producer. They not only make cheese and milk goats, but they also breed chickens, salt sardines, and dig potatoes. They worry about death and taxes and rain, integrity and income. Their eyes glow with missionary zeal when they talk about their work, reflecting a strange, strong hunger that only the deeply obsessed will recognise.

They believe in what they grow and what they deliver with all their hearts. Some of them are Akubra-hatted farmers, some are whizz-bang wheeler dealers, and others are purely skilled craftsmen, but all share a passion for producing the very best.

Take the far-sighted Ian Milburn of Glenloth in the Mallee region, who was able to look beyond traditional wheat farming, and use the land to breed superior corn-fed, free-range squab, chicken, duck, and pheasant. 'It's a classic small business,' he says ruefully. 'You work like hell, pour everything into it, and finally, after five years, you start to see a return. But you have to be committed to get there.'

But not all the great Victorian producers are in the country. Czechoslavakian-born Irena Votavova shares her comfortable middle suburban Melbourne home with around 20,000 garden snails. 'One night soon after I arrived in Melbourne, I went to a French restaurant and ate snails for the first time,' she recalls. 'The next morning, I woke up and announced to the family that we were going into the snail business.'

Business has been growing rapidly since then. Her tiny little *helix aspersa* now crawl over the French bistro plates of Melbourne, the luckiest ones ending up in paper-thin ravioli on a wave of parsley butter on the embossed plates of the acclaimed Paul Bocuse restaurant at Daimaru.

Clockwise from top left: Richard Thomas; smoky French-style sausage;
Jonathon Gianfreda with his Jambon de Bayonne; goats on the lawn at Richard Thomas' 'benevolent laboratory'

AUSTRALIA - A GOURMET'S PARADISE

Another vital link in the city's food chain is Melbourne butcher Jonathon Gianfreda, whose wonderfully smoky French style saucisson Lyonnaise is on the menus of top bistros throughout the country, and whose jambon de Bayonne-style ham has caused an almost mini-revolution in the local small goods industry.

Gianfreda attacks his work with a remarkable passion and intelligence. On nights when he can't sleep, he will sneak into his shop to experiment with a new cut of veal, or to perfect stuffed pig's trotters. He brings his own love of food and his experience of dining in the world's finest restaurants to his craft, but he can still be madly parochial.

'Victorian meat is amazing, mainly because we have the best pastures,' he says. 'Whenever there's a drought or a flood anywhere else, the stock is brought down here to get back into condition.'

According to Gianfreda, the best lamb in the state comes from the rich Gippsland area, particularly around Korumburra, while Sandy Cameron at Meredith near Ballarat produces exceptionally fine milk-fed lambs and, in a new development in the tradition of 'bush mutton', some breeders in north-east Victoria are experimenting with lambs fed on salt bush and clover.

For beef, he leans heavily towards the Angus and Hereford breeds, particularly those found in the High Plains area near Mansfield, although he is quite a fan of the Murray Greys being bred along the Murray basin. His quail and poussin come from Whittlesea, his hare from the Western District, while venison is yet another jewel from the multitude of riches that emanate from the rich and lush Gippsland area.

FRUITFUL BOUNTY Gianfreda might divide the state into lambs and steers, but Terry Greguol of Mario's Quality Fruits in Toorak, a suburb of Melbourne, sees it more in terms of tubers and brassicas. The confidant of many of Melbourne's most respected restaurateurs, Greguol is a walking encyclopaedia on everything that grows in the ground, with an endearing ability to get excited over the sight of a perfect Dutch carrot.

Right: Dairy cows grazing near Warrnambool
Above: Feeding time for calves

FROM COW TO CONSUMER

Bonlac Foods Limited is Australia's largest dairy co-operative and number one processed food exporter.

The Australian owned co-operative, which is based in the dairy-rich state of Victoria, was established in 1986 with the amalgamation of former independent dairying co-operatives. The success of the venture—which has benefited suppliers, customers, shareholders and employees through improved marketing and distribution, reduced operating costs and increased product development—can be measured in its impressive performance with the latest figures showing group sales approaching $1 billion. Turnover has been maintained at twelve per cent compounding growth since formation.

Bonlac, which is headquartered in Melbourne, has 3,200 dairy farming family shareholders, ten factories in Victoria and joint venture operations in Bangladesh and Singapore. It exports to Japan as well as having interests throughout Asia. Half of all products produced by Bonlac are exported to more than fifty countries world wide and its products make up thirty per cent of all Australian dairy exports.

Aided by Victoria's temperate climate and rainfall, Bonlac is an efficient year-round milk producer, with the quality of this milk resulting from an extensive programme that ensures freshness from 'cow to consumer'.

Once the milk has passed rigorous scrutiny at Bonlac's world-class laboratories, Bonlac processes, manufactures and markets a wide range of dairy products which include butter, cheese, powdered and UHT milk, and soft serve ice-cream. Bonlac's major international brands are Red Cow, Falcon and Cow brand and, in Australia, Western Star, Bodalla, Allowrie, Perfect Cheese, Frosty Boy, Mr Whippy and, under licence, the Bega brand.

The success of Bonlac products as a market leader is directly attributable to its impeccable standards, distribution and competitive pricing. Bonlac's factories now have ISO9002 accreditation. Its commitment to quality has instilled a spirit of pride and excellence in all employees, as well as improving lifestyle and returns on investment for Bonlac's dairy farming families.

'Victoria is a world leader in fruit and vegetables,' he says with typical enthusiasm. 'Whether it's our rich volcanic soils, the wind or the sun, I don't know. But whatever it is, this is the perfect state for growing vegetables.'

According to Greguol, the real heart and soul of local vegetable production is the Werribee region which grows most of Victoria's cabbages, cauliflowers and lettuces, closely followed by Cranbourne in the sand belt where families like the Schreurs and the Corrigans specialise in the likes of celery, leeks, parsnips, carrots and spinach.

Then there are the Dandenongs, pioneered by the early Dutch settlers who introduced shallots, salsify and witlof.

The lush Mornington Peninsula is home to Victoria's now-thriving herb and salad green industry. It was here that dedicated and far-sighted growers like Daniel Romaneix and Brian Hussey first led Australia out of the iceberg lettuce age. Where once an 'exotic' salad in this country meant one containing cos and mignonette, these days it is more likely to be a melange of cresses, Dandelion leaves, lamb's lettuce, mitzuna and chervil.

The Peninsula is also where Clive and Penny Blazey established their Diggers Garden Company specialising in seeds producing 'heirloom' vegetables and fruits, varieties that have been passed on from one generation to another. Proving that not all tomatoes are red, the Blazeys have grown yellow, crimson, green, pink, orange and grey, returning colour as well as flavour to the humble tomato.

Potatoes, too, are making a comeback. After the dark ages when our only choice was washed or unwashed, we now have patrone, desiree, toolangi delight, kippfler, bintje, russet burbank, spunta, exeton, kennebec, the all-purpose Ballarat red, and more, thanks to the efforts of the potato research station at Toolangi near Healesville and growers like Geoff and Bronwyn Dobson of Acheron Valley and Mike Cullinan at Bullarook.

For fruit, Greguol singles out the Goulburn Valley for stone fruit and apples, the Dandenongs for berries and the rich north-west around Mildura for its bounty of citrus fruits, grapes, nuts and olives. 'The Italian fraternity can take a big bow for all of that,' says Greguol.

COASTAL DELIGHTS While the Italians were making their mark on our vegetables, the Spanish were just as influential in fishing circles in Victoria, particularly in the early part of this century. Perhaps the best known was the Canals family who opened their Nicholson Street fish shop in 1931.

These days, the shop is run by Peter Canals, a well-known figure at the wholesale market and a prominent spokesman for the industry. In his time, he has supplied fish to just about

Clockwise from top left: The brilliant colour of summer berries; Clive Blazey's exotic salad greens; the remarkable colours and variety of Victorian potatoes; Brian Hussey's lettuce and herbs

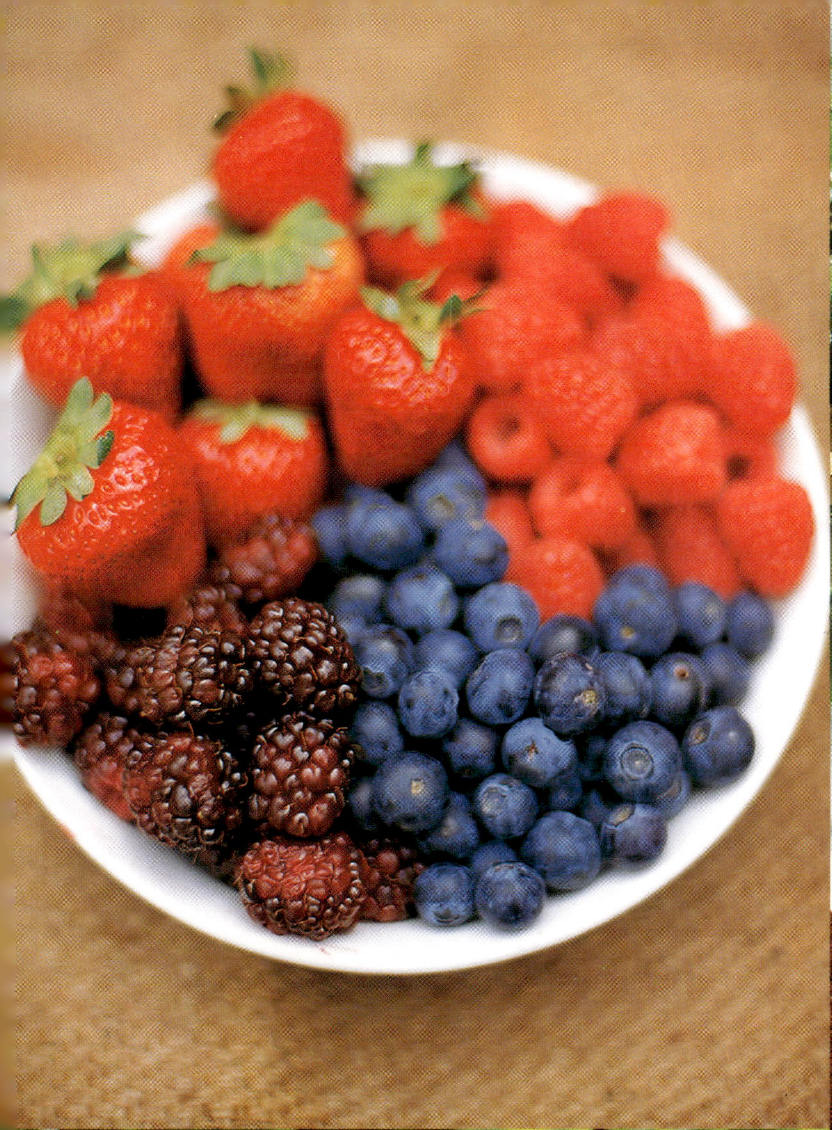
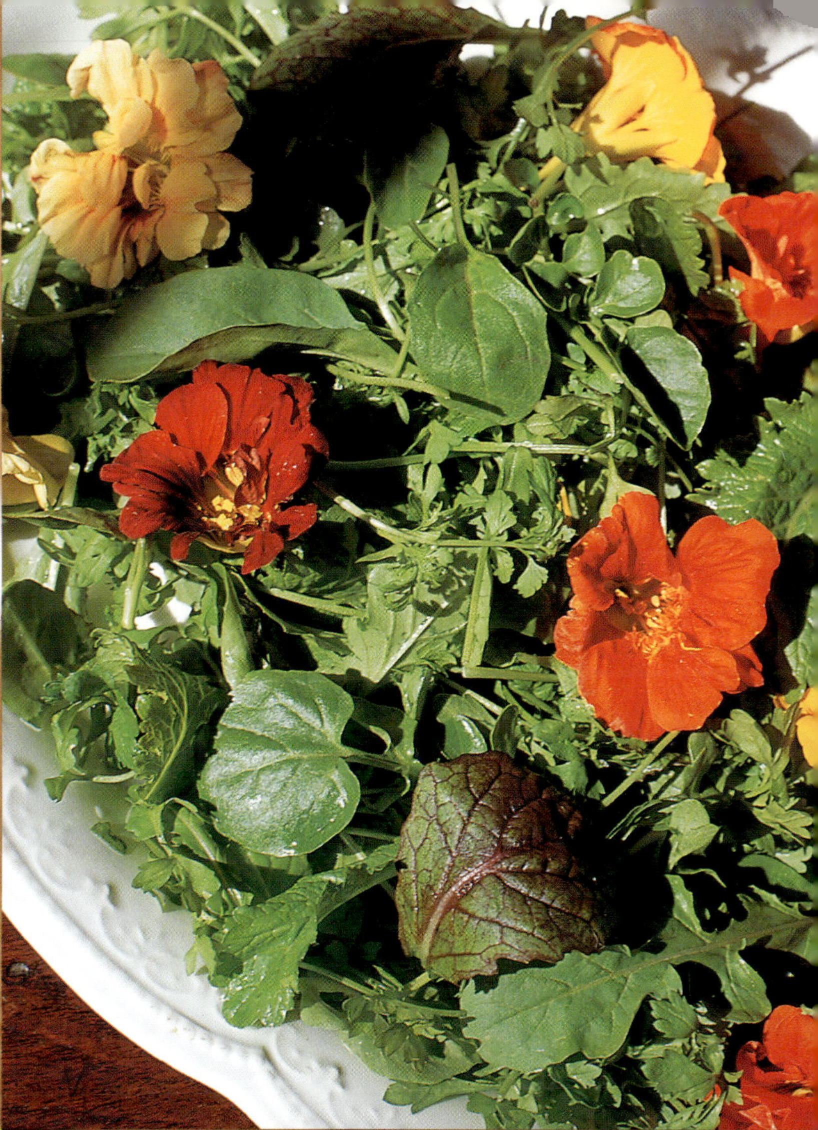
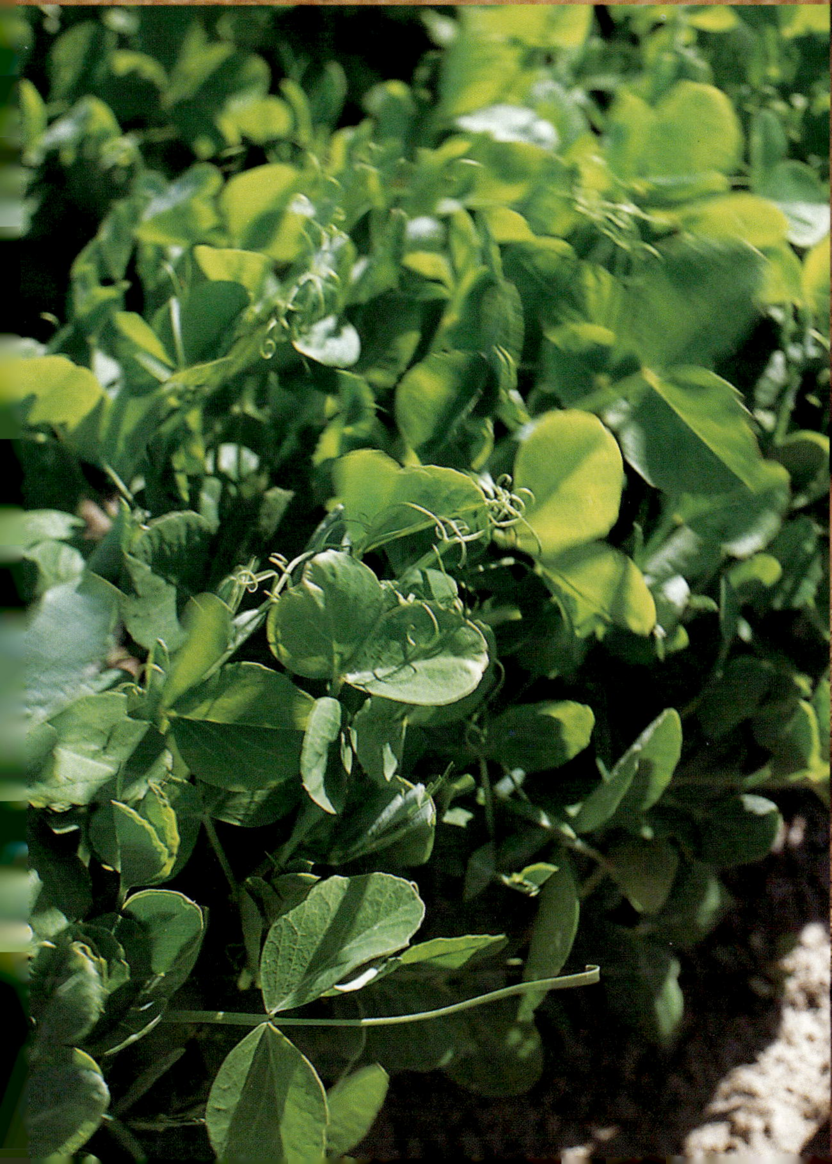
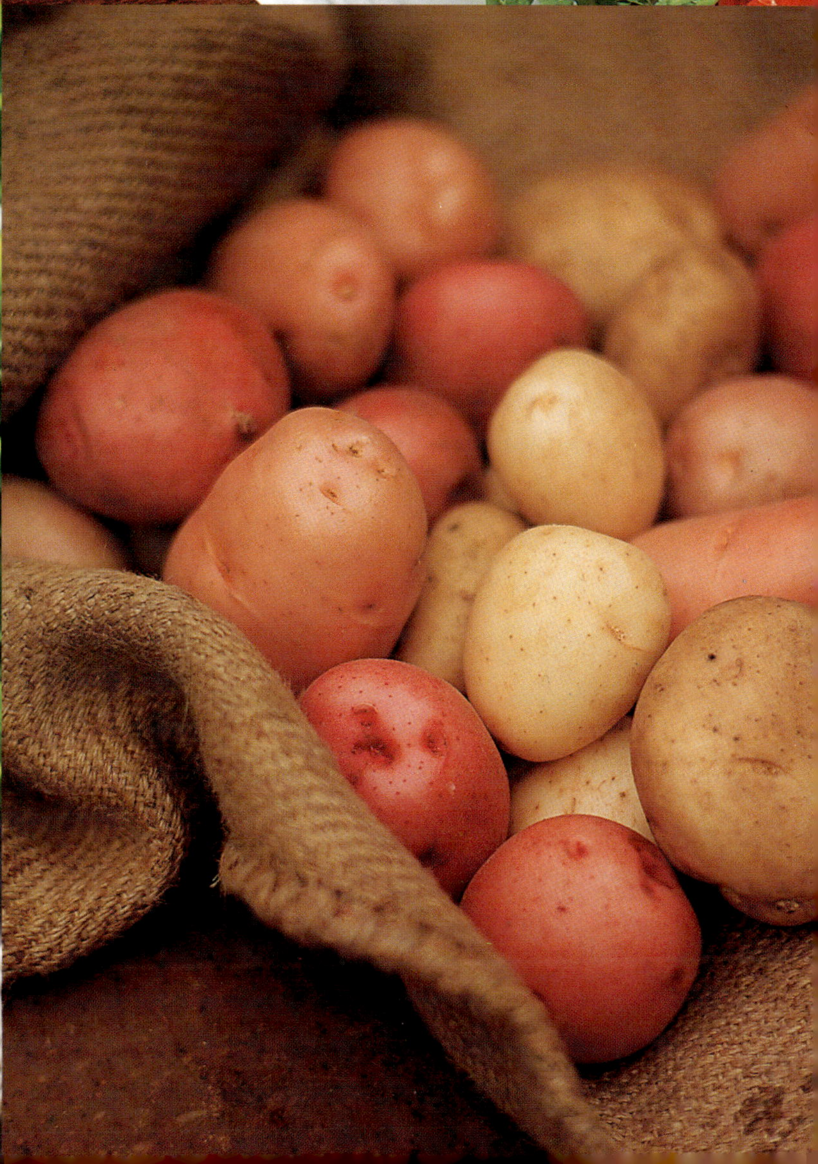

AUSTRALIA - A GOURMET'S PARADISE

every top restaurateur in town including Stephanie Alexander, Jean-Jacques Lale-Demoz, Gloria Staley and Gilbert Lau.

While Canals begrudgingly admits that Victoria doesn't boast the glamour breeds like barramundi, coral trout, red emperor, or the classic rock oyster, he is quick to point out that there is a lot of good eating to be had along the Victorian coast line.

His personal mini piscatorial tour begins at Portland in the west where the deep sea boats bring in plenty of orange ruffy, blue warehou, blue grenadier, ling and blue eye. Then it's on to Port Fairy, Port Campbell and Apollo Bay for rock lobster and maybe some abalone if you're lucky.

Next stop is Port Phillip with a quick call into Geelong, Queenscliff and Portarlington for some of the state's finest snapper, whiting that would rival the best from South Australia, and wonderful farmed mussels.

At San Remo, you'll find that shark becomes a local fish and chip shop treat known as 'flake', as well as good mullet, bream and whiting. Moving on, along the South Gippsland coast around Port Franklin and Welshpool, you'll discover copious amounts of garfish, calamari, rock flathead and whiting. After stocking up on more flathead and whiting and some magnificent wild local mussels at Lakes Entrance, it's on to Mallacoota for the state's best abalone, as well as some good bream and flathead.

But even when you run out of sea, you don't run out of fish in Victoria. Inland, you have yabbies and eels in the Western District, succulent salmon from Rubicon, and rainbow trout from the Goulburn River. Then, of course, there's the Murray cod, Murray perch and Murray crays, even if New South Wales regards the Murray River as its own.

A CORNUCOPIA OF TASTES With so much wonderful produce everywhere you look, it is little wonder that the restaurants of Melbourne are so exciting. There is barely a cuisine that can't be found on one of our famous food streets. The Chinese restaurants in Little Bourke Street in the city are the equal of their Hong Kong counterparts. Walk down Lygon Street in Carlton and suddenly you're in a Roman suburb. Visit Vietnam in Victoria Street, Richmond, and the Mediterranean in Fitzroy Street, St Kilda. In a single block in Brunswick Street, Fitzroy, you can choose between Turkish, Indian, Spanish, Thai, Italian, and modern Melbourne bistro cooking. While much has been written about the comparative merits of Sydney dining and Melbourne dining, they retain distinct differences that can be celebrated by both parties. We treasure our glorious dining-rooms, the sheer Victorian splendour of the Hotel Windsor, the formal drawing-room demeanour of Mietta's, the hallowed halls of Stephanie's and Jacques Reymond, the clubbiness of the marvellous mural room at Florentino and the imposing grandeur of the Flower Drum with its Forbidden City touches and unforbidden pleasures.

Yet at the same time a Melbournian can sniff out a wood-fired pizza oven at 500 paces, and will happily drive to the other side of town for a good caffe latte without giving it a second thought.

Whether it's breakfast at Marios in Fitzroy, morning coffee at Caffe e Cucina in Prahran, an afternoon-pick-me up at the George Cafe, a laid-back dinner at the Stokehouse on the beach at St Kilda, or a glamorous night out at Chinois in South Yarra, there is a quality to the eating that is irrevocably, unmistakably Melbourne.

But if the food has a local flavour, so too does the wine.

COOL CLIMATE WINES Since the 1960s there has been a renaissance in Victoria's wine industry with new wineries opening at such a head-spinning rate, you need to sit down with a glass of something just to contemplate the sheer magnitude of it all.

Wine lovers in Melbourne have a pretty soft time of it. In barely an hour, they can visit the lush Yarra Valley, or the new promised land known as the Mornington Peninsula, while most of the other wine-growing areas are perfect for a leisurely weekend away.

Victoria has become queen of the cool climate wines in this country, and a leader in the crisp, fresh styles that will steer the country into the twenty-first century. The soil, as well as the climate, can take a lot of the credit for the amazing quality of the wines.

Melbourne wine writer Mark Shield once noted that when Roseworthy Agricultural College built a computer model of the most desirable soils and climate for wine production and fed in data from around the country, seventy per cent of the best areas were located in Victoria.

The last rays of sun disappear over the cray pots at Apollo Bay

So what is the classic Victorian wine? Some would say it was sparkling burgundy, a rich, mellow and lively wine developed in the Great Western area, which now even has its own special day, celebrated in June each year. Others would unhesitatingly jump for the meaty reds, or the great fortified wines of Rutherglen, the deliciously sticky tokays and muscats of wineries like Chambers, Bullers, Morris' and Campbells. Then there are those who favour the elegant, beautifully structured chardonnays that have come out of the Yarra Valley in recent years, and the gloriously fresh and feisty pinot noirs of the Mornington Peninsula.

Others, still, say the great Victorian wine is yet to come, and when it does it will be made from an Italian grape variety, like the many being experimented with at the moment by forward-thinking wine-makers like Dromana Estate's Gary Crittenden, the hard-working crew at Brown Brothers at Milawa, and T'Gallant's Kathleen Quealy and Kevin McCarthy.

It's a lucky thing that we have so many wonderful wines to choose from. After all, with such a bounty of great food, great chefs, and passionate producers, Victorians have much that's worth raising a glass to.

Terry Durack

Right and above: Harvesting and sorting, key steps in the production of Rosella's famous tomato soup

A FAMILY FAVOURITE

With 100 years of providing Australian families with delicious, home-style soups, sauces, chutneys and pickles, Rosella is a household name. The distinctive Rosella bird and blue logo, one of the most well-known icons in Australia, signifies quality, reliability and tasty, wholesome foods. It would be hard to find an Australian child who didn't grow up enjoying Rosella's famous Tomato Soup!

Beginning in 1895 as a jam and preserved fruit business run by only two men, Rosella products—now made and marketed by Unifoods, a division of Unilever—are made in the company's plant at Tatura in the fertile Goulburn Valley, a major fruit and vegetable-growing region of Victoria.

Made only from Australia's finest produce, the Rosella brand is most famous for its rich sauced products, which include such established family favourites as Rosella Tomato Sauce, Tomato Soup, Pickles and Chutney and the latest product range Chicken Tonight Simmer Sauces. A wide variety of the freshest, highest-quality Australian vegetables are used, including mushrooms, onions, carrots, cauliflower and, of course, tomatoes. And while other companies produce their tomato sauces from reconstituted tomato paste, Unifoods is the only company in Australia to produce significant quantities of tomato products directly from fresh tomatoes.

The Tatura plant, which employs about 140 people, is one of the largest processors of tomatoes in the southern hemisphere. In view of Unifoods' strong commitment to continually supplying top-of-the-range products—particularly sauces—the company upgraded its factory in late 1994 with the aim of achieving an even more efficient manufacturing process.

Despite being a market leader at home, Unifoods has a number of products made specifically for the export market. Dishes popular in Australia—such as Chicken Tonight and the Raguletto Pasta Sauces—are adapted by specialist home economists and food technologists to suit the local tastes of Asian countries such as Japan, Taiwan and Korea.

With Rosella's superb quality, dependability and rich, healthy flavours, there's no doubt that it will continue to be a trusted name in Australian homes.

AUSTRALIA - A GOURMET'S PARADISE

CADBURY CALLS VICTORIA HOME

Cadbury Australia is an expanding international business which 'still calls Australia home'—and Victoria its home base.

Cadbury's head office and Pacific Rim operations are located on St Kilda Road, a famous tree-lined thoroughfare leading into the centre of Melbourne's business district. Two of Cadbury's major manufacturing plants are also located near Melbourne.

The Cadbury factory at Ringwood is one of the most modern confectionery plants in the Asia Pacific region. The Ringwood plant has continually been enlarged so that today it is a world-class, technologically advanced manufacturing and distribution centre. Cadbury has invested $25 million in a modern high-rise warehouse with a fully computerised and totally automated storage and retrieval system. The warehouse services all of Cadbury's Australian and export markets by providing the freshest products at all times.

At Ringwood, Cadbury manufactures many of its market-leading bar lines, such as Cherry Ripe, Crunchie, Picnic and Europe bars, as well as children's lines such as Freddo and Caramello Koala, and seasonal lines such as Cadbury and Red Tulip Easter and Christmas novelties.

Cadbury's major sugar confectionery factory is located at Scoresby. Like its sister plant, the Scoresby factory has been upgraded and enlarged. It produces Pascall, Molly Bushell and Harlequin sugar confectionery.

Cadbury is Australia's leading confectionery manufacturer in the $1.5 billion Australian confectionery market.

Right: Yarra Valley grapevines in autumn Above: Paul Bocuse restuarant; picnickers on the banks of the Yarra River

A MOUTH-WATERING FEAST

Victoria may be Australia's smallest mainland state but what it lacks in size, it more than makes up for in its harvest of riches—cultural, scenic spectacle, some of the world's finest food and wines and its magnificent capital city, cosmopolitan Melbourne.

The state is a feast for the food and wine-lover. A starting point is a visit to Melbourne's Queen Victoria markets where the eyes feast on mouth-watering displays of fruit and vegetables, meat, fish and delicatessen sections—sourced almost entirely from the state's premium food-producing regions.

The next priority is to visit some of the city's fine restaurants to sample these superb ingredients as interpreted by master chefs at world-renowned restaurants such as Stephanie's, Mietta's, Marchetti's Latin and Paul Bocuse.

Pleasurable eating experiences aren't exclusive to grand dining establishments, however. Melbourne has more than 3,000 restaurants offering over seventy national cuisines. Some streets are famous for their cuisine: Lygon street is 'Little Italy', Acland Street is famous for European cakes and deli items, while Brunswick Street is dotted with Indian, Malay, Japanese, Turkish and more.

Victoria has an impressive 230 wineries spread throughout nine distinct viticultural districts. Several are on Melbourne's doorstep: for example, the glorious Mornington Peninsula and the Yarra Valley.

In the tradition of wine-producing cultures, many regions celebrate the relationship of food and wine in characteristic style. Most famous is Melbourne's annual Food and Wine Festival (February/March)—a veritable showcase of the state's richesse. A highlight on Australia's gourmet calendar, it is one event celebrities from the world stage of food and wine daren't miss.

Tourism Victoria produces a range of publications providing information to visitors on the wide variety of the state's attractions. These include a Touring Guide to the Wine Regions of Victoria, Great Victorian Motoring Holidays and a Victorian Bed and Breakfast Getaways brochure, and, together with the 'family' of regional brochures, they ensure Victoria's food and wine attractions are accessible to all visitors.

SOUTH A

Right: A Barrossa valley vineyard soaks up the unrelenting South Australian sun
Below: The Red Ochre Grill, where bush tucker meets the palate of city dwellers; sand dune-like mountains of salt

154

USTRALIA

Tradition with a Twist

Let's look at what's on the menu right now.

Essence of snapper with seared abalone, pickled ginger and coriander; blue fin tuna in tempura crust with snow peas; kangaroo fillet, calves liver and quince with blackcurrant sauce; charlotte of cumquats and ladyfingers scented with anis. That's from a recent menu prepared by masterchef Urs Inauen, a lecturer at Adelaide's Regency College Hotel School.

Or from the menu at the Red Ochre Grill, the popular restaurant run by South Australia's bush tucker guru Andrew Fielke: hot and sour kangaroo tail soup with Kakadu plums; blue swimmer crab custard in filo pastry with crab and lemon aspen sauce; rabbit fillet with muntries risotto and fresh green peppercorn cream.

THE MELTING POT Local produce subjected to a melting pot of cultural influences, a blend of styles and techniques from all over the world, multicultural, global in character, yet uniquely Australian. It has come together better in Adelaide probably than anywhere else in Australia.

How did this small-city state come to be regarded as the gastronomic capital of Australia by gourmets and food writers in the early 1990s? How is it that, although hard hit by recession and the loss of several of its important 'icon' restaurants, it still manages to earn a respect for its strong food and wine culture which seems out of proportion to its small population of a mere 1.3 million, nine-tenths of it concentrated in Adelaide?

Even more than Sydney or Melbourne, Adelaide's culinary development was retarded by the curse of the Anglo-Saxons who colonised South Australia in 1836. If kangaroo or possum appeared on a dinner table then, as it surely did, it was from necessity rather than choice. For the next 130 years it was to be mutton or beef and the obligatory three veg for South Australians. But, even then, several events took place which came to be of great culinary significance to the state.

The first wave of non-Anglo Saxon migrants arrived in 1838—Silesian settlers led by Pastor Augustus Kavel, escaping religious persecution from what is now northern Germany. This was 150 years before food writer Stephanie Alexander would write in her book *Stephanie's Australia* that 'migrants are Australia's most important gastronomic resource'. It was to be especially true in South Australia, with its small, malleable population and brittle economy, both of which would be readily influenced by future waves of migrants.

The Silesians appeared odd and uncouth to the xenophobic English settlers, who nonetheless welcomed the poultry, butter, vegetables and fruit that these industrious migrants were soon selling from their small farms at Hahndorf and Lobethal in the Adelaide Hills, the Barossa Valley and Klemzig in Adelaide itself.

In the 1840s grapes were planted in the Barossa Valley, by both English and German settlers, starting a wine industry which would grow to be one of the biggest in Australia and, now, one of the most significant in the world. About fifty per cent of Australia's wine is currently produced in South Australia, which has six major wine regions: the Barossa Valley, the Southern Vales, the Adelaide Hills, the Clare Valley, Coonawarra and the Riverland. Apart from their obvious value as wine producers, these regions also provide focal points for the development of regional cuisines, signs of which are now emerging.

Another early planting, which unfortunately didn't survive commercially, was of olive trees. Cuttings were collected from prime olive orchards around Marseille and brought to Australia in 1844. More cuttings soon followed from Lisbon, Nice, Florence and Bari, and in 1851 pioneer colonist Sir Samuel Davenport sent olive oil to the Great Exhibition in London where it was declared to be equal to the best oil from Lucca.

It was clear that the South Australian climate was ideal for olive growing and books were written on its cultivation, but it failed to take root. Perhaps local farmers were too poor to wait seven years for an economic return, and instead went for faster fortunes in wheat, barley and sheep. The legacy of those early olive groves is now spread through the Adelaide Hills where tens of thousands of olive trees still grow, unkempt and in awkward places, picked only by Greeks and Italians who can't believe their good fortune in having such a resource growing wild. Now a new olive oil industry is emerging, with new plantings and new technology.

The way local olive oil is being regarded today is, perhaps, symbolic of the many other culinary opportunities which slipped away from this still predominantly Anglo-Saxon community. Not that we were so different from any other Australians.

Simplicity is best—pure cold-pressed olive oil and olives in oil

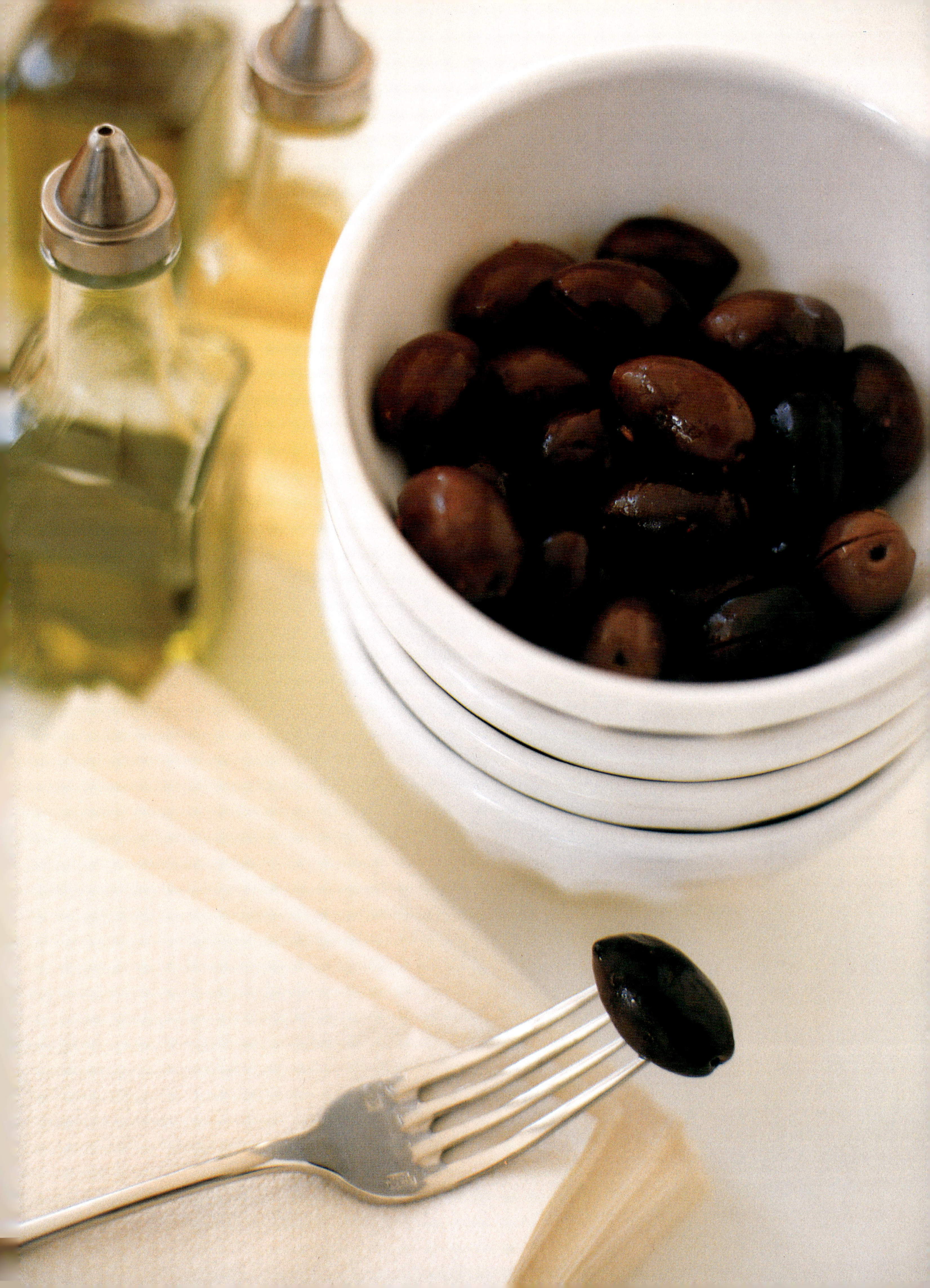

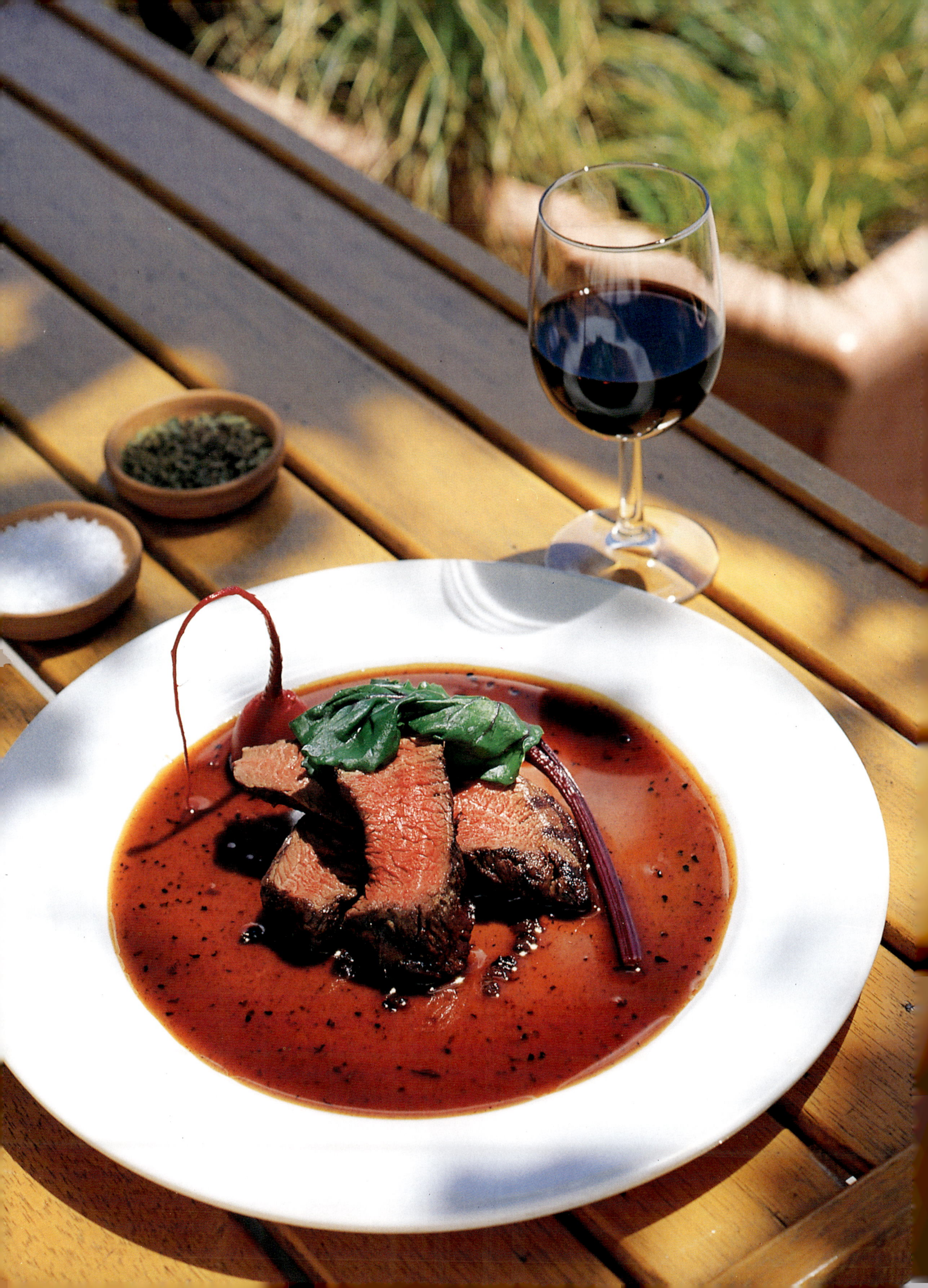

It's probably too simple to attribute the liberalisation of Australian eating habits to various waves of migration. As Michael Symons asks in his book *The Shared Table*, how do we account for the sudden interest in Chinese cooking in the late 1950s when our Chinese population had reached an historic low? How does Australia account for our very early affection for French food, when we have never had a significant number of French migrants?

OPPORTUNITIES FOR ALL Yet in South Australia the influence of German, Greek, Italian, Chinese, Yugoslav and, latterly, Vietnamese migration has shown very clearly in its restaurants. Also significant is the effect some of these groups have had on the market gardens, the markets and shops—the basic food supply.

It started with the Germans, as already mentioned. Then, late last century, Italian migrants—mostly from Molfetta on the Adriatic coast—started a South Australian fishing industry, predominantly in Port Adelaide and Port Pirie.

Here was another missed opportunity for the Anglo-Saxons, almost as pitiful as the olive oil. It would be another seventy years before they would recognise squid or tommy ruffs as good for anything except bait, although even they could not fail to appreciate the extraordinary quality of the local King George whiting, or the prawns and lobsters these Italian fishermen brought in.

Two world wars brought successive waves of soldier settlers, many of whom took up blocks of land in the Riverland, where a major stone fruit and citrus industry would become the basis of the regional economy, along with vast plantings of both table and wine grapes. More soldier settlers went to Kangaroo Island to farm wheat and sheep. Today traditional farming is giving way to alternative food crops in both regions, often very much with an eye to export markets.

Then, of course, in the fifties, all over Australia, came the great post-war migrations from Europe and the culinary transformation of the country began.

It is still a matter of debate as to where and by whom the first espresso coffee was poured in Adelaide. It could have been in 1952 at the Mocca Bar in Hindley Street from one of those wonderful old, glowing Gaggias with pump handles. This event marked the beginnings of civilised culinary life in Adelaide, even though the only decent Italian cooking in the city was in the boarding houses where the young Italian migrants lived.

By the mid-sixties, Adelaide had only half a dozen Chinese restaurants and even fewer Italian. Slowly they crept into Hindley Street—the Sorrento, Pagana's, the Flash coffee bar, Marcellina's, the Star grocery.

Red Ochre Grill's kangaroo fillet with baby beet and a pepperberry glaze

Right: Pure white sea-salt mountains at Price, in brilliant contrast with the bright blue South Australian sky
Above: The familiar Saxa salt shaker

SALT FROM THE SEA

Cerebos products have been inextricably linked with the Australian way, with the culture of Aussie cuisine, for the past three generations. Specialising in condiments (it does best in sauces and gravies, both wet and dry), its brands have very strong, established recognition. Out of its 150 different product lines, Gravox is the big thing at Cerebos, together with Fountain tomato sauce and Saxa salt (open Australia's kitchen cupboards and you will find Saxa in perhaps eighty per cent of them).

When you're onto a good thing, stick to it: although the Australian palate has surely become more sophisticated in the past ten or twenty years, the tradition of 'meat and three veg' is definitely still alive and well (the eight most preferred home-cooked meals revolve around this staple). And the champion is the roast; and Roast and Gravox gravy are synonymous. So Cerebos continues to play an integral part in Australia's food chain.

Cerebos is a quiet achiever (the stamp of the quintessential Australian), a company of steady and unassuming growth. Already it exports to the Pacific Islands and New Zealand, and holds a substantial position in the Asian market through its Cerebos Asia Division (China, a country very interested in sauces, is a place to cultivate interest). And new products are always in the process of development, mostly at the main site in Sydney, and mostly using Australian ingredients. For example, the Saxa range of cooking and table salts uses exclusively Australian sea-salt—from arguably the cleanest beaches in the world—and, through contractors in Parkes, New South Wales, Cerebos grows and processes its own tomato crops for its Fountain range.

With 400 employees and sales offices in every state, the future for Cerebos is one of great expectations. Cerebos will be there to dress the bland, to titillate the palate and, by offering convenience and choice, to make meal-time decisions a pleasure.

Soon the Yugoslavs and Greeks were doing a vigorous trade with barbecue grills, like the Barbecue Inn, and the famous fish and chipperies of Gouger Street—Paul's, George's, Stanley's and the Gouger Cafe—opened and continue to thrive today.

The more 'sensible' Anglo-Saxons still dined at the South Australia Hotel, the Arkaba Steak Cellar, the Starlight Room at the Hotel Australia, or at the Feathers Hotel where one day in 1968 a young Austrian chef named Peter Jarmer started work.

His story is not unique, but it perfectly illustrates the dramatic transition that was about to take place in Australian cooking and in which, as far as Adelaide was concerned, Jarmer was to play a significant role.

He had trained in Austria, worked in Sweden's Opera House restaurant and grand hotel restaurants, and knew how to cook better than all but a few chefs in Adelaide at that time. However, he was forced to take a job as a cook's assistant, just a step up from washing the dishes.

He graduated to cooking pub counter lunches and smorgasbords, then sous chef at the Arkaba Hotel making prawn cocktails, omelettes, three soups and whiting cooked all ways. Then as head chef at Benjamin's, a stylish restaurant by the Torrens Weir, he introduced Adelaide to yabbies, served Swedish-style with dill mayonnaise.

Jarmer recalls that in the early 1970s few customers were interested in yabbies—not when lobster and mud crab were only six dollars per kilo.

He accepted an offer to teach nouvelle cuisine at the new Regency College Hotel School, which itself would go on to play a major influential role in the development of culinary and hospitality skills in South Australia.

Knowing little about nouvelle cuisine he went to Sydney and talked to chefs such as Mogens Bay Esbensen, Damien Pignolet and Michael Manners. He returned so excited he couldn't wait to get back into a restaurant. And he did, in 1981 at Reilly's, which had just been vacated by another highly significant chef, Philip Searle.

Two years later Jarmer would win *The Bulletin* magazine/Quelltaler Wine award for best food in South Australia. The best steak, incidentally, was still at the Barbecue Inn, the best 'ethnic' at the Italian restaurant Ettore, and the best

South Australia - Tradition with a Twist

wine list at Le Paris (in the hands of Nick Papazahariakis, who now has Chloes and still has the best wine list).

This was a marvellously exciting period for Adelaide restaurants. While Jean Mahe was cooking fine, classical French food at L'Epicurean, Philip Searle (at Possums from 1984) was startling the locals with such daring creations such as his famed checkerboard ice-cream, Maggie Beer was just getting going at the Pheasant Farm near Tanunda in the Barossa Valley, and Cheong Liew was cooking electrifyingly original food at Neddy's.

ORIGINAL FOOD When the history of the development of Australian cuisine is written, Cheong will have a chapter to himself, so influential has he been. Coming to Australia in 1973 from Kuala Lumpur as a young engineering student, he dropped out, tried accounting, dropped out, and started making sandwiches for pub lunches. Both his father and grandfather had run restaurants in Malaysia, so he wasn't a total novice.

He finally gravitated in the right direction and became the grill chef at a popular Greek restaurant where he soon started to bend the rules; his lobster à la plaka, for example, featured a white wine sauce with tomato, black olives and lightly melted fetta cheese—heresy to Greeks who had never thought of cooking fetta in their sauces, but it was so delicious it stayed on the menu.

More international boundaries crumbled as Cheong moved on to Jill Heaven's Lord Kitchener's Restaurant, then Moos, another of her restaurants where Cheong brought together all the threads of his experience—Malaysian, Indian, French, Greek and, above all, Chinese.

In 1975, with partner Barry Ross, he opened Neddy's, a small, run-down restaurant in Adelaide's Hutt Street. His hungry mind drew on everything from the more classical training of his fellow chefs to a cookery book from New York's Four Seasons restaurant (where they concentrated on using local ingredients) and a Salvador Dali cookery book whose decorative presentation appealed to Cheong.

Left: Harvesting strawberries for Beerenberg jams
Above: Cheong Liew shares his knowledge with trainee chefs

It suddenly occurred to him that he should call on everything that he knew. It led to an ornamental style, drawing on a broad blend of techniques, making the best possible use of local ingredients.

It predated Ken Hom's East meets West or any other notion of so-called 'fusion' cuisine. It was also a year before Alice Waters presented her first regionally-inspired menu in 1976 at Chez Panisse in California, and it may be that food historians will argue that this was one of the real starting points of Australia's new cuisine.

Cheong had taken a multitude of cuisines with an Australian ingredient to create a perfect multicultural blend. It was unique, not to be found anywhere else in the world.

Cheong believes he was probably the first chef in Australia to put kangaroo on a restaurant menu, and that his salad of Moreton Bay bugs was the beginning of warm salads in this country. His menu would soon include signature dishes such as kangaroo marinated in wine and vinegar, served with mustard and fennel bulb poached in milk; octopus fried in olive oil with avocado and quail egg salad; pot-roasted pigeon finished with parmesan and breadcrumbs; steamed cucumber and lamb's brains with a spicy red sauce; and pork hocks served with wood fungus and yellow ginger-flower rice, which many of Cheong's former customers still believe to be perhaps the best thing they've ever eaten.

REGIONAL CUISINE But if it was Cheong Liew who started to give some definition to what might conceivably be a uniquely Australian cuisine—and there are still many Australians who believe such a thing is unlikely if not impossible—it was Maggie Beer who gave Australia its best articulation of an Australian regional cuisine.

Admittedly she had the good fortune that her husband, Colin, had started his pheasant farm several years earlier in the Barossa Valley, where a strong German culinary tradition had survived in its butchers, bakers and home cooking.

Beer was a city girl, from Sydney, from a family of passionate cooks. In what seemed to her to be a natural adjunct to the farm business, she started a farm shop selling pates, terrines, cooked take-away pheasant, pickled quails eggs and freshly baked bread.

After nine months of this she decided to go the whole hog and open a restaurant, the Pheasant Farm, in 1979—an audacious move given that it was tucked away in the rural backblocks. It seemed the most natural thing in the world to her to look around at that local tradition and the produce it had spawned.

She soon had local growers providing her with mallard ducks, hare shot in nearby vineyards, yabbies from local farm dams, blue swimmer crabs from nearby Port Pareham on St Vincent

Maggie Beer and her irresistible pates, now sold throughout Australia

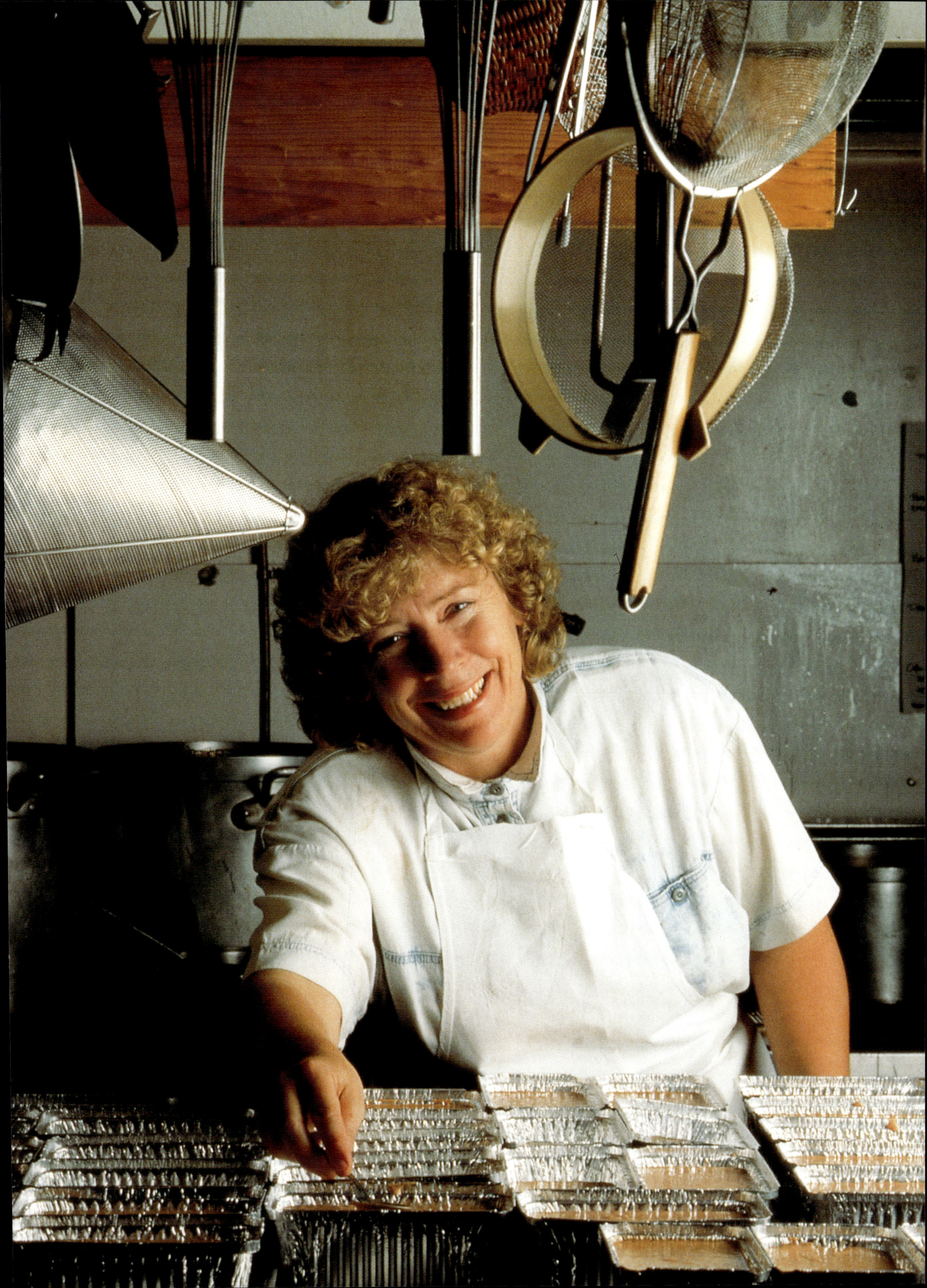

OLIVERHILL
WINERY
KAY BROS
WINERY
CORIOLE
WINERY
SEAVIEW
WINERY
CHAPEL HILL
d'ARENBERG
WINERY
MERRIVALE
WINERY

Gulf, turnips and salsify, wild mushrooms from pine forests at Mount Crawford, the fiddle-head ferns which grew on her property, local pears, quinces and citrus fruit, and she persuaded one of the local butchers to smoke kangaroo when he wasn't smoking bacon and speck.

Just as important to the restaurant's success was its relationship with many of the valley's wine-makers. A synergy developed between chef, produce providers and wine-makers which enabled an intense sense of regionality to be developed and exploited.

Naturally there was pheasant on the menu, roasted hard for twelve minutes—a technique she perfected and taught others. Her favourite pheasant dish, she says, was pheasant roasted with native currants pickled in Pernod, served with braised witlof.

Then there was the saddle of hare served with pickled green walnuts, a hare glaze and spatzle (tiny dumplings); and the roasted pigeon (caught in the coppermine ruins at Burra), served with baby beetroot, skordalia made with walnuts and lots of garlic, and a pigeon glaze.

Her favourite dish of all was duck egg pasta tumbled with shavings of smoked kangaroo, sun-dried tomatoes, pine nuts and Parmigiano Reggiano. A summer variation had the smoked kangaroo tossed with rocket and witlof, topped with fat, pink globules of keta caviar.

It had not been Beer's original intention to make the Pheasant Farm a grand restaurant. We're not haute cuisine, she would say, we're country. But her 'cuisine of the sun' consistently brought national and world recognition, and when it won a *Gourmet Traveller* magazine Restaurant of the Year award the judge, Parisian-based Patricia Wells, remarked that the Pheasant Farm had most captured the mood and spirit of Australia.

The demise of the Pheasant Farm at the end of 1993 left a gap which has not yet been filled, although there are a significant number of restaurants in several other wine regions which are promoting a strong sense of regionality. These include the tiny restaurant attached to Skillogalee winery, Tatehams in Auburn, Vintners and 1918 in the Barossa, Cafe C at Springton, the Uraidla Aristologist and Bridgewater Mill in the Adelaide Hills, and the Salopian Inn and Leonard's Mill further south.

WEEKEND FOR ALL South Australia has, however, developed a series of regional food and wine festivals whose contribution to creating a genuine, egalitarian food and wine culture in the state has been undervalued.

The first was the Clare Gourmet Weekend, started in 1984, a straggling picnic of an event which involved nearly all of the valley's twenty or so wineries and a mixture of local and city chefs. The concept quickly spread to the Barossa Valley which now has both a gourmet weekend and the biennial vintage fest, the Southern Vales, which has a Bushing Festival and,

Clockwise from top left: The spacious, tiered interior of the Granary restaurant at Bridgewater Mill; pork and crab sausages with a chilli and coriander sauce by Libby Tinsley at the Granary restaurant; a collection of local wineries; vines carpet the dry soil of the Clare Valley

AUSTRALIA - A GOURMET'S PARADISE

A BLEND OF CULTURES

Few would dispute the credentials of South Australia as one of the nation's pre-eminent gourmet states. Certainly no one argues that it is Australia's major wine producer. The facts speak for themselves. The state produces more than sixty per cent of Australia's output—almost all of it at the premium end of the market.

South Australia's wine-producing regions also deliver value-added enjoyment in their enormous tourist appeal—as do the many quality restaurants and atmospheric pubs that dot the countryside.

You don't have to be a wine aficionado to enjoy sipping and sampling your way through some of the most heart-achingly beautiful scenery that awaits the visitor to the wine country—but chances are you'll become one.

There's the Barossa Valley with its colourful German traditions, the romantic Clare Valley with its Cornish origins, the sheer spectacle of the Fleurieu Peninsula's Wine Coast and the enchantment of the Adelaide Hills region to name just a few. Each of the regions celebrate the marriage of food and wine in their own memorable style.

Nor do all good things come in a bottle in South Australia. While many of the bottles contain wines easily described as liquid sunshine—which reflect the state's climate and regional diversity—much of South Australia's bounty comes on a plate.

The state can legitimately claim some of the nation's finest restaurants. On a per capita basis, Adelaide has the highest concentration of restaurants in Australia and the quality is uniformly good. The state is also a breeding ground for some of the nation's most highly-regarded chefs.

But fine chefs can only deliver the goods if the goods are worthy. Among South Australia's many attributes is a climate conducive to the

South Australia - Tradition with a Twist

production of fine foods. Its southern seaboard is a vast source of fresh fish—chief among them as many a food lover will endorse—is their superb whiting, South Australian crayfish from Kangaroo Island, and Coffin Bay oysters. South Australian chefs also pioneered the preparation and presentation of kangaroo as a gourmet item. The state also produces a wealth of fine quality fruits, vegetables and excellent meats.

These taste experiences, coupled with romantic stays in charming heritage-style guest accommodation—or sleek, city hotels (if you prefer)—ensure South Australia's enduring appeal. Then too, there's the majesty of its rugged outback regions: the moody beauty of the Flinders Ranges with their spring carpets of wildflowers, the intriguing flora and fauna of Kangaroo Island, and the curious lunar-like landscape of Coober Pedy, the opal mining town where the inhabitants live underground.

Another integral part of South Australia's heritage is its reputation as the Festival State. South Australians love to celebrate. They'll turn any event into a festival—a culture which springs from its robust, cosmopolitan mix of peoples. And the biennial Adelaide Arts Festival is recognised as one of the premier events of its kind in the world, equal in stature to the Edinburgh Festival.

South Australia is truly a state of plenty.

Left: Another stunning day dawns at Port Augusta Far Left: Feasting, dancing and merry-making are all part of the annual Hahndorf Schutzenfest Above: A view of the city of Adelaide with the River Torrens and Festival Centre in the foreground

because it overlooks St Vincent Gulf, a wine and seafood festival called From the Sea and the Vines, and a Harvest Festival in the Adelaide Hills.

The collective impact they have made in exposing large numbers of people to excellent food and wine with a distinct regional bias can't be underestimated. They are attended by up to 20,000 people, only a few of them committed foodies, so the bulk are ordinary citizens who can't avoid in this way becoming more food and wine conscious.

Just as important has been the growing awareness throughout South Australia of the commercial value of regional produce. This is, of course, in keeping with national trends towards rural diversification and export potential, as well as a growing community desire for authenticity—'real' food with real flavour. And regional food producers in South Australia continue to expand and prosper. An oyster industry, for instance, that was once focused only on Coffin Bay, near Port Lincoln, now has sprawled around the West Coast to include half a dozen more localities such as Smokey Bay and Ceduna. Port Lincoln, which hosts one of the largest deep-sea fishing fleets in Australia and is a major source of blue fin tuna, also has a tuna farming industry which is expanding faster than all expectations.

Squid and octopus caught in local gulfs until recently, like the delicious little tommy ruffs, were regarded as no better than bait, now compete for a place on the table with snapper, garfish and the highly-prized King George whiting, which are unique to South Australian waters. Scallop, mussels, abalone (much of it goes to a huge export market in Asia) and blue swimmer crabs are popular and readily available seafoods.

The produce is eclectic and exciting, with varieties extending from bush tucker farmers in the far north growing quandongs, samphire, bush tomatoes and muntries, to olive growers and yabbie farmers in the mid-north—where a start is being made on establishing a sheep's milk cheese industry—and to exotic potato growers in the Adelaide Hills (where up to fifteen varieties are now being grown). Venison, smoked salmon, walnuts, chestnuts, geese, raspberries and milk-fed veal can be found along with more traditional produce.

Typical of the regional potential now being exploited is Kangaroo Island, where comparisons are being drawn with King Island or even Tasmania itself.

Right: Olive groves in the Adelaide foothills where Joe Grilli sources his olives for his premium olive oil Above right:Joseph Foothills extra virgin olive oil, regarded as one of Australia's best olive oils

Depressed rural markets for wheat and wool, and growing local and export demand for clean food, has brought embryonic new products such as sheep's milk cheese and yoghurt, baby lamb, a burgeoning marron industry, free range chickens (the island is free of predators such as foxes), honey, wine, olives, oysters, and development of its traditional lobster (up to 20 tonnes a week in season, mostly exported to Asia) and scale fish industries.

The development of the local olive oil industry is an indication of the enthusiasm and speed with which these new products are being produced. Three years ago South Australia had only two small-scale commercial olive oil producers, Mark Lloyd at his Coriole winery near McLaren Vale, and fellow wine-maker Joe Grilli at Primo Estate on the Adelaide Plains, each of whom produced limited amounts of high quality oil.

Much more oil was pressed from olives growing wild along roadsides and in Hills gullies, the legacy of those early plantings last century, picked by Italian and Greek families who took them to the three or four small presses around the city.

The introduction of two state-of-the-art small olive processing plants in the past two years has provided a major breakthrough, both in production cost and quality. A recent tasting of boutique olive oils in Adelaide showed their number had swelled to at least fifteen.

New olive orchards are being planted, radically different cultivation and picking methods are being considered, and there is hope this will grow into a major new food industry for South Australia.

MARKET DAYS A stroll through Adelaide's Central Market, Australia's oldest city market in one location, vividly illustrates the great diversity and high quality of South Australian produce. Compact and colourful, this market is one of the finest of its kind in the world, fringed by Adelaide's small Chinatown and more than forty restaurants. Fruit, vegetables, herbs and flowers from Adelaide Hills and plains jostle for space with seafood from local gulfs, stalls selling milk-fed veal or kangaroo salami, home-cured prosciutto, local olive oils and cheeses, speciality teas and coffees, prize-winning chocolates, Chinese herbalists, coffee shops and Asian cafes selling the best laksa in town. Although products such as these are now almost taken for granted in Adelaide's better restaurants.

It is also true to say that the huge influx of cafe/bistro establishments, and the closure of some of the city's 'icon' restaurants, has for the time being changed the nature of the city.

But the change has been less dramatic than some people think. Prophets of doom have pointed to an exodus of Adelaide chefs to Sydney, but these were fewer and longer ago than is sometimes remembered.

The overall standard of Adelaide's restaurants remains uncommonly high. Some, such as Nediz Tu where Le Tu Thai and Kate Sparrow have taken over Cheong Liew's mantle, are still among the best in Australia, and absurdly inexpensive by national standards. The old dictum that it is possible to eat better for less in Adelaide than anywhere else in Australia remains true.

More significantly, with few exceptions, those chefs who have closed their restaurants have stayed in South Australia and now contribute to developing its culinary culture in a variety of ways, probably now influencing a broader range of people and tastes than they did when cooking in their inevitably elitist restaurants.

Chefs such as Maggie Beer, Cheong Liew, Urs Inauen, Ann Oliver and Cath Kerry are teaching, writing books, catering and in general acting as culinary ambassadors for the state. The only significant recent departure, Lew Kathreptis, who closed his highly-acclaimed and innovative Mezes restaurant, is cooking at the Australian High Commission in London— another culinary ambassador.

He will almost certainly return because, despite the pressures and frustrations of financially-stressed times, Adelaide remains an exciting place for a chef. It is a small city surrounded by vineyards and farms, where the conjunction of chef, customer, food grower and wine-maker is closer than in any other Australian city.

Nigel Hopkins

Left to right, top to bottom: Joe Grilli, maker of the Joseph Foothills olive oil and also the winemaker at Primo Estate; freshly baked bread; every style of prepared kangaroo meat one could want; deli goods on display at Adelaide's Central Markets; Red Ochre Grill's wallaby and rabbit fillets wrapped in prosciutto with a Madeira and pepper leaf glaze; bursting with colour and freshness, an array of fruit and vegetables at Adelaide's Central Markets; choose from a selection of fresh fruit while walking along Rundle Mall; pick from the best that South Australia has to offer: salsa, chutney, Lemon Aspen dressing, olive oil or Ligurian bee honey; Kate Sparrow and Le Tu Thai

TURKEYS
CHICKENS
DUCKS
GEESE

BULK SPECIAL
2 kg LOTS
6 80
ROO BURGERS
6 150
Quality
KANGAROO SHASLICKS
75
KANGAROO MARINATED
FRUITY APRICOT STEAKS
5.40 kg
KANGAROO BARBEQUE STEAK
5.40 kg

4.99
Csabai
1.49

SWEET MUSCATELS
2.99

MAGGIE BEER'S VIRGIN OLIVE OIL.
$9.50 375ML
EXCLUSIVE TO KANGAROO ISLAND LIGURIAN BEE PURE HONEY

WESTERN A

*Right: The eerie lunar-like landscape of the Pinacles desert, 200 kilometres north of Perth
Above: Harvesting rockmelons in the Ord River, Kununurra; one of Western Australia's key exports, sheep meat*

AUSTRALIA

A Different Time and Space

Arrive in the west, and you can't escape the feeling that you're somewhere very different. The clocks go back two hours, the sun sets in the sea (in the Indian Ocean), and yet it's still Australia! And whether you've taken the long drive across the Nullarbor, spent a couple of nights on the Indian Pacific train or several hours on a plane, the feeling of distance and isolation is palpable.

To the ninety per cent of Australians in the east, the west is the distant, undiscovered part of Australia. Strange, then, that to the overseas visitor, Western Australia is the state most quintessentially Australian. It's Australia in the raw—the way it is internationally imagined. If you think of the Australian lifestyle, the west is where it abounds: sunny, unpolluted and slow-paced. But, most importantly, it's where Australia is at its most spacious. Western Australia's greatest resource is its unspoiled, unpopulated space. Two-and-half-million square kilometres of it shared by only 1.7 million people. That's nearly one and a half square kilometres each!

Western Australia's size also makes it Australia's most diverse state. It's the only one whose boundaries extend from the very top to the very bottom of this grand, old continent and has everything in between: tropics, stark desert, beautiful beaches, awe-inspiring eucalypt forest, and wheat and wool country. Isolated as it is by a 12,500 kilometre stretch of coastline and a vast inhospitable desert, it is hermetically sealed against the rest of the country. There are species of plants and animals in Western Australia that occur nowhere else in the country. This gives the west a look and an atmosphere distinct from the rest of the continent.

It is a different place with a different pace. With such distances to travel, why hurry? In true Australian style the locals have simplified the huge spaces to three points on the compass: 'up north' is anywhere north of Perth, 'down south' is anywhere south of Perth and everywhere else in Australia is 'over east'.

But such generalities hide a multitude of climates. Each point on the compass points the way to a vastly different agricultural landscape. North points the way to Carnarvon vegetables and to the tropical fruits of Kununurra; east is the huge strip of wheat, wool, lamb and beef country; south is the land of vineyards, marron farms, dairy farms and Harvey beef; and west is the Indian ocean and its bounty for which Western Australia is quite rightly famous.

Given its small population and remoteness, it is a shock to visit market stalls or a delicatessen and taste the huge range of locally-produced edibles on offer, or to experience the diversity and quality of wine that the state produces. Walk through Northbridge in Perth and you'll be surprised at the sophistication of the food. Go to a restaurant and you'll find a huge choice of viands: where else can you eat emu, goat, lamb, beef, venison, buffalo, fish, marron, yabbies, oysters, mussels and lobster all farmed in the same state?

This quality and diversity of local produce is highlighted in the superb, more often that not, laid back style of the local restaurants.

IDYLLIC EXPERIENCES In a quiet corner of Perth behind an unpretentious facade lies the sun-drenched courtyard restaurant San Lorenzo. In these rather laid-back surroundings Gary Jones, 1994 winner of the Remy Martin/*Gourmet Traveller* Restaurant of the Year Award, showcases his culinary talents. Jones' spirit and creativity combines classic French technique with Eastern and Asian flavours to produce dishes which metamorphose into a distinctive Australian style.

San Lorenzo takes the tastebuds around the world. In dishes such as kangaroo with spiced lentils, served with tiny samosas filled with minced kangaroo, taste the spice markets of Thailand and India, along with uniquely Australian meat. Western Australian dhufish and scallops also feature on the menu, which captures the flair of Jones' style and the unusual marriage of tastes extracts the maximum flavour from each ingredient.

For casual but elegant dining, again with a West Australian flavour, Gershwin's Restaurant at the Hyatt Regency Perth is worth a visit. Proudly creating innovative 'West Coast Cuisine', the chefs at Gershwin's use the very best West Australian produce to create exciting taste combinations. Chef de Cuisine Mark Sainsbury combines a selection of the ocean's best, such as rock lobster, coral trout, dhufish and scallops, with carefully selected fresh produce from local markets. Signature Gershwin dishes include the succulent West Australian rock lobster served on a bed of bok choy with a wasabi cream sauce and toasted nori or the unbeatable grilleded dhufish with a sweet curry sauce.

Pan-fried local scallops with orange and cardamon sauce, from Gary Jones at San Lorenzo

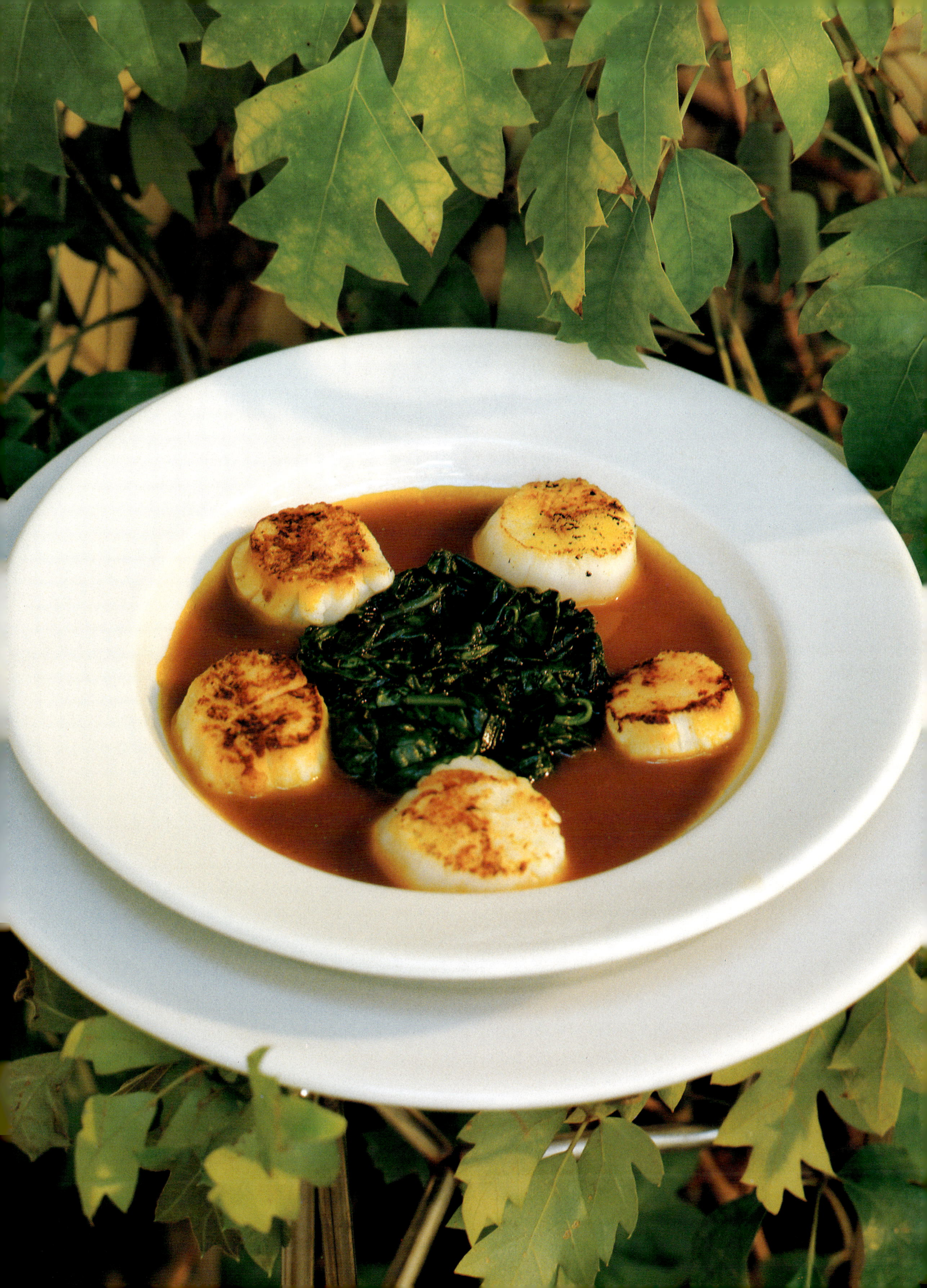

PARTNERS IN EXPORT

From 100 million hectares of farms, gardens and pastoral leases, with the coastline stretching 12,500 kilometres from the tropical north to temperate south, Western Australia offers food, wine and beverages in abundance and a multitude of opportunities for investment.

Milk, honey, grain, fruit, vegetables, meat and seafood all contribute to an annual $5 billion turnover, more than $2 billion of which is earned overseas by exports of raw and processed products.

But Western Australia's food industry, the nation's most diverse, is not only renowned for the quantity of its products. Unpolluted land and waters and rigorous health standards ensure produce of unparalleled quality. The Indian Ocean and vast deserts have isolated its flocks and crops from disease and infestation and its fisheries are regulated to ensure sustainability.

Export-conscious food producers are sharply aware of the need to respond creatively to market demands with new varieties, new technology and competitive prices. Whether meeting growing demand for European style products in nearby South-East Asia, manufacturing Udon noodles for Japan, providing Halal meat to Islamic communities around the world, or taking advantage of out-of-season demand for fruit in Europe, Western Australia's food industry is constantly exploring new opportunities.

Buyers and producers are increasingly looking to indigenous species. Freshwater crustaceans, such as marron and yabby, are flown live to exclusive European restaurants and demand for kangaroo, emu and crocodile meat is growing.

Opportunities for expansion and investment in Western Australia's food industry are almost as plentiful as its products. By the end of the century, Asia's food imports are anticipated to exceed $180 billion and Western Australia is ideally positioned to actively participate.

Western Australia - A Different Time and Space

Relaxation of international trade barriers, comprehensive transport links and advances in handling and storage technologies are increasing industry access to markets further afield. Investment is welcome, both in partnership with existing producers or in new projects, and there are few restrictions on foreign involvement in any part of the food industry.

Western Australia offers relatively inexpensive agricultural and industrial land, a highly skilled workforce and world-class infrastructure. Industry, government and academia work together to ensure that workforce training, production and processing technology and market research are at the forefront of international practice.

International promotion of Australia by government and industry as the source of clean, 'green' food products is complementing the state's already strong market position. Another attraction for investors is Western Australia's affluent and gastronomically adventurous population. Supermarkets, delicatessens and restaurants provide an enormous test kitchen for new products and ingredients, while an ethnically diverse community also stimulates this process.

Thus, high quality pastas, salamis, cheeses and wines originally produced for Western Australians of European origin have become part of the diet of the whole community and are now valuable exports. Similarly, a growing population of Asian origin is generating local production of soy bean curd, Asian-style noodles and a host of Asian horticultural produce.

Western Australia's Department of Commerce and Trade can help buyers contact food and beverage exporters. Information and advice for potential investors—such as investment incentives—are also available.

It's easy to see why the opportunities for investment in Western Australia are as diverse, vast and exciting as the state itself.

Left: Gourmet lettuce Far Left: Honeydew melon ready for picking, Ord River, Kunnunurra Above: Endeavour prawns

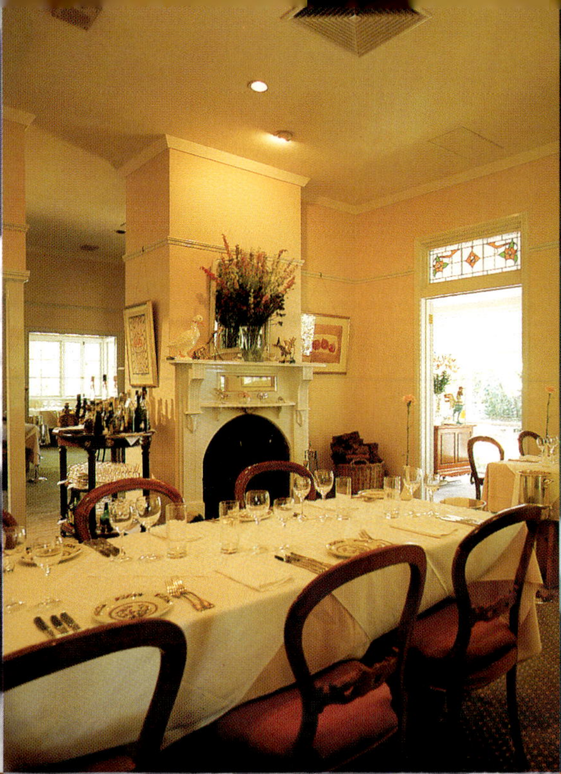
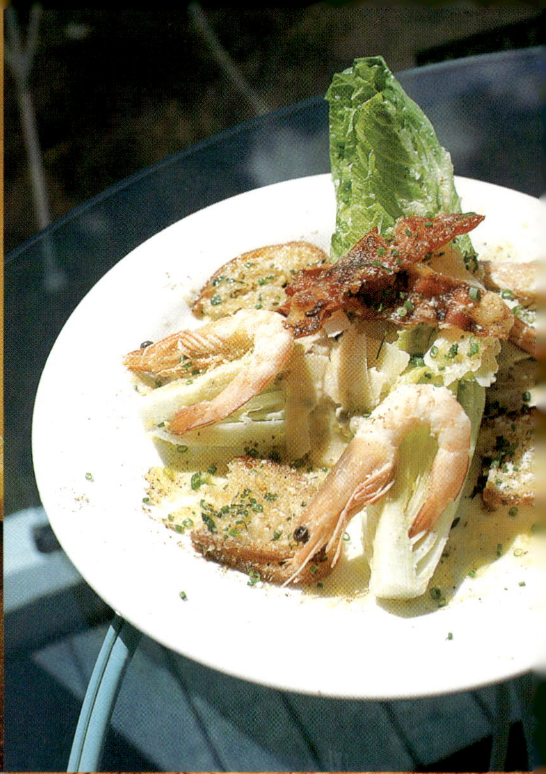
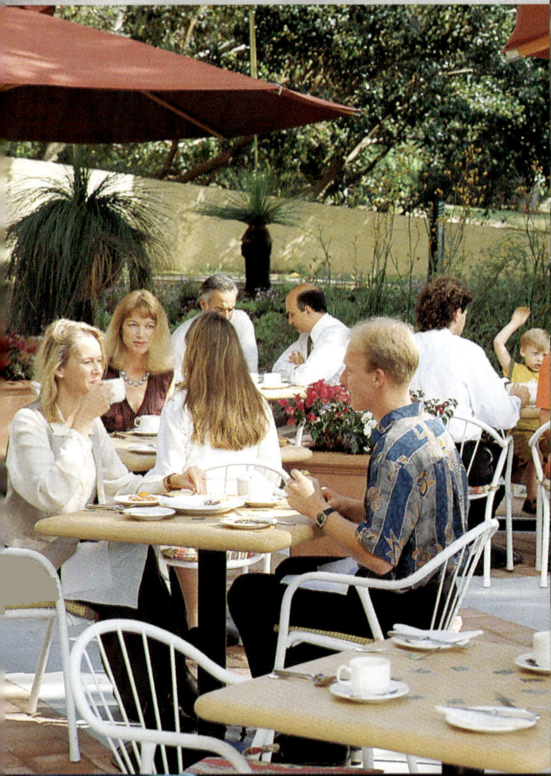
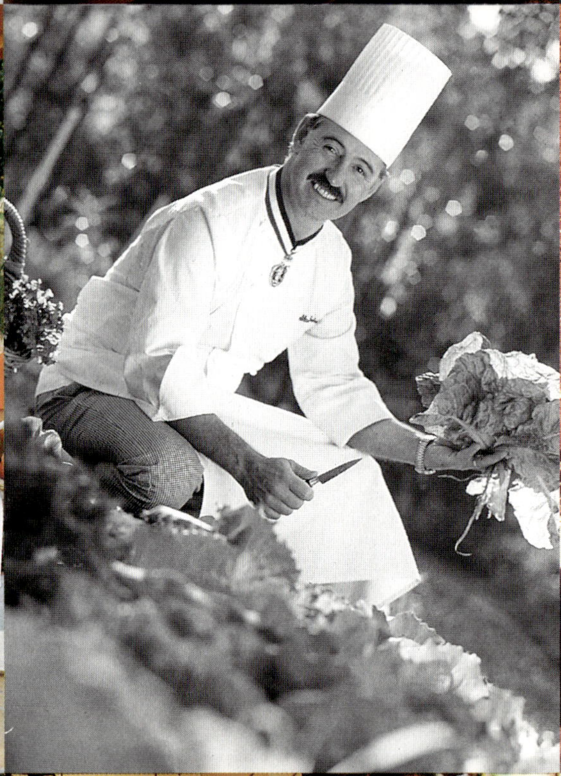
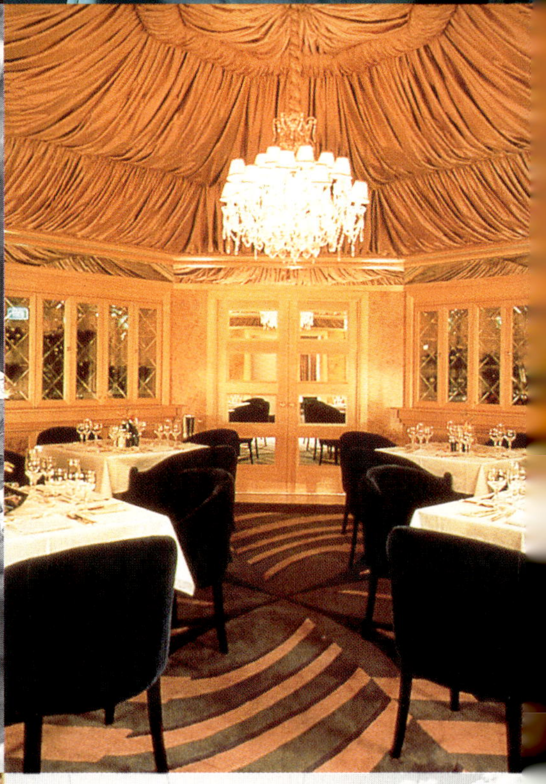
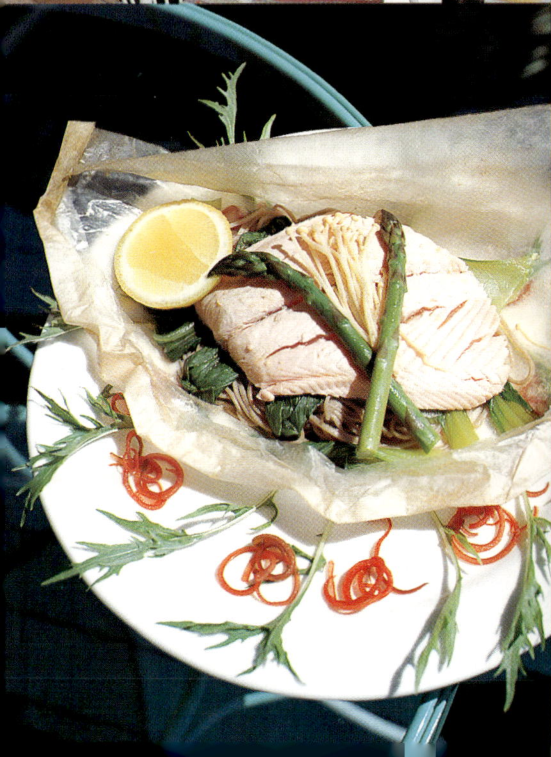
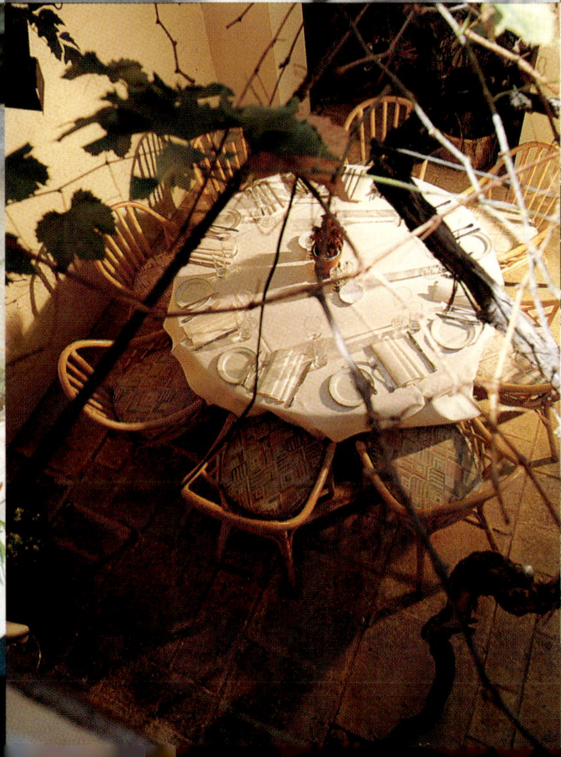
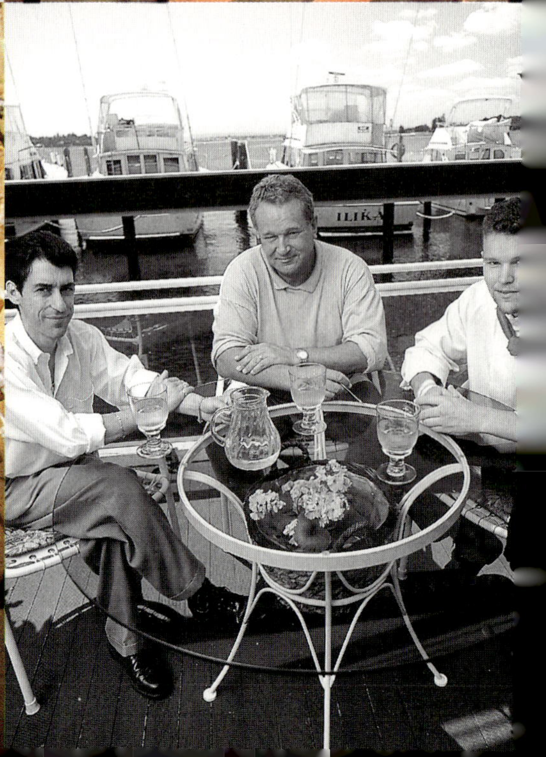

If you prefer arriving for your meal by water, to be greeted by the gentle sounds of a grand piano and an entourage of pelicans and ducks, Mead's Fish Gallery at Mosman Bay on the Swan River is where you should head. With a decade of experience in their previous restaurants, Jo Jo's, Jessica's, Cocos and the Surf Club, proprietors Warren and Linda Mead have created yet another wonderful, idyllic setting for enjoying the best Western Australia has to offer.

Mead's Fish Gallery combines the highly creative elements of numerous members of the Mead family and provides a memorable experience. Succulent oysters, Red Emperor and marron are features of the menu along with contemporary Italian dishes and the best local beef, all of which can be enjoyed while savouring the commanding view of the Swan River with its traffic of boats and majestic yachts.

One of the more out-of-the-way land-based restaurants, but definitely worth the detour from Perth, is The Loose Box restaurant, situated in Mundaring, thirty kilometres east of Perth. Proprietor and executive chef Alain Fabregues uses a selection of unique Western Australian crustaceans such as marron combined with herbs and vegetables grown in the restaurant's grounds to create a total sensory experience.

Awarded the Meilleur Ouvrier de France in 1991 Fabregues joins the Hall of Fame that includes Paul Bocuse, Pierre Troisgros and Roger Vergé, and he surprises those that share his table with fabulous French cuisine that has a definite local flavour.

PIONEERING SPIRIT But things weren't always so bountiful. When the first settlers arrived in 1829, they were faced with a very different picture. There were times when it seemed likely they would starve in the strange environment. The soil near Perth was poor and cropping conditions were quite unlike those of rural England.

But what brought those first settlers closest to starvation is what has made Western Australia's bounty so diverse—it's isolation. Transport has always been expensive or impractical, so Western Australia has had to produce everything. Since those first settlers achieved self-sufficiency, solid primary industries have provided the necessities of life.

It is as if the memories of those first settlers remain as part of the state psyche. The push towards complete self-sufficiency continues. The latest development is the Ord River scheme which grows fruit and vegetables near Kununurra at the very top of the state, 3,000 kilometres north of Perth. The diverse climates of Western Australia have been harnessed to provide fresh produce all year round.

The pattern of most primary industries has been first to supply a domestic need, and then, once the industry is established, to extend into the markets of Asian neighbours.

Left to right, top to bottom: Gary Jones from San Lorenzo; the elegant understated interior of the Loose Box restaurant, Caesar at Meades—baked cheese croutons, crispy pancetta, prawns and crisp salad leaves; for relaxed outdoor dining try Frasers restaurant in Kings Park; Alain Fabregues picks a fresh lettuce from his own garden in the grounds of the Loose Box restaurant; Gershwins restaurant at the Hyatt Regency Perth re-creates the style of the golden era; Tasmanian salmon steamed in a bag with asparagus, bok choy and Japanese noodles, from Meades; the vine-laced courtyard at San Lorenzo's; part of the Meades Seafood Emporium team (left to right): Tony Crucitti, Warren Meade, Josh Meade

AUSTRALIA - A GOURMET'S PARADISE

The state's best example of this is wheat. Most of its production is now exported. The wheatbelt extends for some 16 million hectares, so it's not surprising, then, that Western Australia regularly produces more than a third of Australia's annual crop. Growing conditions are excellent, with winter rains and dry harvesting conditions. Western Australian wheat has an international reputation for its quality, freedom from foreign matter, chemical residues, weather damage and moisture.

The industry has gone through dramatic change. Fifty years ago there was just one grade of wheat. Millers can now access some forty-five different grades to make flour for specific uses. From noodles to foccacia to Arabic flat bread, there's a flour for every purpose. The export noodle market has grown so large it consumes thirty per cent of Australian wheat exports. Western Australia has pioneered the growing of cadoux, a type of wheat ideal for Japanese white noodles, while the standard white wheat is used in the manufacture of Japanese Udon noodles and exported to Japan and other Asian markets. There's even a defined 'noodle zone' in the wheatbelt!

And not to be outdone, Italian pasta, made from high quality Western Australian flours, is now exported to south-east Asia by the Belmar family.

Western Australia also has a reputation for growing some of the world's best lamb. Europe remains one of the main markets despite fierce competition from subsidised European producers. The second largest market is the Middle East, which requires a leaner, lighter meat that fits in perfectly with Western Australia's Merino-based flocks. Lambs are sold to 100 overseas buyers in thirty countries. And the export of beef and live cattle, too, has become a flourishing industry, with Asian markets importing premium quality Western Australian table meat and the United States receiving manufacturing beef for hamburgers.

The state boasts one of Australia's most efficient dairy industries. Western Australian herds produce the highest yield per cow, the highest production per farm and some of the best quality milk in Australia. The dairy industry, too, has been highly active in exports. Western Australia has exported milk for more

Right: Sheep graze in the lush pastures of Western Australia's farming belt Above: fresh cuts of gourmet meat

SUCCULENT FLAVOURS

The Western Australian Meat Marketing Corporation is a statutory authority which was established in the early seventies with the express purpose of marketing Western Australian lamb. Today, the Corporation's distinctive WALAMB brand is readily accepted internationally as a symbol of premium quality, dependability and succulent flavour.

Up until July 1994, the Corporation was responsible for marketing all of Western Australia's lamb. While they have no preferred position on the domestic market, they have been retained by the government of Western Australia as a 'single desk' marketer of Western Australian lamb to the world. In simple language, this means that all exports of lamb must be organised through the Corporation. (They also deal in mutton, goat meat and other meat products.)

More than eighty per cent of sales comprise added-value products. All product is Halal slaughtered and conforms to the exacting health requirements overseen by the Australian Quarantine and Inspection Service.

WALAMB products are supplied either chilled or frozen to customer specification. The latest modified-atmosphere packaging techniques are also utilised to further extend shelf-life. Processing takes place in the Corporation's own internationally-approved works at Spearwood under the highest standards of hygiene and quality control.

Because of Western Australia's open range farming systems, careful husbandry and pollution-free environment, we are able to deliver healthy lambs to the markets of the world, free of chemical or hormone treatments, resulting in naturally lean, tasty and succulent meats perfectly matched to suit the most discerning customers.

The success of the Corporation's performance can be measured by its sales to well over 100 overseas buyers in thirty countries—proof of the wide acceptance of fine, Western Australian lamb, which is acknowledged the world over as a premium product.

than thirty years and now sells fresh milk to Singapore, Malaysia and Hong Kong. More than ninety per cent of ice-cream exported to Japan comes from Western Australia. And Western Australian creams, yoghurts and cheeses are being exported to established dairy markets.

In 1931 the first bananas from Carnarvon arrived in Perth; now these, too, are exported. Just about every primary industry is an export success. The west was quietly tapping into export markets long before it became a national economic imperative.

Another established Western Australian export industry is that of honey; Western Australia's unique array of wildflowers and eucalypts has been providing the world—including the United Kingdom, Germany, Singapore, Japan and the Middle East—with highly distinctive organic honeys for over 100 years.

The last decade has not only seen Western Australian commodities gain export success; a plethora of specialty products has been reaching international kitchens as well. The Department of Commerce and Trade has been actively promoting Western Australian products under the banner 'Land of Plenty' and its efforts, without doubt, are having an effect.

THE LAND OF PLENTY In the export market, Western Australia holds a trump card: diverse produce from unspoiled, unpolluted land. 'Naturally grown' and 'free from disease and chemicals' are all-powerful claims in an increasingly ecologically and health-minded world. Take the example of the capretto (young goat): this is a new export-oriented industry for Western Australia, but already about ninety per cent of production is sold to mainly Swiss hotels and restaurants that demand a product guaranteed free from contamination. Distant from the heavily industrialised world and bound by sea and sand, Western Australia can always make that claim.

The bounty and variety of Western Australia's produce not only meets world demand, it caters to the needs of Australia's changing palate (multiculturalism has left its mark in many areas but perhaps no more so than in our bellies). More than 100 national groups are represented in Western Australia, all of whom bring gastronomical as well as cultural influences. At Fraser's restaurant in Kings Park in Perth you'll find cooking influences from all over the world and a menu that has everything from kangaroo to black chicken, a Malaysian breed whose skin, flesh and bones are as black as coal.

Three families represent what immigration has done for Western Australia's gastronomical landscape and whose names are synonymous with their products. The D'Orsogna brothers arrived in Western Australia in 1949. Their smallgoods have become so successful they're in just about every Western Australian fridge. Mention seafood in a Western Australian context

A field of ripe wheat, Greenough

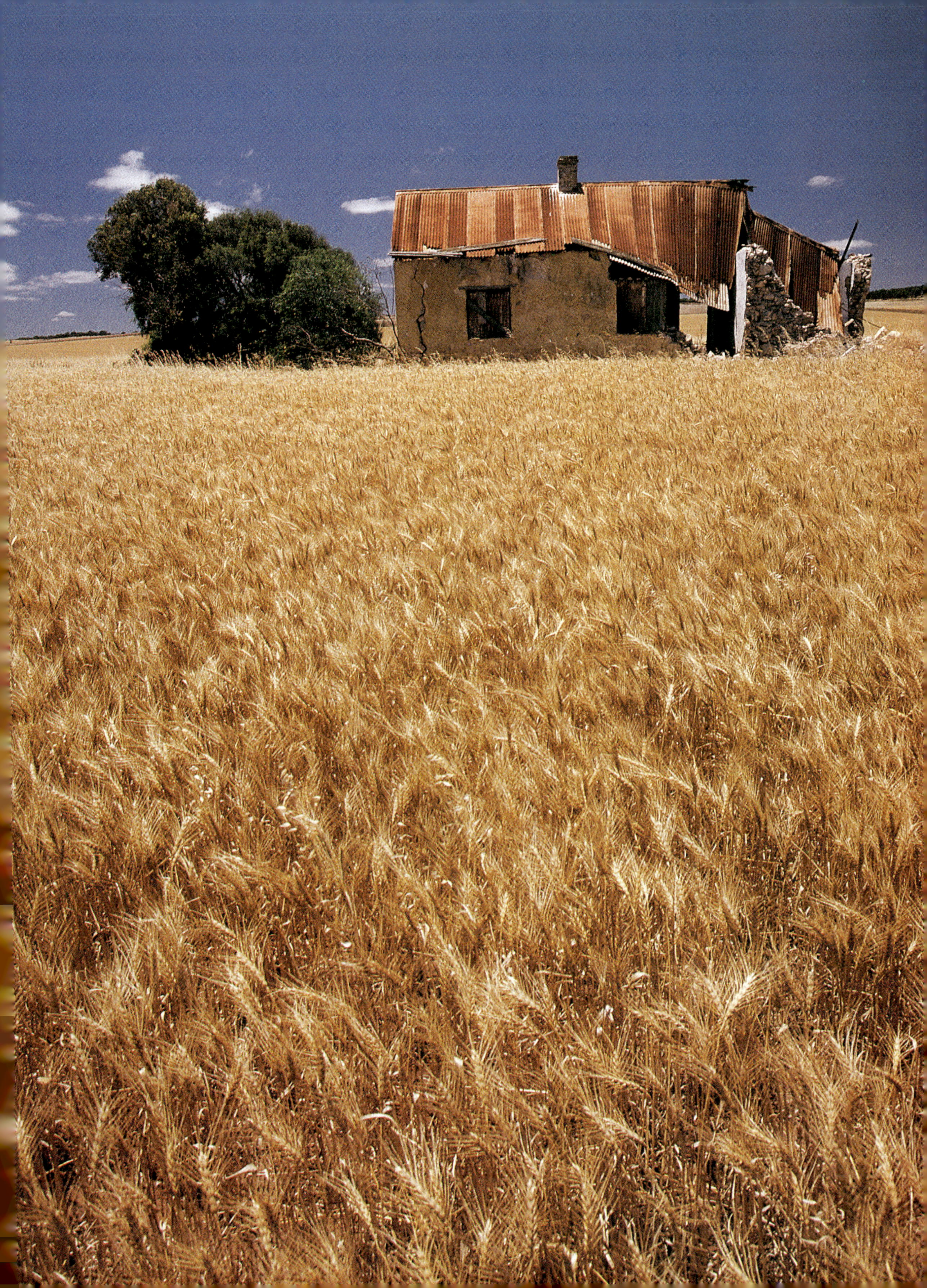

AUSTRALIA - A GOURMET'S PARADISE

and the name Kailis is bound to arise. This family has interests in the sea which stretch all the way from fish and chips to lobsters and pearls.

And the Mendolia family has made a more recent imprint on the consciousness of Western Australian gourmets. Mendolia's Fremantle Sardines began as a sideline to their anchovy business, Auschovies. Australian sardines were once fed to cats or sold as bait and threaded onto hooks to catch fish that people thought made much better eating. It was only as Australians travelled and ate sardines in Spain, Portugal and the rest of the sardine-eating world that we started to look for sardines in Australia. Simultaneously, reports came of how good fish oils are for health. Sardinops Neopilchardus are abundant in fish oil and Fremantle is abundant in sardines.

AN ABUNDANCE OF SEAFOOD

Seafood, forever the gourmet's delight, comprises a major industry for Western Australia and is a way of life for many of the people in the remote communities that dot the vast stretch of coastline facing the Indian Ocean. Like many food industries the fishing and lobster industries have humble origins and were based on the provision of local delicacies for the small communities of Perth and Fremantle. In the last century fishermen in small boats operated in the shallow coastal waters using local knowledge to guide them. Nowadays, fishermen operate from approximately thirty ports along the state's extensive coastline and use the latest mechanical and electronic equipment.

The growth of the seafood industry over the last fifty years has been phenomenal. In 1992-3, 34,535 tonnes of seafood products worth $378 million were taken in the state. A significant proportion of the catch was exported, mainly to lucrative markets in Japan, Taiwan, the United States, Hong Kong and Europe. The unique Western Rock Lobster, the largest single species fishery in Australia, regularly contributes in excess of $250 million to Western Australia's export revenue. In the 1993-4 season rock lobster exports accounted for 11 million kilograms with a value of $333 million live lobster exports making up an increasing proportion of this total.

Right: Unforgettable salamis from D'Orsogna—Di Felino, Ventricina and Casalingo Above: Exquisite prosciutto (Parma) ham is matured on the bone and air-dried for a year

Western Australia - A Different Time and Space

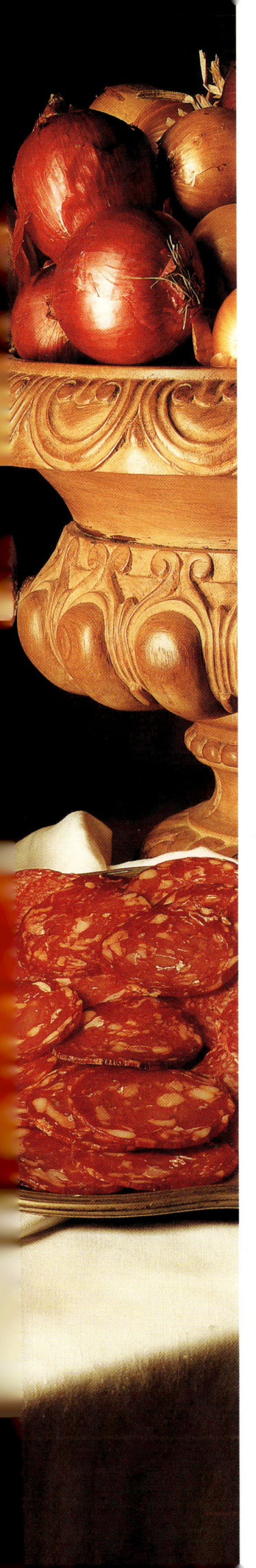

DELECTABLE DELI DELIGHTS

D'Orsogna Limited is a long-established Western Australian smallgoods manufacturer which has a strong market position in Australia and is strengthening its markets in south-east Asia.

The original company was founded in 1949 by the D'Orsogna brothers who are from the Abruzzi region of Italy, a relatively untravelled part of Italy where the gourmet tradition is strong. For Italians like the D'Orsognas who arrived in Western Australia in the thirties, it must have seemed a gastronomical desert. All you could find in a delicatessen was devon sausage.

The brothers brought from their homeland priceless skills in making genuine traditional smallgoods which today form the core product of this successful business. The range now includes the highly prized prosciutto, which is cured and matured on the bone for up to a year. Then there is the delectable salame di felino (pure lean pork flavoured with sherry), a range of salamis to please all palates and specially prepared cooked meats such as pastrami and peppered steak. As well as this the company manufactures various grades of bacon which are sold into high volume market sectors.

D'Orsogna also produces around 200 different types and packs of variety smallgoods such as antipasto packs, delicatessen knobs, polish sausage, strasburg and krakowurst—all prepared in the finest D'Orsogna style.

All of D'Orsogna's products are made from Australian-grown ingredients and, as a result of Australia's rigorous quarantine standards, the country's livestock are largely disease-free. Not only does D'Orsogna take great pride in its traditional heritage, it is also meticulous in maintaining the best standards of practice in quality control and is working towards achieving International Quality Accreditation to ISO9001. The gourmet meats can be trusted for hygienic preparation that is free from artificial enhancers but, most importantly, its products are totally authentic in traditional flavour.

Coupled with its expertise, entrepreneurial vision and dedication to excellence, D'Orsogna Limited's business has become one of Western Australia's great success stories. The company is now poised for even greater success as it expands into overseas markets.

While the main lobster season is between November and June there is a lot of activity between July and September when the lobsters mate and the larvae, or puerulus, are carried offshore over a wide area of the south-east Indian Ocean. The Leeuwin Current, a band of warm, low salinity water of tropical origin travels from Exmouth in the north to Cape Leeuwin in the south and is a critical element in ensuring a bountiful lobster season.

The Western Rock Lobster is renowned for its quality as a cold water lobster and in recent years there has been a massive increase in demand for this lobster in Taiwan, Japan and Hong Kong.

Similarly, Western Australian Tiger, King, Banana and Endeavour prawns are world-renowned for their quality. With up to 100 boats operating up and down the coast $68 million worth of prawns were taken in 1992.

There are two major prawn fisheries along the coast north of the Tropic of Capricorn in Shark Bay near the distinctly tropical town of Carnarvon, 983 kilometres north of Perth, and even further north in the pristine waters of the Exmouth Gulf. Both are 'limited entry fisheries' which means that the fishery resource is carefully managed to protect the breeding base of the fishery to ensure sustainable fishing operations. With twenty-seven boats operating in the Shark Bay area the 1994 season catch totalled 1,200 tonnes while in Exmouth Gulf sixteen boats caught a total of 1,100 tonnes of prawns.

Michael Kailis, founder of the M G Kailis Group, is recognised as the pioneer of the West Australian prawn industry. In the early 1960s he first used converted lobster boats supported by a self-contained processing plant at Learmonth. Nowadays, the prawning operations in Shark Bay and the Exmouth Gulf boast fishing fleets with the world's best processing facilities and shore-based handling depots.

Fish—including the succulent snapper and red emperor—scallops, abalone and shark meat are also major Western Australian industries. Shark Bay is also a major fishery for whiting, while small pilchard fisheries are centred on Albany, located at the bottom of the south coast.

Besides the mainstream seafoods, the marron has long been one of Western Australia's star attractions. Marron is a large, freshwater crustacean similar to a yabbie, up to 38 centimetres in length and is a delicacy much sought after. Marron farms are springing up all over the south of the state and it takes only twelve months to grow a marron to marketable size and they can be exported live or processed. The marron's cousin, the yabbie, is also being farmed in dams in the south of the state and mussels, oysters and rainbow trout are even more recent arrivals.

An aerial view of the pristine Lagoon at Shark Bay

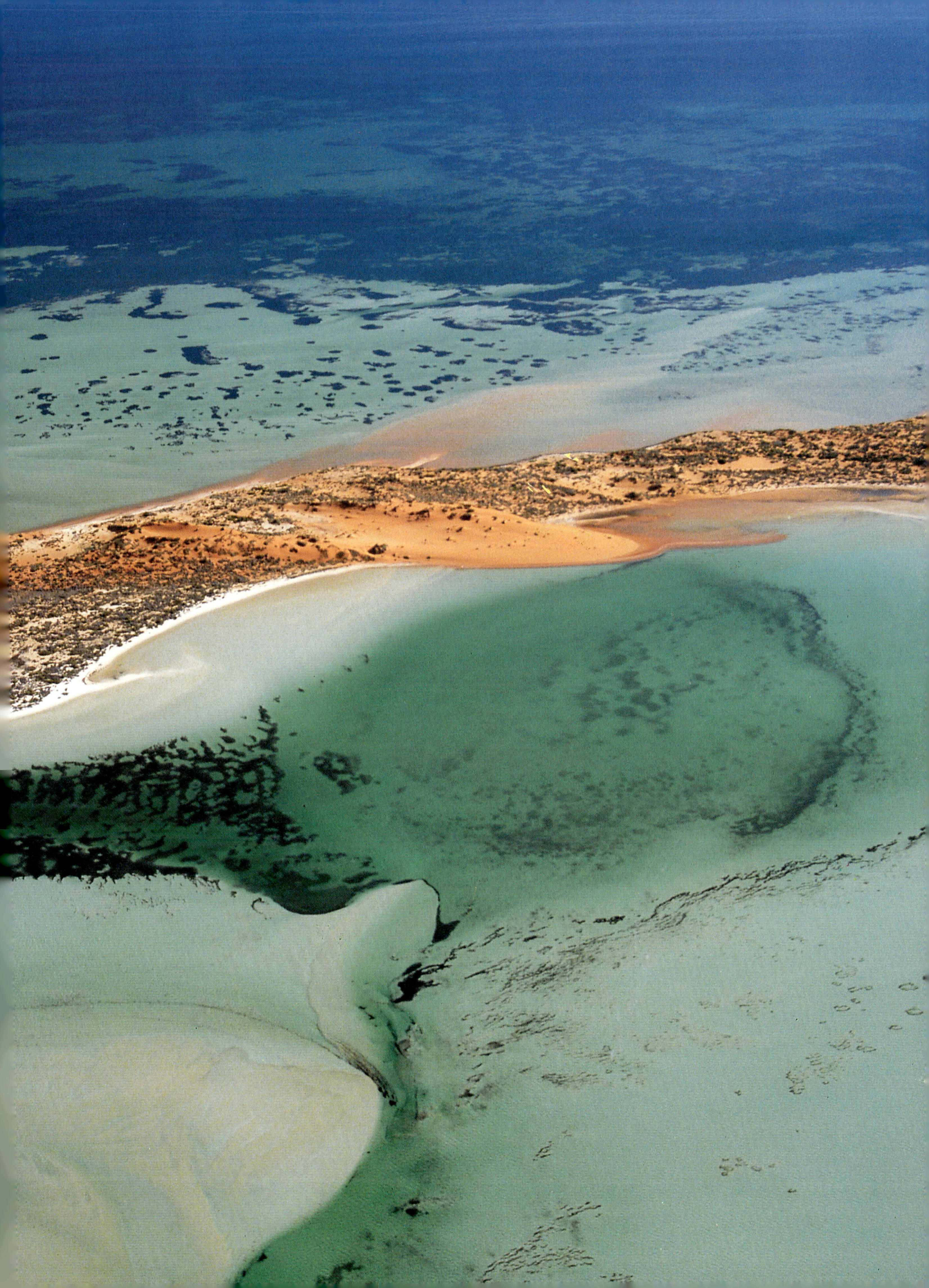

AUSTRALIA - A GOURMET'S PARADISE

PREMIUM SEAFOOD FOR THE WORLD

As a dominant producer of the highest quality Australian seafood, it would be easy for The M G Kailis Group of Companies to content itself with being a big fish in a small pond. But there has never been room for complacency in the way the group does business. Despite its powerful market position and rising international profile, innovation remains a hallmark of the group's activities, both in catching and processing seafood and in devising the best corporate structure to deliver its produce to the tables of the world.

The drive to broaden the group's corporate focus with a fresh and energetic approach has led to a unique partnership between the M G Kailis Group and K G Palmer and Associates Pty Ltd, an international marketing and consultancy firm that was incorporated within the M G Kailis Group structure over three years to 1994.

Established in 1979 by Ken Palmer, the consultancy specialises in the marketing of seafood and still undertakes work for a range of Australian clients, including M G Kailis Group subsidiary companies. When the Kailis Group decided in 1984 to branch out beyond its traditional areas of catching and processing into the realms of marketing and trading, K G Palmer & Associates was the vehicle chosen for the job.

The marriage of the two groups combined the fishing industry expertise, financial strength and reputation for excellence of the M G Kailis Group with the marketing skills of K G Palmer & Associates. Annual seafood sales for K G Palmer & Associates are now in excess of $100 million with over half of this being direct sales for M G Kailis Group subsidiaries.

In its ambition to expand the supply and product range of Australian seafood, K G Palmer & Associates, in 1992, established a trading office in

Western Australia - A Different Time and Space

Cairns, the focal centre of seafood production in Northern Australia.

With the successful development of the Queensland trading operations, the supply of premium seafood products was complimented by the M G Kailis Group acquisition of a Cairns cold storage and packing facility in 1994.

The group is a leading exporter of the world's premium cold-water lobster, the Western Rock Lobster, which is caught in the waters off Dongara, about 440 kilometres north of Perth. It is also the dominant prawning company in Western Australia, including the operation of fifteen out of the sixteen trawlers licensed in the Exmouth Gulf fishery. Exmouth Gulf is renowned for its succulent Tiger, King and Endeavour Prawns which grace the tables in restaurants and homes here and overseas.

An initiative developed by K G Palmer & Associates on behalf of the M G Kailis Group is the commitment to custom packing premium seafood products for an international network of prestigious hotel chains and supplying international flight kitchens.

Already Australia's largest privately-owned marine corporation the M G Kailis Group has matured under the marketing guidance of K G Palmer & Associates into a powerful conglomerate dedicated to supplying quality seafood to the world market.

Left: Waves crash along the sandy coastline of the Exmouth Gulf
Far Left: A fresh catch of brown tiger prawns
Above: Fresh lobster being packed for export

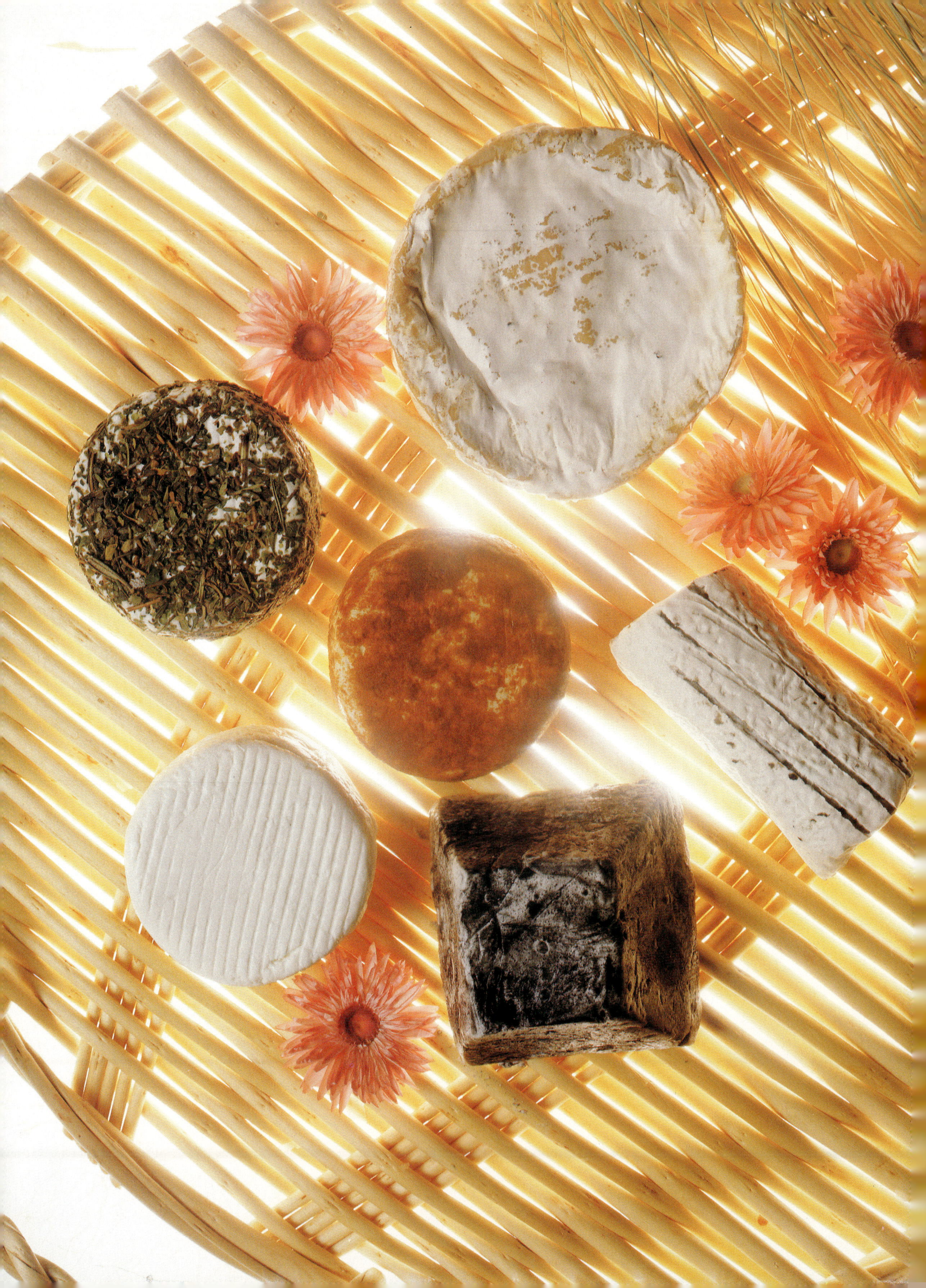

Western Australia - A Different Time and Space

As if enjoying the fresh bounty of the Indian Ocean in a sumptuous seafood meal is not enough the northern coast of Western Australia has a feast of delights. The area between Exmouth and Coral Bay, known as the Coral Coast, is a prime game fishing and diving area. The Ningaloo Reef off Cape Range National Park, is Western Australia's largest coral reef and is home to over 250 types of coral and 500 species of fish. The reef is also home to fascinating wildlife, including the whale shark (the world's biggest fish) as well as being a turtle breeding ground.

OUT OF THE ORDINARY As well as new aquaculture ventures Western Australia is also pioneering emu farming. The breeding stock were brought from an Aboriginal community in the outback. The red, fine-grained meat contains one-third of the cholesterol of beef and, with its delicate flavour, is finding favour not only in Australia but also in export markets, particularly France. The quality of the Western Australian environment is also especially suited to the rearing and production of buffalo, kangaroo, crocodile and venison meat.

In the hills to the east of Perth is the wonderfully named Gidgegannup, home to the most invisible of Western Australia's gourmet successes, Gabrielle Kervella's goats. Tucked away behind the gate and up the driveway, the goats and the dairy are well hidden. It's amazing that the produce of the seventy-odd Saanen and Anglo-Nubian goats can find its way to just about every deli worth the name throughout Australia. The quality of Kervella Goats Cheese is so highly regarded that Gabrielle has even cracked the French-obsessed Singapore market.

VINE AMBASSADORS One of Western Australia's best ambassadors is its wine. The taste of wine speaks of its origins—there are few other natural products whose flavour is so closely related to where it is grown. Western Australian wines are not short on flavour or structure. It has not been by accident or clever marketing that Western Australian wines dominate the premium market—it has been due to sheer quality.

Australia now exports thirty per cent of its production. Ten years ago it was only three per cent. Exports are increasing thirty per cent annually, and all but the smallest Western Australian wineries are reaching those export markets.

Western Australia's wine industry can be divided into three main phases in its 150 years: there is the very old, the new and the very new. Drive through the Swan Valley and you soon realise it's pretty ancient vine territory. In fact, the area was producing wine before South Australia or Victoria. When the Parmelia arrived to found the colony of the Swan River in 1829, on board (apart from optimistic settlers) were vine cuttings. These were planted only two days after arrival on a 20 hectare property at Guildford on the banks of the Swan River.

An inspiring collection of Kervella goat cheeses

MARGARET RIVER CLASSICS

Leeuwin Estate not only has a respected name in Western Australia as a master winemaker, it has gained an enviable reputation on both domestic and international scales for elegant wines of rare quality.

The planting of vines at Leeuwin was inspired in the early 1970s by California's Robert Mondavi, who identified the vineyard site as being ideal for the production of premium wine. Under the direction of the Horgan family and a team of dedicated winemakers, Leeuwin has unashamedly striven for excellence in all facets of the Estate's operations.

The highly accoladed wines in Leeuwin Estate's portfolio are pricey—but perfection doesn't come cheap. You don't win an international profile unless you perform, and Leeuwin Estate does—always. Its premium wines are ranked with the world's finest in international tastings.

The Estate is one of the loveliest imaginable. Its natural amphitheatre is circumscribed by beautiful native timbers forming an arc around a grassy arena—which provide the setting for its world-famous concerts where artists such as Kiri Te Kanawa, James Galway, Ray Charles, Diana Ross, Dionne Warwick, Tom Jones, Julia Migenes, George Benson and a number of international orchestras have all performed.

While the concerts are a sideline, they are fast winning a reputation akin to England's famous Glyndebourne.

Adorning the walls of the winery's award-winning restaurant are paintings by some of Australia's leading artists—including Sir Sidney Nolan, Arthur Boyd and John Olsen—all commissioned to appear on the labels of Leeuwin's finest releases, appropriately labelled the 'Art Series'.

Neighbouring Voyager Estate—originally called Freycinet—has vineyards producing premium wine in the classic style that typifies the Margaret River region. Voyager Estate—with its whitewashed buildings reminiscent of South Africa's Cape Dutch architecture—creates an aesthetic appeal, while its immaculate vineyards leave no doubt that Voyager is here to stay. Voyager currently has 24 hectares of prime Margaret River soil under vine, with plantings of sauvignon blanc, chenin blanc, cabernet franc, semillon, cabernet sauvignon, pinot noir and merlot grapes. Within the next three years, the development plan is for a harvest of up to 20,000 cases.

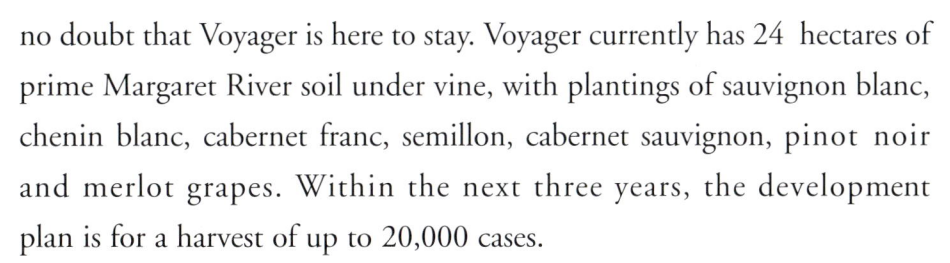

With this in mind, Voyager has been methodically seeking wider domestic and export markets. Wine is being sold to a premium liquor chain in Japan and a UK agent has been introducing Voyager's wines to Britain. There is also solid interest from premium wholesalers in France.

By spring 1995, Voyager Estate will open its doors to the public for tastings and cellar sales. With tourist numbers in the Margaret River area growing by an annual ten per cent, Voyager is sure to become a major attraction.

Brookland Valley Vineyard's excellent wines nearly risk being overshadowed by its wonderful restaurant, Flutes Cafe. It overlooks beautifully tended vineyards—where even the ducks are friendly—and you'll taste some of Western Australia's best produce.

Planted in three stages by the Jones family from 1984 to 1986, and overseen by viticultural gurus Garry Crittenden and Brian Corser, the 20 hectares of vineyards are now at their peak. The vineyard, which was carefully planned, combines the latest technology with traditional practices, resulting in the production of premium wines, consistent in style and quality.

Brookland Valley Vineyard specialises in the production of four wines—chardonnay, sauvignon blanc, cabernet merlot and merlot. Classic winemaking techniques are used, with emphasis on maximising fruit flavours. The wines show a delicate touch with superb drinkability being the optimum criteria. The unique label features a bronze statue of Pan (hence the name Flutes) which is photographed amid splendid Margaret River scenery for each release.

Left: Barrels of Leeuwin Estate wine mature for 17 months in these oak barrels before blending and bottling Far Left: A bronze statue of Pan casts an air of tranquility over the Brookland Valley vines Above: Sunset over Voyager Estate

AUSTRALIA - A GOURMET'S PARADISE

And it was here that the first wine in Western Australia was produced. The property and the old cellar still survive under the control of the Yurisich family. Olive Farm, as it is called, is the oldest operating winery in Australia.

The Swan Valley is a fascinating wine region for its diversity. All types of vineyard, all sizes of winery and all styles of wine are represented. There are back-yarders, family wineries, and publicly listed companies.

The Houghton name looms large in Western Australia's wine industry in the present, the past and, no doubt, the future. Houghton is not only the biggest producer (crushing half of the state's grapes), it is one of the oldest operating wineries.

Until the 1970s the Swan Valley was the Western Australian wine industry. But during the 1970s came the second phase, the discovery of the south-west. Perth doctor Tom Cullity planted the first vineyard at the beautiful site of Vasse Felix. That was 1967. Encouraged by some stunning wines, others soon followed. In 1983 Cape Mentelle's 1982 Cabernet Sauvignon won the Jimmy Watson Trophy; then to prove it was no fluke followed it up in 1984. Leeuwin Estate's Chardonnay was recognised as one of the best Australia had produced and Margaret River was firmly established on the world wine map.

Margaret River now boasts all manner of artists producing their craft from wood, whey, and wine. There are now some forty-odd wineries and two cheese makers: Margaret River Cheese Company which produces excellent brie and camembert, and Fonti whose specialities are ricotta, strachino, havarti and the aged cheddar Metricup Gold. Farms of yabbie and marron, venison and buffalo are also in the district. The place is growing at eleven per cent per annum and doesn't look like stopping.

Margaret River's atmosphere is an intriguing blend of cultures: wine, art, food and surf. It's a pretty attractive combination. Add to that the natural beauty of Margaret River, wineries within easy distance of each other, and only a three-and-a-half hour drive from Perth, and it's not surprising it has become a favourite destination. Guest houses and holiday cottages abound and the winery restaurant has become a phenomenon. Just about every second winery has a restaurant as a sideline to the cellar door. Flutes at Brookland Valley is one of the best. A lovely setting, an eclectic menu which makes extensive use of Western Australian produce and Brookland Valley's wines make it a great spot for lunch or dinner. There are plenty of others up and down the peninsula: Leeuwin Estate, Vasse Felix, Cullen's and Amberly Estate, but probably the most spectacular is Wise Winery whose tables look out over Geographe Bay.

Margaret River is a popular destination. So far the Great Southern has lacked the atten-

Clockwise from top left: Houghtons vineyard in the Swan Valley; keeping an eye and palate on the maturing wine at Leeuwin Estate; the gum tree-lined entrance to Houghton Estate's Vineyard; the superlative association of fine wine, tempting food and the arts at Leeuwin Estates' award-winning restaurant

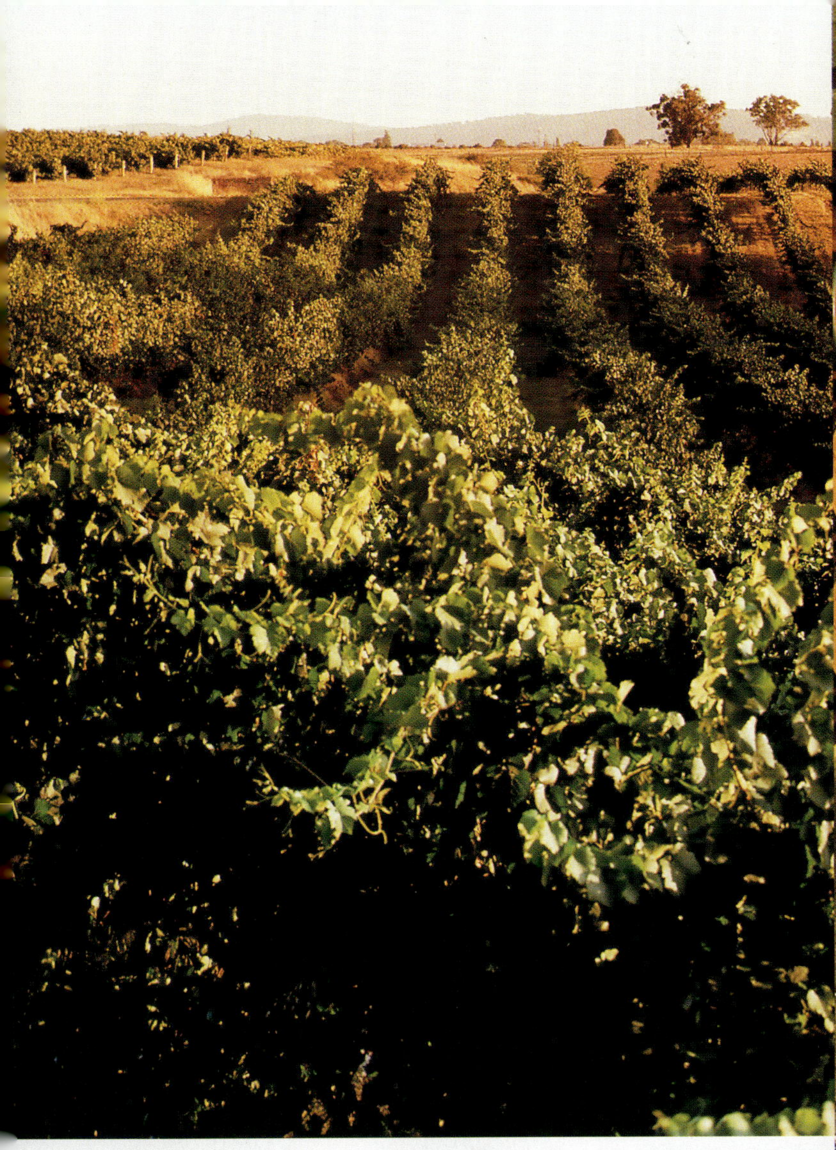

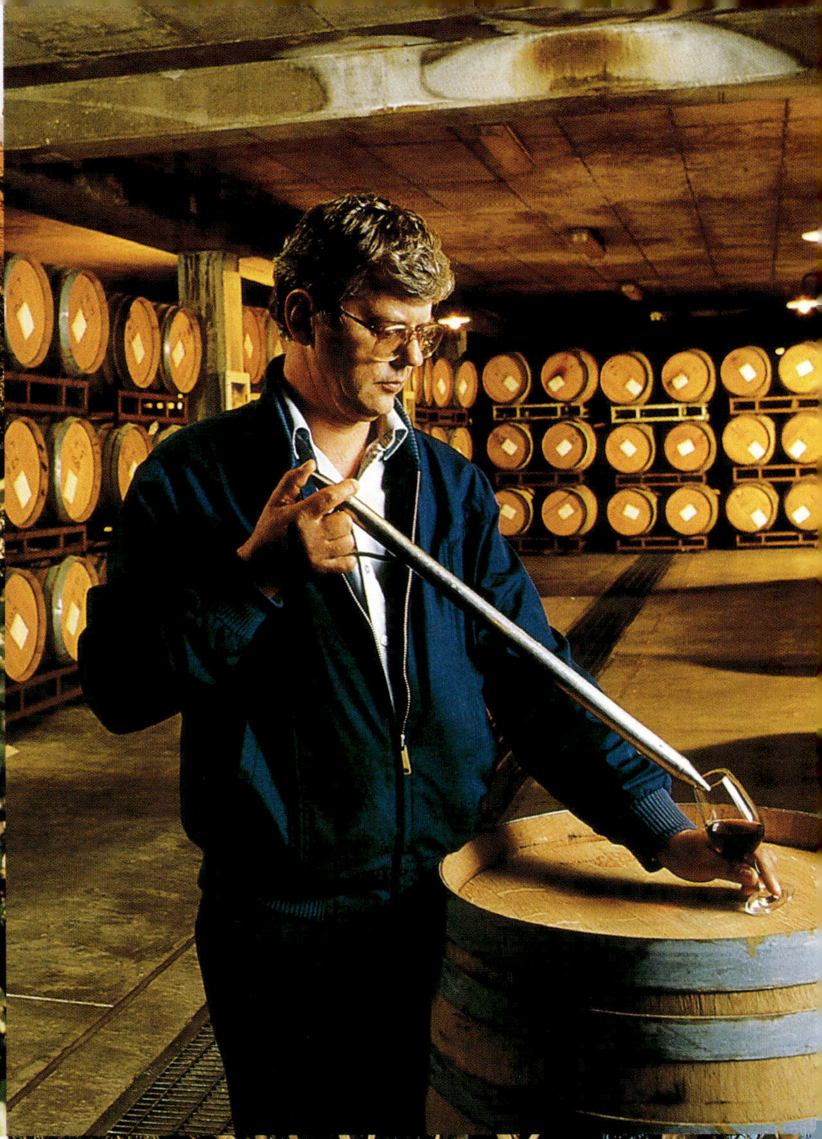

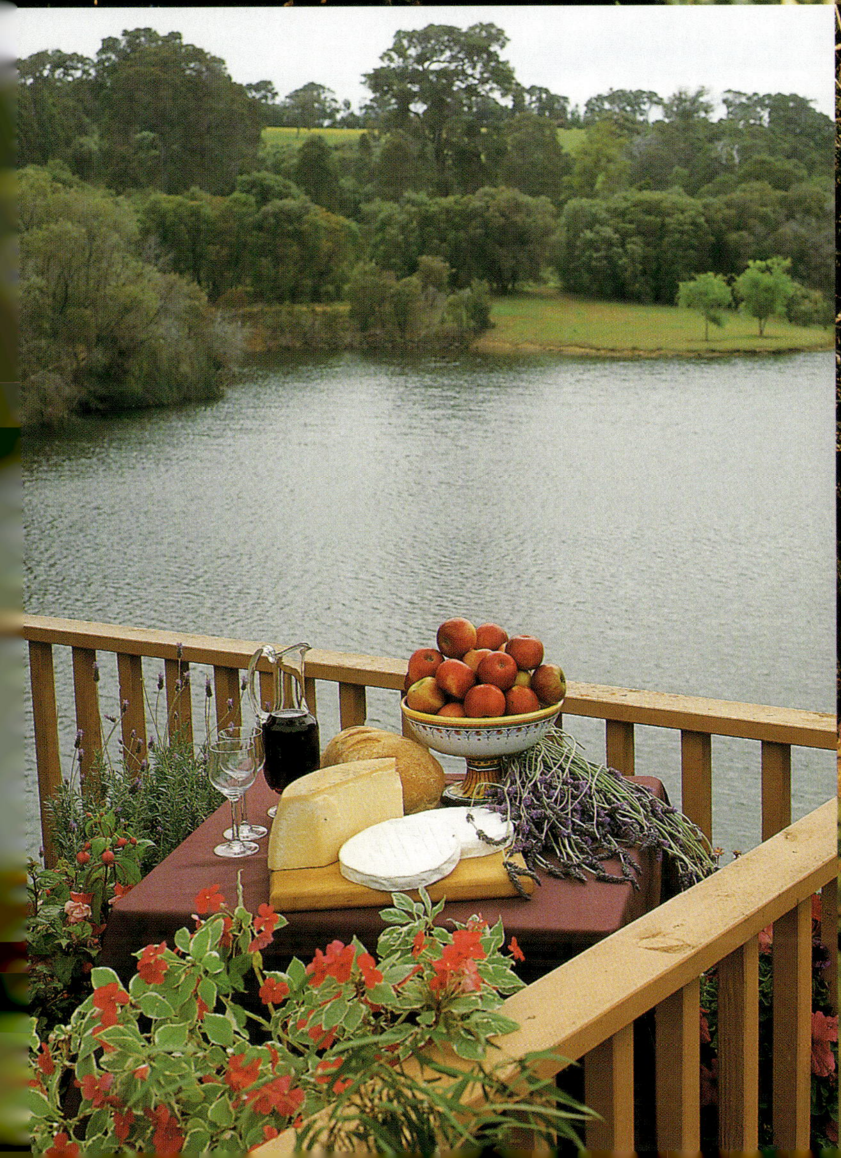

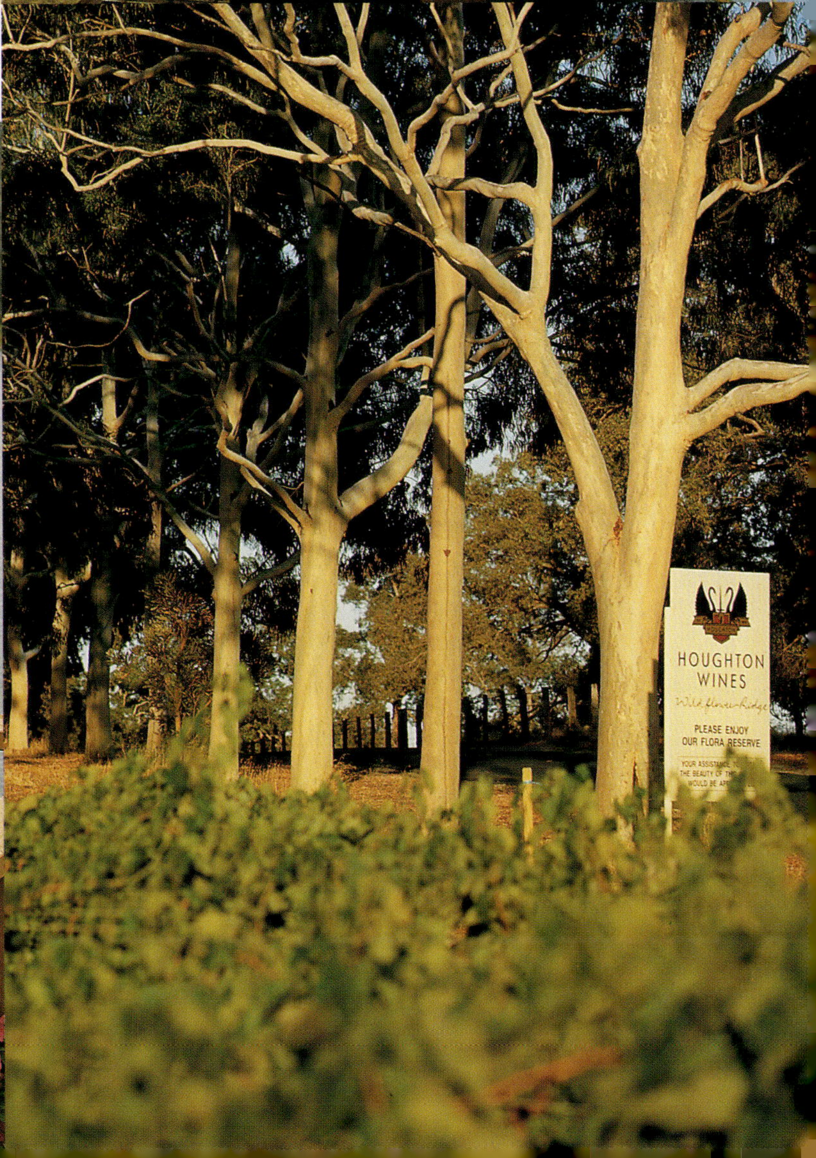
HOUGHTON
WINES
PLEASE ENJOY
OUR FLORA RESERVE

AUSTRALIA - A GOURMET'S PARADISE

ADVENTURES IN EXCELLENCE

A hundred years of quality service has made the Peters and Brownes Group the largest producer and distributor of frozen and chilled food in Western Australia and a major supplier to Asian markets.

The abundance of high-quality raw materials, healthy agricultural regions and fertile wide-open farmlands in Western Australia are essential ingredients for all the Group's products. Peters and Brownes' sophisticated production techniques, international standards of excellence and dedication to meeting customers' needs have resulted in a yearly turnover of over $300 million for the Group.

An important product for the Group is its world-famous Peters ice-cream. The best fresh milk, together with advanced manufacturing methods, have resulted in the Group commanding over sixty per cent of market share in Western Australia in all major segments. The Asian market has enjoyed Peters ice-cream (under various brands) for decades, and the Western Australian Group represents eighty per cent of Australia's ice-cream exports to Japan.

With ice-cream always a preferred treat it's hard to choose a favourite among Peters' delectable range. However, Super Premium Connoisseur is the Group's paramount ice-cream, a fact illustrated when Connoisseur won five awards, including the prestigious Champion Ice Cream, at the 1994 Perth Royal Show. Connoisseur comes in a mouth-watering range of flavours that include Chocolate Obsession, Strawberry Romanoff and New England Butter Pecan.

Another successful member of the Group's 300 gourmet products is its well-loved flavoured milk, made with fresh reduced-fat milk and using only authentic flavourings. Two

Western Australia - A Different Time and Space

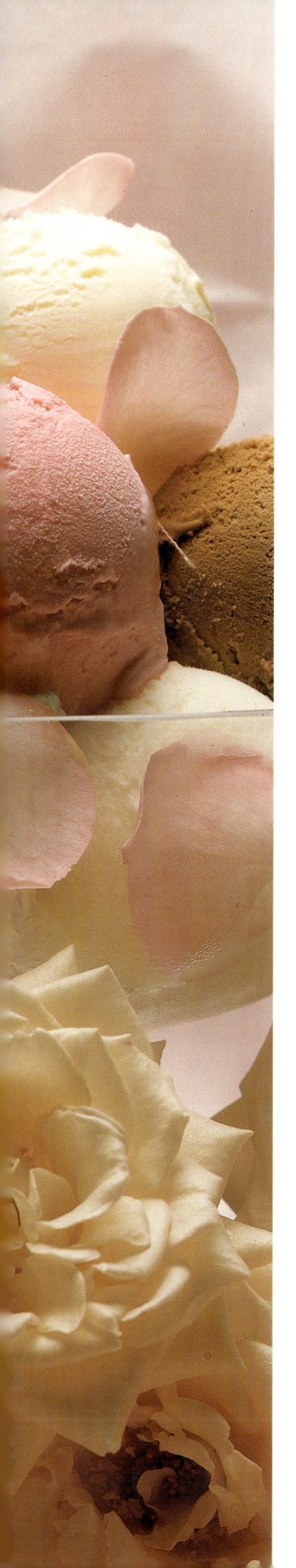

> of the popular flavours are Original Chill, which is made from pure Cadbury chocolate, and Coffee Chill, which contains genuine percolated coffee.
>
> The Group's meat company, Clover Meats, supplies meat for the export, retail and food service markets. Beef, mutton, goat, ram and offal are processed at the company's Halal export abattoir facilities in Perth, the centre of one of the world's best breeding regions for top-quality cattle. Clover Meats are recognised for their quality in the United States, Canada, South-East Asia and the Middle East.
>
> Peters and Brownes is constantly developing new products to meet the needs of domestic and overseas markets. With such commitment, the Group is naturally a key player in the food industry in Western Australia and the world.

tion it deserves; it has a different ambience. Like no other wine region in the state, Great Southern embodies the enormity of Western Australia. There are now nearly twenty wineries open for cellar-door sales spread over an area about 100 kilometres east-to-west and 60 kilometres north-to-south.

It is the biggest designated wine district in the country and quite daunting to the kilometre-weary traveller. It's best to think of the place in its smaller regions and arrive through Frankland River, cruise to Mt Barker, across to Porongurup, down to Albany and out through Denmark.

Apparently it was Maurice O'Shea, legendary wine-maker of the Hunter, who first put the idea into people's heads that the south-western tip of the continent would be a good place to make wine. From way over the other side of Australia he scrutinised the data and (for a Hunter man) blasphemously announced that if he'd had his time over again he'd love to do it in the Albany/Mount Barker region.

The first cuttings were planted in 1965 at Forest Hill, and in 1972 the first cabernet sauvignon from Frankland River was taken up to Houghton and

Left: Not for the faint-hearted! A mountain of mouth-watering ice-creams from Peters and Brownes Far Left: Gourmet cheeses and milk products for the discerning

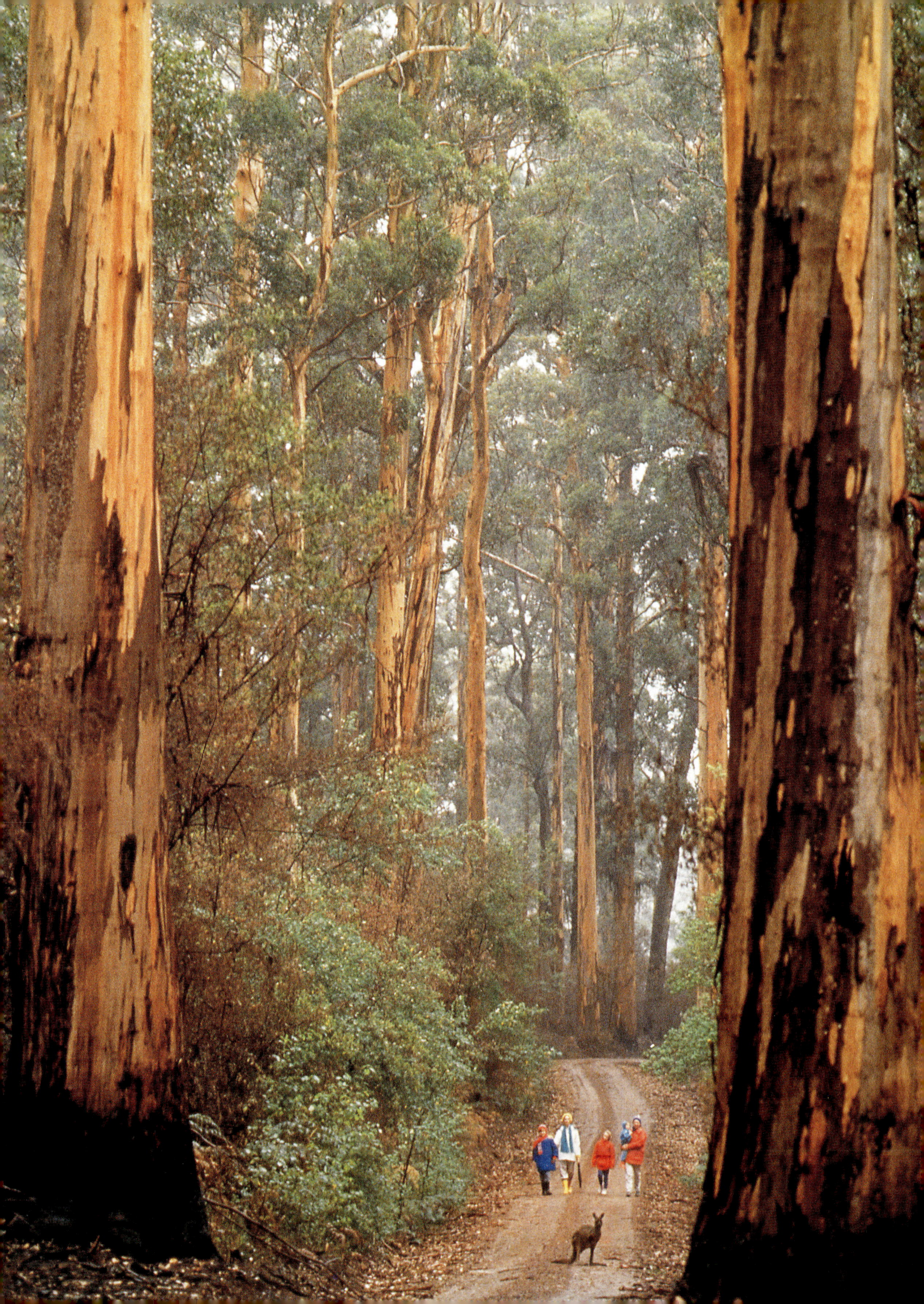

made by Jack Mann. But it is Plantagenet that had the distinction of being the first commercial winery in the area in 1968.

The Great Southern region has shown itself capable of tremendous versatility. The gamut of major grape varieties are represented in wines of stunning quality. Sublime chardonnays and cabernet sauvignons are produced by virtually every winery but there are also specialities such as Plantagenet Shiraz, Alkoomi Malbec and Wignall Pinot Noir.

But without doubt the most spectacular success has come from riesling. Great Southern rieslings have a vibrant, limey intensity and have proved to be extremely long-lived.

If you've never seen the name Warren Valley on a wine label you soon will. It's tagged to be the Margaret River of the twenty-first century. Warren Valley is the new name for the region of Pemberton and Manjimup. Pemberton now has four wineries operating a cellar door with more opening all the time. The Pemberton/Manjimup area is dotted with marron and trout farms which are also open to the public.

The district lies between the Great Southern and Margaret River and has been receiving a tremendous amount of favourable industry interest. The chief wine-maker at BRL Hardy, Peter Dawson (who oversees a fifth of Australia's entire production from just about every region), nominates Pemberton's grapes as the ones he would most like to work with. Plenty of others feel the same way. Domaine Chandon, a Yarra Valley-based company, is already buying chardonnay and pinot noir from the area for its excellent sparkling wine, and Houghton has purchased 200 hectares in the region.

Western Australia is huge in every sense. When it comes to food and wine, its eclectic vastness is mind-boggling. It is not only the diversity of products that is so surprising, it is the quality in each one. But it does stimulate the appetite and, if the essence of good living is quality and variety, then Western Australia has it.

Gregory Duncan Powell

Towering Karri trees dwarf bushwalkers as a wallaby looks on

THE GOLDEN WEST

Of all Australia's states, arguably the one with the greatest mystique is Western Australia.

To many Australians and overseas visitors, it is the quintessential Australia—with its rugged outback, its spectacular coastline, majestic forests and its 2.5 million square kilometres of sheer vastness.

The state has won a place in history for its seemingly limitless resource reserves that include gold, iron ore, oil, gas and minerals. It can also legitimately be described as a 'jewel of a state' with the biggest diamond mine in the world, and easily the most voluptuous pearls. It is a state rich in food and wine, both of which are exported all over the world. In Western Australia big is spelt BIG.

"In 1984 the Western Australian Tourism Commission was established to promote the state. Tourism has become one of the top export industries, along with mineral and cereals."

While the greater part of Western Australia is desert and largely uninhabitable, visitors are surprised to discover a state of great diversity and of spectacular natural scenery as well as a host of man-made tourist attractions.

The starting point for most visitors arriving in Western Australia is the capital, Perth. It is one of the world's loveliest cities, owing much to its handsome setting on the elegant Swan River. And despite its distance from other capital cities, Perth surprises the newly arrived with its sophisticated lifestyle.

It has a truly cosmopolitan identity yet a quality of life that is uniquely Western Australian. There is no shortage of natural playgrounds, spacious parks and expansive waterways. Those who pursue leisure will be delighted by its casino, its world-class restaurants and a splendid cultural calendar.

Western Australia - A Different Time and Space

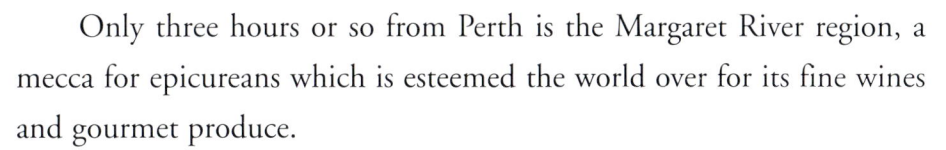

Only three hours or so from Perth is the Margaret River region, a mecca for epicureans which is esteemed the world over for its fine wines and gourmet produce.

To the far north of the state lies the astonishing Kimberley—a region without parallel anywhere in the world. Its natural wonders include the mysterious Bungle Bungle massif, while on the coast is the legendary town of Broome, famous for its pearls, its colourful past and Cable Beach, one of the world's most sublime stretches of white, undulating sand.

Farther south are the famous gorges of the Pilbara, and near Tom Price can be found the magnificent Karijini National Park.

The state also has marine parks rich in vivid corals and a variety of sea life. And who could overlook the famous dolphins of Monkey Mia which enchant visitors from all over the world with their endearing antics.

By contrast, in the southern part of the state lies a gentler region of valleys, pasture lands and magnificent Karri forests—among the world's grandest.

Six hundred kilometres to the east of Perth lie the goldfields and the historic city of Kalgoorlie-Boulder—with a past every bit as evocative in anecdote as the American west, but infinitely more authentic.

Western Australia is everything you've imagined and more. There are a million stories of heroism, courage, riches and romance. Add to these the glorious sunsets, white beaches, rich red soil, a vivid blue sea and the fantastic spirits of the Aboriginal Dreamtime, and you'll find that Australia's golden west rivals anything Hollywood has ever dreamt of. What's more, every bit of it is engraved in reality.

Left: A carpet of wildflowers in bloom in the mid-west
Far Left: Wave Rock, a 15-metre granite formation approximately 2,700 million years old, near Hyden, east of Perth
Above: Shell Beach at Shark Bay

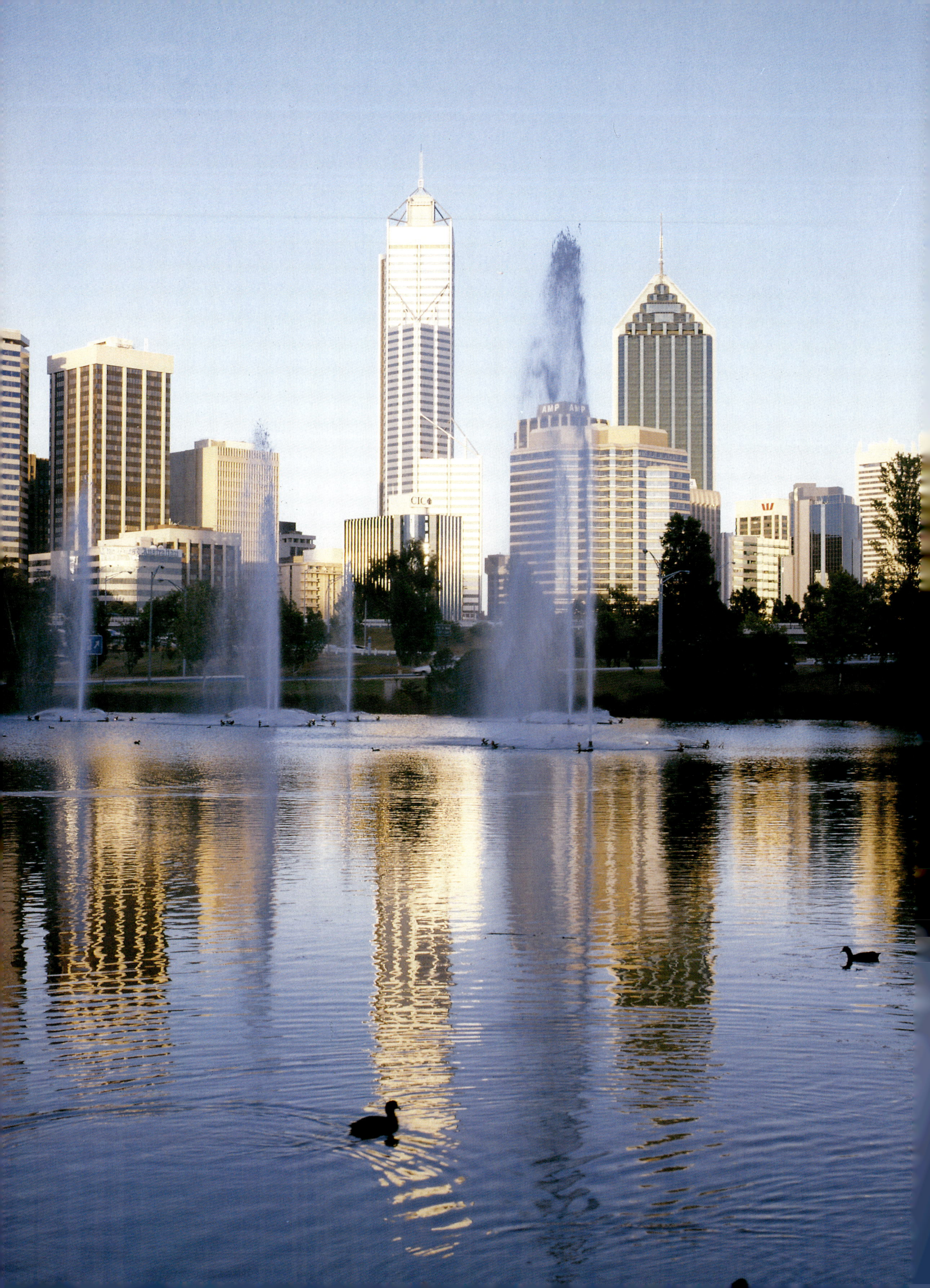
AMP AMP
CIC

A FIVE-STAR OASIS

Hyatt is one of the most highly-respected hotel groups in the world, with 167 hotels and resorts across thirty-one countries. In Australia, they have a well-deserved high-profile as a market leader.

When Australia won the America's Cup in 1983 there was no Hyatt in Perth. Perth only gained the services of a top-class hotel in 1988 when Hyatt assumed management of a new five-star property in Adelaide Terrace. Situated on the banks of the Swan River, the hotel has spectacular views over the Perth foreshores and the beautiful oasis of Kings Park.

A $12 million programme of renovation and refurbishment transformed the hotel into a Hyatt. It is now a hotel with a unique combination of renowned high-quality Hyatt standards of accommodation, meticulous service and the friendly informality which is one of Perth's most revered attributes.

The Hyatt boasts 364 richly furnished rooms with stunning views of the Swan River, the city skyline and the Darling Ranges. An extensive food and beverage service is offered by the hotel, and its three superb restaurants proudly feature the finest of Western Australian produce. In addition, the Hyatt Regency Perth chefs have won the 'Best Establishment' award for the last three years in the prestigious Salon Olympia Culinaire competition.

Gershwin's is the hotel's signature restaurant, where guests are treated to formal five-star dining in either the main dining room, the wine room or a private dining suite. Under a canopy of champagne silk, diners can enjoy creative 'West Coast Cuisine' while listening to an array of unforgettable Gershwin melodies.

Meanwhile, the more relaxed Joe's Oriental Diner presents a variety of Asian-inspired dishes in an atmosphere enhanced by genuine Asian art and antiques. And for yet another memorable dining experience, the Cafe has an excellent buffet as well as an á la carte menu filled with culinary masterpieces. The exhibition kitchen where diners can watch talented chefs at work guarantees the freshness of all the dishes.

With such a diverse range of dining options available, it's little wonder that the Hyatt's restaurants are a favourite among guests and locals alike.

The beautiful Perth skyline, home to the Hyatt Regency

C E L E B

Right: Gourmet chicken barbecued in the great outdoors
Below: Essential cooking utensils for camping; 'Spotted Dog'—damper with raisins

EATING

the Great Outdoors

Australia—the word alone conjures up images of clear blue skies, golden sands, red earth and gum trees. For Australia is blessed with a fortunate climate, with great diversity from the tropical north to the cooler south, from the fertile coastal strip to the expansive grandeur of the interior. Such diversity is reflected in the huge variety of produce which abounds in this land. A country of vast open spaces, an expansiveness which translates into the Australian personality, it is a country which generates spontaneity. The physical space and abundance of fresh produce foster a casual approach like the Australian temperament. Nowhere is there greater celebration of, and in, the great outdoors.

From the first swaggie who boiled his billy of tea on an open campfire to the present day with all manner of exotic seafood, meat and game enhanced by spices and seasonings, Australians have loved to eat and entertain outdoors. First there was an Australian indigenous cuisine, but with the coming of the white man early settlers were isolated in the bush and adopted and then adapted many of the old customs and traditions of Europe. Available ingredients were substituted. Yet even then, the first kitchens were outdoors, later enclosed as lean-tos or cook-out huts. Damper, a kind of bread, became and remains an Australian standby—a simple combination of self-raising flour mixed with a liquid such as water, milk or beer and a little butter (or in modern times olive oil), and cooked in a damp billy on an open fire, around a stick or more recently in the oven.

Today Australia may be a largely urban society but most Australians have come in contact with the actual growing of food with access to orchards, farms and market gardens. This is despite a revival in apartment and inner-city living—yet often even these have a balcony or garden area with, however small, a barbecue. Home ownership is the Australian dream, complete, of course,

AUSTRALIA - A GOURMET'S PARADISE

with backyard. And what better venue to enjoy the fruits of one's labour and land!

Even for travellers and day-trippers, there are excellent facilities elsewhere with public barbecues, either gas or stocked with firewood, at roadside lay-bys, in Melbourne along the banks of the Yarra River, at picnic grounds, beaches and in the bush—though care must be exercised, especially during the bush fire season. Yet even then, gas barbecues are sometimes permitted in contained areas and private gardens. Beer gardens in pubs have long centred around 'cook your own' barbecues with salads and vegetables provided on the side. Many a conversation is struck up over the huge communal grill where some even douse their steak and onions with another Aussie favourite, beer.

Australia, too, is a sports-mad nation—and that again means eating outside. There is a glorious tradition of picnics and marquees—at the Melbourne Cup and other races, and at the polo, football, the beach or when sailing. This tradition extends from the grandest ringside 'box' to the most humble snack in a paper bag eaten sitting on the ground. For entertaining en masse, whole lambs or pigs and butts of beef slowly spit-roasted are popular. And even that Australian icon, the meat pie, has now achieved gourmet status with an annual national competition to find the best meat pie and gourmet meat pie.

Outdoor dining has overtaken more cultural events, too. In Sydney, the Opera, Jazz and Symphony in the Park have become annual summer events. Enthusiasts mark out their 'spot' and picnic all day and well into the night while watching the performances. Shakespeare is performed in the Botanical Gardens in Melbourne, Sydney and Adelaide, with the audience picnicking again on home tucker or that provided by nearby five-star hotels.

A STYLE OF OUR OWN Outdoor festivals have taken on a life of their own, especially in the wine regions of South Australia and Victoria. Leading-edge restaurants have been set up in some wineries, and enthusiasts travel between them, sampling a glass of wine and plate of food at each venue. Music is an integral part, with everything playing from orchestral ensembles to bush bands. Or it may be even the focus, as at Leeuwin Estate's huge annual concert which features high-profile international acts, or Huntington Estate's ten-day festival in Mudgee, headlined by the Australian Chamber Orchestra. In the cities the wine region may come to town, or an area like the world-famous Manly Beach in Sydney will close off the streets to have its own wine and food festival. Some places have semi-permanent Asian-style noodle markets once or twice a week. Most famous of all, perhaps, is Victoria's Harvest Picnic at Ballarat, a huge annual affair taking place outdoors with marquees, tents and thousands of visitors interested in the state's best and finest produce and how it is served. Melbourne also

Left to right, top to bottom: Breakfast at the Melbourne Cup, Australia's premier horse race; a fresh mixed salad, Northern Territory style; The Bacardi Club, part of the Sydney Festival celebrations; sunset over Mirage Hotel, Surfers Paradise, Queensland; dining at sunset at Mindil Market; Boerewors sausages with a tomato, onion and basil sandwich; outdoor eating at the Melbourne Food and Wine Festival; fishing, a leisurely activity; proud fisherman displaying their catch

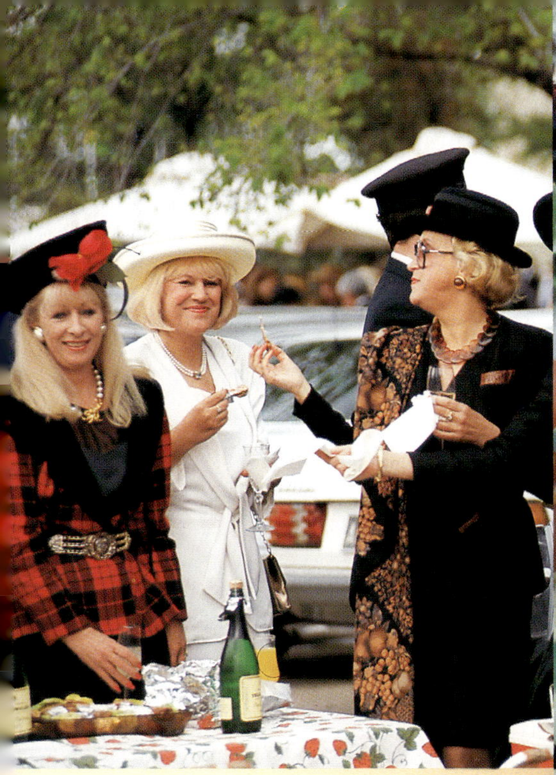
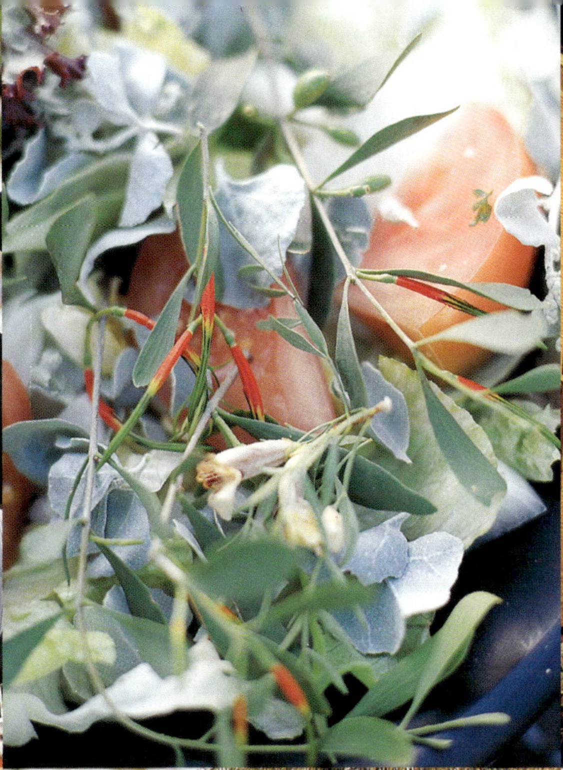
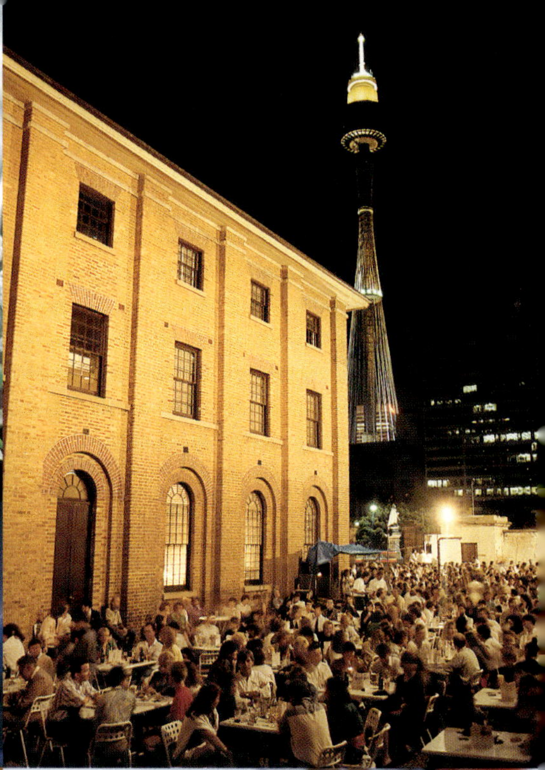
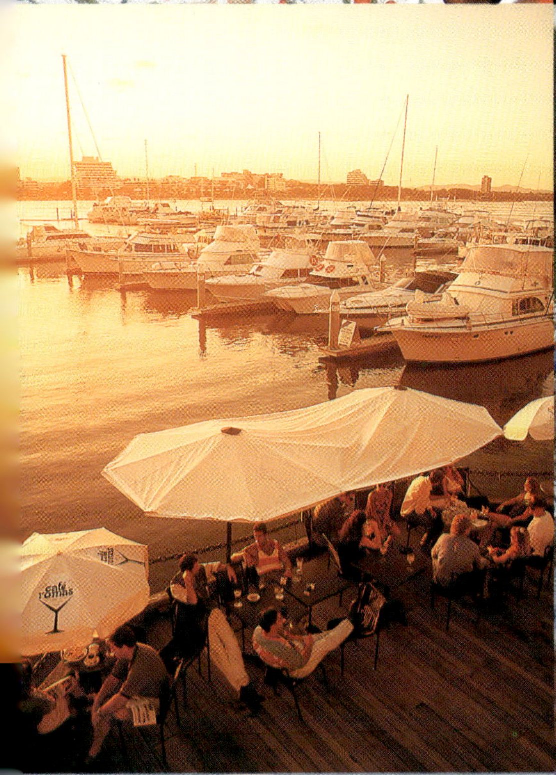
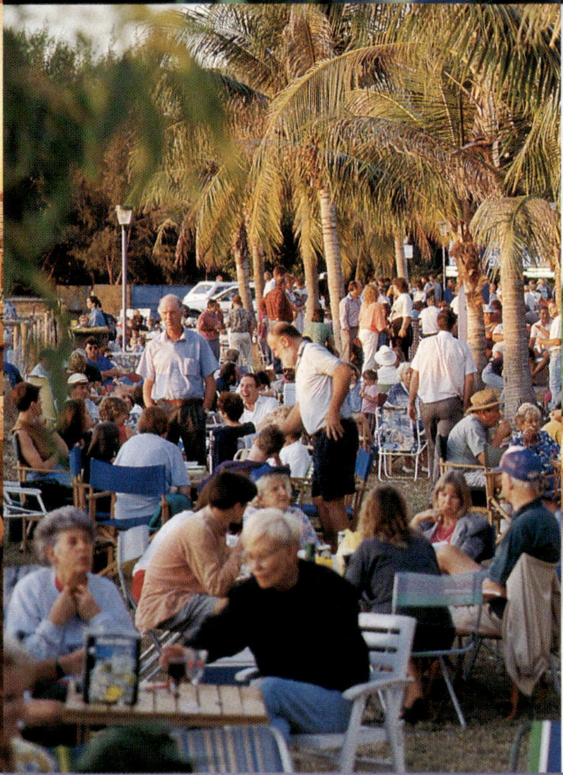
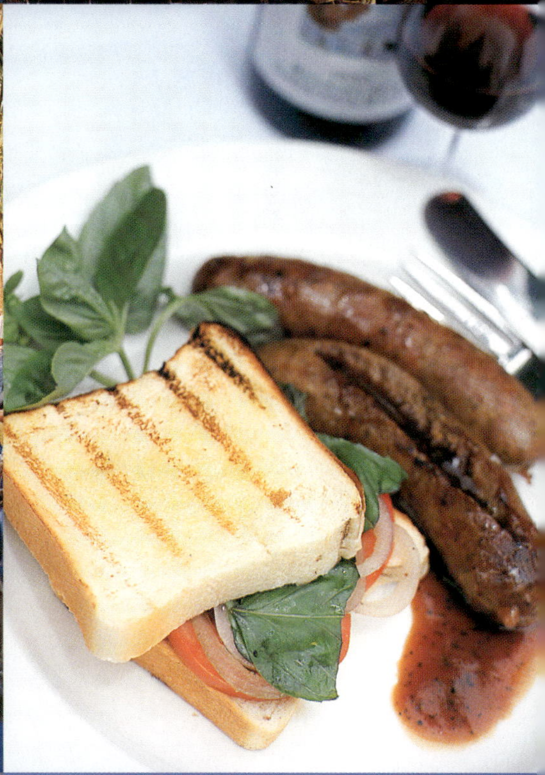
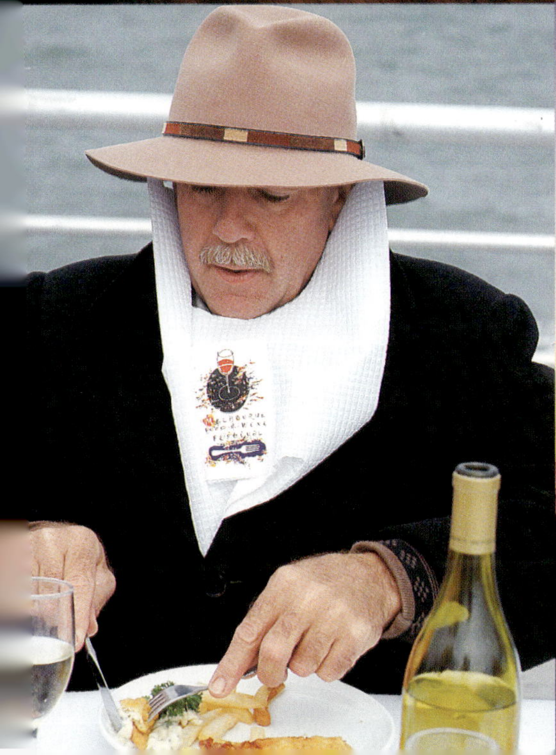
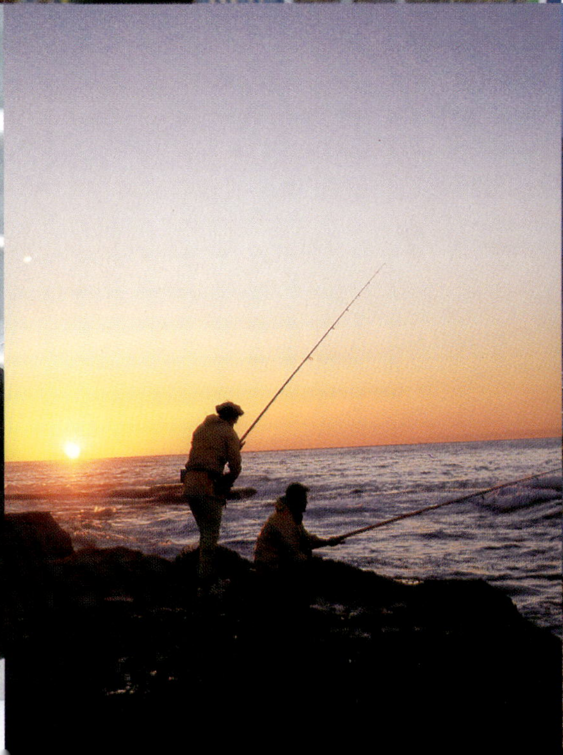
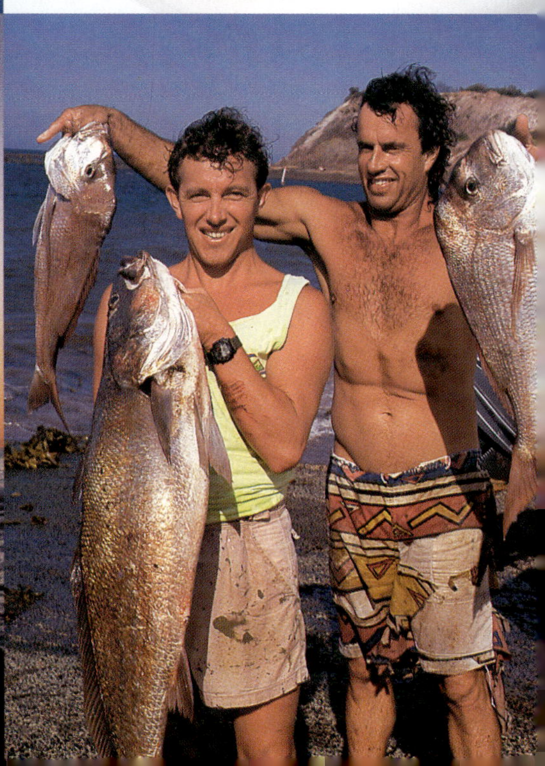

AUSTRALIA - A GOURMET'S PARADISE

COMMITTED TO QUALITY

The Australian Meat and Live-stock Corporation (AMLC) is the national marketing organisation of the meat and livestock industry in Australia. As such, it is responsible for the marketing and promotion of beef, veal and lamb, both in Australia and overseas, as well as mutton, goat, buffalo and offal.

A quality livestock industry began with the arrival of the First Fleet over 200 years ago, when Australia's geographical isolation ensured that only disease-free sheep and cattle survived the long trip from Europe. This isolation also kept Australia free from exotic diseases, and today strict quarantine ensures that no diseases enter the country with animals. However, it was not only a heritage of hardy livestock and geographical isolation that created the industry. Favourable climate and extensive land resources have helped and Australia has also been at the forefront of technological development in livestock production, storage and transportation. The first meat packaging and refrigeration plants were developed here and Australian refrigeration techniques are recognised as among the best in the world.

The AMLC sees as its mission as follows: 'to create a more consumer-oriented meat and livestock industry through leadership in marketing and systems development and so increase industry returns'.

The Corporation is pro-active and innovative, and is responsible for the design and implementation of extensive, coordinated marketing programmes to support domestic and export meat sales. This takes the form of advertising and promotions, merchandising, public relations, constantly updated nutrition/education programmes and market research to identify upcoming consumer trends.

Celebrating the Great Outdoors

In addition, the AMLC supports and encourages new retail and food service products, retailer education, the development of new modern cuts and, in the food service sector, it encourages the innovative use of beef, veal and lamb in new meat dishes.

There is also quality and quantity (quota) control, licensing of meat and livestock exporters, on-line computer sale of livestock (CALM), industry training, systems development and, through AUS-MEAT, a special language to help end-users get the best product and product consistency for their needs.

Control of activities in these areas is central to the AMLC's ability to meet the changing needs of meat consumers in Australia and overseas. Products available for sale in local and international markets need to be the most appropriate for those markets, therefore close liaison with the industry is of paramount importance. This takes place through regular consultation with other industry bodies in developing AMLC research, marketing, promotion and education strategies and programmes.

Left: Peppered steak cooked to perfection
Far Left: British White cow and calf
Above: Lambs grazing in a pristine environment near Armidale, New South Wales

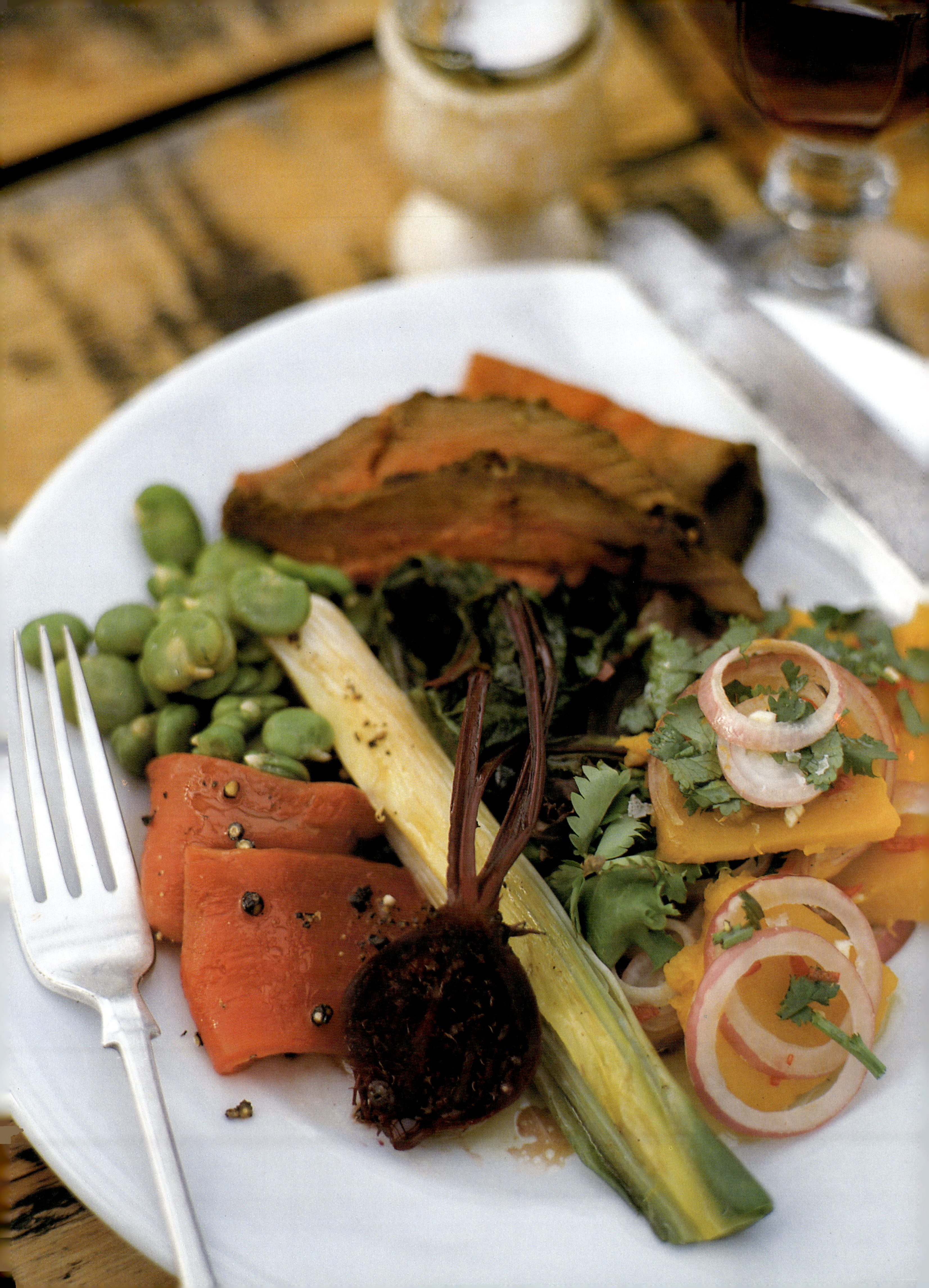

has an impressive Arts Festival every year in spring.

Enjoying the great outdoors is not confined to picnics and barbecues. With the repeal of antiquated laws preventing pavement dining, restaurants are taking advantage of the climate and putting tables and chairs on adjacent parks, pavements and beaches. Fremantle during the defence of the America's Cup in 1987 was a sight to behold—a whole city dining on the sidewalk!

In Melbourne at Southbank there are restaurants which overlook the Yarra River and even a restaurant on a barge during the annual Melbourne Wine and Food Festival. Whole walls of restaurants disappear in Adelaide: they remain glassed-in in winter, but with fine weather in spring and autumn and in extreme summer heat the walls are completely removed—an effective way of bringing the outdoors inside. In Brisbane outdoor dining is centred along the Brisbane River front at Riverside and Kangaroo Point. Further north in Noosa outdoor dining is de rigeur along Hastings Street, the main tourist strip which is right on the beach. Outdoor cafes are also beginning to spring up along the river front at Noosaville. And even in Civic in the centre of Canberra tables clutter the pavement.

Australia is, of course, an island continent and so has a huge range of seafood available both in the waterways and the oceans. This lends itself to instant outdoor cooking and enjoyment. Almost every child in Australia has at some time caught a fish (often a 'tiddler' snared on a piece of string with a bent nail) and asked Mum or Dad to cook it immediately. Prawns and lobster are perennial favourites. But Australians have also broadened their horizons in what fish they will eat. European migrants created a demand for octopus, cuttlefish, squid and calamari (calamari is actually the name for a particular type of squid but it was quickly adopted as a generic term so that consumers would eat something previously thought inedible!). Then mussels, pippies and bivalve molluscs began to appear as well as oysters. Few Australians can deny that oysters freshly opened, full of the tang of the sea, are surely the most perfect food. Local mussels are flung on the barbecue, topped with garlic butter or herbed tomato concasse and eaten, as they are, off the shell.

INFINITE VARIETY In the last decade the Asian influence on seafood has been strongest, with a demand for small whole fish such as silver biddies, garfish and red mullet. Highly-coloured fish have become popular and varieties like catfish are now acceptable. Japanese cuisine has created a demand for sashimi fish—not only tuna but kingfish, garfish and lobster. Yet these premium specimens are eaten, not only as sashimi, but barbecued and grilled.

Rump roast with cumin pepper and sea salt crust served with mixed vegetables

AUSTRALIA - A GOURMET'S PARADISE

Australians no longer only batter and deep-fry such seafood or conceal it in heavy sauces. Often at its best simply butterflied and grilled, it may also show the influences of multicultural Australia: olive or sun-dried tomato butter may be melted quickly over grilled or pan-fried fish; tuna and salmon may be sugar-cured; tuna may be barbecued with a hot wasabi and coriander sauce. Or whole salmon wrapped in foil, filled with dill and lemon, baby octopus cooked in chilli, or whole fish may be steamed Thai style with lemon grass, coriander, ginger and chilli. All these are also enjoyed outdoors, and to accommodate such developments, barbecues themselves have advanced—there are now kettle barbecues, and many others incorporate smoker boxes or woks as well as a hot plate and grill.

Such evolution is not only the domain of the sea. Sheep arrived with the First Fleet and so meat has been an Australian staple from early colonial days, a food also affected since then by diverse influences. Lamb came roasted, as 'mock duck', then was curried and more recently cooked with Middle Eastern spices and couscous. Even the way in which it is butchered has changed, with more modern, lean and boneless cuts branded 'Trim Lamb'. Little steaks or fillets are cooked in minutes, served on focaccia, topped with pesto or accompanied by chargrilled eggplant and capsicum. Tandoori lamb is popular and curry-crusted butterflied leg is sublime.

The T-bone steak is possibly the cut of meat most identified with cooking in the great outdoors. In times gone by it was served with jacket potatoes (wrapped in foil and cooked in the coals of the fire), sour cream, garlic bread and salad. Now the beef is more likely to be eye fillet, thinly sliced and served with a spicy Thai dipping sauce made from vinegar, sugar syrup, fish sauce and coriander. Meat may be chunked and cooked on a skewer, or spare ribs marinated and seared over the open flame. The hamburger has achieved gourmet status and teriyaki marinated chicken drumsticks have become a picnic and children's party stand-by. Chicken breasts are enhanced by 101 different sauces, and even sausages come in innumerable different deluxe flavours. And the old

Right: Chillies, an essential ingredient in many Thai-style dishes
Above: Harvesting the ripest, reddest peppers for Tabasco Pepper Sauce

ADDING A LITTLE ZIP

They say that you can tell the length of a marriage by the level of Tabasco pepper sauce left in the bottle. Not anymore. The distinctive piquant flavour of everyone's favourite pepper sauce has firmly established it as a staple ingredient in contemporary cooking. But most people don't realise that there are 125 years of history in every little red bottle, going all the way back to the American Civil War.

It all began on Avery Island, off the Louisiana Gulf coast, an island that literally sits on a mountain of solid salt. After the war, Edmund McIlhenny returned to the island and nurtured a special variety of red capsicum peppers from Mexico. He experimented with making a sauce by crushing the ripest, reddest peppers, adding half a coffee cup of Avery Island salt per gallon, and letting the concoction age in crockery jars. After thirty days, he added 'the best French wine vinegar' and let the mixture age for another thirty days. After straining the sauce, he filled small cologne-type bottles, which were then corked and dipped in green sealing wax.

Before long the sauce was in such demand that McIlhenny decided to make it commercially. In 1869 he sent 350 bottles of his pepper sauce under the trademark Tabasco to a group of United States wholesalers and, to his delight, the orders poured in.

Since it was introduced to this country over fifty years ago, Australians have realised Tabasco's potential for adding a little zip to everything from breakfast eggs to the incomparable pick-me-up of a Bloody Mary. The versatility of Tabasco suits Australia's busy, outdoor lifestyle, as it's easy to use and adds a richer, fuller flavour to Aussie favourites such as barbeque marinades and sauces, salad dressings and dips. As either a condiment or an ingredient, it can subtly enhance almost every kind of food, from the every-day to the exotic. It's no wonder that Australians are now following the American pattern, where nearly every household has a bottle of Tabasco sauce in the cupboard!

favourite of sausages stuffed with fresh oysters hasn't been forgotten, either!

Farmed game is widely available with smoked quail, an inexpensive option for an easy picnic or quick fling onto the hotplate. Kangaroo, long used only in certain states and for export, is now legalised in others. Far from decimating an exclusively Australian image, the culling is a godsend to farmers and carried out under the most stringent of hygiene conditions. The resulting meat is extremely low in fat yet with all the nutritional benefits of red meat. Ideally served rare, it is perfect for fast and easy outdoor cooking. Indeed, there has been a huge growth in interest in native foods, sometimes called 'bush tucker': wattleseed may appear in damper, lemon myrtle as a flavouring for damper or seafood, bark may take the place of foil to encase fish cooked on the coals and bush tomatoes are used as a relish for barbecued meats.

There is an ever-increasing range of fruit and vegetables available. Australia is such a huge continent that it has every growing condition from sub-tropical to cool, from maritime to inland. Add to this again the influences of migration and ming beans are just as likely to appear alongside a radicchio salad or corn on the cob! Indeed, there are very few things which don't grow in Australia.

Australia is a unique island continent, its geography and climate nurturing the most tremendous range of primary produce. Post-war migration has ensured diversity so that Australia is now a nation with a culinary tradition all its own. Eclectic, yes. But in essence good produce cooked simply to wonderful effect—and where better than in the great outdoors!

Lyndey Milan

Right: A delectable picnic
Above: Carols by candlelight, Myer Music Bowl, Melbourne

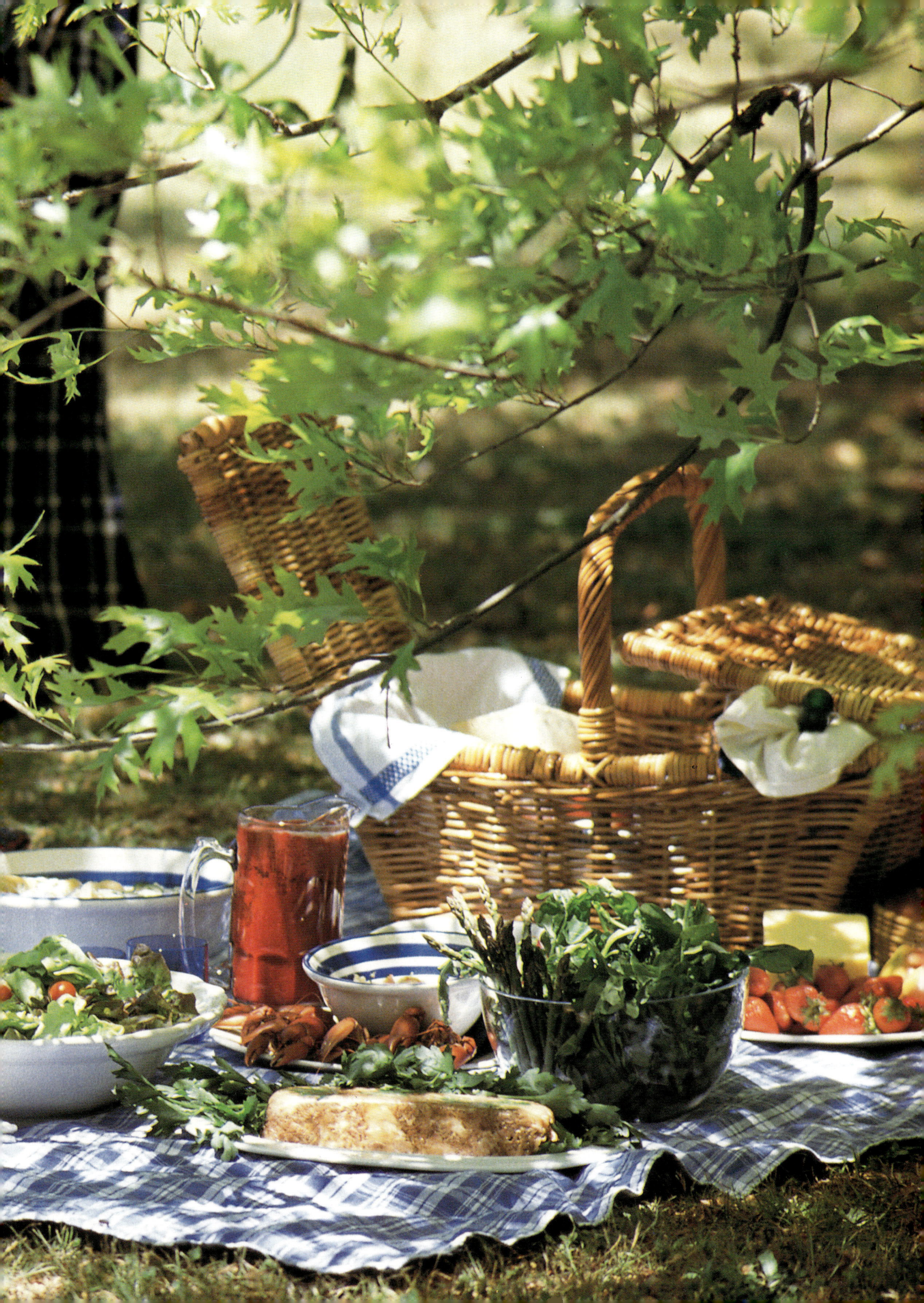

A WONDERF

Right: An aerial photograph of Seppelts Vineyard, South Australia
Above: Ripening black grapes; Rosemount's fertile soil produces wine of exceptional quality

UL BOUQUET

Australia's Wine Heritage

Wine has been made continuously in Australia for almost two hundred years: grapevines arrived with the First Fleet in 1788, and commercial wine production was underway in New South Wales and Tasmania by the 1820s, and in Western Australia, South Australia and Victoria by the 1840s.

Indeed, the first golden age of viticulture occurred in the second half of the nineteenth century. Victoria was the leading wine-producing state, and the development of much of its vineyard area was inextricably linked with the waxing and waning of gold-mining activity across the centre and north-east. They were turbulent times, with fortunes won and lost overnight and with a vast appetite for the finer (though sometimes coarser) things of life. Thus Australia was the foremost market for French champagne. Not all of it was consumed; celebrating goldminers were wont to play skittles with unbroached bottles.

Bubbles of all kinds burst sooner or later—in Australia the great bank crash of 1893 heralded harder times for all. In Victoria the vine louse phylloxera, a series of ill-planned government initiatives (and reversals) and the abolition of protective state excise taxes with federation in 1901 led to the rapid decline of its wine industry and the emergence of South Australia as leader.

NEW DIRECTIONS The opening up of the vast irrigation schemes along the Murray and Murrumbidgee Rivers in the early years of the twentieth century accelerated an already-evident trend away from table wine to fortified wine production, from cool areas to warm ones. The viticultural map shrank rapidly, even though between 1920 and 1926 production rose by 250 per cent; the engine room was South Australia, with wineries in the Southern Vales, Barossa Valley and along the Murray providing three-quarters of Australia's production, ninety per cent of which was fortified wine.

It became imperative to expand markets for the flood of wine. With the dual impact of a federal government export bounty and a United Kingdom 'Empire Preference' excise regime, exports to the United Kingdom soared. Virtually all was fortified wine exported in barrel; between 1928 and 1940 Australia's cumulative exports to the United Kingdom exceeded those of France.

But the sweet, cream sherry and tawny port styles were what the markets of the world demanded at the time, and it was with such wines that Australia re-entered the markets after the conclusion of World War II. Indeed, as late as 1960, over eighty per cent of all wine produced was fortified. However, changes as fundamental as those at the end of the previous century were underway, changes which reflected the wheel turning full circle.

ASTOUNDING SUCCESS For in the last twenty-five years the industry has moved from under twenty per cent table wine to ninety per cent. The number of wineries has increased from 150 to 750. The viticultural map has grown to once again encompass all of the regions which existed in the nineteenth century (many of them in the cooler parts of Australia) and incorporate some new areas. Consumption of wine has risen from five litres to eighteen litres per person per year.

In the last ten years the type of grapes being grown have moved from one third premium to two thirds premium, representing a massive investment in restructuring the vineyards. One dividend has been the increase in exports from eight million to 130 million litres per year, with a further trebling forecast by the year 2000.

If that target is achieved, Australia will move up the international totem pole from its present position as the eleventh largest wine producer in the world. The constraints are more likely to arise from the supply than the demand side. A fifty per cent increase in premium vineyard plantings will have to be completed between 1994 and 1997 at a cost of $500 million. On the demand side of the equation, Australian wines—and Australian wine-makers—have achieved international recognition as some of the world's best in an incredibly short period.

NATURAL ADVANTAGES Yet the foundations were laid over a much longer period, and were at least in part pre-ordained. The Australian soils are very ancient; they are varied, of course, but far larger areas of the country have good viticultural soils than will ever need to be planted. The climate, too, is of ancient origin if one accepts that climate change has always been part of the environment. It is a far more limiting factor than soils: a quick glance at a map will show that with the exception of central and northern Victoria, the Murrumbidgee Irrigation Area of New South Wales and the Riverland areas along the Murray River, all of the

Looking across the vineyard to Robert's restaurant at Pepper Tree in the Hunter Valley

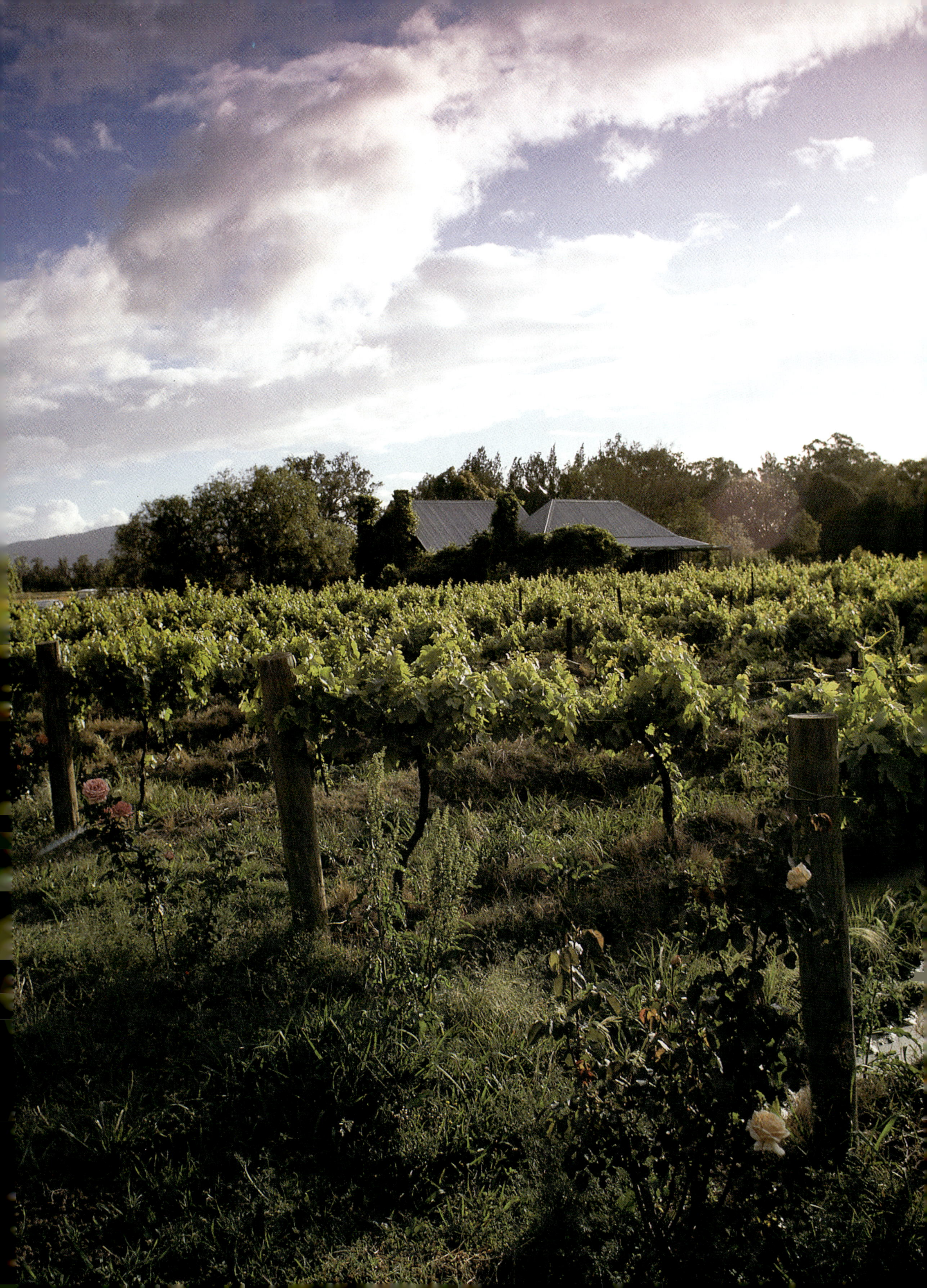

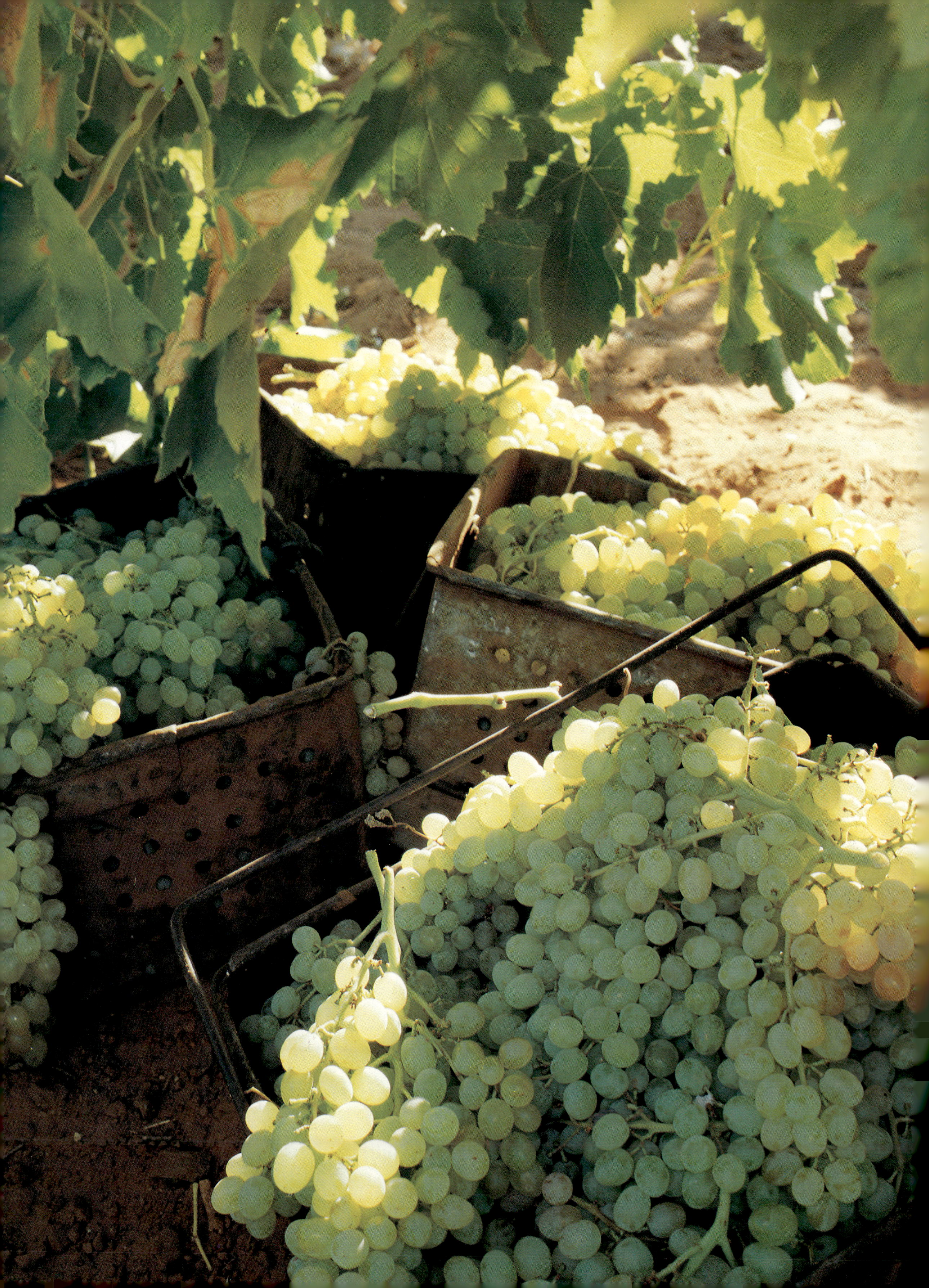

Australian wine regions are clustered on or within 100 kilometres of the coast—and all are in the southern half of Australia.

Even with this limitation, there is tremendous variation in the climate of the various regions. Southern Victoria, Tasmania, the far south-east of South Australia, the Adelaide Hills and the south of Western Australia all have vineyards situated in climates as cool or cooler than that of Bordeaux, France. Certainly, there are much warmer regions in which vintage variation is minimal. Here the grapes are virtually guaranteed to fully ripen without disease or other incident. It is here that the South Australian Riverlands and Murrumbidgee Irrigation Area come into their own, producing two-thirds of the Australian crush. Yields are high, viticultural costs are low, and clever wine-making technology turns the grapes into wine which is the Australian equivalent of vin ordinaire, but which the world markets have judged to be far superior to the vin ordinaire of Europe sold at the same price.

In the domestic market, this wine fills the millions of wine casks, or bag-in-the-box, which Australians have made their own since production techniques were perfected in 1974. Around sixty-six per cent of all wine consumed in Australia is sold in this package. In turn, sixty per cent is dry or near dry white wine, and only eighteen per cent dry red. (Sparkling wine is ten per cent, fortified 8.5 per cent, others 3.5 per cent.) It is no surprise that the introduction of the wine cask coincided with the commencement of the white wine boom in Australia. In 1974 sales of dry white and dry red wine were the same; within ten years those of dry white wine were five times as great as those of red wine.

These changes in Australia coincided with the cultural revolution in all aspects of wine and food which inexorably gathered momentum in the post-World War II years, at first slowly in the 1950s and 1960s, ever faster and more surely in the 1970s and 1980s. Wine may not be the everyday food substance of Italy or France, but its consumption now transcends every barrier of class, race or wealth. It is as widely consumed in the industrial western suburbs of Sydney as it is in the affluent dormitory eastern suburbs; it is enjoyed by young and old alike; it is as much a part of the business lunch as the evening meal at home. Yet none of these things were true at the start of the 1950s, when it was just another form of alcohol, then easier to obtain than beer.

Even this paints an incomplete picture of the changes which have taken place over this time span. In 1959 a total of only seventy tonnes of cabernet sauvignon were crushed in Australia, enough to make 450 cases of wine. In 1993, 38,000 tonnes were vintaged, and the official forecasts for 1996 suggest 72,000 tonnes. The situation with chardonnay is even more

Sultana grapes from the Barossa Valley, traditionally used in the production of ports and other fortified wines

*Right: The lush green rows of
Yalumba's vineyards
Below: The old brandy
still-house at Yalumba*

224

DISTINCTIVE CHARACTER & FLAVOUR

One of the most famous names in the history of Australian wine-making is Yalumba—the flagship of the distinguished South Australian wine company Samuel Smith & Son.

Yalumba is the Aboriginal name given to the family-owned winery in the Barossa Valley by Samuel Smith in 1849. Six generations later, Yalumba is the oldest family-owned winery in Australia and the original vineyard holding of thirty acres has expanded to around 1,100 acres in selected sites around Koppamurra, Coonawarra and Eden Valley.

Some of the wines bearing the proud Yalumba label are the classically elegant and award-winning Yalumba Pinot Noir Chardonnay 'Cuvee One', Yalumba Angas Brut N.V., Yalumba Oxford Landing wines and the premium wines known as 'The Signature', 'The Menzies' and 'The Family Reserve' range.

Other distinctive brands from the company's portfolio include the individual vineyard wines from the prestigious Eden Valley region in South Australia. Pewsey Vale, Heggies Vineyard and Hill-Smith Estate have each established their reputations as small vineyards producing world-class varietal wines.

Historic Pewsey Vale was established in 1847. Situated in the hills overlooking Eden Valley, it became one of the first 'cool climate' vineyards in Australia. Longer, cooler ripening temperatures deliver remarkable grape quality, reflected in the many awards Pewsey Vale wines have received since 1864.

The Heggies Vineyard was established in 1971 and with its beautiful Australian bush setting, interestingly produces wine of the European style. Plantings include the rare Viognier grape as well as Chardonnay, Merlot and Riesling which all show the characteristics of finesse, delicacy and length of flavour, possibly due to the relatively high altitude of 550 metres above sea level.

Today, the family is dedicated to upholding their reputation as producers of fine wines of great character which are marketed in Australia and abroad. Recent successes in a broad range of international competitions have added weight to their enviable industry reputation.

dramatic: none was made before 1971 when Murray Tyrrell in the Hunter Valley and Craigmoor in Mudgee made their first wines. It was not until the end of the 1970s that the first chardonnay was nationally marketed, but even in 1979 there were only 1,500 tonnes crushed. By 1993 the tonnage had increased to 55,000, and will leap to 89,000 tonnes by 1996.

ACROSS THE CONTINENT At the very time Murray Tyrrell was publicly extolling the virtues of chardonnay he was not-so-privately saying that the Hunter Valley produced far better semillon. It is with this variety that the enigmatic climate of this famous region (160 kilometres north of Sydney) is best expressed. If one only looks at the temperature, it has a hot climate, seemingly more suited to fortified wine production than fine table wine. To add insult to injury, the soils are meagre, and nature has a nasty habit of depositing most of the modest rainfall when it is least wanted—right in the middle of vintage.

Yet the region has always been a producer of table, not fortified wine, wine of remarkable finesse and longevity. The answer lies in the relatively high humidity, the afternoon sea breezes and frequently accompanying cloud cover—and those meagre soils. The result is semillon which is almost painfully austere in its youth, but which gradually assumes the aromas and tastes of nuts, honey and lightly browned buttered toast as it becomes ten years old, the best living for more than twenty years.

Cabernet sauvignon came to the Hunter Valley in 1963 at the hand of former surgeon Dr Max Lake, who can fairly claim to have been the first of the 400 or so boutique wine-makers who have since swapped part or all of city lives for weekend and annual holiday wine-making. Just as with chardonnay, there are those who aver that the traditional red grape of the Hunter, shiraz (or hermitage as it was called), makes a better wine than the newcomer of cabernet. Certainly it is that the gently earthy—some say sweaty saddle—regional characters impose themselves on both varieties, producing wines of wonderful, if idiosyncratic complexity.

Mudgee and the Canberra district are the other homes for boutique wineries in New South Wales, the Murrumbidgee Irrigation Area for the vast wineries of de Bortoli and McWilliams. And a rapidly increasing quantity of chardonnay

Moorooduc Estate, Mornington Peninsula, Victoria

A Wonderful Bouquet - Australia's Wine Heritage

is grown at Cowra in south-western New South Wales, but so far there are no wineries there.

Victoria, having shrunk to a mere shadow of its nineteenth century glory, is now resurgent. The number of wineries has increased from thirty to 243 since 1965, the number of wine-growing regions from four to seventeen. The dress circle around Melbourne consists of the Yarra Valley, Mornington Peninsula, Geelong, South Gippsland and Macedon, the closest wineries thirty minutes drive, the most remote ninety minutes drive. The Yarra Valley (in particular), Mornington Peninsula and Macedon are very beautiful regions, with a distinctly European air about them. For one thing, the grass stays green for at least nine months every year, sometimes continuously. For another, they are very cool. Chardonnay and pinot noir are the most important grapes, used to make both sparkling and supremely elegant table wine, although selected sites can and do produce excellent cabernet sauvignon and merlot in warmer vintages.

As one moves north and crosses the Great Dividing Range, the climate—and the feel of the countryside—changes dramatically. Central Victoria witnessed the height of the 'auriferous fever', and Ballarat still retains many of the magnificent buildings erected during the gold rush days, and is a prime tourist destination. If this is gold country, it is also full-bodied dry red country, cool enough to invest the shiraz from around Great Western (another gold town) with pepper and spice aromas reminiscent of the Rhone, but warm enough to give great richness and depth to shiraz, cabernet sauvignon or blends thereof.

Victoria's north-east, lying between Glenrowan (of Ned Kelly bushranger fame) and Rutherglen, makes some of Australia's most distinctive wines. These are the unctuous fortified dessert wines made from brown frontignan (called muscat) and from muscadelle (confusingly called tokay). Long-barrel age in the baking heat of the century-old galvanised iron wineries works the same magic as a trip around the equator did for the wines of Madeira, which these jewels of north-east Victoria most resemble.

Victoria's viticultural map spreads from chilly Drumborg in the far south-western corner to Mildura in the north west across to East Gippsland, over 250 kilometres and four hours drive east of Melbourne. There is little of the state which is not capable of growing grapes, and the spread of vines will doubtless continue well into the next century.

By contrast, the South Australian map has remained far more constant over the last century. The only completely new region established prior to 1990 was Padthaway (in 1963), which is proving to be a portent of things to come. This south-eastern corner of South Australia has been identified by the major companies as a region the potential of which is limited only by the availability of underground water for irrigation and frost control. Vast new vineyards are being established from Robe on the coast across to Bordertown and Keith on the Victorian/South Australian border, all destined to serve the demands of the export market.

Coonawarra (where it all started in the 1890s) remains Australia's most famous region for cabernet sauvignon, although the quality of its shiraz is also exemplary. Padthaway, ninety kilometres north, has proved to be a better white wine region, with chardonnay, sauvignon blanc and rhine riesling leading the way—although as with virtually all Australian wine regions, there is no fixed dichotomy.

Scenically, the laser flat plains of the south-east are uninspiring, and are a disconcertingly long way from Adelaide. Neither complaint can be made about McLaren Vale (skirting the south of Adelaide), the Adelaide Hills (a stone's throw to the east) or the Barossa Valley (to the north). For many, the Barossa Valley is the very heart of the Australian wine industry; certainly it ranks with the Hunter Valley as its best known region.

INTERNATIONAL INFLUENCES Multiculturalism has long been part of Australia's heritage, and nowhere is this more evident than with wine. Germans—principally religious refugees from Silesia—laid the cornerstones of the Barossa Valley from the 1850s; the Swiss were the architects of the Yarra Valley and Geelong in Victoria at the same time; the Dalmatians (of Yugoslavia) came to the Swan Valley around the turn of the century; while successive waves of Italians before and after World War II have played a leading role alongside the McWilliams in the Murrumbidgee Irrigation Area of New South Wales.

The German Lutheran presence in the Barossa Valley is palpably evident wherever you go: the beautifully crafted bluestone and sandstone houses; the place names (Hahndorf, Kaiser Stuhl and so forth); the food (sauerbraten and bienenstuck in place of meat pies and milk shakes); and the wineries—Gramp (of Orlando), Seppelt and Henschke are but a few of many companies founded 150 years ago by Silesian immigrants.

Fittingly, it is the spiritual home of riesling (or rhine riesling as it is known in Australia), however much may be grown these days in the nearby hills which the Barossans call the East Barossa Ranges and which others regard as a northerly extension of the Adelaide Hills. This,

Wining in style—250 guests at Domaine Chandon in Victoria's Yarra Valley

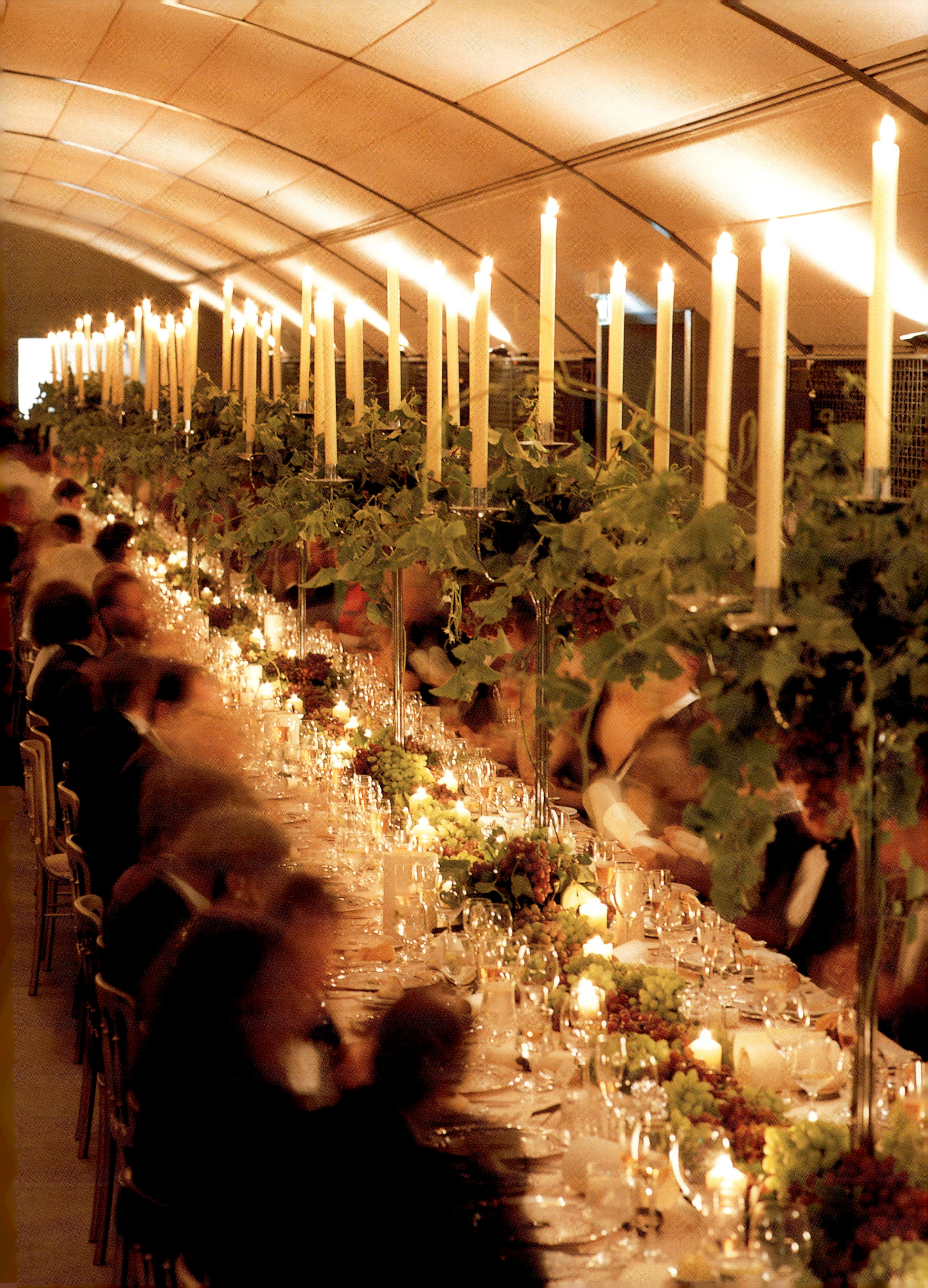

*Right: Impressive views from the
Wise Family Restaurant
Below: One of Wise's many
fine wines*

SPECTACULAR SENSATIONS

The Wise Family Winery & Restaurant is blessed with one of the most spectacular outlooks in the world for enjoying good food and estate-grown wines. The sixty-hectare estate, a three-hour drive from Perth, encompasses the spring-fed Meelup Valley, located on Cape Naturaliste Peninsula, and is the most northern vineyard in the Margaret River region. The restaurant boasts an expansive wine deck overlooking the valley and the clear turquoise waters of Geographe Bay.

Semillon and sauvignon blanc grapes thrive on the gravelly soils of the original Eagle Bay Estate, which was amalgamated with Geographe Estate in 1992. Here the granitic valley soils host the cabernet sauvignon and merlot vines as well as a small planting of pinot noir and chardonnay.

The modern winery produces only 4,000 cases of wine annually, but these wines are served in top restaurants and wine stores around Australia, and are available in Tokyo and San Francisco. Cellar door sales and direct shipping can also be arranged.

The Estate is establishing an impressive reputation for quality wines, due in no small part to the unrelenting passion of proprietor Ron Wise. In the Wise restaurant these wines accompany truly superb cuisine made with local fresh ingredients, such as marron which is supplied by nearby Capel Freshwater Lobsters.

A semillon-sauvignon blend or Wise's classy chardonnay are ideal to sip while enjoying a summer meal on the restaurant's balcony. In winter, the cabernet sauvignon-merlot can be enjoyed by the blazing log fire.

Wine and food fanciers can savour some of life's great pleasures from the spectacularly positioned restaurant on its hilly perch. During the migratory season patrons can see whales frolicking in Meelup Bay. Meelup Spring, located on the estate, was a source of fresh water for American whalers in the early 1800s.

Rustic accommodation is available and guests are invited to participate in vineyard activities by appointment.

For sheer pleasure, visitors to the west should make a Wise choice.

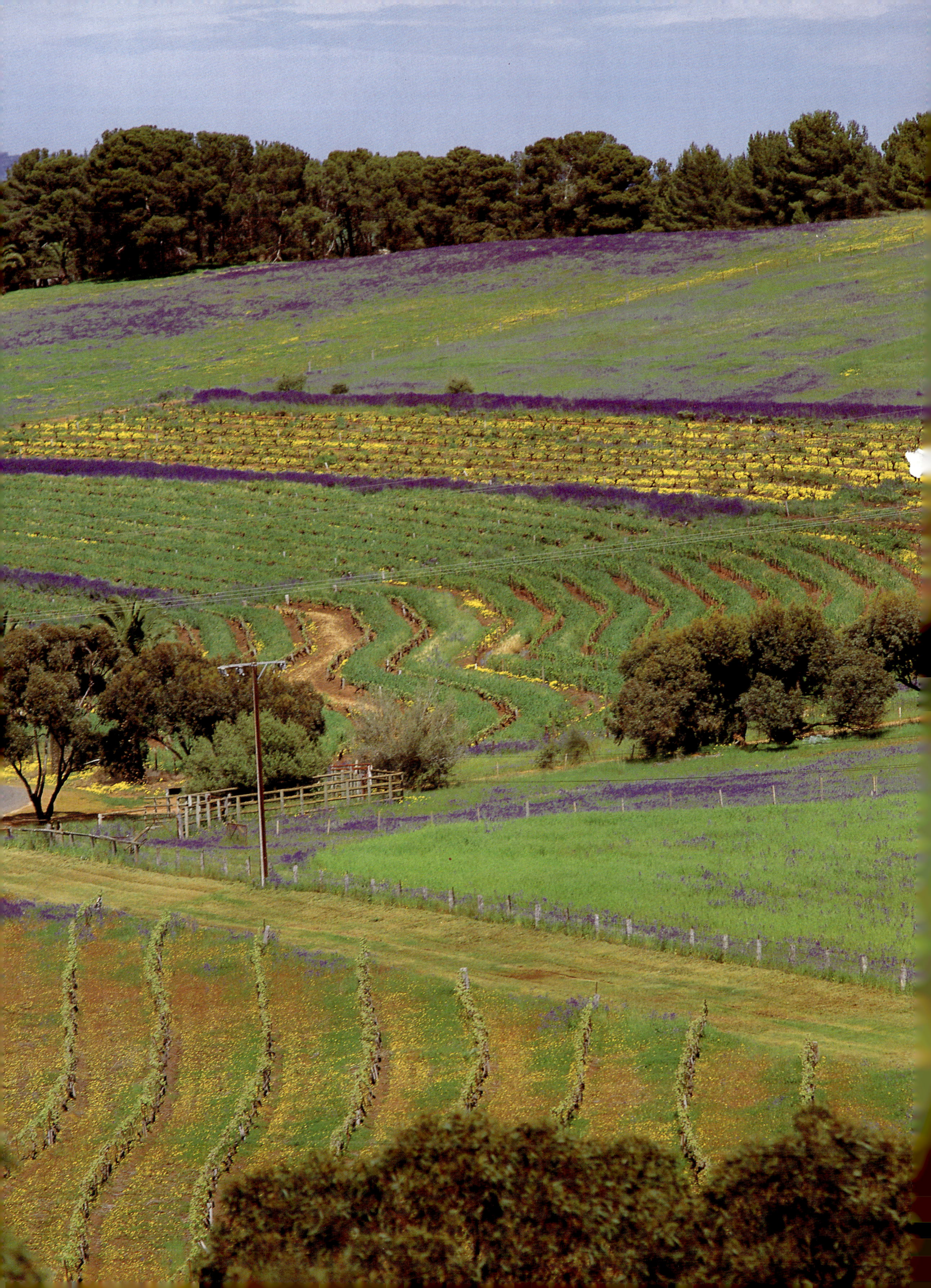

too, is symptomatic of the Barossa Valley as a whole: the majority of the forty-two wineries draw some or most of their grapes from other regions—notably the south-east, the Riverlands and McLaren Vale.

It is also the source of many broodingly rich red wines, none more famous than Penfolds' Grange Hermitage. Its creator, Max Schubert—who died in 1994—is seen by many as Australia's greatest wine-maker. He also believed in regional blending to provide chemical and textural balance in wines, so Grange was always derived from various vineyard (and regional) sources; this appetite for blending is a feature of the Australian industry, covering both regions and varieties, and widely practised by all the medium to large-sized wineries. McLaren Vale (or Southern Vales as the region is sometimes called) is a jack-of-all-trades. Originally famous for its immensely sturdy red wines, often described as ferruginous and prescribed for anaemic patients by English physicians in Victorian times, it is now equally well-known for its chardonnay and sauvignon blanc. In cooler years, indeed, its sauvignon blanc is outstanding, easily Australia's best and offering a real alternative (in a more opulent, tropical/gooseberry mould) to the sauvignons of New Zealand. It is an important supplier of grapes to wineries across Australia, but at the same time was for decades described as the home of the small winery. Its gently rolling hills are as beautiful in winter—when the vineyards are clothed in the gold flowers of soursops growing between the rows of vines—as it is in summer. Like the Barossa Valley, restaurants abound (the Salopian Inn is famous) and accommodation is plentiful.

The diminutive Clare Valley (two hours north of Adelaide) has remained a hidden treasure; only the main street of the town of Clare shows the scars of twentieth-century progress. Together with the Eden Valley (in the northern Adelaide Hills), the twisting, folded dales and streamlets of the Clare Valley make Australia's most famous and finest rhine riesling; bone dry, crisp and—if given the chance—marvellously long-lived. But it also produces high quality shiraz and equally good cabernet sauvignon, the latter sometimes blended with malbec to produce a regional specialty of particular note.

Western Australia's wine industry was focused almost entirely on the Swan Valley for over a century, but since the 1970s the balance has shifted quite dramatically to the Margaret River (220 kilometres south of Perth) and to the Mount Barker/Frankland region, even further away in the far south western corner of the state. The almost feminine softness and intimacy of the Margaret River contrasts with the masculine vastness of Mount Barker/Frankland, yet both share an abundance of Australian trees, shrubs and flowers of greater variety and beauty than any other part of Australia outside the tropical rainforests of Queensland. The strongly

A superbly tended vineyard, typical of the Barossa Valley in South Australia

Right: Rosemount's maturation cellar at Denman
Below: Night harvesting; a reminder of earlier days

AWARD-WINNING WINES

Rosemount Estate is one of the most successful family-owned wine companies in Australia and around the world.

With more than 800 hectares of vines spread across seven vineyards in the Upper Hunter Valley and four vineyards in the Coonawarra, McLaren Vale, Langhorne Creek and Adelaide Hills regions of South Australia, Rosemount produces a range of fine quality wines each year, including premium chardonnay, semillon, sauvignon blanc, cabernet sauvignon, shiraz and merlot.

At Rosemount a successful marriage of traditional winemaking techniques, together with modern technology and sophisticated winery equipment, has created premium wines that now enjoy an exceptional reputation for quality in the highly competitive local and international markets.

The Rosemount story actually has two beginnings. The first revolves around a German settler, Karl Brecht, who planted vines and established a highly successful winery on the fertile soils beside the Goulburn River in the Upper Hunter Valley of New South Wales in 1860.

Brecht's wines were so impressive that they were recognised with Gold Medals in the Great Expositions of Europe and the United States. But Brecht's dream died with him, and the rich Rosemount acres reverted to cattle pastures.

Rosemount's renaissance came in 1969 when the Oatley family purchased the 220-hectare property where the old winery has stood. Bob and his sons quickly recognised the potential of the land they had bought and began planting again, selecting the best classified varieties of the day with a view to growing quality wine grapes from the very outset.

The plan soon payed off, and Rosemount quickly developed a reputation for the quality that has stayed with it to this day. In his Australian Wine Guide the celebrated wine writer James Halliday notes: 'The ability to win gold medals almost at will at national shows is but one indicator of the quality and consistency of all the wines under the Rosemount label'.

'As one goes up the range', Halliday continues, 'complexity, weight and richness all increase, reaching a veritable crescendo with Roxburgh Chardonnay'.

maritime-influenced climate of the Margaret River produces wines of very distinctive styles: bracingly crisp, herbaceous sauvignon blanc and semillon (frequently blended); contrastingly soft and creamy chardonnay; and cabernet sauvignon which somehow manages to simultaneously display bright cherry fruit and a sinewy, almost gravelly, structure.

Rhine riesling has been tried but found wanting in the Margaret River, but comes into its own in Mount Barker/Frankland, piercingly fragrant and with delicate lime-accented flavours. Cabernet sauvignon, too, flourishes here, producing exceptionally elegant yet tightly structured wines which—like the rhine riesling—are very long-lived. The chardonnay reflects the cool climate, with grapefruit and melon aromas and flavours which build with several years in the bottle. Pinot noir, too, is making an emphatic statement in scattered spots throughout the region.

The final outposts of Australian wine are the Granite Belt of southern Queensland and Tasmania. The wineries of the Granite Belt are tiny and sell most of their wine to the passing tourist trade: semillon, chardonnay and shiraz are the mainstays. Tasmania is a far more significant wine-producing region in terms of quality and potential, but provides less than half of one per cent of the national production. It has nine regions, each producing wines of distinctive style. The three best known regions are Pipers Brook, the Tamar Valley and the Derwent Valley, but all nine are extravagantly beautiful. Tasmania may be last and smallest, but it is certainly not least.

James Halliday

The art of making great vintages

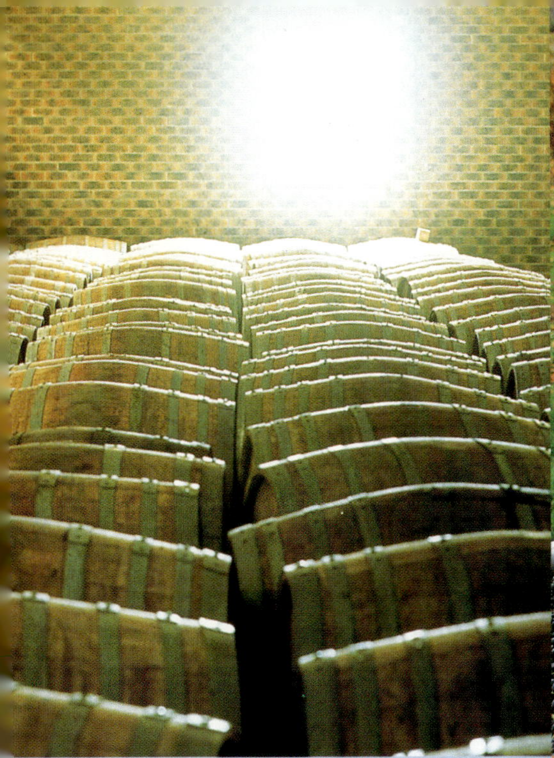
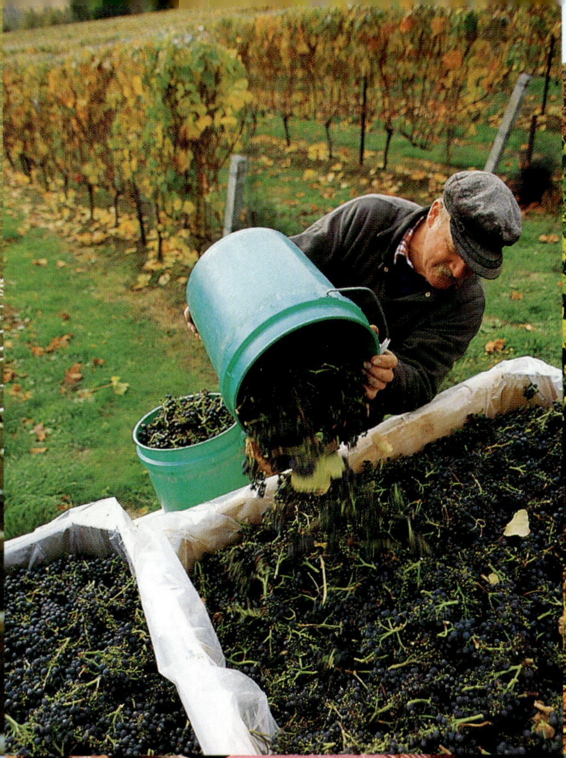
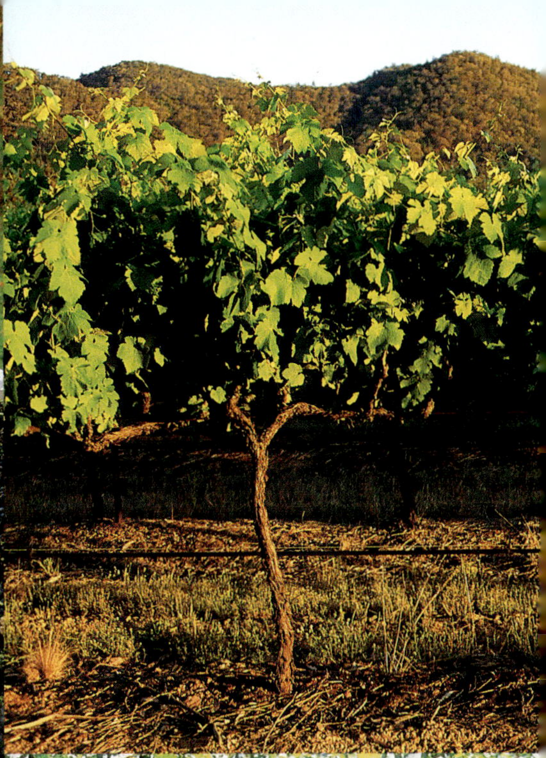
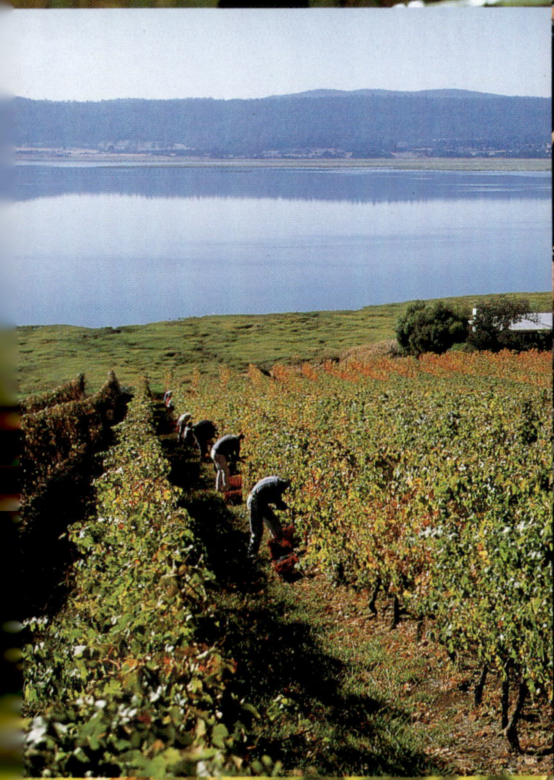
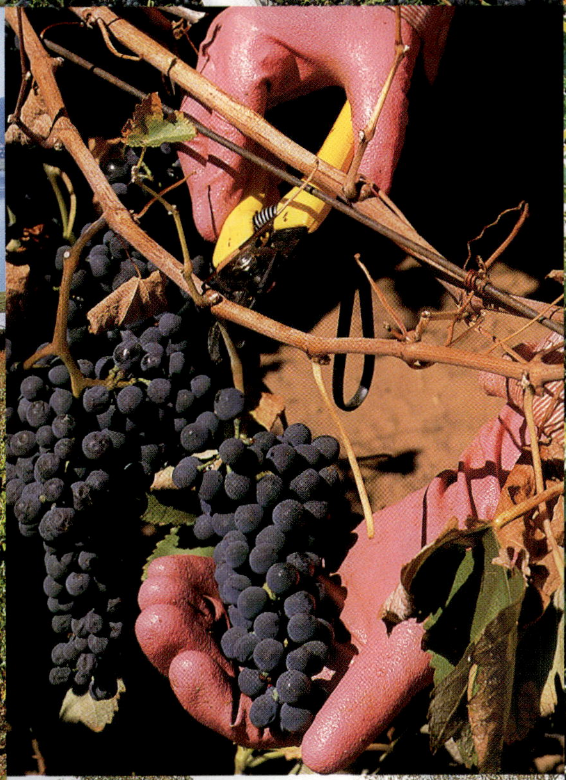
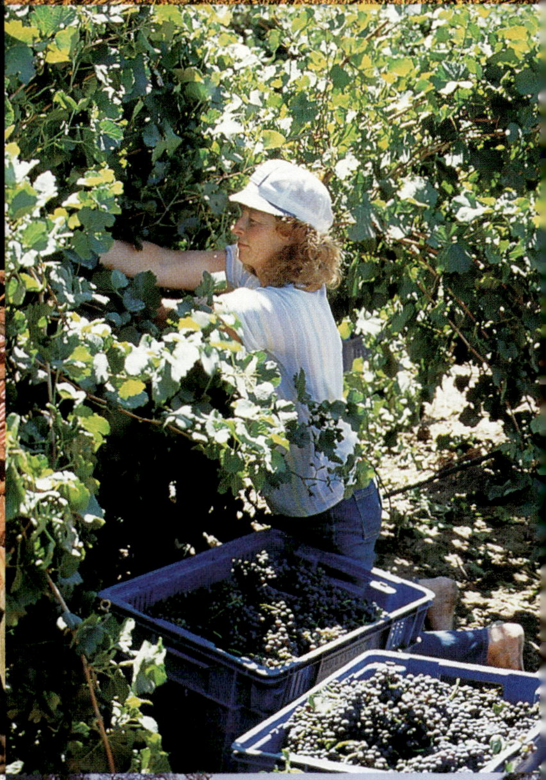
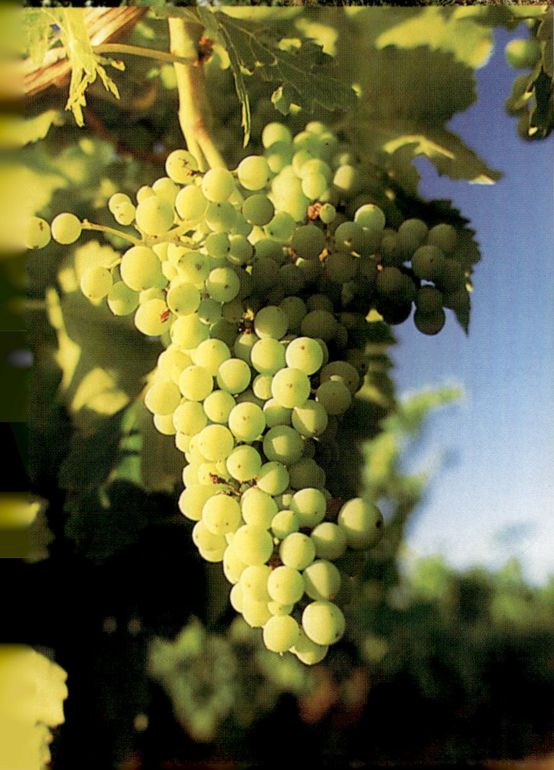
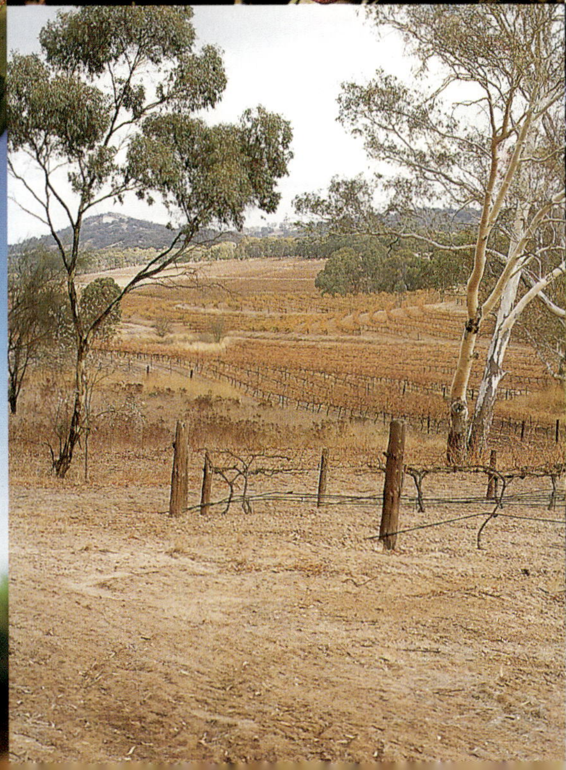
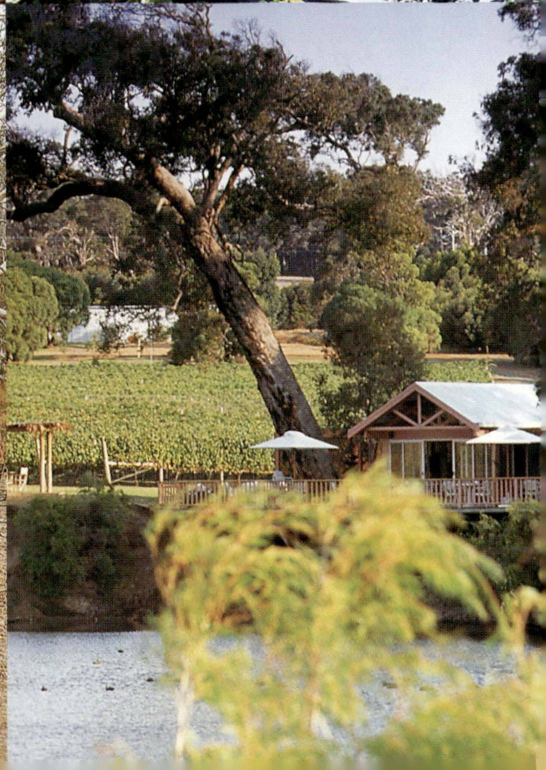

INTERNATIO

Right: Evening light on stooks of hay in central Victoria Below: Grains of black pearl caviar resting on soba noodles from Tables at Toowong; Gambaro's famous fresh seafood platter

238

PROFILE

Made in Australia

Australia has always been a significant exporter of food, reflecting and reinforcing early images of the country as a pastoral paradise. In recent times, overseas demand for Australia's top quality, fresh and manufactured produce has heralded a booming new era, one which means greater export earnings for the country and an ever-increasing image as a sophisticated source of gourmet produce and products.

FRESH FROM AUSTRALIA One of Australia's biggest attributes is its clean environment. But it would be foolish to ignore the fact that much of Australia's increasing success in exporting fresh produce is due to sophisticated, technologically advanced quality control, handling and transport procedures, honed to perfection thanks to Australia's own vast distances. The third element of Australia's gourmet export success rests on nothing more than exquisite taste. English novelist Anthony Burgess once wrote, 'Australian seafood is pregnant with wholesome concupiscence: Aphrodite laughs in every oyster'.

Over the past fifteen years Australia has aggressively developed the niche marketing of its fresh produce. Tasmania now grows the only buckwheat sourced outside Japan for soba noodles. Western Australian chèvre amazes French visitors, while in Queensland it is all but impossible to buy a mud crab with two claws because of exports to the lucrative 'claw-only' market of Hong Kong. Similarly, Germans are wildly enthusiastic for Australian venison.

The same story holds true for Australian wines which have annihilated the international competition at leading wine shows from London to New York to Paris, winning gold medals in all categories. The reasons for the huge success of wine exports are the same as the ones that have kept Australians fiercely partisan about their own wines for years: high quality, reasonable prices and sheer integrity of taste.

BRAND LEADERSHIP

Pacific Brands Food Group is one of Australia's largest consumer branded food companies. The Group is a division of the wholly-owned Australian company Pacific Dunlop Limited, which has a proud and successful heritage dating back more than 100 years.

For generations Dunlop has been a revered name in Australia. Initially synonymous with automotive products and sports equipment, Pacific Dunlop's extensive portfolio today includes construction materials, biomedical products and food—to name a few.

Pacific Brands Food Group is an acknowledged market leader, renowned for the dependability and excellent quality of its brands and innovative food technology.

Among its well-known brands, which are household names, are Edgell-Birds Eye canned and frozen vegetable and fish products, Peters ice creams and Herbert Adams' sweet and savoury pies and pastries, which include the world's most famous pie—the Four'n Twenty.

So great is Herbert Adam's production capacity, it can create 40 million Four'n Twenty pies a year. Put another way, in one hour it can make sufficient pies to feed 100,000 people at the Melbourne Cricket Ground.

To meet Australia's growing demand for pasta, Pacific Brands Food Group pioneered the Latina fresh pasta range—available from supermarket dairy cases and other outlets. Another popular brand is Leggo's, with its authentic Italian pasta products and sauces. (The enormous growth of pasta consumption in Australia—a staggering forty per cent per annum—means that Pacific Brands is a huge processor of Australian-grown durum wheat.)

The Group also meets the needs of health-conscious people with its creative range of Yoplait fresh dairy foods

International Profile - Made in Australia

and Vitari fruit desserts. And soon to be released is a range of French-developed, restaurant-quality gourmet meals, available pre-prepared and chilled from dairy cases.

Fundamental to the success of the Group's food products is its commitment to the highest quality raw produce. The company has harnessed Australia's huge potential in its clean environment and large areas of fertile land, which provide ideal conditions for growing first-quality vegetables for the domestic and Asian markets.

Tasmania is one of the world's most important growing regions for potatoes. The species most in demand is the Russet Burbank. The company's Ulverstone plant in the state's northern 'vegetable bowl' sources product from no fewer than 500 growers.

This state-of-the-art plant is at the 'cutting-edge' of french fry production technology, capable of processing sixteen tonnes of potatoes per hour. So sophisticated is the technology, an imperfection in an individual potato chip can be detected and eliminated from the production line in an instant.

Australia is bountiful as a producer of lush, fresh vegetables like asparagus, peas, carrots, broccoli and more—all processed to quality perfection under the Edgell-Birds Eye brands.

Pacific Brands are dedicated to developing export markets in Asia. It already exports Peters ice-cream to Japan and has a fifty per cent interest in Meadow Gold Investment Ltd Co, China's largest ice-cream producer, and has purchased forty per cent interest in General Pacific Foods Co Ltd of Thailand—owner of the Ducky brand.

As part of its expansion programme, Pacific Brands Food Group has established offices in Tokyo, Hong Kong, Singapore and Auckland.

Far left: Football and Four 'n' Twenty pies, an unbeatable combination
Left: Harvesting golden fields of wheat in Queensland Above: John Farnham in a tomato field producing an Edgell television commercial

Australia's food export market still belongs overwhelmingly to manufactured foods. More and more Asian markets are looking to Australia to provide high-quality products simply because they know there is no cost-cutting with quality ingredients guaranteed by the 'Made in Australia' legend on the label.

Over the past ten years, Australia has doubled its total food exports, fresh and processed, to a massive $11 billion per year. The greatest leaps forward have come from the meat, fish and shellfish, cereal, vegetable, fruit and dairy sections of the industry. Direct wine and beverage exports have increased profits tenfold during the same time to $385 million per year.

This dramatic export growth is exemplified by Orlando Wyndham, winner of the 1993 Australian Exporter of the Year Award and one of Australia's top three wine producers, which now considers itself an international company that just happens to be based in Australia. Similarly, of the thirteen Australian companies in *Fortune* magazine's official 1994 listing of the 500 largest companies in the world, two—Fosters and Goodman Fielder—are in the food and beverage industry.

Not surprisingly, much of this international success story has been played out in the Asian and United States trading arenas, the two regions that account for seventy per cent of Australia's total export trade. Until the recent rise in the value of the Australian dollar, financial experts were worried that many export successes were the result of favourable exchange rates. But the reality, especially in the food and beverage industry, is that the overseas expansion of Australian companies in their aggressive pursuit of expanding markets has been based largely on quality. Many of these companies are now so firmly locked into their Asian and American markets that the further predicted rise in the value of the Australian dollar scheduled for the mid to late 1990s will have a negligible effect on sales.

According to Philip Armbruster at Austrade, 'Australian food exporters have become more specialist and competitive in new categories over the past five years, particularly at the top end of the market. The sales of fresh asparagus to Japan, for example, have grown from zero to $25 million a year since 1990. France now imports $17 million worth of lobster and seafood per year—up from nothing in 1991. The French are also importing Australian snails reared in Victoria.

'But Europe is essentially a closed shop to Australian food exports and that fact, plus our position in the Asia–Pacific region, is the main reason behind the

International Profile - Made in Australia

expansion of Asian markets. Hong Kong has become a particularly fast area of growth and much of the produce we sell to the Territory goes into China. Sales of milk, cheese and butter to Hong Kong have doubled in only two years. Abalone sales are up to $21 million a year but this looks small against $85 million worth of lobster sales.

'Japan continues its love affair with all things Australian. One of the big unsung success stories is cheese. Sales of Australian cheese have surged from $44 million a year to $150 million in just five years. We are now meeting the tough Japanese premium grade meat specifications, with Gilbertson's in Victoria being a market leader, and exports have climbed to $1.58 million a year'.

Advanced technology is playing an important role in Australia's food export expansion. GEMMNET (an acronym for Global Electronic Marketing and Merchandising Network), a revolutionary electronic trading system is now being used by Woolworths for the sales of grocery and fresh food products and is destined to chalk up yet another success for Australia's high-tech communications reputation in the Asia–Pacific Rim. Woolworths is the first retailer subscriber to the GEMMNET network which has the ability to actually show the products to be bought and sold on individual computer screens.

Essentially, sellers list their products and services and allow selected buyers access through subscription from the catalogue. Buyers scan for merchandise and services based on price and quality, negotiate with potential sellers by E-mail, fax or phone, then order by electronic data interchange or fax. Within three years, the project is to have 15,000 suppliers and 1,000 retailer subscribers on the network in Australia and overseas and in the long term, it will cover all products and services.

STRATEGIES FOR SUCCESS Government initiatives have also been important in honing Australia's food reputation overseas. In July 1992, the Federal Government announced its Agri-Food Strategy to further develop an already export-oriented industry, in association with private sector interests. One of the strategies developed was the Clean Food Export programme, under which Australian food is promoted as being 'sourced from a clean environment'.

The campaign identifies Australian manufactured foods with a blue and yellow logo of a globe centred by a stylised map of Australia. The label verifies their origin, builds consumer loyalty and sets high-quality standards for the

Fresh sea urchins for the Japanese market

AUSTRALIA - A GOURMET'S PARADISE

THE FRESH FOOD PEOPLE

If a company promotes itself as 'the Fresh Food People' there is an inherent responsibility to deliver just that—fresh food—otherwise customer loyalty will quickly fall away.

Woolworths sees freshness for the virtue it is. It is committed to ensuring that the quality- and value-seeking customer can purchase the ultimate in freshness for every trading hour of their operations. It is virtually a truism that a garden-fresh item picked the very same morning can be on your table that night—the same can be said of their baked goods and many other fresh food items.

But this commitment doesn't come lightly. Woolworths' management and its team of professional buyers are ever-vigilant for market trends. They continually liaise with growers and buyers for 'the best', while scrutinising the food industry for the exacting standards the company rigorously seeks in guaranteeing swift delivery to maximise market freshness.

While visiting farms and orchards is a vital tool, of equal importance is management's relationship with major marketing authorities such as the Australian Meat and Live-stock Corporation, the Australian Pork Corporation and the CSIRO, as well as consulting with food technologists and nutritionists.

In the 1920s and 1930s the name Woolworths or 'Woolies', as it was affectionately known, was synonymous with good value, cheerful service and customer-friendly prices—a tradition that continues today. Many generations of Australians grew up hearing the name 'Woolies' and the family tradition of shopping at Woolworths is carefully-nurtured to this day. Woolworths 'brand loyalty' has become an enduring 'buy' word in many Australian households.

International Profile - Made in Australia

In the recent past, Woolworths quickly recognised the needs of Australia's constantly changing population-profile. A visit to their mouth-watering displays of crisp, fresh produce or, for that matter, a perusal of the rich variety of smallgoods, cheeses and wide range of delicacies, is testimony of this.

Then there is their broad selection of quality meats available from the self-selection cabinets. Because of Australia's vastness, Woolworths is able to source product from a range of geographic regions each reflecting seasonal variation. They are dedicated to supplying customers with the 'best in season' from the 'best in the region'.

This commitment to customer service and freshness is indicative not only of Woolworths' company philosophy, it also positions Australia as being at the 'cutting edge' of quality food consciousness, a sophistication enriched by its multicultural population.

Woolworths Limited has no historical ties to, or any commercial relationship with, any other company outside Australia of the same name. It is the nation's largest food retailer with over thirty per cent of the Australian grocery market, and with its general merchandise and specialty retail groups, is the second largest retailer accounting for an estimated ten per cent of national retail sales.

Their supermarkets are the largest operating division within the group with over 422 supermarkets trading across Australia in every state and territory, except Victoria where they trade as 'Safeway', and Tasmania where they trade as 'Purity' and 'Roelf Vos'.

Examples of the fine fresh produce available at Woolworths

AUSTRALIA - A GOURMET'S PARADISE

products which seek to participate in the campaign. The logo and associated standards can be compared with the standards set and enforced in the mid-1980s for Australian wine.

1997 has been earmarked as the Year of Good Living Down Under by the Australian Tourism Commission (ATC). According to a recent world survey eating and shopping are the two greatest interests of international tourists, and the ATC is set to showcase the incredible variety, diversity and tastes of Australian gourmet food and wines in the clean, healthy environment they come from.

EXPORTING QUALITY In the current quest of Australia's food export trajectory, the confectionery business, with international sales up 42 per cent in 1993-4 is an outstanding performer. Cadbury Australia has recently invested $70 million in production and warehouse facilities in Australia just to service its Asia–Pacific export markets, now the fastest growing segment of the company's market. Cereal product exports also increased by 26 per cent in 1993-4, thanks to the efforts of companies like Pacific Brands Food Group, makers of pasta and dairy foods, Peters Ice-Creams and Edgell-Birds Eye frozen vegetables. Pacific Brands is an acknowledged leader in developing export trade with Asia, with offices in Tokyo, Hong Kong, Singapore and Auckland. The company also has a fifty per cent stake in Meadow Gold, China's largest ice-cream producer.

Fish products made the second most important contribution to processed food sales at $557 million in 1993-94, a figure bolstered by the efforts of companies like Tassal, one of the largest fully-integrated salmon producers in the world. The French have picked up a taste for our oysters in a big way, says Austrade, especially prime Pacific and golden oysters such as the ones from Cameron of Tasmania, the state's largest and most prestigious oyster producer.

At the 1994 International Wine Challenge held in England, Australian wines received sixty per cent of the awards, despite comprising less than ten per cent of entries. Of the fourteen trophies awarded, Australia won five—two by Penfolds and one each by Yalumba, Rosemount and Tim Knappstein Wines.

Right: A dairy cow grazes on the pastures of the Atherton Tablelands Above: The best of fresh Australian dairy produce

D A I R Y   G O O D

Behind its tranquil rural image, Australia's dairy industry is big business on both a domestic and world scale. Australian exports of dairy foods represent over $1 billion per year, or 500,000 tonnes of product.

Australia is an ideal dairy nation. The country's dairy-producing regions have a mild climate, adequate sunshine and appropriate levels of rainfall. Such a climate allows Australian herds to be pasture-fed throughout the entire year, avoiding the northern hemisphere practice of keeping cows indoors during freezing winters. This results in pure, high-quality dairy milk—a naturally rich source of calcium and beta carotene (vitamin A).

The Australian Dairy Corporation (ADC) is a statutory authority which performs a series of valuable, industry-specific roles: domestic and international marketing and promotion; planning and information—which involves the collection, analysis and dissemination of a wide range of industry data; and the management of a farmer-funded market-support scheme.

The promotional role of the ADC is designed to improve attitudes to and use of Australian dairy foods on export and domestic markets. On export markets, this non-branded promotion works in conjunction with Australian exporters' individual efforts, while on the domestic market a more general promotional effort is pursued.

Meanwhile, the ADC also conducts commercial activities on international markets. Through agency arrangements the ADC exports cheese to Japan and the United Kingdom on behalf of Australian manufacturers. The intention behind these arrangements is the maximisation of Australia's competitive position in markets with limited access or where import arrangements require some countervailing market power.

Furthermore, the ADC owns a commercially-operated trading subsidiary company, Austdairy Limited. Austdairy exports dairy commodities and technical/managerial services to clients in markets around the world. These activities assist the long-term development of new dairy market opportunities for Australian companies.

Over recent years, our wine-makers have come to expect a high degree of success at overseas wine exhibitions. In the United States, Italy, France and especially Britain, where wine connoisseurship is an art form, Australian wines have consistently taken more than their share of trophies and gold medals in open competition with the world's best.

Major English and American wine judges and specialist wine writers are giving high ratings to Antipodean wines. 'The Aussies have perfected the technique of capturing a strong fruit flavour in all their wines,' writes English Master of Wine Jane Hunt. 'And what is more, they offer incredible value for money.'

The wines are soft, flavoursome and fruity, ready to be enjoyed as soon as the cork is pulled—exactly what today's modern wine drinker wants. Their appreciation calls for no prior wine knowledge on the part of the consumer, yet an educated palate immediately discerns that the wine is well-made. To the delight of the diminishing band of people who enjoy mature wines, Australian reds (and quite a few whites) behave impeccably when cellared.

Will Australia be able to provide enough wine to satisfy the increasing thirst of export and domestic markets? Probably not in the short term, but substantial new plantings of vines are going ahead, and the more bounteous 1994 vintage (725,00 tonnes, compared with 610,000 tonnes in 1993) will offer some relief from the tight supply situation affecting the industry.

The ten largest wine-makers account for 85 per cent of the beverage wine produced in Australia. Southcorp Wines encompasses fourteen labels, including the high-flyers Penfolds, Lindemans, Seppelt, Wynns and Seaview. Other major wine companies, whose products are sold throughout the world, include BRL Hardy, Orlando-Wyndham and McWilliam.

Samuel Smith & Son, Australia's oldest family-owned wine firm, is well-known for its range of products under the Yalumba, Hill-Smith Estate, Pewsey Vale and Heggies Vineyard labels. Samuel Smith & Son's dynamic chief executive, Robert Hill Smith, has recently initiated wine-making ventures in New Zealand, France and California.

Rosemount Estate is a Hunter Valley-based family company which, although only twenty-five years old, has built an extensive domestic and export business on quality red and white table wines. It exports fifty per cent of its annual production of almost nine million bottles, mainly to Britain and other ECU countries and to the United States. Rosemount has its own marketing companies in the United Kingdom and United States, and keeps its products in the public eye with a string of international wine show successes.

In the south-west corner of Western Australia, a group of Margaret River wineries is producing some exciting wines. Leeuwin Estate is in a class of its own, commanding premium

A Hunter Valley vineyard

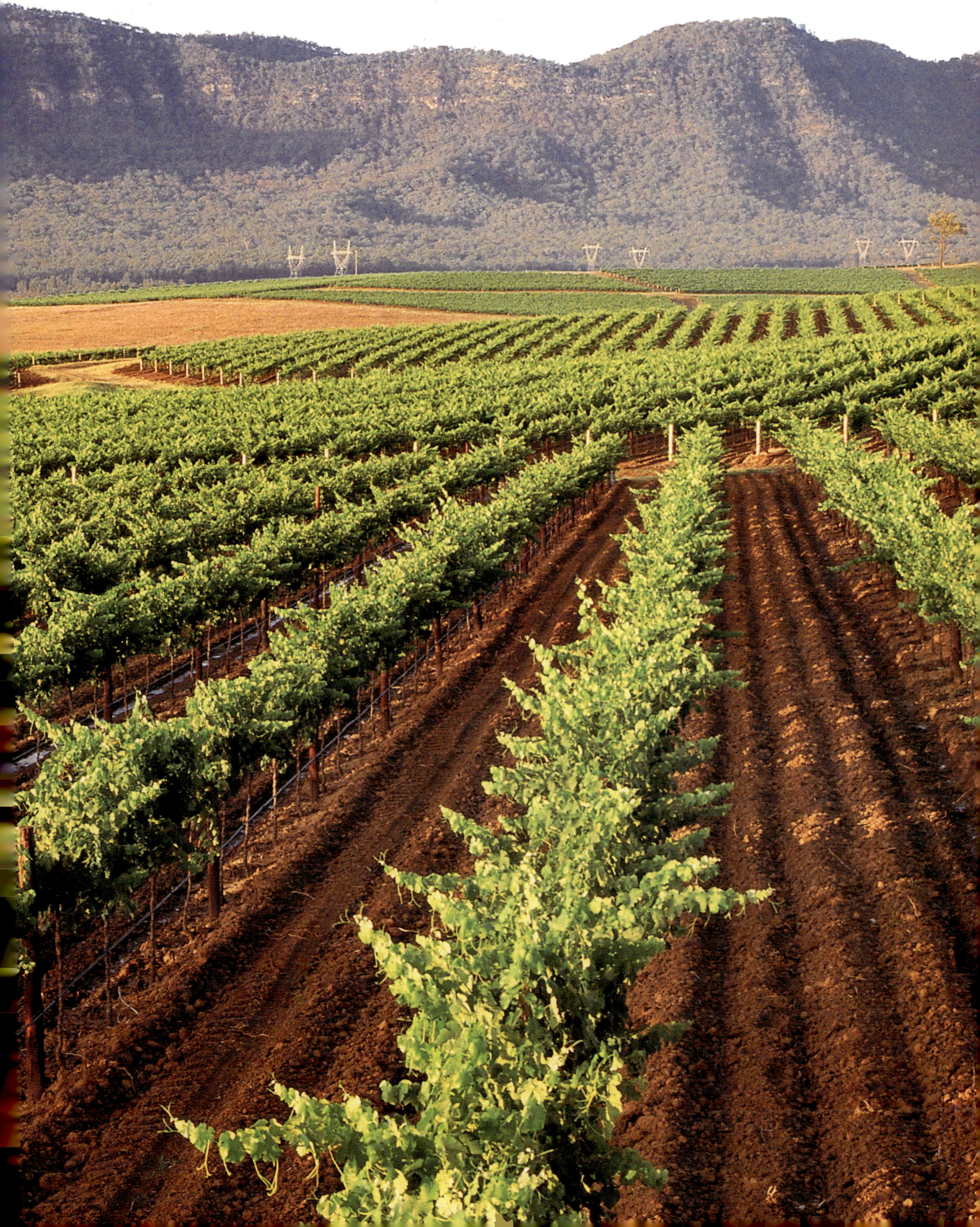

AUSTRALIA - A GOURMET'S PARADISE

THE AUSTRALIAN AIRLINE

Every Australian who has ever travelled abroad knows the feeling. And these days, the feeling is getting even stronger.

You step inside the jet that is going to take you from some far-flung corner of the world back home, and you are met with broad grins and cheery welcomes that make you feel as though you have arrived already.

That's the secret of Qantas—an airline that reflects the spirit of its homeland more distinctly than just about any other airline on earth, and that has taken the best things about the Australian culture and turned them into a massive global business.

In 1994, the airline launched an initiative which has implanted the airline's spirit even more deeply with a powerful television campaign constructed around Peter Allen's hit ballad 'I Still Call Australia Home'.

But there is far more to the initiative than simply the television campaign. The 'new' Qantas offers radical improvements in cabin interiors, in seats and leg room and in meal service. Lighter, fresher menu selections are offered on domestic services with more flexible cabin service in First and Business Class.

A la carte dining has been introduced in First Class on selected international flights. Passengers can choose to eat something light or more substantial when it suits them and have it cooked to order. From the emphasis on fresh, Australian-grown produce to the consideration of passenger comfort, Qantas reflects the strengths and increasing confidence of an airline preparing for a new millennium.

Qantas began life very nearly three quarters of a century ago under true pioneering conditions—as Queensland and Northern Territory

International Profile - Made in Australia

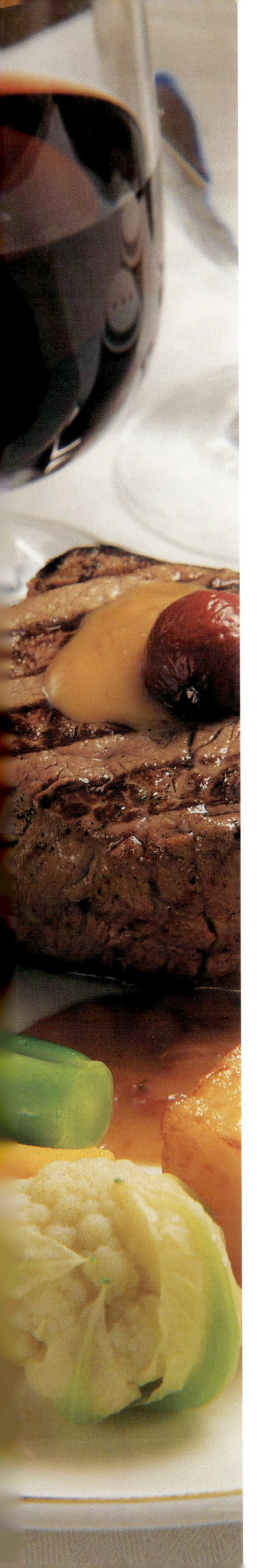

Aerial Services, in the dust-dry Queensland outback town of Winton on 16 November 1920.

The 'fleet' then consisted of a single-engined biplane with which the airline provided links, as required, between isolated outback townships and communities. The fleet had expanded sufficiently by 1922 for Qantas to operate its first scheduled services, and by 1935 was sophisticated enough for the airline's first international link—between Australia and Singapore—to be established.

But what a difference sixty years can make. From that first overseas operation, which helped to create an Australia to Britain service in association with British Airways' predecessor Imperial Airways, Qantas has captured the world.

There are now 128 'roo-tailed' aircraft criss-crossing Australia and encircling the globe—fifty-five of those wide-bodied jet airliners including eighteen of the latest Boeing 747-400 Longreach aircraft.

But apart from providing a service that gives Australia a presence in every corner of the world, Qantas is a very substantial business. Some $6.6 billion in total revenue was earned in 1993-94, including almost $5 billion in passenger revenue of which 70% came from overseas operations.

It's a long way from Winton, but the 'roos are still flying, the grins are still broad', and flying home by Qantas still, somehow, can make you feel glad to be home.

Far left and left: Qantas typically uses home produce to provide meals of supreme quality Above: Qantas' promotional jet with artwork depicting Aboriginal Wunala Dreaming

prices for its top drops. 'Our "Art Series" Chardonnay and Cabernet Sauvignon are well-received in the twelve countries to which we export,' says Leeuwin's Denis Horgan. The immaculate vineyards of Voyager Estate, Brookland Valley and its wonderful restaurant, Flutes, and the Wise Family Winery and Restaurant are further attractions which make the three-hour drive from Perth worthwhile.

Over the past few years, discerning wine buffs have begun to realise that we are producing some magnificent fizz, expertly made by the traditional champagne method, using the classic grape varieties chardonnay, pinot noir and meunier. Croser, Jaansz, Mountadam, Yalumba 'D', Clover Hill, Edwards & Chaffey and Yellowglen Cuvee Victoria are all well-balanced and complex, with fine yeast character and palate structure.

A number of Australian producers are helped by specialist advice from France. Domaine Chandon, owned by Moet & Chandon, and Blue Pyrenees, part of the Remy group (Krug, Charles Heidsieck, Piper Heidsieck), would appear to have an unfair advantage. Yet Seppelt Salinger, Southcorp's flagship, was awarded the trophy for best sparkling wine at Australia's 1994 National Wine Show—and more than 50 per cent is earmarked for export. Whichever way you look at it, Australian wines appear to have a sparkling future.

ENERGY AND EXCITEMENT After the excesses of the 1980s, the last years of the twentieth century were slated to become a time of restraint, yet, gastronomically we are in the midst of the most exciting period in Australian culinary history, and as the facts above show, the movement spills over strongly to our food exports. With exciting trade developments like the strengthening of APEC (Asia-Pacific Economic Region), Australia is set to add a predicted $15 billion to its export successes and there's little doubt that the food and wine industries will play a big part.

Elisabeth King and Alan Hill

International Profile - Made in Australia

INNOVATIVE OUTPUT

The growth of Green's Foods Limited has been spectacular: from the small sugar packing group that Howard Green and his son Nelson founded in 1978, it is now a national food organisation, with more than 600 employees, and is listed on the Australian Stock Exchange. Production and distribution facilities are located in New South Wales, Western Australia, Tasmania and South Australia, with distribution centres in Queensland and Victoria. Recent figures show that it is still expanding at the rate of about twenty per cent a year.

Green's supply dry groceries, convenience foods, snacks, beverages and pet foods (in proprietary and house brands often specially formulated for customers) to all major food chains in Australia. These products range from such commodities as flour and sugar to microwaveable meals and breakfast cereals. One of the company's great success stories is Green's Pancake Shake, one of the major items in the cake mix category.

Green's main concern is that products meet consumer needs in convenience, quality and value for money. Commitment to the marketing of new products (forty to sixty a year) is focused both on Australian demands and on the special needs of the international market.

The company's export drive centres around its distribution points in fifteen Asian and Pacific countries and its subsidiary manufacturing and marketing companies in the United Kingdom and Vietnam. For those overseas markets, Green's aim is to be competitive and innovative as well as mindful of cultural differences that can require products to be fine-tuned to local tastes.

Green's has a competitive edge that goes a long way. Look at its approach: target a specific sector of the food product market, identify a need, and launch a product to meet that need within a couple of months (compare that with competitors' twelve to eighteen months). An intelligent and fast-paced approach to marketing and manufacturing have made Green's the success it is today.

Far left: Freshly baked muffins and slices
Left: A colourful array of beans, pulses, seeds and spices

AUSTRALIA - A GOURMET'S PARADISE

FOR LOVERS OF FINE CHOCOLATE

Cadbury Australia is an Australia-based confectionery manufacturer which markets some of the world's best-loved chocolates and confectionery products.

With manufacturing plants in six countries and a factory currently being built in Beijing, Cadbury is an integral part of the global Cadbury Schweppes Group whose products are enjoyed every minute of the day by millions of people in over 170 countries.

The success of Cadbury is due to the fact that it has carved out a leadership position by offering lovers of fine chocolate four essential ingredients: product quality, taste, excitement and, above all, enjoyment.

Combined with these talents Cadbury has a remarkable track record of innovation. The company has created a solid reputation as a marketeer and is known for its new product development, creative packaging, unique advertising and merchandising, extensive distribution network and after-sales service.

Cadbury is now taking its brand names into new markets with products such as the all-new range of novelty Cadbury Ice Cream and Cadbury Mousse, a new dairy dessert.

It is this vitality and commitment to innovation which is at the core of Cadbury's diverse range of chocolates and confectionery products which include block chocolates, chocolate bars, children's products, boxed chocolates, sugar confectionery, seasonal lines and chocolate foods.

CADBURY AND THE PACIFIC RIM Asia and the Pacific Rim are among the most competitive consumer markets in the world. With a major part of the world's population living in this area, the Asia Pacific represents an exciting opportunity for Cadbury. Cadbury has already had an incredible record of success marketing and merchandising many of its famous brand names throughout the region.

With a strong support team located in Melbourne at the head office of its Pacific Rim Operations, Cadbury is combining its marketing initiative and product development skills to expand into south-east Asia.

Cadbury's Pacific Rim operations include the Cadbury Malaysia plant at

International Profile - Made in Australia

Shah Alam near Kuala Lumpur where Cadbury moulded blocks, bar lines and Trebor sugar confectionery are made.

P T Trebor Indonesia in Jakarta produces sugar confectionery under the Trebor brand and bar lines and snack lines, while CRP Indonesia is a chocolate manufacturing plant located in East Jakarta.

Cadbury Singapore is a marketing and sales operation which imports product from Australia. Cadbury Japan distributes Trebor and Cadbury products into the growing Japanese market.

In 1993 Cadbury entered into a joint venture with the Beijing General Corporation for Agriculture, Industry and Commerce to build a major manufacturing plant near Beijing. The project is being managed by Cadbury Australia and production is scheduled to begin in 1995.

In places where the company does not have its own manufacturing, Cadbury's wide range of top-quality chocolate and confectionery products are imported from Australia, New Zealand, Indonesia and Malaysia.

Expansion of Cadbury's international operations is targeted at marketing on a country-by-country basis into such places as Hong Kong, Taiwan, Japan, Thailand, the Philipines, Papua New Guinea and the Pacific Ocean nations. Exports to these and other countries are now the fastest growing segment of Cadbury Australia's total local production capacity.

Cadbury's mission in the Asia Pacific is to give everyone the pleasure of tasting its distinctive products.

To highlight how serious it takes this calling, Cadbury Australia recently invested over $70 million in production and warehousing facilities in Australia to service this market. Continuous upgrading of facilities maintains Cadbury's world-class production procedures and stringent quality assurance practices.

Research and development also plays a major role in giving Cadbury a leading edge in product quality and product "development", and major technology and manufacturing improvements are continually being made along with advancements in computer systems, telecommunications, merchandising and distribution. Now that's commitment.

Ever-popular Cadbury Dairy Milk Chocolate

AUSTRALIA - A GOURMET'S PARADISE

GOOD LIVING DOWN UNDER

The expectations of today's traveller have become ever more challenging for tourism commissions and independent travel operators the world over. Australia is no exception. This country is, however, perfectly positioned to meet the needs of the special interest traveller with a host of experiences unequalled elsewhere.

'Special Interest' travel has emerged as the major growth area in world tourism. While it isn't always the reason for travel, the special interest focus adds to the total quality experience, and can often influence the decision to visit a specific destination.

While today's travellers are increasingly selective, this doesn't necessarily translate into a desire for more and better luxury accommodation. More often than not, it means that the traveller is seeking a first-hand experience of indigenous or regional culture—fascinating foods and wines, encounters with flora and fauna and geographic spectacle.

Australia—the island continent—is admirably equipped to deliver these ingredients. It is a land of adventure with vast open spaces, a staggeringly beautiful coastline and an ancient Aboriginal culture.

To meet the challenges of the 'new breed' tourist, the Australian Tourist Commission has designed an ongoing series of promotions highlighting specific areas of interest. 1995 will celebrate Australian Art and Culture, while 1996 will focus on Festivals. And 1997 will acknowledge Good Living—the bountiful gourmet foods and wines that only Australia's clean, green environment and richly diverse culture can deliver.

The principal function of the Australian Tourist Commission is to market Australia as the exhilarating destination it is, while the 'Special Interest Travel' programme is designed to build vital links between the

International Profile - Made in Australia

tourist industry, organisations and individuals who are involved in special interests and events. Winemakers and restaurateurs play an integral role in these promotions. No quality travel experience is complete without the 'companionship' that good food and good wine provide.

Another important attribute of Australia's food and wine producing regions is their ideal climate and growing conditions, which not only contribute to the excellence of the produce and wines but also enhance the tourist experience. These regions also cherish their historic traditions which are often reflected in heritage accommodation as well as regional cuisines.

Australia's extraordinary cultural diversity has given birth to a broad range of gastronomic experiences which can be enjoyed equally in smart city restaurants, brasseries and bistros as well as captivating country locations. Even Australia's famous pubs now offer quality contemporary cuisine as well as some great 'old favourites', such as steak and chips.

While the Australian Tourist Commission's international promotion, Good Living Down Under, will not be launched until 1996, the Commission has already produced a food and wine portfolio, titled Food and Wine in Australia, as a background for overseas public relations consultants and media with a series of tours designed for international wine and food writers.

The results of these promotions have yielded winning results. One eminent Asian publication devoted an entire edition to the excellence of Australia's food and wine.

Until recently, many overseas visitors had no concept of the astonishing variety of Australia's restaurants, freshness of produce, originality and expertise of our chefs and world-class wines. But now the secret is out.

Far left: Moreton Island, one of the many beautiful islands off the Queensland coast
Left: Lush rainforest Above: Everlasting Daisies, Western Australia

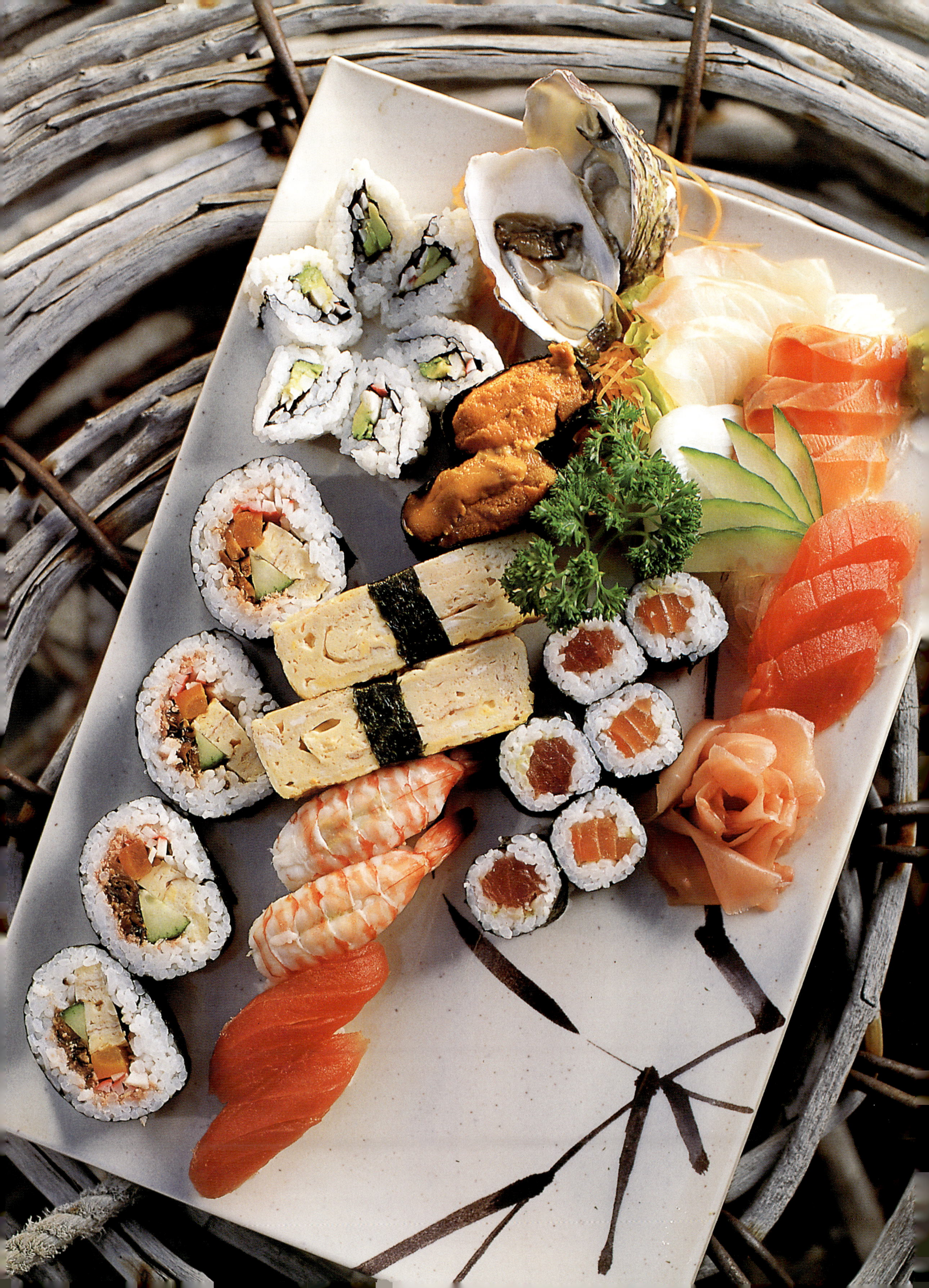

Sponsor's Directory

Lead Sponsor

AMERICAN EXPRESS INTERNATIONAL, INC

ARBN 000 618 208

Registered Head Office
Ground Floor
92 Pitt Street
Sydney NSW 2000
Tel:(02) 239 0666
Fax:(02) 235 0192

John Schaap *Chief Operating Officer - Australia, New Zealand, South Pacific.*
Alberto Modolo *Chairman - Australia, New Zealand, South Pacific.*

Travel Service Offices:

Centrepoint
City Walk and Petrie Plaza
Canberra ACT 2601
Tel: (06) 247 2333
Fax: (06) 257 3472

105 Elizabeth Street
Melbourne VIC 3000
Tel: (03) 608 0333
Fax: (03) 600 0750

Perry House
131 Elizabeth Street
Brisbane QLD 4000
Tel: (07) 229 2022
Fax: (07) 229 1610

21 Cavill Avenue
Surfers Paradise QLD 4217
Tel: (075) 38 7588
Fax: (075) 38 6361

13 Grenfell Street
Adelaide SA 5000
Tel: (08) 212 7099
Fax: (08) 231 0526

78 William Street
Perth WA 6000
Tel: (09) 426 3777
Fax: (09) 481 4312

74A Liverpool Street
Hobart TAS 7000
Tel: (002) 343 711
Fax: (002) 312 618

American Express Travel Related Services Company, Inc., a wholly-owned subsidiary of American Express Company, is the world's largest provider of travel and financial services in over 160 countries. Products include the American Express Card, Corporate Card, Travellers Cheques and Travel Services.
Refer to page 21

A combination sushi dish from Shigryuki Hatano at Orizuru Sushi Bar

Major Sponsors

AUSTRALIAN MEAT AND LIVE-STOCK CORPORATION

227 Elizabeth Street
Sydney NSW 2000
Tel:(02) 260 3111
Fax:(02) 267 6620

John Kerin *Chairman*
Bruce Standen PhD *Managing Director*

17th Floor
750 Lexington Avenue
New York NY 10022
Tel: (212) 486 2405
Fax: (212) 355 1471

World Trade Center Building
PO Box 29
Trade Center
241 Hamamatsucho
Minato-Ku
Tokyo 105 Japan
Tel: (3) 3435 5785
Fax: (3) 3438 1677

5th Floor
Yateem Centre
PO Box 5622
Almutanabi Road
Manama Bahrain
Tel: (973) 244009
Fax: (973) 245086

11th Floor
Kyobo Building
1 Chongro l-ka
Chongro-ku Seoul 110-714
Korea
Tel: (822) 720 7091
Fax: (822) 733 8337

Trade Names:

Aussie Beef
Trim Lamb
Fresh Australian Range Lamb

The AMLC is a statutory authority with the primary responsibility of marketing Australian meat and livestock in Australia and overseas.
Refer to pages 103, 210-211

Major Sponsors

AUSTRALIAN TOURIST COMMISSION

Level 4
80 William Street
Woolloomooloo NSW 2011
Tel:(02) 360 1111
Fax:(02) 331 3385

John Hutchison *Managing Director*
Carole Hancock *General Manager Operations*

Branch Offices:

2121 Avenue of the Stars
Suite 1200
Los Angeles CA 90067 USA
Tel: (310) 552 1988
Fax: (310) 552 1215

Gemini House
10-18 Putney Hill
Putney London SW15 6AA
Tel:(081) 780 2227
Fax:(081) 780 1496

Central Plaza
Suite 1006
18 Harbour Rd
Wanchai Hong Kong
Tel:(852) 802-7700
Fax:(852) 802 7700

Sankaido Building
8th Floor
9-13 Akasaka 1-Chome
Minato-ku Tokyo 107 Japan
Tel:(03) 3582-2191
Fax:(03) 3589-5352

The Australian Tourist Commission is a statutory authority set up to market Australia internationally as a tourist destination. Its principle objectives are to increase the number of visitors to Australia from overseas, maximise the benefits to Australia from overseas visitors and ensure that Australia is protected from adverse environmental and social impacts of international tourism. The ATC is based in Sydney and has offices in every major market around the world.

Refer to pages 246; 256-257

Major Sponsors

CADBURY SCHWEPPES PTY LTD - CONFECTIONERY DIVISION

ACN 004 551 473

636 St Kilda Road
Melbourne VIC 3004
Tel:(03) 520 7444
Fax:(03) 520 7400

Kevin Hayes *Chairman and Managing Director*

Branch Offices:

323-351 Canterbury Road
Ringwood VIC 3134
Tel: (03) 210 1461
Fax: (03) 879 6696

74 Biloela Street
Villawood NSW 2163
Tel: (02) 727 8555
Fax: (02) 724 6557

Cadbury Road
Claremont TAS 7011
Tel: (002) 49 0108
Fax: (002) 73 2151

188 Welshpool Road
Welshpool WA 6106
Tel: (09) 458 6999
Fax:(09) 356 2638

Cnr Adam Street & South Road
Hindmarsh SA 5007
Tel: (08) 346 1631
Fax: (08) 340 1854

Cnr Medway Street & Shoebury Street
Rocklea QLD 4106
Tel: (07) 848 0099
Fax:(07)892 1684

Trade Names:

Cadbury
Red Tulip
MacRobertson
Europe
Pascall

Cadbury Schweppes Pty Ltd is a wholly-owned subsidiary of Cadbury Schweppes Plc, one of the world's largest confectionery and beverage companies. Cadbury is the market leader in all major segments of the Australian confectionery industry. Household names include Cadbury Dairy Milk, Red Tulip, Cadbury Bournville Cocoa, Fry's Bars, Twirl, Flake, Cherry Ripe, Crunchie, Picnic, Roses as well as Pascall and Molly Bushell products. The confectionery division is also responsible for the management of Cadbury Confectionery operations throughout Asia and the Pacific Region.

Refer to pages 28-29; 51; 123; 152; 246; 254-255

Major Sponsors

CANTARELLA BROTHERS PTY LTD

ACN 000 095 607

118 Wetherill Street
Silverwater NSW 2128
Tel:(02) 748 0299
Fax:(02) 748 1915

Leslie Schirato *Managing Director*
Muzio Cantarella *Director*

Branch Offices:

628-632 Smith Street
Clifton Hill VIC
Tel:(03) 489 9011
Fax:(03) 486 2468

46 First Street
Brompton SA
Tel:(08) 346 2399
Fax:(08) 346 7647

12 Lathe Street
Virginia QLD
Tel:(07) 865 2099
Fax:(07) 865 2118

10-12 Fargo Way
Welshpool WA 6106
Tel:(09) 451 4544
Fax:(09) 451 5773

80 Kembla Street
Fyshwick ACT
Tel:(06) 280 4154
Fax:(06) 280 7330

Trade Names:

Vittoria Coffee
Cavalli Lambrusco
Jarlsberg Cheese
Barilla Pasta
Giralda Olive Oil
King Oscar Sardines

Vittoria Coffee is wholly owned by Cantarella Brothers Pty Ltd. An Australian Company with an Italian heritage. Vittoria has achieved the position of the largest pure coffee company in Australia. Cantarella Brothers reputation of supplying premium quality European products is second to none.

Refer to pages 24-25

Major Sponsors

DAVIDS LIMITED

ACN 000 031 569

13 Bessemer Street
Blacktown NSW 2148
Tel:(02) 208 1500
Fax:(02) 208 1555

John J David *Executive Chairman*
Jeffrey J David
John M Patten *Joint Group Managing Directors*

Branch Offices:

Davids Distribution Pty Ltd
37 Bessemer Street
Blacktown NSW 2148
Tel: (02) 208 1222

Davids Distribution Pty Ltd
Cnr Nyrang & Mildura Streets
Fyshwick ACT 2609
Tel: (06) 295 2566

Davids Vic Distribution Pty Limited
75-79 Fitzgerald Road
Laverton VIC 3028
Tel: (03) 206 5222

Davids Distribution Pty Ltd
628-648 Kingston Road
Loganlea QLD 4131
Tel: (07) 884 2222

Davids SA Limited
410-450 Findon Road
Kidman Park SA 5025
Tel: (08) 352 9595

Davids Asia Pty Ltd
37 Joo Koon Circle
Jurong 2262 Singapore
Tel:(0011) 65 862 5411

Supermarkets:
Rainbow IGA Supermarkets
Festival IGA Supermarkets
Foodtown Supermarkets
Welcome Mart Supermarkets
Clancy's Food Stores
Jewel

Product:
IGA and Black & Gold

David's is Australia's leading independent grocery wholesaler and also owns a 50% interest in ALM which is Australia's leading independent wines and spirits wholesaler. Since 1927, Davids has remained committed to it's basic business philosophy to deliver "the lowest possible prices and the best customer service".
Refer to pages 100-101

Major Sponsors

PACIFIC BRANDS FOOD GROUP

ACN 004 085 330

19-25 Camberwell Road
Hawthorn East VIC 3123
Tel:(03) 275 1400
Fax:(03) 882 9544

Grant Latta *Managing Director*
Jeff Cox *Financial Controller*

Branch Offices:

Herbert Adams Bakeries
41-125 Tennyson Street
Kensington VIC 3031
Tel:(03) 279 9777
Fax:(03) 376 4813

Peters Foods
254 Wellington Road
Mulgrave VIC 3170
Tel:(03) 565 7777
Fax:(03) 562 1827

Edgell-Birds Eye
1279 Nepean Hwy
Cheltenham VIC 3192
Tel:(03) 581 4444
Fax:(03) 581 4423

Socomin International Fine Foods
Thackray Road
Port Melbourne VIC 3207
Tel:(03) 676 8200
Fax:(03) 676 8262

Pasta House MFG Co. Pty Ltd
4 Ricketts Road
Mount Waverley VIC 3149
Tel:(03) 544 8777
Fax:(03) 543 5838

Dugan Food For Gifts
127 - 131 Bamfield Road
West Heidelberg VIC 3081
Tel:(03) 457 5500
Fax:(03) 457 5381

Fleury Michon
19 - 25 Camberwell Road
Hawthorn East VIC 3123
Tel:(03) 275 1400
Fax:(03) 882 9544

Edgell Fresh
403 Pacific Highway
Artarmon NSW 2064
Tel:(02) 436 8888
Fax:(02) 906 8575

Major Brands include:

*Pacific Brands Food Group is one of Australia's largest consumer branded food companies, with an extensive portfolio of market-leading brands with annual sales in excess of $1.1 billion. The Group has a total commitment to international growth and expansion into Asian markets with regional offices established in Tokyo, Hong Kong, Singapore and Auckland. PBFG has invested in a network of joint ventures in Asia, including significant ice cream businesses in China and Thailand.
Refer to pages 240-241; 246*

Major Sponsors

QANTAS AIRWAYS LIMITED

ACN 009 661 901

Level 9
Building A
Qantas Centre
203 Coward Street
Mascot NSW 2020
Tel: (02) 691 3636
Fax: (02) 691 3339

Gary Pemberton *Chairman*
James Strong *Managing Director*

395-403 King Street
Hammersmith London W6 9NJ
Tel: (081) 846 0466
Fax: (081) 846 0526

Suite 600
N Continental Blvd
El Segundo California 90245
Tel: (310) 535 1950
Fax: (310) 535 1989

300 Orchard Road
06-05/08 The Promenade
Singapore 0923
Tel: 730 9256
Fax: 737 5839

942/145 Cham Issara Building
Rama IV Road
Bangkok Thailand
Tel: (2) 236 0305
Fax: (2) 236 9196

Refer to pages 92; 105; 250-251

Major Sponsors

SOUTH AUSTRALIAN TOURISM COMMISSION

South Australian
TOURISM COMMISSION

Levels 7&8
178 North Terrace
Adelaide SA 5000
Tel:(08) 303 2390
Fax:(08) 303 2296

Geoff Coles AM *Chairman of the Board*
Michael Gleeson *Cheif Executive Officer*

Branch Offices:

Melbourne Travel Centre
25 Elizabeth Street
Melbourne VIC 3000
Tel:(03) 614 6522
Fax:(03) 629 3445

13-14 Mezzanine Floor
93 William Street
Perth WA 6000
Tel:(09) 481 1268
Fax:(09) 324 1390

247 Pitt Street
Sydney NSW 2001
Tel:(02) 264 3375
Fax:(02) 264 1006

612 Kingston Road
London SW 20 8DW
Tel:(44 81) 544 9844
Fax:(44 81) 544 9843

Suite 9
8 Guthrie Street
Paddington QLD 4064
Tel:(07) 368 4126
Fax:(07) 368 4199

Trade Names:

South Australian Short Breaks

The principal objectives of the SATC are to promote SA's image as an appealing tourist destination and to provide a high quality of information and services to people all over the world. It also aims to stimulate the development of new tourist facilities.

Refer to pages 168-169

Major Sponsors

SPOTLESS CATERING

SPOTLESS SERVICES LIMITED

ACN 005 309 320

20 Blackwood Street
North Melbourne VIC 3051
Tel:(03) 320 9222
Fax:(03) 328 4109

Brian S Blythe *Chairman*
Ron B Evans *Managing Director*

Branch Offices:

123 Gotha Street
Fortitude Valley QLD 4006
Tel:(07) 252 9500
Fax:(07 252 2688)

55 Sussex Street
Sydney NSW 2000
Tel:(02) 367 7444
Fax:(02) 367 7466

30 O'Rorke Road
Penrose Auckland
New Zealand
Tel: 579 5666
Fax: 579 0382

183 Melbourne Street
North Adelaide SA 5006
Tel:(08) 239 1444
Fax:(08) 239 1423

The Garden Park Office
345 Harborne Street
Herdsman Park WA 6017
Tel:(09) 242 1966
Fax:(09) 242 2406

8 Montpelier Retreat
Hobart TAS 7000
Tel: (002) 235 488
Fax: (002) 240 496

Spotless Catering Services Ltd
O'Brien Catering
Nationwide Field Catering
Nationwide Facilities Management
Servicemaster

Spotless Catering forms part of Spotless Services Limited—a wholly owned Australian public company. The Management of catering and allied services is the core business activity of Spotless Catering with some 700 operations throughout Australia and New Zealand.

The scope and expertise of Spotless extends across a range of environments: worksite cafeteria's, corporate boardrooms, sporting venues, cultural and arts centres, airports, hospitals, defence bases and remote mining locations.

Spotless aim to provide customers and clients with the highest possible standard of service enjoying food served professionally and with enthusiasm by efficient, competent staff who take pride in being of service to others.

Refer to pages 40-41

Major Sponsors

WESTERN AUSTRALIAN TOURISM COMMISSION

6th Floor
16 St Georges Terrace
Perth WA 6000
Tel: (09) 220 1700
Fax: (09) 220 1702

Kevin Harrison *Chairman & Chief Executive Officer*
Tony Serra *General Manager - Tourism*

The role of the Western Australian Tourism Commission is to accelerate the sustainable development of the tourism industry for the long term social and economic benefit of the state.
Refer to pages 202-203

Major Sponsors

WESTERN AUSTRALIAN DEPARTMENT OF COMMERCE AND TRADE

170 St George's Terrace
Perth WA 6000
Tel:(09) 327 5666
Fax:(09)327 5542

Hendy Cowan *MLA Deputy Premier and Minister for Commerce and Trade*
Bruce Sutherland *Chief Executive Officer*

Western Australian Government Overseas Offices:

Europe
Western Australia House
115 Strand
London WC2R OAJ
England
Tel:(71) 240 2881
Fax:(71)240 6637

Hong Kong
Suite 702-3
Ocean Centre
5 Canton Road Tsimshatsui
Kowloon Hong Kong
Tel:(852) 735 7557
Fax:(852) 736 3397

Japan
7th Floor
Sankaido Building
9-13 Akasaka 1-Chome
Minato-ku Tokyo 107 Japan
Tel:(03) 3585 0807/8
Fax:(03) 3582 9592

Malaysia
4th Floor
UBN Tower Letter Box51
10 Jalan P Ramlee
Kuala Lumpa 50250 Malaysia
Tel:(03) 201 8175/6
Fax:(03)201 8177

Indonesia
World Trade Centre
J1 Pemuda
27-31 Surabaya
East Java 60275 Indonesia
Tel:(31) 519 123
Fax:(31) 519 118

The Department of Commerce and Trade is committed to the growth of internationally competitive manufacturing and service industries able to capture new national and international markets and to compete against imports.

Refer to pages 178-179; 184

Major Sponsors

WOOLWORTHS SUPERMARKETS

'The Fresh Food People'
WOOLWORTHS

(a Division of Woolworths Limited.)

ACN 000 014 675

Cnr Fairfield and Dursley Roads
(National & NSW offices)
Yennora NSW 2165
Tel:(02) 892 7111
Fax:(02) 892 7599

John Brunton *Managing Director Supermarkets*

Branch Offices:

Woolworths *(QLD)*
Fox Road
Acacia Ridge QLD 4112
Tel:(07) 213 4111
Fax:(07) 213 4333

Woolworths *(SA-NT)*
80-88 Rundle Mall
Adelaide SA 5000
Tel:(08) 205 5300
Fax:(08) 205 5336

Woolworths *(WA)*
123 Kewdale Road
Kewdale WA 6105
Tel:(09) 351 5222
Fax:(09) 351 5199

Safeway *(VIC)*
522 Wellington Road
Mulgrave VIC 3170
Tel:(03) 263 2444
Fax:(03) 263 2899

Purity *(TAS)*
20 Lampton Ave
Derwent Park TAS 7009
Tel:(002) 72 4066
Fax:(002) 73 1396

Roelf Vos *(TAS)*
5 Trotters Lane
Prospect TAS 7250
Tel:(003) 44 8866
Fax:(003) 43 1723

Brand Names:

Home Brand
Naytura
Beattie's Lolly Shop

The Supermarket Division is the largest division of Woolworths Limited and as such is the No.1 Food Retailer in Australia with over 30 per cent of the Australian Grocery Market. In addition to being the market leader in groceries, the Division is the largest retailer of fresh foods in the country.

Refer to pages 243-245

General Sponsors

AUSTRALIAN DAIRY CORPORATION

1601 Malvern Road
Glen Iris VIC 3146
Tel:(03) 805 3777
Fax:(03)885 6748

Grahame Tonkin
Managing Director
Ken Baxter *Chairman*

Branch Offices:

NSW/QLD/ACT Regional Office
Suite 37 103 Majors Bay Rd
Concord NSW 2137
Tel:(02) 743 3321
Fax:(02)736 2116

SA/WA/NT Regional Office
48 Greenhill Rd
Wayville SA 5034
Tel: (08) 373 0747
Fax: (08) 272 5476

VIC/TAS/ Regional Office
1601 Malvern Road
Glen Iris VIC 3146
Tel: (03) 805 3805
Fax: (03) 885 6748

ADC
5th Floor
Kokusai Hamamatsucho
Building
9-18 Kaigan 1-Chome
Minato-Ku
Tokyo 105 Japan
Tel: (0011) (813) 3432 3522
Fax: (0011) (813) 3432 3518

Refer to page 247

BOC GASES AUSTRALIA LIMITED

ACN 000 029 729

The BOC Gases Building
799 Pacific Highway
Chatswood NSW 2067
Tel: (02) 936 3666
Fax: (02) 415 1777

Barry Beecroft
Managing Director and
Regional Director South Pacific

20 Charles Street
Paramatta NSW 2150
Tel: (02) 689 4800
Fax: (02) 689 4930

90 Bell Street
Preston VIC 3072
Tel: (03) 287 8444
Fax: (03) 284 0382

1688 Ipswich Road
Rocklea QLD 4106
Tel: (07) 212 4222
Fax: (07) 212 4111

Cnr Jervois Street &
Ashwin Parade
Torrensville SA 5031
Tel: (08) 354 9111
Fax: (08) 43 5778

590 Hay Street
Subiaco WA 6008
Tel: (09) 381 0444
Fax: (09) 381 4678

Trade Names:

Gas and Gear Centres
Argoshield
KwikFreeze
Healthizone
Insectigas
Pestigas
Bactigas
Cellamix
Deodourgas
Gasmatic
Mr. Gaspo

Refer to page 53

General Sponsors

BONLAC FOODS LIMITED

ACN 006 483 665

566 St Kilda Road
Melbourne VIC 3004
Tel:(03) 270 0922
Fax:(03) 270 0911

William H Hill *Chairman*
W Ian Gresswell *Managing Director*
Robert C A Paterson *General Secretary*

State Sales Offices:

64-128 Bridge Road
Dandenong VIC 3175
Tel:(03) 798 2222
Fax:(03) 798 7996

Suite 103, 30 Cowper Street
Parramatta NSW 2150
Tel:(02) 633 9877
Fax:(02) 891 3433

3/17 Hayling Street
Salisbury QLD 4107
Tel:(07) 277 8177
Fax:(07) 875 1415

99 Halifax Street
Adelaide SA 5000
Tel:(08) 223 6177
Fax:(08) 223 3919

Unit 5/12 - 14
Burton Street
Cannington WA 6107
Tel:(09) 451 8884
Fax:(09) 356 2792

Refer to page 145

CAMERON OF TASMANIA PTY LTD

ACN 009 579 168

Main Road
Dunalley TAS 7177
Tel:(002) 535 111
Fax:(002)535 278

Ian Cameron *Managing Director*
Michael Cameron *General Manager*

Trade Names:

Cameron of Tasmania Pty Ltd
Premier Oyster Company
Royal Tasmanian Oysters

Refer to pages 127; 246

General Sponsors

CASCADE BREWERY COMPANY PTY LTD

ACN 058 152 195

2nd Floor
152 Macquarie Street
Hobart TAS 7000
Tel:(002) 218 300
Fax:(002) 243 446

Steve Rutledge *General Manager*
Duncan Hall *Company Secretary*

Refer to pages 118-119

Trade Names:

Cascade Ultra-C Blackcurrant Fruit
Juice Syrup
Cascade Raspberry Fruit Juice Syrup
Cascade Slam Carbonated Cordial
Cascade Apple Isle Sparkling Apple Juice
Mercury Cider

CEREBOS (AUSTRALIA) LTD

ACN 004 304 803

92-96 Station Road
Seven Hills NSW 2147
Tel:(02) 624 5200
Fax:(02) 674 2887

John Mulford *Chairman*
John Toynbee *Managing Director*

Branch Offices:

Suite 3, Level 1
14 Wellington Street
Arcacia Ridge QLD 4110
Tel:(07) 277 7633
Fax:(07) 277 0138

Unit B 11 Hudson Avenue
Castle Hill NSW 2154
Tel:(02) 899 6011
Fax:(02) 634 1808

Refer to pages 154; 160-161

2215 Dandenong Road
Mulgrave VIC 3170
Tel:(03) 547 0733
Fax:(03) 547 9930

46A Beulah Road
Norwood SA 5067
Tel:(08) 363 0013
Fax:(08) 363 1247

3 Miles Road
Kewdale WA 6105
Tel:(09) 353 2588
Fax:(09) 353 1081

Trade Names:

Gravox
Fountain
White Crow
Saxa
Salad Magic

General Sponsors

CURTIN FOODSERVICE EQUIPMENT

ACN 001 040 428

222 Coward Street
Mascot NSW 2020
Tel:(02) 693 5988
Fax:(02) 317 3185

Ken Hudson *Managing Director*
Jack Scott *Director Sales & Marketing*

Branch Offices:

Curtin (Qld) Pty Ltd
215 Jackson Road
Sunnybank Hills QLD 4109
Tel:(07)344 2444
Fax:(07)345 6403

J Curtin Pty Ltd
Unit 17 477 Warrigal Road
Moorabbin VIC 3189
Tel:(03) 555 4322
Fax:(03) 553 4653

Curtin SA Pty Ltd
6-10 Lamont Street
Croydon Park SA 5008
Tel:(08) 340 1677
Fax:(08) 340 1897

Lenny's Commercial Kitchens
6 O'Malley Street
Osborne Park WA 6017
Tel:(09) 446 6322
Fax:(09) 446 4156

Frig-Com Tasmania
94 Hopkins Street
Moonah TAS 7009
Tel:(002) 284 821
Fax:(002) 284 822

Trade Names:

Zanussi, Blodgett, Pitco,
Scotsman, Carpigiani,
Alto-Shaam, Curtin,
Groen, Henny Penny,
Nieco, ISA, Magi Kitchen.

Refer to page 57

D'ORSOGNA LIMITED

ACN 063 427 752

Cnr Stock Road & Leach Highway
Melville WA 6156
Tel:(09) 337 3444
Fax:(09) 314 1380

Neil Hamilton *Chairman*
Bob Bishop *Managing Director*

Branch Offices:

Doro Distributors
Kintore Lane
Mile End SA 5031
Tel:(08) 434 409
Fax:(08) 352 3583

Conga Victoria
70 Bell Street
Preston VIC 3072
Tel:(03) 487 9530
Fax:(03) 4840764

Conga NSW
62 Cosgrove Road
South Strathfield NSW 2136
Tel:(02) 742 5822
Fax:(02) 742 5625

Kosmos Food Distributors
Lot 9251
Delatour Street
Coconut Grove
Nightcliff NT 0810
Tel:(089) 480 038
Fax:(089) 480 207

Pt. Indoguna Utama
JL. Taruna No.8
Pondok Bambu
Jakarta 13430
Indonesia

Trade Names:

Prosciutto - Parma Ham
Capocollo (Coppa)
Mortadella
Pastrami
Ventricina

Refer to pages 186-187

General Sponsors

R J GILBERTSON PTY LTD

ACN 004 147 228

Kyle Road
Altona North VIC 3025
Tel:(03) 392 6222
Fax:(03) 391 5339

George Gilbertson *Chairman*
Malcolm Slinger *Managing Director*

Branch Offices:

R J Gilbertson (Southern) Pty Ltd
King Island Branch
Aerodrome Road
Curry, King Island TAS 7256
Tel:(004) 621 477
Fax:(004) 621 671

Adelaide Branch
702 Main North Road
Jepps Cross SA 5094
Tel:(08) 349 5100
Fax:(08) 260 1195

R J Gilbertson (Queensland) Pty Ltd
South Armidale Road
Grafton NSW 2461
Tel:(066) 422 733
Fax:(066) 426 502

Longford Meat Company
Tanney Road
Longford TAS 7301
Tel:(003) 911 509
Fax:(003) 912 115

Refer to pages 114; 129; 243

GREEN'S FOODS LIMITED

ACN 058 023 260

29 Glendenning Road
Glendenning NSW 2766
Tel:(02) 832 3555
Fax:(02) 832 3096

Duncan McDonald *Chairman*
Nelson Green *Managing Director*

Branch Offices:

8 Wadhurst Drive
Boronia VIC 3155
Tel:(03) 800 1922
Fax:(03) 800 2138

433 Logan Road
Stones Corner
QLD 4120
Tel:(07) 394 8394
Fax:(07) 847 2138

17-21 Clovelly Avenue
Royal Park SA 5014
Tel:(08) 341 1866
Fax:(08) 341 1578

199 Georgetown Road
Launceston TAS 7520
Tel:(003) 261 833
Fax:(003) 264 275

1-7 Ilda Road
Canning Vale WA 6155
Tel:(09) 455 1011
Fax:(09)455 4877

Trade Names:

Green's
Prepact
Blue Banner (Pickled Onions)
Supercoat (Pet Care)
Poppin (Popcorn)
Green's Breakfast Cereals
Bakers Own

Refer to pages 252-253

General Sponsors

H J HEINZ COMPANY AUSTRALIA LTD

ACN 004 200 319

Princes Highway
Dandenong VIC 3175
Tel: (03) 212 3757
Fax: (03) 212 5506

Terry Ward *Chairman*
D A Irving
*Area Director Australasia
- Heinz/Wattie's*

Branch Offices:

2nd Floor
1-7 Jordan Street
Gladesville NSW 2111
Tel: (02) 817 1577
Fax: (02) 817 1665

6/321 Kelvin Grove Rd
Kelvin Grove QLD 405
Tel: (07) 356 8344
Fax: (07) 356 7421

46 Nelson Street
Stepney SA 5069
Tel: (08) 362 5634
Fax: (08) 362 4266

Unit 6
4 Brodie Hall Drive
Bentley WA 6102
Tel: (09) 470 3266
Fax: (09) 470 3323

39 Overseas Drive
Noble Park VIC 3174
Tel: (03) 795 8144
Fax: (03) 701 0470

Trade Names:

Heinz
Weight Watchers
Greenseas
PMU
Epicure
Wattie's
Golden Days
Farex

Refer to pages 186; 188-191

HYATT REGENCY PERTH

ACN 053 688 118

99 Adelaide Terrace
Perth WA 6000
Tel:(09) 225 1234
Fax:(09) 325 8899

George Benney *General Manager*
Richard Russ *Financial Controller*

Branch Offices:

Hyatt International Hotels
Level 2
153 New South Head Road
Edgecliff NSW 2027
Tel:(02) 327 2622
Fax:(02) 327 3619

Trade Names:

Cafe
Gershwin's
Joe's Oriental Diner
La Strada Coffee Terrace

Refer to pages 110-111

General Sponsors

M G KAILIS EXPORTS PTY LTD

ACN 008 698 630

50 Mews Road
Fremantle WA 6160
Tel: (09) 335 1133
Fax: (09) 335 1197

Micheal Kailis CBE AM Cit WA
Chairman
George Kailis *Managing Director*

M G Kailis (1962) Pty Ltd
4 Brady Road
Dongara WA 6525
Tel: (099) 271 106
Fax: (099) 271 385

M G Kailis Gulf Fisheries
Pty Ltd
Exmouth Road
Learmonth WA 6707
Tel: (099) 492 576
Fax: (099) 491 032

Broome Pearls Pty Ltd
125 Blackman Street
Broome WA 6725
Tel: (091) 921 295
Fax: (091) 922 597

Independent Mini Coldstores
41 Joan Street
Cairns QLD 4870
Tel: (070) 316 162
Fax: (070) 517 258

Trade Names:

Seasnap
Seabird
Seachoice

K G PALMER & ASSOCIATES PTY LTD

ACN 008 860 473

Suite 6, 24 Riseley Street
Applecross WA 6153
Tel: (09) 316 1822
Fax: (09) 364 2860

Refer to page 139

Alex Kailis *General Manager*
Ken Palmer *Executive Director*

Trade Names:

Palcon

LACTOS PTY LTD

ACN 009 479 869

Old Surrey Road
Burnie TAS 7320
Tel:(004) 31 2566
Fax: (004) 31 2647

Russell Paterson
Managing Director
Alan Jarman
Company Secretary

Refer to pages 176; 205

Branch Offices:

7 Conifer Crescent
Dingley VIC 3172
Tel:(03) 558 1433
Fax:(03) 558 0801

Suite 8
1059-1063 Victoria Road
West Ryde NSW 2114
Tel:(02) 874 9421
Fax:(02) 874 9419

Parent Company
Bongrain SA
Le Moulin a Vent
78280 Guyancourt
Versailles France
Tel:(1) 30 43 81 01
Fax:(1) 30 43 83 90

Trade Names:

Heritage, Domaine, St Claire
Mersey Valley, Lady Nelson

General Sponsors

NATIONAL DAIRIES TASMANIA LTD

ACN 009 482 124

215 Lenah Valley Road
Lanah Valley TAS 7008
Tel:(002) 3250700
Fax:(002) 325 791

John Watson *General Manager*
John Corrigan *Operations Manager*

Branch Offices:

Old Surrey Road
Devonport TAS 7310
Tel:(004) 24 1681
Fax:(004) 24 8432

Refer to page 112

266 York Street
Launceston TAS 7250
Tel: (003) 31 6166
Fax: (003) 31 9548

Trade Names:

Tasmaid
Milk
Cream
Yogurt
Custard
Sour Cream
Pura

Milk
Light Start
Skimmm

PETERS AND BROWNES GROUP

ACN 008 668 602

22 Gedes Street
Balcatta WA 6021
Tel:(09) 344 9344
Fax:(09) 344 9300

Graham Laitt *Managing Director*
Gad Raveh *Chairman*

Refer to pages 198-199; 246

Trade Names:

Brownes
Peters
Clover Meats
Clover Smallgoods
Milne Feeds

General Sponsors

ROSEMOUNT ESTATE

ACN 000 786 676

18 Herbert Street
Artarmon NSW 2064
Tel:(02) 439 3222
Fax:(02) 906 2613

Robert Oatley *Chairman*
Christopher Hancock Hon MW
Managing Director

Branch Offices:

Rosemount Estate Wines Ltd
Hatchlands
East Clandon Guildford
Surrey GU4 7RT UK
Tel:(44 1483) 211466
Fax:(44 1483) 211717

Rosemount Estates Inc.
583 First Street West
Sonoma CA 95476 USA
Tel:(707) 996 4504
Fax:(707) 996 5063

Refer to pages 234-235; 248

Rosemount Estates Pty Ltd
26 Virginia Street
Virginia QLD 4014
Tel:(07) 265 6999
Fax:(07) 265 3599

Rosemount Estates Pty Ltd
252 Cambridge Street
Wembley WA 6014
Tel:(09) 382 2233
Fax:(09) 388 3154

Rosemount Estates Pty Ltd
58 Duerdin Street
Clayton North VIC 3168
Tel:(03) 562 5770
Fax:(03) 562 5793

Rosemount Estates
14 Ingoldby Rd
McLaren Flat SA 5171
Tel: (08) 383 0001
Fax: (08) 383 0456

Trade Name:

Rosemount Estate

Key Products:

Hunter Valley Chardonnay
Hunter Valley Fume Blanc
Hunter Valley Semillon
South Australian Shiraz
South Australian Cabernet Sauvignon
Show Reserve Hunter Valley Chardonnay
Show Reserve Coonawarra Cabernet Sauvignon
Balmoral Syrah
Roxburgh Chardonnay

TABASCO PEPPER SAUCE

ACN 008 419 501

33 Hope Street
Ermington NSW 2115
Tel:(02) 857 2000
Fax:(02) 858 5721

Bruce McGilvray *Managing Director*
Ian Sanders *Finance Director*

Branch Offices:

Refer to pages 214-215

33 Hope Street
Ermington NSW 2115
Tel:(02) 857 2000
Fax:(02) 858 5721

212 Chesterville Road
Moorabbin VIC 3189
Tel:(03) 553 4144
Fax:(03) 553 4238

Cnr Wilkie & Station Road
Yeerongpilly QLD 4105
Tel:(07) 848 3532
Fax:(07) 892 2976

5 Graham Street
Adelaide Airport SA 5000
Tel:(08) 234 3866
Fax:(08) 234 3858

382 South Street
O'Connor WA 6163
Tel:(09) 331 2222
Fax:(09) 337 9509

49-51 Dowling Street
Launceston TAS 7250
Tel:(003) 34 5473
Fax:(003) 31 2197

General Sponsors

TASMANIA DEVELOPMENT AND RESOURCES

22 Elizabeth Street
Hobart TAS 7000
Tel: (002) 335 888
Fax: (002) 335 800

Chris Brooks *Chief Executive*
Andrew Reeves *Executive General Manager Development*

Refer to pages 107; 126

TASMANIA DEPARTMENT OF TOURISM SPORT AND RECREATION

Level 15
Trafalgar Centre
110 Collins Street
Hobart TAS 7000
Tel: (002) 308 153
Fax: (002) 308 353

Bob Morris *Director/Secretary*
David Riley *Director Marketing Strategy and Services*

Refer to pages 130-131

TASSAL LIMITED

ACN 009 548 770

5 Franklin Wharf
Hobart TAS 7000
Tel:(002) 240 355
Fax:(002) 240 373

Peter Shelley *Managing Director*

Trade Names:

Royal Tasmanian Abalone
Royal Tasmanian Lobster
Royal Tasmanian Salmon
Royal Tasmanian Seafood

Refer to pages 114-115; 246

General Sponsors

TOURISM NEW SOUTH WALES

Tourism New South Wales

140 George Street
Sydney NSW 2000
Tel:(02) 931 1111
Fax:(02) 931 1490

Tony Thirlwell *Chief Executive & General Manager*
Wolfgang Grimm *Chairman*

Branch Offices:

NSW Travel Centre
19 Castlereagh Street
Sydney NSW 2000
Tel:(02) 231 4444
Fax:(02) 232 6080

Refer to page 97

388 Bourke Street
Melboune VIC 3000
Tel:(03) 670 7461
Fax:(03) 642 1260

Cnr King William & Grenfell Streets
Adelaide SA 5000
Tel:(08) 231 3167
Fax:(08) 231 9560

40 Queen Street
Brisbane QLD 4000
Tel:(07) 229 8833
Fax:(07) 221 3129

As well as overseas offices in
London
Tokyo
Singapore
Los Angeles
Auckland

Trade Names:

Tourism New South Wales
NSW Travel Centres

TOURISM VICTORIA

You'll love every piece of Victoria

55 Swanston Street
Melbourne VIC 3000
Tel:(03) 653 9777
Fax:(03) 653 9755

David Grant *Chairman*
Robert Annells *Chief Executive*

Branch Offices:

403 George Street
Sydney NSW 2000
Tel:(02) 299 2288
Fax:(02) 299 2425

16 Grenfell Street
Adelaide SA 5000
Tel:(08) 231 4129
Fax:(08) 231 9627

Refer to pages 152-153

Overseas Offices:

United States
Tel:(310) 552 5344
Germany
Tel:6162 85550
Singapore
Tel:2555 6888
Taiwan
Tel:757 6482
Japan
Tel:(33) 582 2789
Korea
Tel:(2) 793 1853
Hong Kong
Tel:587 1181
New Zealand

General Sponsors

UNIFOODS

(A division of Unilever Australia Ltd)

ACN 004 050 828

20-22 Cambridge Street
Epping NSW 2121
Tel:(02) 869 6100
Fax:(02) 869 6150

Jeff Fraser *Chairman Unilever Australasia*
Enzo Allara *Managing Director Unifoods*

Brand Names:

Rosella
Continental
Raguletto
Chicken Tonight
Refer to page 151

WESTERN AUSTRALIAN MEAT MARKETING CORPORATION

823-827 Wellington Street
West Perth WA 6005
Tel:(09) 420 0200
Fax:(09) 481 3026

J.C. (Con) Goosens *Chairman*
Johnathan Burston *Chief Executive*

Brand Names:

WALAMB
WAMMC

Refer to pages 182-183

General Sponsors

WESTINGHOUSE APPLIANCES

ACN 000 029 407

175 Bonds Road
Riverwood NSW 2210
Tel:(02) 717 2288
Fax:(02) 717 2208

John Hanna
Managing Director Email Limited
Colin Forster
*Executive General Manager
Marketing Email Major
Appliance Group*

Refer to pages 46-47

Branch Offices:

6 Selhurst Street
Coopers Plains QLD 4108
Tel:(07) 344 5076
Fax:(07) 344 4420

70 Burnley Street
Richmond VIC 3121
Tel:(03) 254 3822
Fax:(03) 254 3820

616 Torrens Road
Woodville North SA 5012
Tel:(08) 203 8441
Fax:(08) 347 1644

2 Geddes Street
Balcatta WA 6001
Tel:(09) 442 6555
Fax:(09) 442 6550

WINNING APPLIANCES PTY LTD

ACN 002 193 688

177 Phillip Street
Redfern NSW 2016
Tel:(02) 698 8099
Fax:(02) 319 6734

John Winning
Managing Director
Bill Winning *Director*
Richard Winning *Director*

Branch Offices:

113 Alexander Street
Crows Nest NSW 2065
Tel:(02) 438 2611
Fax:(02) 906 2997

Refer to pages 34-35

Paramatta Industrial Estate
Unit 5A 6 Boundry Road
Northmead NSW 2152
Tel:(02) 630 0588
Fax:(02) 630 0594

Micheal's Of Brighton
757 Hampton Street
Brighton VIC 3186
Tel:(03) 592 6400
Fax:(03) 593 1008

Authorised Franchise Agents For:

St George
Miele
Gaggenau
Omega Smeg
Westinghouse
Vulcan Chef
Kleenmaid
Ilve
Fisher & Paykel
General Electric
Blanco
Bosch
*And many other brands

General Sponsors

WISE WINERY

ACN 008 996 156

Eagle Bay Road
Cape Naturaliste Peninsular
via Dunsborough WA 6281
Tel:(097) 55 3331
Fax:(097) 55 3979

Ron & Sandra Wise *Proprietors*
Tim Wise *Manager*
Mark Ravenscroft *Winemaker*
Adam Lane *Executive Chef*

Refer to pages 230-231

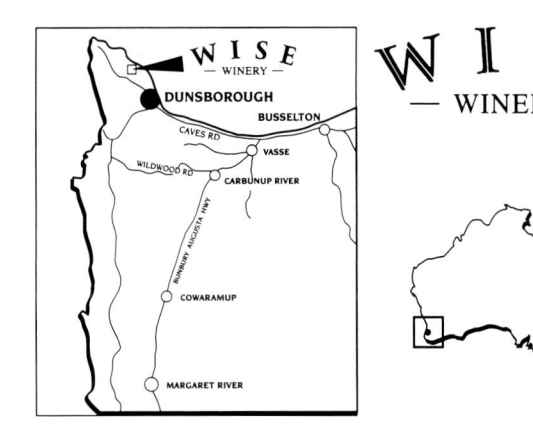

BROOKLAND VALLEY VINEYARD PTY LTD

ACN 008 909 064

PO Box 180
Cowaramup WA 6284
Tel:(097) 55 6250
Fax:(097) 55 6214

Michael Wright *Owner Managing Director*
Stuart Pym *Wine Maker*
Michael Melsom *Viticulturalist*
Elizabeth Summerhayes
Director Sales and Marketing

LEEUWIN ESTATE

ACN 008 689 110

18 High Street
Fremantle WA 6160
Tel: (09) 430 4099
Fax: (09) 430 5687

Malcolm Jones *Managing Director Vineyard*
Deirdre Jones *Managing Director Restaurant &
Accomodation*
Liza Jones *Sales & Marketing Manager*

VOYAGER ESTATE (WA) PTY LTD

ACN 009 399 446

12/10 Johnston Street
Peppermint Grove WA 6011
Tel:(09) 385 3133
Fax:(09) 383 4029

Denis Horgan *Founder*
Tricia Horgan *Founder*

Refer to pages 194-196; 252

General Sponsors

YALUMBA WINERY

Yalumba Winery
Eden Valley Road
Angaston SA 5353
Tel:(085) 613 200
Fax:(085) 613 393

Graham Brooke *Chairman*
Robert Hill Smith
Managing Director

Branch Offices:

205 Grote Street
Adelaide SA 5000
Tel:(08) 231 3963
Fax:(08) 231 0863

13 Shoebury Street
Rocklea QLD 4106
Tel:(07) 892 5022
Fax:(07) 892 4633

109-113 Hyde Street
Footscray VIC 3011
Tel:(03) 689 1122
Fax:(03) 687 7261

114 Radium Street
Welshpool WA 6106
Tel:(09) 451 9822
Fax:(09) 458 7198

Centurm Place
6-8 Crewe Place
Roseberry NSW 2018
Tel:(02) 313 8244
Fax:(02) 313 6129

Trade Names:

Yalumba Fine Wines
Yalumba Angas Brut N.V.
Yalumba Oxford Landing
'The Menzies'
'Antipodean'

Refer to pages 224-225; 248

Photograph Credits

Whilst all care has been taken to identify the photographic sources in this book, the publisher expressly disclaims all and any liability to any person in the event that the publisher has been unable to identify a source or where a source has been incorrectly identified.

About Face Restaurant 79; The Adelphi Hotel 43; A Gourmet Traveller/Simon Griffiths 19, 166; Australian Dairy Corporation 246; Australian Dried Fruits Association 221; Australian Meat & Live-Stock Corporation 210; Australian Tourist Commission 86, 89, 104, 120, 132, 135, 174, 211, 246, 256; Baretti Restaurant 43; Bathers Pavilion 96, 102; BOC Gases Ltd; Bonlac Foods Limited 144; Brookland Valley Vineyard 194; Cadbury Confectionery 28, 29, 50, 51, 254; Camerons Oysters; Cantarella Brothers 24-25; Cascade Beverages 109, 118; Cerebos (Aust) Pty Ltd 154, 160; The Curtin Group 57; Darley Street Thai 19, 38; Davids Limited 100, 101; D'Orsogna Limited 186; Florentino Restaurant 135; The Flower Drum 19; Franks, Belinda 5, 12, 89; Gambaros Restaurant 79, 238; Garvey, Robert 197; Gebecki,Michael 1, 222; R J Gilbertsons Pty Ltd; Green's Foods Limited 252; Griffiths, Simon 20, 142, 226; Hancock, Grant 158, 163, 166, 170, 173; Hatch, Peter 135, 141-142,147; Heinz & Co Pty Ltd 138; Hendrie, Peter 209; Houghton Estate 197; Hyatt Regency Perth 180; Il Centro Restaurant 11, 80; Illustrations 204; Image Bank 152, 209; The Inter-Continental 38; Joyce, Ray 90, 106, 109, 113, 114, 116, 120-122, 124, 126, 128, 218, 237, 258; Kidd, Paul B. 209; K G Palmer & Associates Pty Ltd 179, 190; Lactos Master Cheesemaker 110; Leeuwin Estate 194, 197; The Loose Box 180; Lung, Geoff endpapers, 12, 58, 61-63, 65-67, 206; Meades 180; Melbourne Food And Wine Festival 209; Mesclun 30, 38, 52, 89; National Dairies Tasmania Ltd; Pacific Brands Food Group; The Park Hyatt Hotel 36; Peters & Brownes Group 198; Pier Nine Restaurant 79; The Pier Restaurant 38; Photo Index 189; Qantas Airways Ltd 92, 250, 251; Queen Victoria Markets 135; Ravisi's 37; Rosemount Pty Ltd 56, 234; Rowland, Peter 26; San Lorenzo Restaurant 180; Seper, George 89; South Australian Tourism Commission 165, 168-169; Spotless Catering 40-41; Stepnell, Ken 84, 144, 166, 168, 238; Stock Photos Pty Ltd 2-3, 209; Stock Photos/Bill Bachman 54, 72, 130, 174, 178, 185; Stock Photos/Benoji 218; Stock Photos/Gary Chowanet 12; Stock Photos/Roger Du Buisson 154, 237; Stock Photos/Robert Della Piana 216; Stock Photos/Ron Galete 71; Stock Photos/Gary Lewis 166; Stock Photos/Peter McNeill 249; Stock Photos/Lance Nelson 52, 68, 71, 132, 173, 237; Stock Photos/Paul Steel 237; Stock Photos/Rolf Richardson 232; Tabasco Pepper Sauce 214; Tables of Toowong 75, 238; Tasmania Department of Tourism, Sport and Recreation 130, 237; Tassal Ltd 114; Tourism New South Wales 86, 95, 96, 99, 102, 149; Tourism Victoria; Unifoods-A Division of Unilever Australia Ltd 150; Vogue Entertaining/Tony Amos 15, 19; Vogue Entertaining/Greg Barrett 206; Vogue Entertaining/Simon Griffiths 19, 26, 55; Vogue Entertaining/John Hay 48, 50; Vogue Entertaining/Andrew Hetsmann 237; Vogue Entertaining/Richard Ludbrook, 6; Vogue Entertaining/Geoff Lung 38, 136, 157, 209, 212, 217, 229; Vogue Entertaining/George Seper 26, 38; Vogue Entertaining/Petrina Tinslay, 14, 16, 19, 23, 30, 33, 38, 44, 173, 177; Vogue Entertaining/Rodney Weidland 15, 19, 26, 30; Voyager Estate 195; Weiss, Glen 11, 38, 71, 75, 76, 79-80, 83, 238; Western Australian Department of Commerce and Trade; The Western Australian Meat Marketing Corporation 174, 182; Western Australian Tourism Commission 191, 200, 202, 203, 237; Westinghouse Appliances 46, 47; Winning Appliances Pty Ltd 8, 34; Wise Winery 230; White, Jill 14; Woolworths-The Fresh Food People 56, 244-245; Yalumba Winery 224, 237.

Glossary

Abalone a marine mollusc with a bowl-like shell bearing respiratory holes. The flesh is used for food and the shell for mother-of-pearl ornaments

Akubra traditional Australian hat made from rabbit felt

Apple Isle Tasmania

Billy tea tea made in a billy can (cylindrical container with close-fitting lid)

Bush the Australian countryside

Bush mutton sheep meat originating from the bush

Bush tucker natural food, as found in the bush

Cockatoo a crested parrot, often white, white and yellow, pink or red

Damper bush bread made from a simple flour and water dough with or without a raising agent, cooked in coals or in a camp oven

Dugong an aquatic herbivorous mammal with flippers, found in tropical coastal areas of the Indian Ocean

Eucalyptus a species of tall tree native to the Australian region, often yielding valuable timber and some an oil, used in medicine as a germicide and expectorant

Hobby farm a farm maintained for interest's sake, not usually the owner's chief source of income

Kakadu plums a native Australian fruit

Kiwi a New Zealander

Koori an Aborigine

Lemon aspen a type of poplar

Myrtle a shrub of Southern European origin with evergreen leaves, fragrant white flowers and aromatic berries

Marron a large freshwater crayfish of Western Australia

Mash mashed potatoes

Moreton Bay Bug (Balmain Bug) an edible, curiously flattened crustacean, first discovered in Sydney Harbour, closely related to the shovel-nosed lobster

Muddies large edible mud crabs

Muntire a prostrate shrub found in dry sandy areas of Victoria and South Australia

Outback remote sparsely populated back country

Pandanus a tropical and sub-tropical tree or shrub having a palm-like or branched stem, long, narrow, rigid, spirally arranged leaves and often prop roots

Pippies edible, smooth-shelled, burrowing, bivalve molluscs

Protea any of the shrubs and trees native to South Africa with cone-like flower-heads

Quandong an Australian tree yielding an edible drupaceous fruit whose seed has an edible kernel

Rambutan a red plum-sized prickly fruit

Salmi a ragout or casserole especially of partly-roasted game birds

Samphire an umbelliferous maritime rock plant with aromatic fleshy leaves used in pickles

Scampi large prawns

'Spaghetti Mafia' an affectionate nickname for the Italian immigrants who introduced Australians to the world of pasta

Spruik to harangue or address a meeting

Swaggie (Swagman) a man who travels about the country on foot, living on his earnings from occasional jobs, of gifts of money and food

Toflerization as embraced by Alvin Tofler, author of *Future Shock*

Top end the northern part of the Northern Territory in Australia

Tyros a beginner in learning anything, a novice

Upped the ante to increase the stakes (in a bet for instance)

Warrigal a dingo, the native Australian dog

Witchetty grub any of the various large, white, edible, wood-boring grubs that are the larvae of certain Australian moths and beetles

Yabbies Australian freshwater crayfish

Writers

TERRY DURACK
Currently the restaurant reviewer for *The Sydney Morning Herald*, and columnist and national reviewer for *Gourmet Traveller*.

MICHAEL GEBICKI
A freelance writer and photographer. He lives in Sydney with his wife and two daughters.

JAMES HALLIDAY
A senior wine show judge and a recipient of international writing award, Halliday is a prolific writer with 27 books published and over 2,000 newspaper and magazine articles to his credit.

BOB HART
Queensland-born food writer and bon vivant who has worked in marketing and journalism in London and Los Angeles. Currently employed by *The Herald & Weekly Times* in Melbourne where he continues to write on food.

ALAN HILL
Worked for twenty years in the wine industry as an export consultant for Australian wineries and as a wine and travel writer. His work is published in *Vogue Living, Vogue Entertaining, Australian Gourmet Traveller, Winestate* and international airline magazines.

JUDITH HIRST
For many years a contributing editor and freelance writer for a variety of Australian and international publications including *Vogue, Gourmet Traveller, Belle* and *Elle*, providing articles on travel, food and entertainment style.

NIGEL HOPKINS
A senior feature writer, food writer and restaurant reviewer for *The Advertiser* in Adelaide and has contributed to a wide range of national and international publications.

ELISABETH KING
A leading Australian food and travel writer and a food columnist for leading Australian publications such as *Gourmet Traveller, The Sydney Morning Herald, Winestate, Panorama* and *Vogue Entertaining Guide*. Co-authored *The World's Finest Foods* for Random House in America.

ANNA MACDONALD
A freelance book and magazine editor who currently co-edits the entertaining pages of Vogue. She lives in Sydney with the artist Mario Dalpra and her nine-year old son.

LYNDEY MILAN
A Sydney-based 'foodie' who presents a food and wine segment on Radio 2UE and a cooking feature on the *At Home* show on Channel 7. Also a committee member of the Wine Press Club.

MAGGIE OEHLBECK
A freelance writer and editor specialising in travel, food, wine, fashion, beauty and business. She was also features editor for *ITA* magazine and now contributes to *The Sydney Morning Herald, BRW, The Australian,* and *Gourmet Traveller* .

GREG DUNCAN POWELL
A freelance specialist wine writer who writes for *Vogue Entertaining*. He is writing a novel set in 14th century France. He lives on the South Coast of New South Wales.

JEAN STOREY
A food-editor-writer and travel writer for *The Sun-Herald*, Sydney. Previously Editor on Staff at the *Readers Digest*, she is a columnist for the *Sydney Morning Herald* and *The Australian* and a food book reviewer for various journals.

ANTONIA WILLIAMS
A New Zealander who spent half of her life in London, where she worked mainly as a editor and writer on English *Vogue*. Now a Sydney-based freelance writer, her subject matter is style in all its manifestations from fashion to food, she contributes to many publications including *Vogue* and *Vogue Entertaining*.